PENGUIN BOOKS
How Language Works

David Crystal was born in 1941 and spent the early years of his life in Holyhead, North Wales. He went to St Mary's College, Liverpool, and University College London, where he read English and obtained his Ph.D. in 1966. He was a lecturer in linguistics at the universities of Bangor and Reading, becoming Professor of Linguistic Science at Reading in 1975, and is now Honorary Professor of Linguistics at the University of Wales, Bangor. He is editor of *The Penguin Encyclopedia* and related publications, the former editor of the Cambridge family of general encyclopedias, compiler of several dictionaries and author of publications on the theory and practice of reference works. He currently directs a company which manages a large reference database and which is developing systems for improving document classification and internet search. A past president of the Society of Indexers, in 2001 his book *Words on Words* (co-authored with Hilary Crystal) was awarded the Wheatley Medal for an outstanding index. In 1995 he was awarded the OBE for services to the English language.

How Language Works

David Crystal

PENGUIN BOOKS

PENGUIN BOOKS

Published by the Penguin Group
Penguin Books Ltd, 80 Strand, London WC2R 0RL, England
Penguin Group (USA) Inc., 375 Hudson Street, New York, New York 10014, USA
Penguin Group (Canada), 90 Eglinton Avenue East, Suite 700, Toronto, Ontario,
Canada M4P 2Y3 (a division of Pearson Penguin Canada Inc.)
Penguin Ireland, 25 St Stephen's Green, Dublin 2, Ireland
(a division of Penguin Books Ltd)
Penguin Group (Australia), 250 Camberwell Road, Camberwell, Victoria 3124, Australia
(a division of Pearson Australia Group Pty Ltd)
Penguin Books India Pvt Ltd, 11 Community Centre, Panchsheel Park, New Delhi – 110 017, India
Penguin Group (NZ), 67 Apollo Drive, Mairangi Bay, Auckland 1310, New Zealand
(a division of Pearson New Zealand Ltd)
Penguin Books (South Africa) (Pty) Ltd, 24 Sturdee Avenue, Rosebank, Johannesburg 2196, South Africa

Penguin Books Ltd, Registered Offices: 80 Strand, London WC2R 0RL, England

www.penguin.com

First published 2006
Published in paperback 2007
2

Set in TheAntique
Printed in England by Clays Ltd, St Ives plc

ISBN: 978-0-141-01552-1

www.greenpenguin.co.uk

Penguin Books is committed to a sustainable future
for our business, our readers and our planet.
The book in your hands is made from paper
certified by the Forest Stewardship Council.

Contents

Preface   xi

Introducing language

1 How what works?   1
2 How to treat body language   5
3 How we use the 'edges' of language   11

Spoken language

4 How we make speech sounds: phase 1   18
5 How we make speech sounds: phase 2   25
6 How we transmit sounds   32
7 How we hear speech sounds   39
8 How we perceive speech   44
9 How we describe speech sounds   51
10 How we describe consonants and vowels   58
11 How we organize the sounds of speech   66
12 How we use tone of voice   73
13 How children learn speech sounds: the first year   79
14 How children learn speech sounds: later years   85
15 How speech can go wrong   90

Written language

16 How we write 97

17 How we make writing systems: early times 105

18 How we make writing systems: modern times 113

19 How we read 121

20 How we write and spell 127

21 How we learn to read and write 133

22 How reading and writing can go wrong 140

23 How writing and speech differ 147

24 How the electronic medium differs 153

Sign language

25 How sign language works 159

26 How sign languages vary 164

Language structure

27 How the brain handles language 171

28 How to investigate language structure 180

29 How we mean 186

30 How we analyse meaning 192

31 How we learn vocabulary 198

32 How children learn to mean 204

33 How dictionaries work 210

34 How names work 217

35 How vocabulary grows 224

36 How we study grammar 230

37 How words work 236

38 How we classify words 242

39 How sentences work 247

40 How we learn grammar 254

Discourse ✳

41 How we discourse 260

42 How conversation works 267

43 How we choose what to say 275

44 How we can't choose what to say 282

Dialects

45 How we know where someone is from 289

46 How to study dialects 295

47 How we know what someone is: the ethnic issue 302

48 How we know what someone is: the social issue 309

49 How we know who someone is: the stylistic issue 316

50 How we know where someone is: the contextual issue 322

51 How dialects differ from languages 329

Languages

52 How languages die 336

53 How languages are born 343

54 How language began 350

55 How language changes 357

56 How language families work 364

57 How the Indo-European family is organized 371

58 How other Eurasian families are organized – part one 380

59 How other Eurasian families are organized – part two 387

60 How the Indo-Pacific island families are organized 393

61 How African families are organized 397

62 How American families are organized 403

Multilingualism

63 How multilingualism works 409

64 How we cope with many languages: translate them 416

65 How we cope with many languages: supplement them 423

66 How we cope with many languages: learn them 430

67 How we cope with many languages: teach them 437

68 How we cope with many languages: plan them 444

69 How not to look after languages 451

Looking after language

70 How to look after languages: recognizing principles 457

71 How to look after languages: recognizing functions 462

72 How to look after languages: recognizing varieties 469

73 Teaching people to look after languages 477

Further Reading 485

Index 487

List of Figures

1 General arrangement of the vocal organs   19
2 The main parts of the tongue   30
3 Movement of a single air particle   33
4 Sine waves of equal frequency but different amplitude   36
5 Waveforms of a vowel [a:] and consonant [s:]   38
6 Anatomy of the ear   40
7 The International Phonetic Alphabet   54
8 The cardinal vowel diagram   63
9 Vowels in Received Pronunciation   64
10 Egyptian hieroglyphs over time   110
11 Sumerian pictograms related to cuneiform   112
12 Some alphabetic systems   114
13 Anatomy of the eye   122
14 Two-handed and one-handed finger-spelling   169
15 Different views of the brain   172
16 Surface areas of the cortex   175
17 Lexical isoglosses for -r in Britain   298
18 Some words for *father* in Indo-European   366
19 The Indo-European family of languages   367

Preface

I know an artist who has spent his whole life painting a still-life, in innumerable versions, in order to get it right. I know another who continually repaints a scene, in various lights and circumstances, in order to obtain fresh insights into it. There is no end to the process. It is always the next work which will achieve the longed-for resolution.

The study of language is no different. I have lost count of the number of times I have tried to introduce this subject to one readership or another. There are, I imagine, only so many ways of telling the language story, but one goes on looking for new angles, new insights. The present book has been an interesting exercise in taking familiar ideas and rethinking them with a focus on the 'how' rather than on the 'what', 'why', 'where', or 'when'. I have quite consciously incorporated material from my earlier expositions displaying those other emphases, but I hope I have managed to present it here in a fresh and interesting way.

It is not necessary to read the book 'from left to right'. Each chapter is designed as a self-contained unit, and there are many cross-references to associated chapters. This is the distinctive feature of any 'how' approach. The section in a car manual which tells you about its tyres can be read independently of the one which tells you about its lights.

This is a book about how language works, not about how the study of language works. That would be called 'How linguistics works' – or perhaps better, 'How linguists work'. I am a linguist, so you will see from these pages how I work, how I think about language. But there is no attempt in these pages to represent the full range of opinions – at times often very divergent – about the way language can or should be studied. This is above all a personal account. Nor is there much on the methodology of linguistic enquiry: while I talk a lot about child language, for example, I do not say anything about the range of methods that linguists use when they are investigating child language. I have therefore included a short bibliography of further reading for those who reach §73 and wish to take such things further.

David Crystal
Holyhead, April 2005

1
How what works?

'Language', the title of this book says. But what is meant by 'language'? Consider the following expressions:

body language
spoken language
written language
sign language
computer language
the French language
bad language
animal language
the language of birds
the language of cinema
the language of music
the language of love

Plainly the word is being used in many ways – some technical, some figurative – and the senses go in various directions. If a reviewer were to remark, after an impressive orchestral concert, 'The conductor and the musicians were all speaking the same language', we would interpret this to be a comment about their playing, not their chatting. And the same point applies to other linguistic terms, when used in special settings. I have seen books called *The Grammar of Cooking* and *The Syntax of Sex*. The first was a collection of recipes – as was the second.

How Language Works is not about music, or cookery, or sex. But it is about how we *talk* about music, cookery, and sex – or, indeed, about anything at all. And it is also about how we write about these things, and send electronic messages about them, and on occasion use manual signs to communicate them. The operative word is 'how'. It is commonplace to see a remarkable special effect on a television screen and react by exclaiming 'How did they do that?' It is not quite so usual to exclaim when we observe someone speaking, listening, reading, writing, or signing. And yet if anything is worthy of exclamation, it is the human ability to speak, listen, read, write, and sign.

An alien visitor to Earth might well wonder what was going on. It would see humans approach each other, use their mouths to exchange a series of noises, and – apparently as a result of making these noises – cooperate in some activity. It would see human eyes look at a set of marks inscribed on a surface, and the eye-owners then behaving in the same way – going out of one door rather than another in a theatre, for instance. Rather less often, it would see some humans using their hands and faces to achieve the same results that others obtain through the use of their mouths. In each case it might think: 'How did they do that?' And in each case the answer would be the same: 'through the use of language'.

But our alien would also observe other kinds of behaviour. It would see humans smiling and frowning at each other, or waving and gesturing, or stroking and kissing. It would notice that the effect of carrying out these actions was similar in some respects to that produced by the use of spoken noises, written marks, and manual signs. It might well reflect: can these actions therefore be called 'language' too?

Our alien would also see apparently similar behaviour among other species. It would see a bee find a source of nectar, return to a hive, and perform a series of dance-like body movements. Other bees would then move off in the direction of the nectar. Animals of all kinds would seem to be sending information to each other in analogous ways. Is this the same sort of behaviour as the humans are displaying, our alien observer might think? Do animals also have language?

These questions involve more than hypothetical extraterrestrials.

Terrestrial observers also need to be able to answer them, as a preliminary stage in the study of language. If we pick up a manual called *How Cars Work*, we do not expect to find in it chapters on bicycles and lawn-mowers. Nor, in *How Language Works*, will there be much space devoted to the use of facial expressions and body movements or to the way animals communicate. Why not?

Modes of communication

Because not all of these forms of communication are *language*, in the sense of this book. *Communication* is a much broader concept, involving the transmission and reception of any kind of information between any kind of life. It is a huge domain of enquiry, dealing with patterned human and animal communication in all its modes. Those who study behaviour usually call this domain *semiotics*. *Linguistics*, the science of language, is just one branch of semiotics.

There are five modes of human communication, because there are only five human senses which can act as channels of information: sound, sight, touch, smell, and taste. Of course, if you believe in telepathy, you would need to recognize a 'sixth sense' available for communication; and perhaps there are life forms which interact using still other modes, such as the non-visible areas of the electromagnetic spectrum. But the five traditional human sensory modes are all we need to put the subject of this book into a more general perspective.

The information we send and receive using these modes is usually called the *meaning* of our communication. But the five modes are not equally relevant for the transmission and reception of meaning. In fact, two of them play hardly any role at all in human beings – the *olfactory* (smell) and *gustatory* (taste) modes. We do not routinely emit smells in order to communicate with others (the controlled flatulent behaviour of some small boys notwithstanding), and there is a very limited amount of information about the outside world which we can receive through the mediums of smell and taste. By contrast, the use of sound – the *auditory-vocal* mode – is fundamental to the notion of language, and the properties of this mode will form the major part of this book (§4). Speech is the primary manifestation of language, in all cultures.

The *tactile* and *visual* modes fall somewhere between these two extremes. They are often technically described as being channels of *nonverbal communication* because the way in which we use facial expressions, gestures, and touch behaviour seems to contrast with the words and sentences we describe as *verbal* language. But ordinary people do not talk about nonverbal communication. Instead, they simply refer to *body language*.

Is this use of 'language' the same as the one we use when we talk about speech, writing, and signing, or about English, French, and Chinese? Should large sections of this book be devoted to how facial expressions and manual gestures work? The answer is no, and to understand why we need to briefly consider the differences between what is involved in nonverbal tactile and visual communication, on the one hand, and in language, on the other. We shall see that these differences also enable us to disregard animal communication, as well as the other figurative applications of the term. We shall be left with a trinity of mediums – speech, writing, and sign – which manifest our concept of 'language'.

2
How to treat body language

When people talk about body language (§1), they are referring to those features of bodily behaviour which are under some degree of conscious control, and which they can therefore use to express different sorts of meaning. The meanings involved are all fairly 'primitive' expressions of attitude or social relationship, such as affection, aggression, sexual attraction, greeting, congratulation, gratitude, surprise, and the signalling of attention. Both tactile and visual modes of communication are employed.

The tactile mode

The tactile mode of nonverbal communication operates when parts of the body make planned physical contact with other people. A very wide range of meaningful activities is expressed by such contact, as this small selection of terms suggests:

dig, embrace, hold, jog, kick, kiss, nudge, nuzzle,
pat, pinch, punch, shake, slap, spank, tickle

They operate within a complex system of social constraints. Some of the acts tend to be found only in private – notably, sexual touching. Some are specialized in function: examples include the tactile activities which we permit from doctors, dentists, hairdressers, or tailors. And some are restricted to certain ceremonies or occasions – a handshake which signals a formal agreement, for example, or a laying on of hands in the context of religion or healing.

The communicative value of tactile activities is usually fairly clear within a culture, but there are many differences across cultures. Some societies are much more tolerant of touching than others, so much so that a distinction has been proposed between *contact* and *non-contact* societies – those that favour touching (such as Arabs and Latin Americans), and those that avoid it (such as North Europeans and Indians). In some cultures, conversationalists touch each other two or three times a minute; in others, no touching takes place at all.

Related to our use of body contact is the way we use body distance and orientation to communicate meaning. There are norms of proximity within a culture (*distance zones*) which can inform us about the social relationship between the participants. Latin Americans, for example, prefer to stand much closer to each other during a conversation than do North Europeans. In a traditional caste system, such as in India, the acceptable distance zones between the members of different castes can vary greatly – from less than 2 metres to over 20.

The visual mode

We use the visual mode to communicate nonverbally in several ways. We can gesture, vary our facial expressions, make eye contact, and alter our body posture. Each of these behaviours performs a variety of functions. Movements of the face and body give clues to our personality and emotional state. The face, in particular, signals a wide range of emotions, such as fear, happiness, sadness, anger, surprise, interest, and disgust. Many of the expressions vary in meaning across cultures, and we have to learn how to interpret the sometimes very subtle movements in the faces of people whose racial characteristics differ from our own.

In addition, the face and body send signals about the way a social interaction is proceeding. We use *eye contact* to show who is the focus of our communication, in a group, or to prompt a person to speak next. We use *facial expressions* to give feedback to others about how we are receiving their message, expressing such meanings as puzzlement or disbelief. We use our *body posture* to convey our attitude towards an interaction – for instance, whether we are interested or bored. Several kinds of social context are associated with specific facial or body behaviours, such as waving upon meeting or taking leave. Ritual or official occasions are often associated with gesture and posture – as with kneeling, standing, bowing, and blessing.

Some visual effects are widely used in the cultures of the world. An example is the *eyebrow flash*, used unconsciously when people approach each other and wish to show that they are ready to make social contact. Each person performs a single upward movement of the eyebrows, keeping them raised for about a sixth of a second. The effect is so automatic that we are hardly ever conscious of it. But we become uneasy if we do not receive an eyebrow flash when we expect one (from someone we know); and to receive an eyebrow flash from someone we do not know can be uncomfortable, embarrassing, or even threatening.

Most gestures and facial expressions, however, differ across cultures. Sometimes the differences are very noticeable, especially when we visit a society which uses far more gestures and facial expressions than we are used to (e.g. Italian, compared with British) or far fewer (e.g. Japanese, compared with British). We even coin phrases to express our sense of these differences, as when an English person describes Italians as 'talking with their arms' or Westerners refer to people from oriental countries as 'inscrutable'.

Even when a visual effect seems to be shared between societies, we have to be careful, for it can convey very different meanings. A thumbs-up sign has a positive 'all is well' or 'I am winning' meaning in Western Europe, the USA, and other cultures influenced by its use as a symbol of combat survival in Roman times. But in the Arab world, as well as in parts of West Africa and Asia, it is a symbol of insult, equivalent to giving someone 'the finger' ('up yours!') in the West. As a consequence, it was never entirely clear, during the aftermath of the Iraq War of 2003, when Iraqis were seen on television giving a thumbs-up to American troops, whether this was the traditional gesture being used as an insult or whether it was the Western version being adopted as a sign of cooperation and a symbol of freedom.

Conversely, a particular meaning can be conveyed by a variety of different visual signals. To express humility or deference, for example, Europeans tend to extend or lower their arms, and they sometimes bow their heads. But in other cultures we find more profound bowing, using the whole of the upper half of the body, as well as crouching, crawling, and prostration. We also see other kinds of hand or arm movement, such as the placing of the palms together in an upward orientation (as in the Indian subcontinent).

Properties of language

Body language is evidently an important means of human communication, and when it comes to basic emotions and social relationships, it is a familiar experience that a gesture, facial expression, or piece of bodily contact can 'speak louder' than words. However, the potential of body language to express meaning is very limited, compared to that which is made available through speaking, writing, or signing. Language, as we shall discuss it in this book, displays certain properties which enable us to express far more than any piece of nonverbal communication could ever do. We can express our surprise or anger using our bodies; but if we want to explain why we are surprised or angry, we need to use language.

Probably the most remarkable property of language is the way it enables us to talk about virtually anything we want. And if it lets us down, by not immediately providing the required words and sentences, we change it so that it will do so. This is what is meant when we say that human language is *productive*. Productivity is the capacity to express and understand a potentially infinite number of utterances, made by combining sentence elements in new ways and introducing fresh combinations of words. Most of the sentences we read in a book are original, in the sense that no one has used those particular combinations of words and constructions before. Nor is there any limit to the length of a sentence: any sentence can be made longer by using *and* (or some similar word) to attach another piece of utterance. Similarly, there is no limit to the number of words in a language; new words are being invented every day.

By contrast, there is no productivity in tactile or visual body language. The number of tactile or visual body signals in everyday behaviour is very small – a matter of a few hundred only (compared to the million or more words in a language such as English) – and they do not increase very easily. We can readily invent a new word – I can do so now, and talk about 'bodylinguistic' behaviour – but it strains the imagination to think what we could do if we were asked to invent a new facial expression or bodily gesture. Nor do these nonverbal features combine to produce a wide range of varying sequences, as we routinely encounter with sentences. Only in the world of artistic expression, such as in the various forms of Indian dance, do we find a significant expansion of the body-language repertoire, in the codified hand signs known as *mudras*.

Another important difference between language and body language lies in the far greater structural architecture of speech, writing, or sign. Language makes use of two fundamental levels of structural organization. At one level, we find the use of sounds or letters – *t, s, e*, and so on – which have no intrinsic meaning. We cannot sensibly ask 'What does "s" mean?' At another level, we find these sounds or letters combining in different ways to form elements that do convey meaning – the words, phrases, and sentences. We can sensibly ask 'What does "sit" mean?'

This property is called *duality of structure*, or *double articulation*, and it is not present in body language. The movements which form the signals of body language always convey some kind of meaning. If I raise my left eyebrow significantly, or smile, or give a thumbs-up sign, the action automatically sends a meaning, and within a culture this meaning remains the same whenever the same action is used. We cannot build up a wide range of body-language 'sentences' which mean something different from the meaning of the elements they contain. Body language cannot be analysed into two levels of structure.

For the same reasons, we cannot call 'animal communication' language. The facial expressions, gestures, and tactile behaviours of the animal kingdom lack productivity and duality of structure in the same way that human body language does. Even the most sophisticated kinds of behaviour, such as bee-dancing or birdsong, are highly limited in what they can do, compared with language. Bees can 'talk' about nectar but not about much else.

There are several other important differences between animal communication and language. In particular, language enables us to talk about events remote in space or time from the situation of the speaker: I can talk about what happened in the near or remote past and speculate about the near or remote future. This property of language – often called *displacement* – is something which goes well beyond the capabilities of animal signals, which reflect stimuli (such as the presence of danger or the direction of a food source) encountered in the animal's immediate environment.

Despite some superficial similarities, so-called 'body language' and 'animal language' are very different from what happens in language, in the sense of this book. I find it clearer to avoid the use of the term *language* altogether, in fact, and to describe these phenomena in more general terms – as *body communication* and *animal communication*. There is nothing wrong with the 'language' metaphor, of course, as long as we realize that that is what it is – no more than a vague approximation to the structurally complex and multifunctional behaviour we find whenever we speak, write, or sign.

3
How we use the 'edges' of language

The contrast between what counts as language and what does not is usually clear enough, once we look for evidence of productivity and duality of structure in communicative behaviour (§2). But the boundary is fuzzy at times. In particular, some non-linguistic forms of behaviour, both vocal and visual, can be adapted so that they take on some of the functions of language. There are also some features of language which are decidedly less complex than others, and where it is unclear whether they should count as part of language or not.

Making vocal noises

The vocal organs (§4) can be used to make a wide range of noises that are definitely not linguistic. They express only a biological state, and communicate no cultural meaning. Examples are coughing, sneezing, and snoring, as well as the various voice qualities which signal a physical condition, such as hoarseness. It makes no sense to talk about 'snoring in English', nor do we expect a foreign language course to teach us how to cough. But a phenomenon such as whistling does something more than just express a basic biological or psychological state.

When we blow air through tensed and rounded lips, we form a primitive musical instrument, and a note is the result. We can alter the pitch level by moving the tongue and cheeks to change the shape of the inside of the mouth. We can alter its loudness by blowing harder. And we can alter its quality (making it soft or shrill) by altering the tension of the mouth muscles or putting our fingers against the lips to make the sound sharper. It does not come naturally. Children have to learn to whistle. And the behaviour is subject to social factors: usually it is boys and men who whistle.

People most often use whistling to carry musical melodies, and some professional whistlers have developed this musical skill into an art form. Some people are able to mimic birdsong or other animal noises. But these imitative abilities have no more linguistic significance than the phenomena they imitate. We move in the direction of language only when individual whistles are used conventionally in a culture to express a specific and shared meaning. Examples include the 'wolf-whistle', the whistle which calls sharply for attention, the whistle of amazement, and the whistle of empathy ('gosh!'), which is often more a breathy exhalation than an actual whistle.

We see the communicative potential of whistling at its most developed in the case of the so-called *whistle languages*, found in some Central and South American tribes, as well as in the occasional European community, such as in the Pyrenees, Turkey, and the Canary Islands. Conversations have been observed between people standing at a considerable distance from each other, especially in mountainous areas, carried on entirely in whistles. The whistled conversations deal with quite sophisticated and precise matters, such as arranging a meeting or selling some goods.

Whistled speech closely corresponds to the tonal and rhythmical patterns of spoken language, and is especially complex when the whistlers speak a language in which pitch levels (tones) are important, such as some languages of Central America. With very few exceptions, each 'syllable' of whistle corresponds to a syllable of speech. Ambiguity is uncommon, because the topic of the conversation is usually something evident in the situation of the speakers. However, it is important for both speakers to use the same musical key, otherwise confusion may arise.

Whistled dialogues tend to contain a small number of exchanges, and the utterances are short. They are most commonly heard when people are at a distance from each other (e.g. when working the land), but they can also be found in a variety of informal settings. Although women are able to understand whistled speech, it is normally used only by and between men.

The whistling is a substitute for speech. The whistlers stop whistling when they are within normal speaking range of each other, and talk in the normal way. For this reason, whistled speech has been called a speech replacement, or *surrogate*. Because it is used only in certain circumstances, and can convey only a limited range of meanings, and is not used equally by all members of the community, it does not really correspond to the complexity and functional breadth of a spoken language. But it is certainly a step in that direction.

Being paralinguistic

There are a number of vocal noises which can be 'superimposed' on the stream of speech. It is possible, for example, to speak while sobbing, crying, laughing, or giggling, or we can introduce a tremulous 'catch' in our voice. The auditory effects are usually immediate and dramatic – though the meaning conveyed is sometimes unclear, and always subject to cultural variation. A giggle can convey humour, innuendo, sexual interest, and several other nuances. In Britain it is most commonly used in joking; in Japan it is more often a sign of embarrassment.

We can also change our tone of voice by altering the quality of the sound we produce in the vocal tract (§5). Normally, the sound produced by our vocal folds yields a vibrant voicing which we hear in every vowel and in most of the consonants. But it is possible to speak without producing any voicing at all. The phenomenon is called *whispering* – and whisper conveys meaning, usually a 'conspiratorial' effect of some kind. A related effect is *breathy* voice, where extra breath is heard on top of what we are saying. We produce breathy voice after exercise, when we are 'out of breath'; but it is also possible to introduce a breathy voice when we are at rest, and it then conveys a meaning. I once heard two neighbours talking about a woman who had returned from a holiday, saying that she was 'brown all over'. The words 'all over' were uttered in a breathy tone. It seems she really was.

Several other tones of voice can be consciously made by altering the way in which we make sounds resonate in our mouths and nose. We can *round* our lips so that everything we say comes out in a tone which we associate with baby-talk or talking to animals ('Who's a lovely little baba/budgie, then?'), though we also use the effect when addressing those with whom we are most intimate. We can add a *nasal* tone of voice if we want to add a mildly 'camp' effect to what we are saying – something which the British comedian Kenneth Williams used routinely. And we can make our vocal folds move very slowly, to produce an effect often called *creaky voice* or *vocal fry*. This was something horror-movie star Vincent Price used to do when he wanted to sound especially menacing, but it is also associated with such attitudes as disparagement and doubt.

These effects all add an emotional colouring to the voice, and their sound quality and use are conditioned by the language and culture of the speaker. When we speak French we have to learn to round our lips to express attitudes in different ways from the way we round them when we speak English. When we learn Portuguese we find that nasal tones of voice are used differently. And when foreigners learn English, they have to do different things too: Finns learning English have to stop 'creaking' their voice so much, for otherwise they give the impression of being perpetually disparaging. These effects all seem to be linguistic in character.

On the other hand, they are plainly not like vowels and consonants, or words and phrases, in the way they are formed and used. They do not show the productivity and duality of structure (§2) which we associate with the rest of language. In many ways they are more like the facial expressions and body gestures of visual communication. This suggests they are *not* really linguistic in character.

We need a way of talking about vocal effects which are on the boundary between the linguistic and the non-linguistic, showing some but not all of the properties of language, and the term *paralanguage* has been devised to fill the bill. The *para-* prefix is from Greek, expressing the notion of 'alongside' or 'above and beyond'. Effects like giggle and whisper are said to be paralinguistic in character, and some scholars include facial expressions and gestures under this heading as well.

Using manual signals

Many gestural systems have emerged to facilitate communication in particular situations. They are often referred to as *sign languages*, but few have developed any degree of structural complexity or communicative range, and it is therefore important to distinguish them from sign language proper – the natural signing behaviour which has evolved for use among deaf people (§25). Nonetheless, they are a definite advance on the 'basic' kinds of body language that are seen in everyday interaction (§2).

Several professions use sets of conventional signals. Sports players and officials can use hand and arm gestures to show the state of play, or an intention to act in a certain way. Groups of performers (such as acrobats or musicians) use them to coordinate their activities. In casinos, officials use them to report on the way a game is going, or to indicate problems that might affect the participants. In theatres and cinemas, ushers use them to show the number and location of seats. In sales rooms, auctioneers use them to convey the type and amount of selling and buying.

People controlling cranes, hoists, and other equipment can signal the direction and extent of movement. In aviation marshalling, ground staff can send visual information about the position of an aircraft, the state of its engines, and its desired position. Firemen can send directions about the supply of water, water pressures, and the use of equipment. Divers can communicate depth, direction, and time, and the nature of any difficulties they have encountered. Truck drivers can exchange courtesy signals, give information about the state of the road, or show they are in trouble. Environmental noise may make verbal communication impossible (e.g. in cotton mills), so that workers start signing to each other.

Race-course bookies send hand and arm signals about the number of a race or horse, and its price. In radio and television production, producers and directors can signal to performers the amount of time available, instructions about level of loudness or speed of speaking, and information about faults and corrections. Religious or quasi-religious groups and secret societies often develop ritual signing systems so that members can recognize and communicate with each other. Some monastic orders have developed signing systems of considerable sophistication, especially if their members are vowed to silence, as in the case of the Trappist monks.

But in none of these cases are we dealing with systems containing thousands of expressive possibilities, as we are with 'language proper', or with signed sentences of any complexity. They all lack productivity and duality of structure (§2), and they are meaningless outside of the situations for which they were devised. A Trappist monk would make little headway signing at a football referee, and vice versa. These signalling systems are highly restricted methods of communication, invented to solve a particular problem. They are a step or so above basic body gestures, but not much more than that.

There are only a few cases where the visual and tactile modes have been adapted to perform a truly linguistic function, providing alternative modes of communication to that which we encounter most commonly in the auditory-vocal behaviour we call 'speech'. Most obviously, the visual mode is used in writing, and there have been several writing-based visual codes, such as semaphore and Morse. Writing can involve a tactile dimension, too, as when visually impaired people receive written information through their finger-tip contact with the sets of raised dots known as braille. Tactile codes also exist, in which sounds or (more usually) letters are communicated through touch; and touch is critical when deaf-blind people use their hands to sense the movements of another person's vocal organs while speaking. Finally, facial expression and gesture is crucially involved in deaf signing – which, as we shall see (§25), is very different from the signing systems described above or the everyday gestural behaviour used by hearing people.

Speech, writing, sign: these are the three mediums which define the conceptual domain of any book on language. And the natural place to begin is with speech. Of all the modes of communication (§1), the auditory-vocal medium is the one which has been most widely adapted for purposes of human communication. All children with their sensory and mental faculties intact learn to speak before they learn to write. Only in the case of a child born deaf is there a natural opportunity to learn a non-auditory system. Moreover, all languages exist in spoken form before they are written down. Indeed, some 40% of human languages (over 2,000 in all) have never been written down. For their speakers, the topic 'how language works' could mean only one thing: 'how speech works'.

4
How we make speech sounds: phase 1

The parts of the body used in the production of speech are called the *vocal organs*, and there are more of them than we might expect. We have to take into account the *lungs*, the *throat*, the *mouth*, and the *nose*. Inside the mouth, we must distinguish the *lips*, the *tongue*, the *teeth*, the roof of the mouth (or *palate*), and the small fleshy appendage hanging down at the very back of the palate (the *uvula*). Inside the throat, we find the upper part, or *pharynx*, operating in a different way from the lower part, or *larynx*. And within the larynx (§5) we need to recognize the important role of the *vocal folds*, located behind the Adam's apple. The space between the vocal folds is known as the *glottis*. There is a lot going on at the same time, when we speak.

The pharynx, mouth, and nose form a system of hollow areas, or cavities, known as the *vocal tract*. (Some speech scientists include the larynx and lungs under this heading as well.) When we move the organs in the vocal tract, we alter its shape, and it is this which enables the many different sounds of spoken language to be produced. In fact, it is the remarkable versatility of the human vocal tract which is so noticeable when we compare humans with their nearest animal cousins, the primates.

The primate vocal tract is very different from that found in humans. Primates have long, flat, thin tongues, which have less room to move. Their larynx is higher (§5), and there is little sign of a pharynx. They are

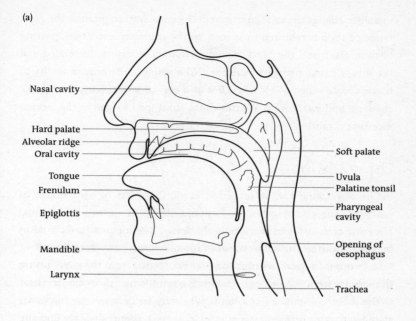

(a)

Nasal cavity

Hard palate
Alveolar ridge
Oral cavity

Soft palate

Tongue
Frenulum

Uvula
Palatine tonsil

Epiglottis

Pharyngeal
cavity

Mandible

Opening of
oesophagus

Larynx

Trachea

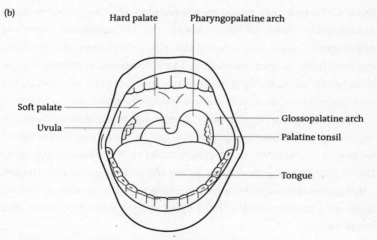

(b)

Hard palate   Pharyngopalatine arch

Soft palate

Uvula

Glossopalatine arch

Palatine tonsil

Tongue

Fig. 1. General arrangement of the vocal organs

unable to change the configurations of the vocal tract to produce the great range of sounds required in speech. In the course of evolution, posture became erect, and the head moved forward. The larynx descended and the long, flexible pharynx developed. The result is the human ability to make a wide range of sounds – but at a cost of less efficient breathing, chewing, and swallowing. We can choke from food lodged in the larynx; monkeys cannot.

Using the lungs

Before any sound can be produced at all, there has to be a source of energy. In speech, this takes the form of a stream of air, which in normal circumstances is set in motion by the lungs. The lungs act as a kind of bellows, allowing air to flow inwards and outwards, as we breathe.

In order to speak, we must first inhale. Signals from the nerve centre in the brain stem (where our breathing is controlled) cause certain muscles in the chest to contract. In particular, the muscles between the ribs cause the ribs to move upwards and outwards. At the bottom of the chest cavity there is a dome-shaped muscle (the *diaphragm*) which separates the lungs from the lower parts of the abdomen. The rib movement causes the diaphragm to move downwards. The result is to expand the chest, and thus the lungs, temporarily causing the air pressure in the lungs to be reduced. Air immediately flows into the lungs, in order to equalize the pressure with that of the atmosphere outside the body.

We then exhale. We contract the chest, and thus the lungs, by lowering the ribs and raising the diaphragm, forcing the air out. This is the air we use for speaking. We never exhale all the air. Only about a quarter of the air in the lungs is used while we are engaged in normal conversation – though the amount increases to some extent if our speech becomes loud or effortful, as in shouting, acting, singing, public speaking, or producing a 'stage whisper'.

Lung air is technically called *pulmonic* air (from the Latin word for 'lung', *pulmo*), and when pulmonic air flows outwards, it is said to be *egressive*. The vast majority of speech sounds are made using pulmonic egressive air. It is also possible – though not usual – to speak while the air-stream is flowing inwards to the lungs, as we inhale. This would be called pulmonic *ingressive* air. We do occasionally hear this air-stream used when someone is trying to talk while laughing or crying, or when out of breath. Words such as *yes* and *no* are sometimes said with an ingressive air-stream, when we use a 'routine' tone of voice to acknowledge what someone is saying. An alternate use of egressive and ingressive air-streams is sometimes heard when people are counting rapidly, 'under their breath'. But ingressive speech is of poor quality, muffled, and croaky, and many people find it unpleasant to listen to. It is never put to routine use in everyday speech.

The sequence of events involved when we breathe in and out is known as the *respiratory cycle*. Normally, the two halves of this cycle are nearly equal in duration; but when we speak, the pattern changes to one of very rapid inhalation and very slow exhalation. The rate at which we breathe also changes. When we are silent and at rest, our average rate is 12 breaths a minute, so the time we take to inhale and exhale is about 2.5 seconds each. During speech, we cut down the time for inhaling to as little as a quarter of a second, and we regularly extend the time for exhaling to 5 or 10 seconds or more, depending on our voice control, emotional state, and other such factors. This altered pattern of breathing enables our exhalations to 'carry' much larger amounts of speech than would otherwise be the case. In everyday conversation, it is perfectly normal to produce 250 to 300 syllables in a minute.

Not using the lungs

The vowels and consonants of English, as of most languages, are all made using pulmonic egressive air. But there are a few types of speech sound which do not use an air-stream from the lungs, and these are encountered in many languages of the world.

Probably the most distinctive type of non-pulmonic sound is the *click*. Click sounds are sharp suction noises made by the tongue or lips. For example, the noise we write as *tut tut* (or *tsk tsk*) is a pair of click sounds, made by the tongue against the top teeth (*dental* clicks). In English they are used to express disapproval. Throughout the Near East a single such click is widely used to express negation. Another type of click uses the side of the tongue (a *lateral* click), made as a noise of encouragement – usually just to horses or other animals, but occasionally to other human beings. A click sound made with the lips puckered is known as a *bilabial* click – it is often used as a 'kiss at a distance'. In each of these cases, we can breathe in and out, quite independently, while making the click sounds. This shows that the lungs are not involved in their production.

In European languages, isolated click sounds are often heard as meaningful noises, but they are not part of their system of vowels and consonants. However, in many other languages, clicks *are* used as consonants. Best known are some of the languages of southern Africa, often referred to as *click languages*. The Khoisan languages, which include the languages of the Khoikhoin and San tribes, have the most complex click systems, using many different places of articulation in the mouth, and involving the simultaneous use of other sounds made in the throat or nose. There are no less than forty-eight distinct clicks in one such language, !Xū (the '!' in the name represents one such click).

Although we think of clicks as relatively 'quiet' sounds, they can be pronounced with considerable force. Miriam Makeba's 'click songs' were very popular in the 1960s. A native speaker of Xhosa, she used several words containing click consonants in her singing, achieving notable effects by articulating them with great resonance.

Some languages use other types of non-pulmonic sound. We can use the space between the vocal folds, the *glottis*, to start an air-stream moving. A number of languages make use of sounds based on this principle, referred to as the *glottalic* air-stream mechanism. When the glottis makes the air move inwards, the sounds are called *implosives*. Implosive consonants occur in many languages, but are particularly common in Native American and African languages. To European ears the effect is of the sounds being 'swallowed'.

When the glottis makes the air move outwards, the sounds are called *ejectives*. Ejective consonants are widely used in the languages of the

Caucasian family, and also in many Native American and African lan-guages. They may even be heard in certain accents and styles of English. Speakers from the north of England quite often use them at the ends of words, in place of the usual [p], [t], or [k].* And regardless of the accent we use, if we speak in a tense, clipped manner, the effect is one of the sounds being 'popped out' at the end of a word.

Making unusual sounds

In special circumstances, people can speak using an abnormal air-stream mechanism. It is possible to compress air within the cheek-space and use that to carry speech – the so-called *buccal* voice. This is best known through the voice of Walt Disney's Donald Duck. It is also possible to make sounds using air rising from the stomach or oesophagus (the pipe leading from the pharynx to the stomach), as in a belch. This speech has a characteristic-ally 'burpy' quality, but it is used in a sophisticated way by many cancer-sufferers who have had a diseased larynx surgically removed. It is called *oesophageal* voice.

We can make other vocal effects, but they are better considered as emotional noises than speech sounds. For example, a short popping sound made with the lips, but with the sound sent outwards rather than sucked inwards, is fairly common in French, where, along with a distinctive hand gesture and shrug of the shoulders, it means roughly 'I couldn't care less' or 'It's not my fault'. A longer rasping sound, made by the tongue protruding slightly between the lips, is a signal of contempt in many languages – what in Britain is called a 'raspberry'. Some people flap the tongue noisily between their lips when they wish to show hesitation.

Finally, we should note that the vocal tract can produce several other kinds of sound which are not used in spoken language at all – or only in a highly idiosyncratic way. For instance, we can scrape or knock the teeth together, flap the tongue against the floor of the mouth, or make a sucking

---

* When a symbol appears in square brackets, it represents a sound. For example, [p] represents a voiceless sound made with both lips – technically, a 'voiceless bilabial plosive' (see pp. 59–60).

noise with the tongue against the inside of the cheek. If listeners hear such noises, they would not usually interpret them as attempts at communication.

The auditory-vocal channel of communication can evidently be put to work in the service of language in a variety of ways. But out of all the possibilities, one way stands supreme. Most of the sounds made by human beings in the 6,000 or so languages of the world (§51) use an outward flow of lung air. And the diversity of these sounds is made possible by a collaboration between larynx, mouth, and nose.

5
How we make speech sounds: phase 2

Before we can speak, lung air has to be converted into audible vibrations, and to do this we use the various organs within the vocal tract (§4). The most important source of vibration for the production of speech sounds is in the lower region of the tract, at the *larynx*.

From a biological point of view, the larynx acts as a valve, controlling the flow of air to and from the lungs, and preventing food, foreign bodies, or other substances from entering the lungs. Also, by closing the vocal folds, it is possible to build up pressure within the lungs, such as would be required for all forms of muscular effort, as in lifting, defecating, and coughing. In the course of evolution, the larynx has been adapted to provide the main source of sound for speech. However, its position in front of the lower pharynx (which leads to the stomach) presents a complication, because food and liquids must therefore pass the entrance to the windpipe on their way to the stomach. (This complication does not exist in other animals, where the larynx is positioned higher up.) To solve the problem, a leaf-shaped cartilage known as the *epiglottis* is pulled across the entrance to the larynx as part of the mechanism of swallowing, thus preventing these substances going in the wrong direction.

The larynx is a tube consisting of cartilages with connecting ligaments and membranes, within which are housed two bands of muscular tissue, the *vocal folds* (or *cords*). The location of the larynx can be easily felt because its front part, the thyroid (or 'shield-like') cartilage, forms a prominent angle in the neck, known as the *Adam's apple* (it stands out more sharply in men). Two other cartilages work along with the thyroid to define the area of the larynx, and the movements of all three help to control the way the vocal folds vibrate.

The opening between the vocal folds, the *glottis*, is quite a small area. In men, the inner edge of the folds is usually between 17 and 24 mm; in women it is even smaller, from about 13 to 17 mm. But despite their small size, the vocal folds are remarkably versatile. Their tension, elasticity, height, width, length, and thickness can all be varied, owing to the complex interaction of the many sets of muscles controlling their movement. These movements take place very rapidly during speech, and produce several kinds of auditory effect.

How we use the larynx

To make voiced sounds

The most important effect is the production of audible vibration – a buzzing sound, known as *voice* or *phonation*. All vowels, and most of the consonants – such as [m], [b], and [z] – make use of this effect. It is in fact possible to feel the vibration. One way is to place the forefinger and thumb on either side of the Adam's apple, and compare the effect of saying a sound which is voiced, such as [zzz], with a sound which has no voice, such as [sss]. Alternatively, we can sense the resounding effect of vocal-fold vibration by making these sounds while putting a finger in each ear.

To make pitch movements

Each pulse of vibration represents a single opening and closing movement of the vocal folds. In adult male voices, this action is repeated on average about 120 times (or *cycles*) a second – corresponding to a note on the piano about an octave below middle C. In women, the average is just less than an octave higher, about 220 cycles a second. The higher the pitch of the voice, the more vibrations there will be. A new-born baby's cry averages 400 vibrations a second.

An individual is able to alter the frequency of vocal-fold vibration at will, within certain limits, to produce variations in pitch and loudness which can convey contrasts of meaning. This linguistic use of pitch and loudness is described in such terms as *intonation*, *tone*, *stress*, and *rhythm*, and is discussed separately in §12.

To make glottal stops

The vocal folds may be held tightly closed – as happens when we are holding our breath. When they are opened, the released lung air causes the production of a *glottal stop*, heard very clearly in the sharp onset to a cough. A glottal stop is used as a consonant sound in many languages of the world. In British English, it is especially noticed in dialects that have been influenced by London speech (in such words as *bottle*, where it replaces the sound [t]).

To make glottal friction

If the vocal folds are kept wide apart, air expelled with energy will produce an audible hiss as it passes through the glottis – an effect that is often used as an [h] consonant sound in languages. Several paralinguistic vocal effects also use glottal friction, such as whispered and breathy voice (§3).

How we articulate

Once the air-stream passes through the larynx, it enters the long tubular structure known as the *vocal tract* (§4). Here it is affected by the action of several mobile vocal organs – in particular, by the tongue, soft palate, and lips – which work together to make a wide range of speech sounds. The production of different speech sounds through the use of these organs is known as *articulation*.

In addition, sounds produced within the larynx or vocal tract are influenced by the inherent properties of the cavities in the throat, mouth, and nose through which the air-stream passes. These cavities give sounds their *resonance*. Several kinds of resonance can be produced, because the vocal tract is able to adopt many different shapes. The most familiar one is nasal resonance, which is heard when we allow air to emerge through the nose. A 'nasal twang' is a feature of many regional accents, as well as of some physical disabilities.

When we describe articulation, it is usual to distinguish between those parts of the vocal tract that can move under the control of the speaker (the *active articulators*), and those which stay in one position at all times (the *passive articulators*). The chief passive articulators are:

- the upper teeth, especially the incisors, which are used to form a constriction for a few sounds, such as the first sound of *thin*;
- the ridge behind the upper teeth, known as the *alveolar ridge*, against which several speech sounds are made, such as [t] and [s]; and
- the bony arch behind the alveolar ridge, known as the *hard palate*, which is used in the articulation of a few sounds, such as the first sound of *you* [j].

All other organs are mobile, to a greater or lesser extent.

Articulating sounds with the pharynx

The *pharynx* is a long muscular tube leading from the laryngeal cavity to the back part of the oral and nasal cavities. It cannot be moved very much, but it is possible to make it narrower or wider, and this constriction can be used to make a consonant sound or to add a *pharyngeal* effect to another sound. *Pharyngealized* consonants and vowels can be heard in several languages, such as Arabic.

Articulating sounds with the soft palate

The *soft palate* is a broad band of muscular tissue in the rear upper region of the mouth. It is also known as the *velum* (the Latin for 'veil'). Its most noticeable feature is the *uvula* – an appendage that hangs down at the back of the mouth, easily visible with the aid of a mirror. In normal breathing, the soft palate is lowered, to permit air to pass easily through the nose – though of course the mouth may be open as well.

In speech, there are three main ways in which the soft palate affects the quality of sounds:

- it may be raised against the back wall of the pharynx so that air escapes only through the mouth; this produces a range of *oral* sounds – such as all the vowels and most of the consonants of English;
- it may be lowered to allow air to escape through the mouth and nose; this is the position required to produce *nasalized vowels*, as in French *bon* 'good', Portuguese, and many other languages; and
- it may be lowered, but the mouth remains closed; in this case all the air is released through the nose, resulting in such *nasal consonants* as [m] and [n].

Articulating sounds with the lips

The *lips* may be completely closed, as for [p] or [m], and this is the normal position for consonant sounds in English. But they may also be held apart in varying degrees to produce the friction of certain kinds of consonant, as in the *b* of Spanish *saber* 'know'. The lips also make the various kinds of rounding or spreading used on vowels – for example, the rounded lips of *boo* vs. the spread lips of *bee*.

Articulating sounds with the jaw

The mandible bone, which forms the *jaw*, permits a large degree of movement. It controls the size of the gap between the teeth, and strongly influences the position of the lips. Speakers sometimes adopt open or closed jaw positions – as when someone speaks 'through gritted teeth'.

Articulating sounds with the tongue

Of all the mobile organs, the *tongue* is the most versatile. It is capable of adopting more shapes and positions than any other vocal organ, and thus enters into the definition of a very large number of speech sounds: all the vowels, and most of the consonants. It is a three-dimensional muscle, the whole of which can move in any of three main directions:

- upwards/forwards, as in the [i:] of *bee* (the colon represents a long vowel);

- upwards/backwards, as in the [uː] of *boo*; and
- downwards/backwards, as in the [ɑː] of *bah*.

In addition, we can alter the shape of the tongue, in any position. For example, some muscles raise or lower the tongue tip, or move it to the left or the right. Others move the tongue sideways, or form a groove along the middle – an important feature of the articulation of [s].

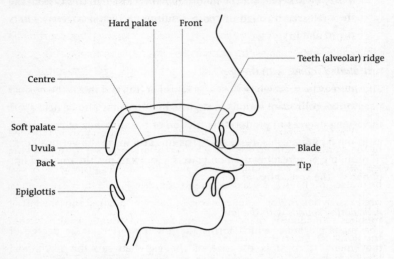

Fig. 2. The main parts of the tongue

There are no obvious anatomical sections to the tongue, so to classify how sounds are made with this organ we have to relate the position of the tongue to the upper part of the mouth.

- the *tip* or *apex* of the tongue is the very front extremity – used, for example, in producing the *th* sounds in words like *thick* and *this*;
- the *blade* of the tongue is the tapering part opposite the teeth ridge – used in producing such sounds as [l], where the blade is pressed against the ridge;
- the *front* of the tongue is the part opposite the hard palate, easily visible when we look inside the mouth; it is high in the mouth when

we pronounce such vowels as the [i:] in *bee* or the [j] consonant at the beginning of *yet*;

- the *back* of the tongue is the part opposite the soft palate, less easily visible when we look inside the mouth, but which comes into view when we put out our tongue; it makes contact with the palate when we pronounce such consonants as the [k] in *car*, and is very low in the mouth when we respond to a doctor's instruction to 'say ah';
- the *centre* of the tongue is between front and back, opposite where the hard and soft palate meet; it is used in making a few consonants and vowels, such as the *central* vowel [ə] heard in such words as *the*; and
- the *rims* are the edges of the tongue, important as part of the articulation of [l] and a few other sounds.

The importance of the tongue in speech production is even reflected in the words and idioms we use. When we want someone to stop talking we can say 'hold your tongue'; someone who is fluent or persuasive can be praised for having 'a good tongue in your head'; and the word is often used as a synonym for 'language' – as in 'foreign tongues' and 'the gift of tongues'. The identity of 'speech', 'language', and 'tongue' is also seen in the Romance languages, where all three notions are expressed by Latin *lingua* and its derivatives, such as French *langue*, Italian *lingua*, and Spanish *lengua*.

6
How we transmit sounds

When we speak, we produce energy in the form of sound. Sound energy is a pressure wave consisting of vibrations of molecules in an elastic medium – such as a gas, a liquid, or certain types of solid (e.g. along a telephone wire). For the study of speech production, the normal way of propagating sound is through the air. Air particles are disturbed through the movements and vibrations of the vocal organs, especially the vocal folds (§5). When we study speech reception (§7), air is not the only medium involved. The process of hearing requires the sound vibrations in air to be transformed into mechanical vibrations (through the bony mechanism of the middle ear), hydraulic changes (through the liquid within the inner ear), and electrical nerve impulses (along the auditory nerve to the brain).

When an object vibrates, it causes to-and-fro movements in the air particles that surround it. These particles affect adjacent particles, and the process continues as a chain reaction for as long as the energy lasts. If there is a great deal of energy in the original vibration, the sound that is produced may be transmitted a great distance, before it dies away. But the air particles themselves do not travel throughout this distance. The movement of each particle is purely local, each one affecting the next, in much the same way as a long series of closely positioned dominoes can be knocked over, once the first domino is pushed. However, unlike dominoes, air particles move back towards their original position once they have transmitted their movement to their neighbours. The movement is wave-like, backwards and forwards.

The way air particles move can be compared to a pendulum or a swing. At rest, a swing hangs down vertically. When it is put in motion, a backwards movement is followed by a forwards movement, on either side of the rest point, as long as there is energy available to keep the swing moving. This to-and-fro movement is called *oscillation*. Similarly, air particles oscillate around their rest point. As a particle moves forward, it compresses the adjacent particles and causes a tiny increase in the air pressure at that point. As it moves back, it decompresses these particles and causes a decrease in pressure. We can draw a graph of the pressure wave that is built up when particles move in this way. This graph is called a *waveform*. It is usual to draw waveforms as patterns from left to right, on either side of a horizontal line representing the passage of time. The simple movement of a single particle would look like this:

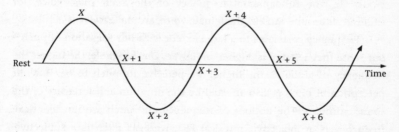

Fig. 3. Movement of a single air particle

Simple waveforms consist of a single pulse of vibration that repeats itself at a constant rate. The result is a *pure tone*. Pure tones are rarely heard in everyday life. Most sounds are complex, consisting of several simultaneous patterns of vibration. To produce a pure tone, you need a special electronic machine, or a device such as a tuning fork. When a tuning fork is struck, it vibrates with a single tone. The prongs of the fork move to and fro at a fixed rate. When the fork is held to the ear, we hear a pure tone.

Generating frequency

A single to-and-fro movement of an air particle is called a *cycle*, and the number of cycles that occur in a second is known as the *frequency* of a sound. Frequency used to be measured in *cycles per second* (*cps*), but this unit has been renamed *hertz* (abbreviated *Hz*), named after the German physicist Heinrich Rudolf Hertz (1857–94), who first broadcast and received radio waves. The basic frequency at which a sound vibrates is known as the *fundamental frequency*, generally abbreviated as F_o and pronounced 'F nought'.

The range of frequencies that a young normal adult can hear is extremely wide – from about 20 to 20,000 Hz. It is not possible to hear vibrations lower than this (*infrasonic*) or higher than this (*ultrasonic*). However, the frequencies at both ends of this range are of little significance for speech: the most important speech frequencies lie between 100 and 4,000 Hz. The fundamental frequency of the adult male voice, for example, is around 120 Hz; the female voice, around 220 Hz (§5).

Frequency correlates to a large extent with our sensation of *pitch* – our sense that a sound is 'higher' or 'lower'. On the whole, the higher the frequency of a sound, the higher we perceive its pitch to be. But our perception of pitch is also affected by the duration and intensity of the sound stimulus. The notions of frequency and pitch are not identical: frequency is an objective, physical fact, whereas pitch is a subjective, psychological sensation.

One way of relating the physical notion of frequency to our sense of pitch is to relate familiar musical notes to fundamental frequency. Middle C has a frequency of 264 Hz. Middle A is the note sounded by the oboe when an orchestra is tuning up: that is 440 Hz. By comparison, the top note of a seven-octave piano is 3,520 Hz, and the bottom note is 27.5 Hz.

Making harmonics

The sound produced by an object vibrating in a periodic way involves more than the basic waveform. Other amounts of energy are also generated by the same vibration, all of which are correlated with the basic wave in a simple mathematical relationship: they are all multiples of the fundamental frequency. Thus an F_o of 200 Hz will set up a 'sympathetic' set of frequencies at 400 Hz, 600 Hz, and so on. These multiples are known as *overtones*, or *harmonics*, and numbered in sequence. In physics (but not in music), F_o counts as the *first* harmonic. So, in this example, 400 Hz would be the second harmonic, 600 Hz the third harmonic, and so on. This kind of framework is especially useful in analysing vowels, certain consonants, and patterns of intonation (§12).

Depending on the nature of the vibrating object (for example, the material it is made of, or its thickness), different sets of harmonics are established, and these are heard as differences in sound *quality*, or *timbre*. The difference we hear between two voices, or two musical instruments, when they produce a sound of the same pitch and loudness, is a contrast of timbre caused by the different harmonics.

Varying intensity

The extent to which an air particle moves to and fro around its rest point is called the *amplitude* of the vibration. The greater the amplitude, the greater the *intensity* of the sound, and along with other factors (such as frequency and duration) the greater our sensation of *loudness*. In the diagram on p. 36 we see three waves of equal frequency but of different amplitude. In each case, one complete vibration lasts 10 msec (the frequency is thus 100 per second, or 100 Hz). But (a) has twice the amplitude of (b), and (b) has twice that of (c).

To measure sound intensity, we need a basic, internationally accepted reference level for sound pressure in air. This *sound pressure level* identifies the threshold at which a sound can be heard. Departures from this reference level are then measured in units called *decibels* (*dB*), named after Alexander Graham Bell (1847–1922), the American inventor of the telephone. Thus, to say that a sound is 90 dB means that it has an intensity which is 90 dB greater than the reference level.

We are able to hear a vast range of sound intensities. A loud shout is

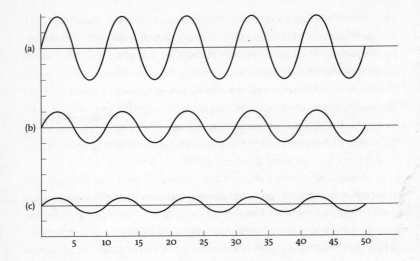

Fig. 4. Sine waves of equal frequency but different amplitude

a million times more powerful than a whisper. It has been estimated that the human ear is sensitive to about 10 million million (10^{13}) units of intensity. To enable analysts to cope with such large amounts, sound intensities are related to each other as ratios, using a logarithmic scale. An increase of 10 dB is roughly equivalent to a doubling of loudness. 30 dB is twice as loud as 20 dB, 40 dB is twice as loud as 30 dB, and so on. In this way, 10^{13} units can be 'reduced' to a scale of 130 decibels – a scale that more accurately reflects the way in which we sense differences of loudness between sounds.

We can get a sense of the decibel scale if we note the differences between familiar sounds.

- The rustle of leaves would be about 10 dB.
- The ticking of a watch held to the ear would be about 20 dB.
- A whispered conversation would be about 30 dB.
- An old-style typewriter in a quiet office would be about 40 dB.
- A car 10 metres away would be about 60 dB.
- Very busy city traffic would be about 70 dB.

- A noisy tube train would be about 80 dB.
- A pneumatic drill at 1 metre distance would be about 90 dB.
- An amplified rock band would be about 120 dB (at least).
- A four-engined jet aircraft at 30 metres distance would be about 130 dB.

At around 120 dB, the sensation of hearing is replaced by one of pain.

It is also possible to work out average intensity values for individual speech sounds. Vowels with the mouth wide open (such as [a:]) are the most intense sounds, followed by vowels made higher up in the mouth (such as [o:] and [i:]) and vowel-like sounds such as [r] and [l]. Much less intense are sounds involving a weak level of friction, such as [f], or those involving an articulatory closure and release, such as [p]. The decibel difference between adjacent sounds can be quite large. In a word like *thorn*, the increase in intensity from the first sound to the second is nearly 30 dB.

Making complex tones

Most sources of sound produce complex sets of vibrations, and this is always the case with speech. Speech involves the use of complex waveforms because it results from the simultaneous use of many sources of vibration in the vocal tract (§4–5). When two or more pure tones of different frequencies combine, the result is a *complex tone*.

There are two kinds of complex tone. In one type, the waveform repeats itself: a *periodic* pattern of vibration. In the other, there is no such repetition: the vibrations are random, or *aperiodic*. Speech makes use of both kinds. The vowel sounds, for example, display a periodic pattern; sounds such as [s] are aperiodic.

It is possible to make an acoustic analysis of the complex wave involved in a particular sound and present its various components in the form of a sound *spectrum*. When we do this it becomes possible to see various 'peaks' of acoustic energy, reflecting the main points of resonance in the vocal tract. These peaks are known as *formants*, and they are

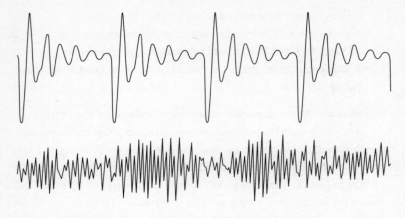

Fig. 5. Waveforms of a vowel [aː] and consonant [sː]

numbered from lowest to highest: the *first* formant (F_1), the *second* formant (F_2), and so on. For a vowel like [iː], as in *bee*, spoken by a man at a fundamental frequency of 120 Hz, the F_1 would peak at 360 Hz, the F_2 at 2,280 Hz, and the F_3 at 3,000 Hz.

Formant structure is a major feature of speech sounds that involve vocal-fold vibration (§5) – which means all the vowels and all the voiced consonants, such as [b] and [n]. It is the formant pattern (especially the disposition of the first two formants) that enables us to tell vowels apart, or to recognize two vowels as being the 'same', even when produced by different speakers. And vowel formants can also help in identifying the character of adjacent consonant sounds.

7
How we hear speech sounds

The first step in the reception of speech – or of any sound – takes place when the sound waves arrive at the ear. From there, sound is transmitted along the auditory nerve to the brain. The process is a complex one, involving several distinct stages which reflect the main anatomical division of the ear into outer ear, middle ear, and inner ear.

The outer ear

The outer ear consists of two parts. The visible part is known as the *auricle* or *pinna* – a structure consisting of several rounded prominences formed mainly from cartilage. The pinna has a minor role to play in the reception of sound: it helps to focus sound waves into the ear, and assists our ability to detect the source of a sound. It also protects the entrance to the auditory canal, both from physical attacks and from excessive amounts of sound. By pressing the central part of the pinna with the finger, it is possible to cover the entrance to the canal, thus considerably reducing the amount of sound entering the ear.

From here, the *external auditory canal* leads to the *eardrum*. The canal is about 2.5 cm long and contains hairs and glands that secrete wax, a substance that acts as a filter for dust, insects, and other tiny substances that might approach the eardrum. The canal acts as a small amplifier for certain sound frequencies (between 3,000 and 4,000 Hz – see §6), thus

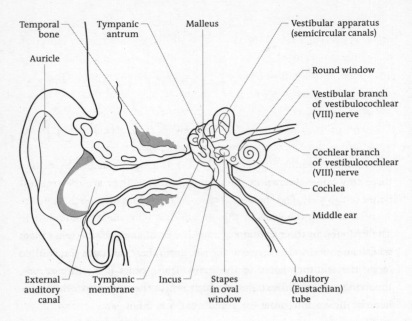

Labels on figure:
Temporal bone
Auricle
Tympanic antrum
Malleus
Vestibular apparatus (semicircular canals)
Round window
Vestibular branch of vestibulocochlear (VIII) nerve
Cochlear branch of vestibulocochlear (VIII) nerve
Cochlea
Middle ear
External auditory canal
Tympanic membrane
Incus
Stapes in oval window
Auditory (Eustachian) tube

Fig. 6. Anatomy of the ear

making weak sounds at these frequencies more perceptible. It also helps to protect the eardrum to some extent from changes in temperature and humidity as well as from physical damage – though no canal has yet proved capable of withstanding the ingenious attempts of young children to insert all kinds of implements inside their ears!

The middle ear

The eardrum separates the outer ear from the middle ear. It is roughly circular in shape, lying at an angle of about 55° across the whole of the external auditory canal. It consists of a fibrous tissue with important elastic properties that enable it to vibrate when sound waves reach it. The shape and tension of the eardrum cause the vibrations to be focused at a prominence near its centre, from where they are transferred to the first of the bones of the middle ear, which is firmly attached to the membrane.

The chamber of the middle ear lies within the bones of the skull, about 15 mm high. It is filled with air, because there is a direct connection to the nose and throat via the *Eustachian tube* – named after the Italian anatomist, Bartolommeo Eustachio (1520–74). This tube is normally closed, but such activities as yawning or swallowing open it. In this way, the air pressure level on either side of the eardrum is maintained.

The primary function of the middle ear is to change the sound vibrations at the eardrum into mechanical movement – which will in turn be transmitted to the fluid-filled inner ear. It does this using a system of three tiny bones, known as the auditory *ossicles*. They are the smallest bones in the body, and the only ones to be fully formed at birth. They are suspended from the walls of the middle ear by ligaments, and are delicately hinged together so that vibrations can pass smoothly between them into the inner ear. The three bones have been given Latin names according to their shape: the *malleus* 'hammer', which is attached to the eardrum, the *incus* 'anvil', and the *stapes* (pronounced *stay-peez*) 'stirrup'. The stapes fits into the *oval window* – an opening in the bony wall separating the middle ear from the inner ear.

This may seem an unnecessarily complicated system of getting vibrations from point A to point B, but it is known to have several advantages. In particular, the process acts as a kind of leverage system, enabling the vibrations to be greatly amplified (by a factor of over 30 dB) by the time they reach the inner ear. As the inner ear is filled with fluid, vibrations would very readily get lost without this amplification. Also, the bony network of the middle ear helps to protect the inner ear from sudden, very loud sounds. The muscles that control the movement of the eardrum and the stapes function in such a way that they lessen the chances of massive vibrations damaging the inner ear. However, the time it takes for these muscles to react is not so rapid that the inner ear can be protected from all such sounds, and cases of damage to the eardrum or inner ear do occur.

The inner ear

This is a system of small interconnecting cavities and passageways within the skull. It contains the *semi-circular canals*, which control our sense of balance, and the *cochlea*, a coiled cavity about 35 mm long, resembling a snail's shell. The main function of the cochlea is to turn the mechanical vibrations produced by the middle ear into electrical nerve impulses capable of being transmitted to the brain.

The cochlea is divided along most of its length into an upper chamber (the *scala vestibuli*) and a lower chamber (the *scala tympani*), separated by the *cochlear duct*. Both chambers are filled with a clear, viscous fluid known as *perilymph*. Vibrations enter this fluid via the oval window and the scala vestibuli, and are transmitted all the way around the cochlea. They pass from upper to lower chamber through an opening in the cochlear duct at its apex, and finish at a sealed opening in the wall of the middle ear, called the *round window*.

The cochlear duct is separated from the scala tympani by the *basilar membrane*, and is filled with fluid known as *endolymph*. This membrane is very thin at the base of the cochlea (about 0.04 mm) and gets thicker as it approaches the apex (about 0.5 mm). It is thus able to respond differentially to incoming vibratory pressures: high frequencies (§6) primarily affect the narrow end; certain low frequencies activate the entire membrane.

Resting on this membrane is the highly sensitive organ of hearing, called the *organ of Corti*, discovered by the Italian anatomist Alfonso Corti (1822–76), and it is this which translates the mechanical movements of the membrane into nerve impulses. It contains a systematic arrangement of cells covered with very fine hairs, distributed in rows and layers along the membrane. These *hair cells* act as sensory receptors, picking up the pressure movements in the endolymph. Electrochemical changes take place, which activate the fibres of the auditory nerve. The signals are then sent the short distance along this nerve to the temporal lobe, via the brain stem and mid-brain, where they are interpreted as speech sounds.

Do we need two ears?

Two ears are a great asset. They enable us to be more precise in our judgement of the position of a sound source – an important factor in listening to people in a group, or heeding the direction of a vocal warning. This happens because a sound source is usually nearer one ear than the other; as a result, the signals to each ear will be slightly out of phase, and one will be more intense. The brain resolves these differences and makes a judgement about localization. Sometimes there is ambiguity (when a sound is reflected by a nearby object, for example), in which case we have to 'search' for the sound source by moving the head.

The value of two ears is most evident in cases of hearing loss in one ear. The 'good' ear copes well with a single speaker in a quiet room; but in contexts where sound is coming in from several directions (such as in a meeting), the listener finds localizing the source of sound very difficult, and may look for the speaker in the wrong direction.

We should also note that the brain uses our two ears in different ways. One ear may have an advantage over the other for certain types of sound. This can be shown in tests of *dichotic* listening, where different signals are presented simultaneously to each ear, and listeners hear one sound ahead of the other. This shows that one ear transmits a sound to the brain more readily than the other. It is an important research technique in the study of speech perception.

8
How we perceive speech

Just as the vocal organs have evolved to facilitate the production of speech, so the auditory system seems 'tuned' to receive speech patterns. When we hear sounds, we hear them as either speech or non-speech; there seems to be no middle ground. No matter how hard we try, we cannot hear speech as a series of acoustic hisses and buzzes, but only as a sequence of speech sounds. This is the kind of observation that has motivated the field of *speech perception* – the study of the way speech sounds are analysed and identified by the brain.

Speech perception is part of the general subject called *auditory perception* – the study of the way we take in any kind of sound stimulus, from music to barking dogs. Several factors are involved, and thus to say that we have 'heard' a sound can mean several different things.

- The body may react physiologically to the presence of a sound stimulus, but we are not consciously aware of it. Such involuntary reflexes can be seen through variations in the rate of our breathing or heartbeat, and in a few other ways.
- A sound is consciously detected. This is how the term *heard* is normally used. For this to happen, of course, there has to be a certain minimum amount of stimulation. The sound has to be *audible*.
- Sounds may be perceived to be the same (*recognized*) or different (*discriminated*). An important question is how different two sounds

have to be in order for the brain to perceive that they are different. There has to be a minimum difference in magnitude – a *just noticeable difference*. Our ability to detect and discriminate sound is known as auditory *acuity*.

- The brain is able to focus on certain aspects of a complex auditory stimulus and to ignore others: the phenomenon of *auditory attention*. When we begin to 'hear attentively', we are said to be *listening*. The concepts of *hearing* and *listening* are therefore not the same, and should always be carefully distinguished.

Finding the units of speech

The basic question in speech perception is how the brain manages to find linguistic units – the vowels, consonants, syllables, words, and so on – within all the auditory noise that surrounds us. When several people are talking at once in a crowded room, we are able to 'tune in' to one speaker and to ignore the others. If we hear our name spoken nearby, we can readily attend to that conversation, even at the risk of disregarding the person we are supposed to be listening to. Such *cocktail-party phenomena* illustrate the human ability to pay attention to some incoming sound stimuli and to ignore others – what is known as *selective listening*. How does the brain select auditory information so impressively?

Those complications are avoided when we are listening to just one speaker, but even a one-to-one interaction is not a simple process. What we receive from a speaker is a continuously varying waveform (§6). If we record that waveform, we find that the linguistic units are not neatly demarcated by pauses or other boundary markers. Sounds run into each other. Yet when we are listening we hear this waveform as a sequence of sounds and words. How is the brain able to analyse this signal so that the language units can be identified?

When we start to analyse the signal, we find other intriguing issues. If we hear different instances of a particular sound, we have no difficulty recognizing them as 'the same'. We hear the [b] sounds in *bee, bay, bar, able*, and *rob* as the same. But when we examine the relevant parts of the waveform, we find that a [b] before an [iː] vowel, as in *bee*, does not have exactly the same waveform as the [b] before an [ɑː] vowel, as in *bar*. Instances of [b] at the beginning of a word also differ from those at the end. Moreover, the articulation of [b] by different people will result in different waveforms because their regional accents and individual voice qualities will not be the same. It will vary, further, when people adopt different tones of voice (such as a whisper), or when it is said in a noisy situation. How does the brain recognize a [b] sound when there is so much variation?

In normal speech, people produce sounds very quickly (twelve or more segments per second), run sounds together, and leave sounds out. Nonetheless, the brain is able to process such rapid sequences, and cope with these modifications. For example, in the word *handbag*, the *nd* is actually pronounced as [m] in colloquial speech, because of the influence of the following [b]; but the word is still interpreted as *hand* and not *ham*. How does the brain carry out such partial identifications?

Looking for acoustic cues

One reason why we are able to recognize speech, despite all the acoustic variation in the signal, and even in very difficult listening conditions, is that the speech situation contains a great deal of redundancy – more information than is strictly necessary to decode the message. The wide range of frequencies found in every speech signal presents us with far more information than we need in order to recognize what is being said. Just some of this information forms the relevant distinguishing features of the signal – features that have come to be known as *acoustic cues*.

The main research technique has been to create artificial sounds using a *speech synthesizer* – an electronic device that generates sound waves with any required combination of frequency, intensity, and time (§6). In the classic experiments using this device, the synthesizer was fed simplified acoustic patterns – a sound with two formants at certain frequencies, for example – and the researchers could then see whether the sound that emerged was recognizable as a certain vowel. Or, a sequence of formants, formant transitions, and bursts of noise could be synthesized, to see if listeners would perceive a particular sequence of consonant and vowel.

Using this technique, researchers found it was possible to establish the crucial role of the first two formants (§6) for the recognition of vowels. Similarly, the technique showed how we distinguish between voiceless and voiced consonants, such as [b] vs. [p] – it largely depends on the onset time of the vocal-fold vibration. And, in an important series of experiments, it was shown how the transitions of the second formant between a consonant and a vowel are especially important as a means of telling us where in the mouth the consonant is being made.

Such findings have laid the foundation for speech perception studies, and the way we perceive vowels and consonants is now quite well understood. But a great deal still remains to be explained. For example, the acoustic values cited for the various sounds are averages, and do not take into account the many differences between speakers. Males, females, and children will produce the same vowel with very different formants, and it is not yet clear how we make allowances for these differences – for example, enabling us to judge that a male [a] vowel and a female [a] vowel are somehow the 'same'. Nor is it obvious how we handle the difference between stressed and unstressed sounds, or other modifications that result from the speed of connected speech.

How we perceive continuous speech

A great deal of research has been carried out on the auditory perception of isolated sounds, syllables, or words. In connected speech, however, very different processes seem to operate. We do not perceive whole sentences as a sequence of isolated sounds. And it turns out that the grammar of the sentence and the meaning of the words strongly influence our ability to identify linguistic units.

In one study, acoustically distorted words were presented to listeners both in isolation and in context. The context helped the listeners to identify the words much more accurately. In another study, single words were cut out of a tape recording of clear, intelligible, continuous speech. When these were played to listeners, there was great difficulty in making a correct identification. Normal speech proves to be so rapidly and informally articulated that in fact over half the words cannot be recognized in isolation – and yet we have little trouble following it, and can repeat whole sentences accurately.

Another feature of continuous speech perception is that we 'hear' sounds to be present, even if they are not. In one experiment, sentences were recorded with a sound electronically removed, and replaced with a cough or buzz. Most listeners, when asked if there were any sounds missing, said no; and even if told that a substitution had been made, most were unable to locate it. In another study, people listened to one of four sentences, in which a sound (marked *) had been replaced by a cough, and were asked to identify a word which ended in *eel*.

It was found that the *eel was on the axle.
It was found that the *eel was on the shoe.
It was found that the *eel was on the orange.
It was found that the *eel was on the table.

People responded with *wheel*, *heel*, *peel*, and *meal* respectively, demonstrating the influence of grammar and meaning in perceptual decision-making.

Results of this kind suggest that speech perception is a highly active process, with people making good the inadequacies of what they hear arising out of external noise, omitted sounds, and so on. A further implication is that models of speech perception based on the study of isolated sounds and words are of little value in explaining the processes that operate in relation to connected speech.

Do we listen actively or passively?

There are two main views of speech perception. In one view, we are thought to play an active role in speech perception, in the sense that when we hear a message, we decode the sounds with reference to how we would pronounce them when we speak. Our knowledge of articulation (§5) acts as a bridge between the acoustic signal and the identification of linguistic units. One major approach, proposed in the 1960s, is called the *motor theory* of speech perception. This theory argues that we model internally the articulatory movements of a speaker. We identify sounds by sensing the articulatory gestures that must have produced them – as if we were 'saying' words to ourselves to match the incoming speech. Another approach is known as *analysis by synthesis*. Here, we are assumed to make use of a set of mental rules to analyse an incoming acoustic signal into an abstract set of features. We then use the same rules to synthesize a matching version in production. Our perceptual system compares the acoustic features of the incoming signal with the ones it has generated itself, and makes an identification.

In the second view, listeners play a passive role. We simply hear a message, recognize the regular distinctive features of the waveform, and decode it. Listening is therefore essentially a sensory process, with the pattern of information in the acoustic stimulus directly triggering a response in the brain. No reference is made to a mediating process of speech production (except in difficult conditions, such as noisy speech situations). Several mechanisms have been proposed. One approach proposes a system of *template matching* – we match incoming auditory patterns to a set of abstract speech patterns (such as vowels and syllables) that have already been stored in the brain. Another suggests we use *feature detectors* – special neural receptors (analogous to those known to exist in visual processing) that are capable of responding to specific features of the sound stimulus, such as a particular formant, noise burst, or other general feature.

Both approaches have their strengths and weaknesses. Active approaches plausibly explain how we are able to adjust to such differences as speaker accent, voice quality, and speed of speech. And several kinds of experiment can be interpreted to support this view. In 'shadowing' studies, for example, people are asked to repeat what someone says as quickly as possible, without waiting for the speaker to finish. We are evidently able to carry out this task at great speed, copying sounds even before we have heard all the acoustic cues. To do this, we must be making active use of our knowledge of linguistic structure.

However, there are arguments against a wholly active view of speech perception. There are many cases of people who cannot speak, for pathological reasons (§15), but who can understand well. And it is possible to understand the speech of stutterers, foreigners, young children, and others where it is not possible to make a simple articulatory match. The passive approach does not encounter these problems. On the other hand, it has in turn been criticized for underestimating the variability of the link between acoustic signals and linguistic units, and for presenting an account in which the processes of speech production and those of speech perception are seen as entirely separate. It therefore seems likely that some combination of active and passive theories will be required, in order to provide a satisfactory explanation of how we perceive speech.

9
How we describe speech sounds

The description and classification of speech sounds is the main aim of *phonetic science*, or *phonetics*. We can identify sounds with reference to their production (or *articulation*) in the vocal tract, their acoustic transmission, or their auditory reception. The most widely used descriptions are *articulatory*, because the vocal tract provides a convenient and well-understood reference point (§5); but auditory judgements play an important part in the identification of some sounds (of vowels, in particular).

An articulatory phonetic description generally makes reference to the following factors.

How we use the air-stream
The source and direction of air flow identifies the basic class of sound. The vast majority of speech sounds are produced using pulmonic egressive air (§4).

How we use the vocal folds
We need to consider the variable action of the vocal folds – in particular, the presence or absence of vibration (§5). *Voiced* sounds are produced when the vocal folds vibrate; *voiceless* sounds are produced when there is no vibration, the folds remaining open. Other vocal-fold actions are sometimes referred to, such as the way the glottis works when it produces a glottal stop (p. 27).

How we use the soft palate

We must note the position of the soft palate (§5). When it is lowered, air passes through the nose, and the sound is described as *nasal* or *nasalized*; when it is raised, air passes through the mouth, and the sound is *oral*.

Where we make the articulation

Place of articulation refers to the point in the vocal tract at which the primary closure or narrowing is made, such as at the lips, teeth, or hard palate. We may also need to take into account accompanying *secondary* constrictions or movements.

How we make the articulation

Manner of articulation refers to the type of constriction or movement that takes place at any place of articulation, such as a marked degree of narrowing, a closure with sudden release, or a closure with slow release.

How we use the lips

The position of the lips is an important feature of the description of certain sounds (especially vowels), such as whether they are *rounded* or *spread*, *closed* or *open*.

Whether we use other factors

In very precise descriptions of speech sounds, we may need to note other factors, such as the relative position of the jaw or the overall shape of the tongue.

Coarticulating

What is so impressive about speech is that all these factors are operating at the same time, and we describe a single speech sound with reference to all of them. In addition, we have to remember that a 'single' speech sound is something of a fiction. The vocal organs do not move from sound to sound in a series of separate steps. Speech is a continuously varying process (§6), and sounds continually show the influence of their neighbours.

For example, if a nasal consonant such as [m] precedes an oral vowel such as [a], some of the nasality will carry forward, so that the onset of the vowel will have a somewhat nasal quality. The reason is simply that it takes time for the soft palate to move from the lowered position required for [m] to the raised position required for [a]. It is still in the process of moving after the articulation of [a] has begun. Similarly, if [a] were followed by [m], the soft palate would begin to lower during the articulation of the vowel, to be ready for the following nasal consonant.

When sounds involve overlapping or simultaneous articulations in this way, the process is known as *coarticulation*. If the sound becomes more like a following sound (its *target*), we are dealing with *anticipatory* coarticulation; if the sound displays the influence of the preceding sound, we are dealing with *perseverative* coarticulation. Anticipatory effects are far more common: a typical example in English is the way vowel lip position affects a preceding [s]. In such words as *see*, the [s] is pronounced with spread lips, anticipating the spread-lipped vowel. In such words as *sue*, the [s] is pronounced with rounded lips, anticipating the round-lipped vowel.

Using the International Phonetic Alphabet

The set of factors listed above is the basis of the International Phonetic Alphabet (or IPA). In 1886, a small group of language teachers in France who had found the practice of phonetics useful in their work formed an association to popularize their methods. They called it the Phonetic Teachers' Association, and in 1897 the name was changed to the International Phonetic Association. One of the first activities of the Association was to develop the idea of a phonetic transcription, and the first version of the IPA was published in August 1888. The latest revision is reproduced on p. 54.

The chart shows all the consonants and vowels, as well as many diacritics used to identify subtle differences of pronunciation, along with symbols for clicks (§4) and pitch variations (§12). In the main table, we see the place of articulation of consonants changing as we move across the

Consonants (Pulmonic)

	Bilabial	Labiodental	Dental	Alveolar	Postalveolar	Retroflex	Palatal	Velar	Uvular	Pharyngeal	Glottal
Plosive	p b			t d		ʈ ɖ	c ɟ	k g	q ɢ		ʔ
Nasal	m	ɱ		n		ɳ	ɲ	ŋ	ɴ		
Trill	ʙ			r					ʀ		
Tap or flap				ɾ		ɽ					
Fricative	ɸ β	f v	θ ð	s z	ʃ ʒ	ʂ ʐ	ç ʝ	x ɣ	χ ʁ	ħ ʕ	h ɦ
Lateral fricative				ɬ ɮ							
Approximant		ʋ		ɹ		ɻ	j	ɰ			
Lateral approximant				l		ɭ	ʎ	ʟ			

Where symbols appear in pairs, the one on the right represents a voiced consonant. Shaded areas denote articulations judged impossible.

Consonants (Non-Pulmonic)

Clicks	Voiced implosives	Ejectives
ʘ Bilabial	ɓ Bilabial	ʼ as in:
ǀ Dental	ɗ Dental/alveolar	pʼ Bilabial
ǃ (Post)alveolar	ʄ Palatal	tʼ Dental/alveolar
ǂ Palatoalveolar	ɠ Velar	kʼ Velar
ǁ Alveolar lateral	ʛ Uvular	sʼ Alveolar fricative

Suprasegmentals

ˈ	Primary stress	ˌfoʊnəˈtɪʃən
ˌ	Secondary stress	
ː	Long	eː
ˑ	Half-long	eˑ
˘	Extra-short	ĕ
.	Syllable break	ɹi.ækt
ǀ	Minor (foot) group	
‖	Major (intonation) group	
‿	Linking (absence of a break)	

Tones and word accents

Level		Contour	
e̋ or ˥	Extra high	ě or ˩˥	Rising
é ˦	High	ê ˥˩	Falling
ē ˧	Mid	e᷄ ˧˥	High rising
è ˨	Low	e᷅ ˩˧	Low rising
ȅ ˩	Extra low	e᷈ ˧˩˧	Rising-falling etc.
↓	Downstep	↗	Global rise
↑	Upstep	↘	Global fall

Vowels

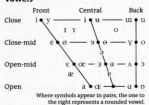

Where symbols appear in pairs, the one to the right represents a rounded vowel.

Other Symbols

ʍ	Voiceless labial-velar fricative
w	Voiced labial-velar approximant
ɥ	Voiced labial-palatal approximant
ʜ	Voiceless epiglottal fricative
ʢ	Voiced epiglottal fricative
ʡ	Epiglottal plosive
ɕ ʑ	Alveolo-palatal fricatives
ɺ	Alveolar lateral flap
ɧ	Simultaneous ʃ and x

Affricates and double articulations can be represented by two symbols joined by a tie bar if necessary. k͡p t͡s

Diacritics

Diacritics may be placed above a symbol with a descender, e.g. ŋ̊

Voiceless	n̥ d̥	Breathy voiced	b̤ a̤	Dental	t̪ d̪
Voiced	s̬ t̬	Creaky voiced	b̰ a̰	Apical	t̺ d̺
ʰ Aspirated	tʰ dʰ	Linguolabial	t̼ d̼	Laminal	t̻ d̻
More rounded	ɔ̹	ʷ Labialized	tʷ dʷ	Nasalized	ẽ
Less rounded	ɔ̜	ʲ Palatalized	tʲ dʲ	ⁿ Nasal release	dⁿ
Advanced	u̟	ˠ Velarized	tˠ dˠ	ˡ Lateral release	dˡ
Retracted	i̠	ˤ Pharyngealized	tˤ dˤ	˺ No audible release	d˺
Centralized	ë	~ Velarized or pharyngealized	ɫ		
Mid-centralized	ě	Raised	e̝ (ɹ̝ = voiced alveolar fricative)		
Syllabic	ɹ̩	Lowered	e̞ (β̞ = voiced bilabial approximant)		
Non-syllabic	e̯	Advanced Tongue Root	e̘		
˞ Rhoticity	ɚ	Retracted Tongue Root	e̙		

Fig. 7. The International Phonetic Alphabet

How Language Works

table from left to right, with the front of the mouth imagined to be on the left. The various manners of articulation are shown as rows in this table. Pairs of voiceless and voiced consonants are shown side by side, with the voiceless member on the left. Vowels, similarly, are shown in a diagram (§10) representing the central area of the mouth, with the vertical dimension showing tongue height and the horizontal dimension showing tongue position towards the front (on the left) and back (on the right) of the mouth.

The IPA looks complex, but this is because of its basic principle that there should be a separate letter for each distinctive sound, and that the same symbol should be used for that sound in any language in which it appears. The languages of the world display a very wide range of sounds, so most of the cells in the table are filled. On the other hand, there are several gaps: languages do not use all the possibilities available in the vocal tract.

Many of the symbols are familiar, to European eyes, because the originators of the alphabet decided to use letters of the Roman alphabet wherever possible, and to introduce new letters and diacritics only when absolutely necessary. However, with only twenty-six letters to play with, many adaptations had to be made, and some completely new symbols had to be devised. Several of these special letters have proved to be useful outside of phonetics, being used as part of new orthographies devised for previously unwritten languages.

Despite the aims of the IPA, alternative phonetic transcriptions for English vowels have appeared. The word *seat* might appear as [si:t], [sit], [siyt], or in some other way. The alternative symbols reflect different interpretations by phoneticians of the relationships between the sounds. For example, if they analysed the difference between English *seat* and *sit* as being essentially a contrast of vowel length, they might transcribe the two words as [si:t] and [sit] respectively, showing the length by the colon. On the other hand, if they saw the difference as essentially involving a contrast of vowel quality – one vowel being articulated in a different place from the other – they might transcribe as [sit] and [sɪt] respectively, using different symbols and no length mark. A transcription such as [siyt] would suggest that the vowel in *seat* has two distinct elements. In each case, the choice of symbols draws our attention to different aspects of the way the vowels are produced.

Distinguishing vowels and consonants

The two labels, *vowel* and *consonant*, are probably the most familiar of all the terms used in the description of speech, but we nonetheless need to use them with great care, to avoid mixing up two different kinds of definition.

In a phonetic definition, we distinguish vowels from consonants in terms of how they are articulated in the vocal tract, and the associated patterns of acoustic energy. In this approach, we define consonants as sounds made by a closure in the vocal tract, or by a narrowing which is so marked that air cannot escape without producing audible friction. Vowels are sounds that have no such stricture: air escapes in a relatively unimpeded way through the mouth or nose. It is therefore relatively easy to 'feel' the articulation of consonants; whereas vowels, involving only slight movements of the tongue and lips, are difficult to locate in this way, and are easier to distinguish on auditory grounds.

In a linguistic definition (strictly speaking, a phonological definition, §11), we distinguish vowels from consonants in terms of how these units are used in the structure of spoken language. In this approach, we define consonants (C) as the units that typically occur at the edges of syllables; vowels (V) are the units that typically occur at the centre of syllables. For example, in the syllables *pet* /pet/, *cat* /kat/, and *ten* /ten/, the syllable structure in each case consists of a central unit and two marginal units, to produce the pattern CVC. (The forward slashes, / /, are used whenever we want to identify sounds from a linguistic point of view.)

In the case of most sounds, the phonetic and the phonological approaches coincide. For example the sounds usually written as *p*, *f*, and *m* are 'consonants' from both points of view: they involve closure or audible friction; and they function at syllable margins, e.g. *map* /map/, *pit* /pit/; there are no such syllables as /mpf/ or /mfp/. Similarly, the sounds represented by *a*, *i*, and *e* are 'vowels' from both points of view: they are produced without audible friction; and they occur at the centres of syllables, in such words as *cap* /kap/, *hit* /hIt/, and *set* /set/.

However, there are a few problem cases. With the sounds usually written in English as *l*, *r*, *w*, and *y*, the two sets of criteria conflict:

- From a phonetic point of view, they are articulated without audible friction, and acoustically they display a similar energy pattern to that displayed by [a], [i], etc. A [w] is really a very short [u]. A [j] is a very short [i]. They must therefore be considered as vowels.
- From a linguistic point of view, these units typically occur at the margins of syllables, as in *let* /let/, *rat* /rat/, *wet* /wet/, and *you* /juː/. They must therefore be considered as consonants.

The usual way of handling this problem is to say that these four units are neither consonants nor vowels but midway between these categories. They are, in short, vowel-like consonants, and might be described either as *semi-consonants* or *semi-vowels*. In practice, we usually describe [l] and [r] as *approximants* or *frictionless continuants*, and [w] and [j] as *semi-vowels*.

As an endnote to this section, I should emphasize that, in this part of the book, all talk of vowels and consonants is with reference to speech and not writing. In written English, for example, the 26 letters of the alphabet comprise 5 vowels and 21 consonants. In spoken English, there are 20 vowels and 24 consonants. It is this discrepancy, of course, which underlies the complexity of English spelling (§20).

10
How we describe consonants and vowels

Describing consonants

We usually describe consonants with reference to the four criteria described in §5.

- their place of articulation in the vocal tract;
- their manner of articulation in the vocal tract;
- the state of vibration of the vocal folds – whether vibrating (voiced) or not (voiceless); and
- the position of the soft palate – whether raised (oral) or lowered (nasal).

The present section concentrates on pulmonic egressive sounds (§4), which make up the vast majority of the sounds of speech.

Varying the place of articulation

Two reference points are involved in defining where we make consonants: the part of the vocal tract that moves (the *active* articulator) and the part towards which it moves or with which it makes contact (the *passive* articulator) (§5). Eleven possible places are used in speech.

Bilabial

We use both lips to make the articulation, e.g. [p], [b], [m].

Labiodental

We make the lower lip articulate with the upper teeth, e.g. [f], [v].

Dental

We make the tongue tip and rims articulate with the upper teeth, e.g. [θ], [ð], as in *thin* and *this* respectively.

Alveolar

We make the blade (and sometimes the tip) of the tongue articulate with the alveolar ridge (§4), e.g. [t], [s].

Postalveolar or *palato-alveolar*

We make the blade (and sometimes the tip) of the tongue articulate with the alveolar ridge, at the same time raising the front of the tongue towards the hard palate, e.g. [ʃ], [ʒ], as in *shoe* and French *je* respectively.

Retroflex

We curl the tip of the tongue back to articulate with the area between the rear of the alveolar ridge and the front of the hard palate. Retroflex sounds are heard in many Indian English accents, and the 'dark' American English and British West Country use of *r* is often retroflex.

Palatal

We make the front of the tongue articulate with the hard palate, e.g. [ç], [j], as in German *ich* and *ja* respectively.

Velar

We make the back of the tongue articulate with the soft palate, e.g. [k], [g].

Uvular

We make the back of the tongue touch the uvula, e.g. [R], as in French *rue* (in certain accents).

Pharyngeal

We make the front wall of the pharynx (in the region of the epiglottis) articulate with the back wall, as can be heard in Arabic.

Glottal

We make the vocal folds come together to cause a closure or friction, e.g. [h], [ʔ] (the glottal stop). This is a rather different method of articulation from any of the other consonants.

Varying the manner of articulation

There are four main kinds of constriction made by the articulators in producing consonants, and these provide us with the basis of classification. The constriction might be total, partial, narrowed, or intermittent.

Consonants which make a total closure

Plosives

We make a complete closure at some location in the vocal tract, and raise the soft palate. Air pressure thus builds up behind the closure, which we then release explosively, as in [p] and [b]. The broader category of *stop* includes closures produced by other air-streams (§4), as well as plosives.

Nasals

We make a complete closure at some location in the mouth, and lower the soft palate so that air escapes through the nose, as in [m] and [n]. Nasals are usually voiced, but they can be voiceless, as in the Welsh word *mhen* 'my head'. Voiceless nasals are shown with the diacritic [ₒ] under a symbol, as in [m̥].

Affricates

We make a complete closure at some location in the mouth, and raise the soft palate, exactly as for plosives. Air pressure builds up behind the closure, but we then release it slowly (compared to a plosive release). The first element of the sound has a sharp plosive character, but this is followed by an element of audible friction, as in [tʃ] and [dʒ], heard in English *church* and *judge* respectively.

Consonants which make a partial closure

Laterals

We make a closure at one location in the mouth, but in such a way that we allow the air to escape around the sides of the closure. Various kinds of *l* sound are the result, as in *leap* and *peel*. They are called *laterals* because of the way we involve the sides of the tongue in the articulation.

Consonants which use a narrowing

Fricatives

We make two vocal organs come so close together that the movement of air between them causes audible friction, as in [f], [z], and [h]. The term *fricative* reflects the nature of the sound produced.

Consonants which make an intermittent closure

Rolls or Trills

We make one articulator tap rapidly against another. Most often this is the tongue tip tapping against the alveolar ridge or the back of the tongue tapping against the uvula, and these articulations produce the different kinds of *trilled r*. Examples can be heard in the *r* sound of Welsh or Scottish English, as well as in many French and German accents.

We make one articulator produce a single tap against another, as in some pronunciations of the *r* in *very*, or the *d* in *ladder*. In such cases the tongue tip taps once against the alveolar ridge. In Spanish a contrast is made between a trilled and a flapped *r*, as in *perro* [pero] 'dog' and *pero* [peɾo] 'but'.

Describing vowels

We usually describe vowels with reference to four criteria.

- the part of the tongue that is raised – front, centre, or back (§5);
- the extent to which the tongue rises in the direction of the palate. Normally, we recognize three or four degrees: *high*, *mid* (often divided into *mid-high* and *mid-low*), and *low*. Alternatively, we can describe tongue height as *close*, *mid-close*, *mid-open* and *open*;
- the position of the soft palate – raised for oral vowels, and lowered for vowels which have been nasalized; and
- the kind of opening made at the lips – various degrees of lip rounding or spreading.

It is difficult to be precise about the exact articulatory positions of the tongue and palate because the tongue movements are very slight, and they give us very little internal sensation. We cannot easily feel where the tongue is in the mouth when we produce a vowel, though it is possible to develop this skill through phonetics training. Nor are absolute values possible (such as saying that the tongue has moved *n* millimetres in a certain direction), because mouth dimensions are not the same between speakers. We therefore tend to make vowel judgements on the basis of auditory criteria, in association with a limited amount of visual and tactile information.

The first widely used system for classifying vowels was devised by the British phonetician Daniel Jones (1881–1967). The *cardinal vowel diagram* is a set of standard reference points based on a combination of articulatory and auditory judgements. The front, centre, and back of the tongue are distinguished, as are four levels of tongue height:

- the highest position the tongue can achieve without producing audible friction;
- the lowest position the tongue can achieve; and
- two intermediate levels, dividing the intervening space into auditorily equidistant areas.

The grid provides a basis for vowel classification, along with information about the accompanying position of the lips. Jones called the main vowel-points 'cardinal' vowels, giving them numbers, and distinguished a primary series (1–8) from a secondary series (9–16), adding two further points (17–18). Each of these vowel-points was also given a phonetic symbol, and these are shown in the diagram (repeated here from p. 54).

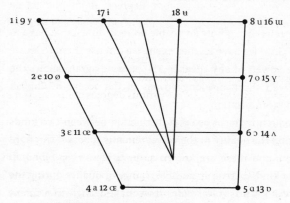

Fig. 8. The cardinal vowel diagram

The distinction between primary and secondary cardinal vowels is based on lip position. The first five primary vowels are all unrounded: front [i], [e], [ɛ], and [a], and back [ɑ]. The remaining three back vowels are rounded: [ɔ], [o], and [u]. In the secondary series, the lip position is reversed: the first five are rounded: front [y], [ø], [œ], and [Œ], and back [ɒ]. The remaining three back vowels are unrounded: [ʌ], [ɤ], and [ɯ]. The two other vowels represent the high points achieved by the centre of the tongue: they are unrounded [ɨ] and rounded [ʉ].

It should be emphasized that the cardinal vowels are not real vowels:

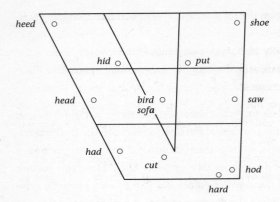

Fig. 9. Vowels in Received Pronunciation

they are invariable reference points (available on recordings) that have to be learned by rote. Once we have learned them, we can use them to locate the position of the vowels of any speaker. The above diagram shows the location of the eleven short and long vowels in the accent of English known as Received Pronunciation.

Languages frequently make use of a distinction between two kinds of vowels. In one kind the quality of the vowel remains constant throughout the articulation, and these are known as *pure vowels*, or *monophthongs*. In the other kind, there is an audible change of quality during the vowel, and these are known as *vowel glides*. If we make a single movement of the tongue during a glide, we call the effect a *diphthong*. If we make a double movement of the tongue, we call it a *triphthong*. Diphthongal glides in English can be heard in such words as *say* [seɪ], *fine* [faɪn], *cow* [kaʊ], *boy* [bɔɪ], and *so* [səʊ]. Triphthongal glides are found in certain pronunciations of such words as *fire* [faɪə] and *power* [paʊə] – often represented in literary writing in such a way as *fiyuh* and *powuh*.

Describing slight differences

There are many tiny differences in the articulation of vowels and consonants. An [e] or [p] sound in one language may not be made in exactly the same way as the [e] or [p] sound in another. Phoneticians have therefore devised a set of symbols which can be used to show these very small differences. They usually take the form of a small *diacritical* mark, such as an accent, dot, or dash, attached to a more prominent symbol.

For example, when we make a consonant such as [s] or [d] we do not normally round the lips; but it is perfectly possible to produce the sound with a rounded quality. Indeed, this happens routinely in English when these consonants are followed by a rounded vowel, such as the [uː] in *soon* and *do*. If we want to draw attention to this 'secondary' feature of articulation, we can do so by attaching a diacritic to the main symbol, as in [sʷ] or [s̜].

Similarly, we can show the way we vary the articulation of a vowel by using diacritical marks:

- a vowel which is made a little lower than a cardinal position can be shown with the symbol [˕], as in [e̞];
- a vowel which is made a little higher than a cardinal position can be shown with the symbol [˔], as in [e̝];
- a vowel which is made a little further forward than a cardinal position can be shown with the symbol [˖], as in [u̟];
- a vowel which is made a little further back than a cardinal position can be shown with the symbol [˗], as in [u̠];
- a vowel which is made more towards the centre of the mouth can be shown with the symbol [¨], as in [ë];
- a vowel which is more rounded than normal is shown with the symbol [˒], as in [ɔ̹];
- a vowel which is less rounded than normal is shown with the symbol [˓], as in [ɔ̜].

Variations of this kind are especially important when trying to capture the distinctive features of different accents (§45).

11
How we organize the sounds of speech

Phonetics is the study of how speech sounds are made, transmitted, and received (§9). It is a subject that requires as its source of data a human being with a functioning set of vocal organs. The person's particular language background is not strictly relevant: phoneticians would draw the same conclusions about the production of speech whether they were studying speakers of English, Hindi, or Chinese.

But English, Hindi, and Chinese are very different languages, using sounds in very different ways. We therefore need a different focus when we study how languages use sounds, and this is what *phonology* provides. The aim of phonology is to discover the principles that govern the way sounds are organized in languages, and to explain the variations that occur. We begin by analysing an individual language to determine which sound units are used and which patterns they form – the language's *sound system*. We then compare the properties of different sound systems, and work out hypotheses about the rules underlying the use of sounds in particular groups of languages. Ultimately, phonologists want to make statements that apply to all languages.

The distinction between phonetics and phonology can be seen from a second point of view. The human vocal apparatus can produce a very wide range of sounds; but only a small number of these are used in a language as units to construct all of its words and sentences. Some languages use very small numbers of sound units – Rotokas, in the Pacific

Islands, has only 11. By contrast, !Xū in southern Africa has 141. English (in some accents) has 44. Whereas phonetics is the study of *all* possible speech sounds, phonology studies the way in which a language's speakers systematically use a *selection* of these sounds in order to express meaning.

There is a further way of drawing the distinction. No two speakers have anatomically identical vocal tracts, and thus no one pronounces sounds in exactly the same way as anyone else (§8). There is even a considerable amount of variation in the sounds of a single speaker. Yet when using our language we are able to discount much of this variation, and focus on only those sounds, or properties of sound, that are important for the communication of meaning. We think of our fellow-speakers as using the 'same' sounds, even though acoustically they are not. Phonology is the study of how we find order within the apparent chaos of speech sounds.

Identifying phonemes

Phonological analysis relies on the principle that certain sounds cause changes in the meaning of a word or phrase, whereas other sounds do not. An early approach to the subject used a simple methodology to demonstrate this. It would take a word, replace one sound by another, and see whether a different meaning resulted. For example, we hear *pig* in English as consisting of three separate sounds, each of which can be given a symbol in a phonetic transcription: [pɪg]. If we replace [p] by, say, [b], a different word results: *big*. [p] and [b] are thus important sounds in English, because they enable us to distinguish between *pig* and *big*, *pan* and *ban*, and many more word pairs.

In a similar way, [ɪ] and [e] can be shown to be important units, because they distinguish between *pig* and *peg*, *pin* and *pen*, and many other pairs. And so we could continue, using this technique – the *minimal pairs* test – to find out which sound substitutions cause differences of meaning. The technique has its limitations (it is not always possible to find pairs of words illustrating a particular distinction in a language), but it works quite well for English, where it leads to the identification of forty-four important units. In the earliest approach to phonological analysis, these 'important units' are called *phonemes*.

Phonemes are transcribed using the normal set of phonetic symbols (§9), but within forward slashes, not square brackets – /p/, /b/, /ɪ/, etc. This shows that the units are being seen as part of a language, and not just as physical sounds.

Identifying allophones

When we try to work out the inventory of phonemes in a language, using this approach, we soon come across sounds that do not change the meaning when we make a substitution. For example, the consonants at the beginning of *shoe* and *she* feel as if they are the same, but in fact they have very different sound qualities (p. 53). For *shoe*, the lips are rounded, because of the influence of the following [u] vowel; for *she*, the lips are spread. If we now substitute one of these sounds for the other, we do not get a change of meaning – only a rather strange-sounding pronunciation. There is only one phoneme here, which we can represent as /ʃ/, but it turns up in two different phonetic 'shapes', or variant forms, in the two words. These phonetic variants of a phoneme are known as *allophones*.

When we study a new language, it is important to pay careful attention to the phonetic variations which occur, to ensure that we make the right decisions about which sounds count as phonemes and which count as allophones. We do not know this information in advance; we have to work it out. And in doing so we have to be ready to cope with differences between the way sounds work in different languages. Sound differences that separate allophones in English may separate phonemes in another language, and vice versa – a principle that is clearly illustrated by the *l* sounds of such words as *leaf* and *pool*. The first *l* (*clear l*) is articulated much further forward in the mouth than the second (*dark l*) – as we can feel if we say these sounds slowly to ourselves. In English, these are allophones of a single /l/ phoneme. In Russian, however, they are different phonemes.

Identifying distinctive features

We need to recognize smaller units than the individual phoneme, in order to explain how sets of sounds are related. We can see this by comparing any two contrasting phonemes in English, using the articulatory criteria introduced in §10.

- /p/ and /b/ differ in one respect only: /p/ is voiceless, and /b/ is voiced. In other respects, they are the same: they are both bilabial, plosive, oral, and pulmonic egressive;
- /p/ and /g/ differ in two respects: there is a contrast of voicing, and there is also a contrast in the place of articulation – bilabial vs. velar;
- /p/ and /z/ differ in three respects: this time, there is a contrast in the manner of articulation (plosive vs. fricative), alongside the contrasts in voicing and place.

All phonemic segments in a language can be analysed in this way, either from an articulatory or an acoustic point of view, and the result is a set of contrasting components known as *distinctive features*. The English segment /p/, for example, is a combination of the features of *voicelessness*, *plosiveness*, and *bilabiality*. We can show these features by giving them values, symbolized by the signs + and –, as in [±voice], [±nasal]. For example, [n] is both [+nasal] ('has nasality') and [+voice] ('is voiced'); [p] is [–nasal] ('has no nasality') and [–voice] ('is not voiced'). Once we have worked out the set of these contrasts which distinguish phonemes, we can apply them to all the segments that turn up in a language.

Identifying phonological rules

In traditional accounts of phonology, we would describe a sound as occurring in a particular position within a syllable or word, and that is all. We would not refer to our knowledge of the relationships that exist between the various types of sound in different words and phrases. Yet this information is essential if we are to understand the way sounds systematically relate to each other and to the grammar and lexicon of a language.

To illustrate this point, we may consider such pairs of words as *telegraph* and *telegraphy*. A phonological analysis of these words is not complete simply by giving each a phonemic transcription: /ˈteləɡrɑːf/ vs. /təˈleɡrəfɪ/. We also need to show that, despite the different patterns of vowels within them, the pronunciations are systematically related, with other pairs of words in the language displaying the same kind of relationship, such as *microscope* and *microscopy*. Once we know the *rule* underlying such pairs of words we can apply it to new words that we have not heard before. For instance, if I invent a new device called a *blipograph*, we intuitively know that there must be a subject called *blipography*. Or the other way round: if I say I am studying *blipography*, you would deduce that there must be *blipographs*.

A major focus of phonological investigation is to work out the rules which relate sets of words of this kind. In the present example, one rule would show how the stress shifts predictably between the words. Another would show how the vowel qualities change as a consequence of the stress shift. If we worked out these rules, we could then see whether all such words in the language followed them, or whether there were any exceptions.

We do not restrict phonological rules to making statements about the sound patterns of a particular language. We also use them to demonstrate the similarities and differences between the sound systems of different languages. Are there rules like *telegraph/telegraphy* in other languages – possibly in all languages? The formulation of phonological rules is a critical step along the road to discovering the universal principles governing the use of sound in language.

Identifying syllables

We need to recognize several other important notions, to explain what is happening in sound systems. One of the most important is the *syllable*. This is a notion that we intuitively recognize. We say such things as, 'Shall I put it in words of one syllable?', and most of us would be able to break a long word down into its syllables, or speak it out 'syllable by syllable'.

There are also several writing systems in which each syllable is represented by a symbol (§18).

Identifying syllables is more difficult to do than might at first appear. A syllable is plainly a unit of sound that is larger than a single segment and usually smaller than a word, but it is not always easy to define the number of syllables in a word or to identify where one ends and the next begins. Do such words as *fire*, *meal*, and *schism* have one syllable or two? Do *meteor* and *neonate* have two syllables or three? And in a word like *master*, where do we draw the line? Should the syllable division be *ma-ster*, *mas-ter*, or *mast-er*?

In a phonological approach, we focus on the way sounds combine in a language to produce typical sequences. Syllables are seen as combinations of vowels and consonants (§10). Vowels (V) are now defined as units which can occur on their own, or which appear at the centre of a sequence of sounds. Consonants (C) are units which cannot occur on their own, or which appear at the edge of a sequence. Typical sequences in English are CV *see*, CVC *hat*, CCVC *stop*, and CVCC *pots*. We need to think of these words as sound-sequences, of course, not as spellings – *see*, for example, is /si:/.

In this way the range of syllable types used in a language can be identified and different languages compared. For example, some languages use only V or CV syllables (e.g. Hawaiian); others use several consonants before and after the vowel. English can have as many as three consonants before a vowel (CCC, as in *strap* and *sprig*) and up to four afterwards (CCCC, as in *glimpsed* and *twelfths*). Here too we need to think of these words as sound-sequences – the end of *twelfths*, for example, is /l + f + θ + s/.

Not all combinations of consonant and vowel can occur in a language. In English, we can combine /s + t + r/ to produce such words as *string* and *strength*. But we cannot combine /ʃ + t + r/. There is no word beginning with *shtr*. On the other hand, German has several words beginning with this sequence, such as *Strang* ('cord') and *Strand* ('beach'). Although the initial letter of these words is *s*, it is pronounced [ʃ].

The syllable, in this view, takes its place as an important abstract unit in explaining the way vowels and consonants are organized within a sound system. There is, moreover, evidence for the psychological reality of syllables from the study of speech errors. When we make a 'slip of the tongue', we mix up the parts of two successive words, substituting one sound for another. The kinds of substitutions usually display the influence of syllabic structure: for example, initial consonants tend to replace each other. We often say such things as *feak and weeble* (for *weak and feeble*), swopping the initial consonants; but it would be most unusual to say *leak and keeble*, putting an end consonant in an initial position. This suggests that a slip of the tongue is really a slip of the phonological part of the brain (§27).

12
How we use tone of voice

It ain't what you say, but the way that you say it. 'What we say' derives from the way we use the segments of speech – the vowels and consonants which combine to produce syllables, words, and sentences. But at the same time as we articulate these segments, our pronunciation varies in other respects. We make use of a wide range of *tones of voice*, and these change the meaning of what we say. The effects do not apply to individual segments: we use them with words, phrases, sentences, and even whole discourses. That is why they are often called *nonsegmental* or *suprasegmental* features of language.

There are a very limited number of ways in which we can vary our speech to produce different tones of voice.

- we can vary the pitch of the voice, saying something at high or low levels, or gradually moving between one pitch level and another as we speak;
- we can vary the loudness of the voice, saying something at loud or soft levels, or gradually increasing or decreasing in loudness as we speak;
- we can vary the speed at which we speak, saying something rapidly or slowly, or gradually increasing or decreasing in speed;
- we can vary the rhythm with which we speak, producing different kinds or patterns of rhythmical 'beats';

- we can vary the amount of silence we introduce into our speech, by using various lengths of pause; and
- we can vary the timbre of our voice, using the range of paralinguistic articulations which can be made in the vocal tract (§3).

The first four of these possibilities are collectively known as the *prosodic features* of language – a broader sense of *prosody* than that found in the study of literature, where it refers to the metrical patterns found in lines of poetry.

Tones of voice vary greatly from language to language. No two languages have the same system. Even if two languages share a particular phonetic feature, they may not use it in the same way. An example is the monotone pitch pattern. A level tone conveys boredom or sarcasm when it is used at the end of a sentence in English. But it has no such meaning at the end of a sentence in Russian. At the same time, we have to recognize that some tones of voice are widely used. People all over the world express their anger by speaking with increased loudness, raised pitch height, and faster speed. That behaviour may well be universal.

Identifying tones of voice

The most important prosodic effects in a language are conveyed by the linguistic use of pitch – the *intonation* system. We use different levels of *pitch* (*tones*) in particular sequences (*contours*, or *tunes*) to express a wide range of meanings. For example, all languages seem to make use of the difference between a falling and a rising tune, and this is widely interpreted as expressing a contrast between 'stating' and 'questioning'. In English orthography, the contrast is signalled by the use of punctuation, as in *They're outside.* vs. *They're outside?* In speech, a much wider range of tones is available to express various nuances and degrees of emphasis. A bored tone of voice might be signalled by a monotone; a surprised tone by extra pitch height. Punctuation is unable to do more than hint at such nuances: *They're outside??!, They're outside . . . ?*

Another important prosodic feature is *loudness*, which is used to convey gross differences of meaning, such as the increased volume usually associated with anger, as well as the fine contrasts heard on the different syllables in a word, as in *regular*, *regard*, and *deregulate*. The loudness of a syllable (§11) is usually referred to as its level of *stress*; the syllables are said to be *stressed* or *unstressed*. The term *accent* is also often used (but in a very different sense from §45). If we said a syllable was *accented* or *unaccented*, we would be referring to the way it had been made more prominent or less prominent due to the combined use of pitch and loudness.

Variations in *tempo* provide another parameter. It is possible to speed up or slow down the rate at which syllables, words, and sentences are produced to convey several kinds of meaning. In many languages, a sentence spoken with extra speed conveys urgency, whereas slower speed conveys deliberation or emphasis. A rapid, clipped single syllable may express irritation; a slowly drawled syllable, greater personal involvement. A drawled tone of voice can be written down using punctuation: *'Ye-e-s,' said Jim*. A clipped tone cannot. It could be hinted at only through the use of an appropriate word: *'Yes,' snapped Jim*.

Pitch, loudness, and tempo combine to make up a language's expression of *rhythm*. Languages vary greatly in the way in which they make rhythmical contrasts. English uses stressed syllables produced at roughly regular intervals of time (in fluent speech) and separated by unstressed syllables – a *stress-timed* rhythm which we can tap out in a 'tum-te-tum' way, as in a traditional line of poetry: *The curfew tolls the knell of parting day*. In French, the syllables are produced in a steady flow, resulting in a 'machine-gun' effect – a *syllable-timed* rhythm which is more like a 'rat-a-tat-a-tat'. In Latin, it was the length of a syllable (whether long or short) which provided the basis of rhythm. In many oriental languages, it is pitch height (high vs. low).

How we use tones of voice

Intonation, along with the other prosodic and paralinguistic features of language, performs a variety of different functions.

To express emotion

The most obvious function is to express a wide range of attitudinal meanings – excitement, boredom, surprise, friendliness, reserve, and many more. We only have to listen to a speech read by a number of different actors to appreciate the remarkable amount of emotional expression that can be conveyed by the voice.

To organize grammar

Intonation and pause play an important role in the marking of grammatical contrasts. The identification of such major units as clause and sentence (§39) often depends on the way pitch contours break up an utterance; and several specific contrasts, such as question and statement, or positive and negative, often rely on intonation. Many languages make the important conversational distinction between 'asking' and 'telling' in this way, e.g. *She's here, isn't she?* (where a rising pitch is the spoken equivalent of the question mark) vs. *She's here, isn't she!* (where a falling pitch captures the force of the exclamation mark).

To give shape to words

In many languages, the syllables in a word are each pronounced with a certain level of prominence. Usually, three levels are recognized: *primary* or *main* stress; *secondary* stress; and *unstressed*. In a word like *photograph*, *pho* has the primary stress, *graph* has a secondary stress, and *to* is unstressed. Sometimes, pairs of phrases can be distinguished by stress: if I see a *hot dog*, I am looking at a warm animal; if I see a *hot dog*, I am looking at something to eat. In some languages, the syllable which carries the primary stress in a word is predictable. Welsh is a case in point: the primary stress almost always falls on the next-to-last syllable in a word. English is not predictable in this way.

To distinguish word meanings

In well over half the languages of the world, it is possible to change the meaning of a word or phrase simply by changing the pitch level at which it is spoken. Languages that allow this are known as *tone languages*, and the distinctive pitch levels are known as *tones* or *tonemes*. In Mandarin Chinese we find such words as *ma*. Spoken with a high-level tone, it means 'mother'. Spoken with a high-rising tone, it means 'hemp'. Spoken with a low-falling-rising tone, it means 'horse'. And spoken with a high-falling tone, it means 'scold'.

To draw attention to meaning

The prosody conveys a great deal about what is new and what is already known in the meaning of an utterance – what is referred to as the *information structure* of the utterance. If we say *I saw a blue car*, with maximum intonational prominence on *blue*, the pronunciation presupposes that someone has previously queried the colour; whereas if we emphasize the *I*, it presupposes a previous question about which person is involved. It would be very odd for someone to ask *Who saw a blue car?*, and for the reply to be *I saw a blue car*!

To characterize a discourse

Prosody is not only used to mark the structure of sentences; it is also an important element in the construction of larger stretches of discourse (§41). In radio news-reading, for example, paragraphs of information are given a distinctive melodic and rhythmical shape. As the news-reader moves from one item of news to the next, the pitch level jumps up, then gradually descends, until by the end of the item the voice reaches a relatively low level. Sermons, sports commentaries, and several other types of spoken discourse have a distinctive prosody.

To help us learn

Prosody can help us organize language into units that are more easily perceived and memorized. If we want to learn a long sequence of numbers, it is much easier if the sequence is divided into rhythmical 'chunks'. It is not easy to remember *8, 5, 3, 7, 9, 6, 2, 1, 8, 4*; but it is much easier to remember *8, 5, 3, 7, 9 – 6, 2, 1, 8, 4*. The ability to organize speech into prosodic units is also an important help when children are learning to talk, or when we are learning a foreign language.

To identify individuals

Tone of voice can mark personal or group identity – what has been called an *indexical* function (§44). We can often tell who is talking by recognizing the characteristic tones of voice they use. In particular, these features help to identify people as belonging to different social groups and occupations, such as preachers, street vendors, and army sergeants.

Can we speak out of tune?

Prosody – and intonation in particular – has often been called the 'melody' or 'music' of speech, but the analogy is not really a good one. There are two main differences. Music, typically, is composed to be repeated; speech, typically, is not. And, if we examine modern Western music, we find tones that have been given absolute values, whereas those of speech are relative.

The consequences of this second point are far reaching. Notes have fixed frequencies (e.g. middle C now has a frequency of 264 Hz: see §6), and instruments can be tuned to ensure that their notes are compatible. But speech is not like this. Men, women, and children use tones with the same linguistic function (for stating, asking, etc.), yet produce them at widely differing frequencies. Moreover, two people of the same sex may both use the 'same' rising tone to ask a question, but one may produce it with a higher frequency range than the other. And even within a single speaker, the pitch at which a tone is produced may vary from one moment to the next, without this affecting the meaning of what is said.

Language is not affected by these biological or random variations. The tones of intonation are relative, not absolute. People are not instruments. They do not speak out of tune.

13

How children learn speech sounds: the first year

Children learning the sounds of speech have quite a mountain to climb. In English, for example, they have over forty vowels and consonants to learn (§10), some 300 ways in which these combine to produce syllables (§11), and several dozen patterns of stress and tones of voice (§12). But by three the basic pronunciation system is established, and by five there is very little left to learn.

It is often thought that nothing much happens linguistically in the first year of life. Indeed, most people think that babies do not 'start to talk' until they are about one year old and say their 'first word'. But long before we hear them produce intelligible words, they are learning a great deal about sounds – in particular, about the basic phonetic functions on which speech depends (§5). Unless they can focus their auditory attention (listening), discriminate sounds from each other, and recognize sounds when they hear them repeated, they will make little progress in learning to speak.

Speech reception

Even very young babies display a remarkable range of auditory abilities. There have been several experiments in which different sounds are played to babies, and their responses monitored. For example, day-old babies have been played their mother's voice speaking normally, the same voice speaking abnormally (in a monotone), and a stranger's voice: only the first caused them to attend. Other studies have shown how babies turn their heads towards the source of a sound within the first few days of life, and prefer human voices to non-human sounds as early as two weeks. Abilities of this kind are so apparent that researchers have concluded that some auditory training must begin within the womb.

An auditory ability to discriminate certain pairs of consonants or vowels (e.g. [pa] vs. [ba]) is present from around four weeks, and this ability to discriminate becomes increasingly sophisticated in subsequent months. The early onset of this ability supports the idea that children's perceptual apparatus is in some way 'programmed' to discriminate speech sounds – that they are born with special *feature detectors* that respond to the acoustic properties of speech.

While babies are developing their perceptual abilities, they are also improving their speech comprehension. Between two and four months, they begin to respond to the meaning of different tones of voice, such as angry, soothing, or playful voices. From around six months, they can recognize the way some utterances relate to particular situations or behaviours – as when people say *Bye-bye* or *Clap hands*. Some individual words may be recognized, such as names of family members, or basic responses (e.g. *No*). Most children understand several words by the end of the first year.

Also during the first year, babies are learning how people use language – their 'pragmatic' skills (§43). One of the most obvious yet remarkable facts of life is that, from the moment a baby is born, a mother holds it in front of her, and talks to it – despite the fact that she knows it does not yet have any language! Mothers seem to have an instinct to promote communication as soon as possible, using the child's earliest biological noises as stimuli for conversation. Cries, burps, sneezes, and other vocalizations are seized upon and interpreted. The mother is very ready to ascribe intentions to the baby's utterances and to build them into a conversation – something she does not do with its non-vocal activities, such as head movements or arm waving. The conversational pressure can be quite intense: in one study, over 100 utterances were used by a mother while attempting to elicit a burp from a three-month-old: *Where is it?, Come on come on come on, You haven't got any, I don't believe you*, etc.

The foundations of conversation are being laid in these early interactions. The mother's behaviour is not random (nor, indeed, is the behaviour of other caretakers). She uses a large number of questions, followed by pauses, as if to show the baby that a response is expected and to provide an opportunity for it to respond. She continually greets the baby, even after very short periods of separation. Moreover, she talks to the child at length only when the child is (in principle) in a position to reply. While the baby is feeding, for example, mothers tend to remain silent, taking up the conversation only when the baby ceases to suck or needs to be winded. This cyclical pattern of speech and silence anticipates the fundamental structure of older conversations.

There are many changes in conversational style during the first year. At around five weeks, the exchanges become more emotive, as smiling develops. The mother's utterances change as the baby's vocalizations grow. At around two months, the emergence of cooing (see below) elicits a softer voice. Some time later, the baby begins to laugh, and the mother's voice becomes more varied in response. As the child starts to take interest in the environment and looks around, the mother speaks more loudly, drawing attention to different objects. Her intonation becomes more exaggerated, and she often repeats her sentences. Simple face-to-face games are played (such as peep-bo, or peekaboo), promoting a great deal of communication.

After six months, the baby's more purposeful movements and explorations produce more extended commentaries by the mother. She no longer responds to every vocalization that is produced, but focuses special attention on those that are more structured in character – in particular, on the first babbled utterances. Between eight and ten months, babies attempt to attract the attention of others by pointing. They begin to 'follow' adult conversations, looking first at one person, then at the other. By the time their first words appear, babies have learned a great deal, both from observation and from practice, about what a conversation is and how to participate within it.

Speech production

And during all this time, what is the baby producing, by way of speech? To begin with, very little. Over the first few weeks of life, a baby's vocal sounds reflect only its biological state and activities. States of hunger, pain, or discomfort that cause crying and fussing are known as *reflexive noises*. Breathing, eating, excreting, and other bodily actions concerned with survival cause a wide range of *vegetative* noises, such as sucking, swallowing, coughing, and burping.

It is not easy to attribute clearly different functions to cries at this age. Hunger and pain cries tend to merge into a single distress cry, though pain cries are often much tenser and have a different rhythm. Discomfort cries are usually much shorter (less than a second) and occur in brief sequences. Vegetative noises are even shorter and contain more consonant-like sounds. There is nothing language-specific about these early sounds, though they do have some features in common with later speech. An air-stream mechanism is being used to produce noise (§4); there is rhythmical vocalization; the vocal folds are being used to produce pitch patterns: all of these are fundamental characteristics of later speech.

Between six and eight weeks the first cooing sounds are produced, generally when the baby is in a settled state. These sounds develop alongside crying, gradually becoming more frequent and more varied, as the child responds to the mother's smiles and speech. They are quieter, lower pitched, and more musical than crying, usually consisting of a short, vowel-like sound preceded by a consonant-like sound made towards the back of the mouth. Many have nasal quality.

Later in this period, cooing sounds are strung together – often ten or more at a time. These strings are not pronounced in a rhythmical way; there are no clear intonational contours. However, some of the sequences (such as [ga] and [gu]) do begin to resemble the syllables of later speech. Then, at around four months, the first throaty chuckles and laughs emerge.

During the cooing stage, babies seem to be performing the first gross activities required for the production of speech. The tongue begins to move vertically and horizontally, and the vocal folds begin to be used in coordination with it. There is a great deal of lip movement and tongue thrusting, which it is thought may be a form of imitation. This then leads, between twenty and thirty weeks, to vocal play.

The sounds of vocal play are much steadier and longer than those of cooing. Most segments last over one second, and consist of consonant + vowel-like sequences that are frequently repeated. They are usually at a high pitch level, and involve wide glides from high to low. A considerable range of consonant and vowel qualities is apparent. In due course, the sounds combine into longer sequences, to produce the first babbled utterances. There seems to be a strong element of practice in the activities of this period, but it also provides a great deal of enjoyment for parent and child alike.

Babbling emerges between twenty-five and fifty weeks. This is initially much less varied than the sounds of vocal play. A smaller set of sounds is used with greater frequency and stability, to produce the [bababa] and other sequences known as *reduplicated* babbling (because of the repeated use of the same consonant sound). About half-way through the period, this develops into *variegated* babbling, in which consonants and vowels change from one syllable to the next (e.g. [adu]). The rhythm of the utterance and the syllable length at this point are much closer to that found in speech. Babbled utterances seem to have no meaning, though some may resemble the words of later speech.

It used to be thought that there was no link between babbling and spoken language. The child was imagined to be trying out every possible sound in a random manner, and that babbling would stop before speech began. Recent studies have shown that this is not the case. In many cases, babbling continues long after speech begins – sometimes as late as eighteen months. Nor are the sounds of babbling a random selection: most babbling consists of a small set of sounds very similar to those used in the early language to be spoken by the child. The brain seems to be controlling the development of babbling and early speech in a similar way, so that a set of well-practised sounds is available for use at the time when children become intellectually capable of using sound for the communication of meaning.

Between nine and eighteen months, we find the appearance of melodic utterance. Variations in pitch, rhythm, and tone of voice (§12) become a major feature of child utterance towards the end of the first year. Parents begin to sense intentions behind these utterances, with their more well-defined shape, and often attribute meanings to them, such as questioning, calling, greeting, or wanting. Games and rituals may develop their own melodic contours. The children start using individual syllables with a fixed intonation, producing *proto-words*, where the sounds are clear, but it is not possible to be sure what they mean.

These are the first real signs of language development, and children growing up in different language environments begin to sound increasingly unlike each other. It is not possible, on the basis of the vocalization alone, to distinguish an English, French, and Chinese child at birth, or at any of the stages up to around nine months. But once intonation and rhythm begin to appear, the differences in language background are striking.

14
How children learn speech sounds: later years

By the time children are a year old, they have learned a great deal about the way adults use sounds to express differences in meaning (§11), but their ability to produce these sounds lags some way behind. Some one-year-olds can recognize several dozen words, involving a wide range of vowels and consonants, but their own ability to pronounce these words may be restricted to just two or three consonants and a single vowel.

One child at thirteen months could use only [b], [d], and [a], but he used these sounds to express a variety of words – for example, [ba] was used for *baby*, *bath*, *cup*, and *Peter*. By fifteen months, he had added [m], [p], and [u] to his repertoire, and was thus able to distinguish a much larger number of words. He also began to use some of these consonants at the ends of words as well as at the beginning; for example, [pu] was used for a nasty smell, and [up] was used for *up*. By age two, he was using over a dozen consonants and vowels, and was able to pronounce over 200 words in an intelligible (though often immature) manner.

Learning vowels and consonants

It is not possible to make precise predictions about the order in which children come to use new sounds. A particular sound often used in a child's environment (such as in the name of a sibling or a pet) can cause that sound to be used much earlier than it otherwise might. Some children have 'favourite' sounds, which they introduce into many words, whether the sound is in the adult version or not; others 'avoid' sounds – for example, persistently dropping certain consonants at the ends of words. There may also be a great deal of variation in the way target sounds are produced – one child pronounced *blanket* as [bwati], [bati], [baki], and [batit], within a few hours of each other. Another produced ten different forms of *pen* within a single half-hour!

Nonetheless, as a result of several studies, we can see a number of general trends in the way children change the sounds of the language, when they attempt to use them.

- They tend to replace fricative consonants (p. 61) by stops, e.g. *see* is pronounced [tiː].
- They tend to replace velar consonants (p. 59) by alveolar ones, e.g. *gone* is pronounced [dɒn].
- They avoid consonant clusters, e.g. *sky* is pronounced [kaɪ].
- They tend to omit consonants at the ends of words, e.g. *hat* is pronounced [ha].
- They often drop unstressed syllables, e.g. *banana* becomes [nana].

As words become longer, sounds in one part of a word can alter the pronunciation of sounds in other parts. This tendency for sounds to *harmonize* is found with both consonants and vowels. Harmony between consonants is found in such pronunciations of *dog* as [gɒg] or [dɒd], with identical (or near-identical) consonants. Harmony between vowels would be heard if *window* were pronounced for example as [wowo] or [wada].

Among the early vowels to appear are [iː] as in *me*, [ɪ] as in *pig*, [a] as in *cat*, [ɑː] as in *baa*, [ɔː] as in *saw*, [ʊ] as in *put*, and [aɪ] as in *mine*; but by age four all the vowels and diphthongs have some degree of use. The first consonants appear at around the end of the first year, but are acquired between two and four years of age. Consonants are more likely to be first used correctly at the beginnings of words; consonants at the end tend to emerge later. After four, there are just a few consonants that still pose problems of articulation or discrimination, such as [θ], [ð], and [ʃ] – *that*, for example, might be pronounced 'dat'. The more complex consonant clusters (such as /str-/) are also fairly late to come under complete control – *string*, for example, is often pronounced 'stwing'.

A very interesting effect is known as the *fis phenomenon*. Several studies have reported intriguing conversations between a young child and an adult, showing that there can be a big difference between what children hear and what they can say. The phenomenon was first reported by US psycholinguists Jean Berko and Roger Brown in 1960 in the following way:

> One of us, for instance, spoke to a child who called his inflated plastic fish a *fis*. In imitation of the child's pronunciation, the observer said: 'This is your *fis*?' 'No,' said the child, 'my *fis*.' He continued to reject the adult's imitation until he was told, 'That is your fish.' 'Yes,' he said, 'my *fis*.'

The effect has been referred to as the *fis* phenomenon ever since. Such reports indicate that children know far more about adult phonology than their own pronunciation suggests.

Learning to reduplicate

During the second year, an important feature of children's pronunciation is an effect known as *reduplication*. This happens when the different syllables of a word are pronounced in the same way. In one child, *water* was pronounced [wowo], *bottle* as [bubu], and *window* as [mumu]. Even monosyllabic words can be reduplicated, as when *ball* becomes [bobo]. Children do not all reduplicate to the same extent. With some children, most words are affected, and the process can be observed for several months. In other cases, there may be very few words involved, and the effect may last only a few days.

The purpose of reduplication has been much discussed. It may be partly motivated simply by the need to play with sounds or to practise them. But it is more likely that the process helps children as they try to cope with the pronunciation of more complicated words. A word like *tiger*, with its changes of consonant and vowel, would be difficult for an eighteen-month-old to learn at one go. Reduplication would give the child a chance to master the pronunciation in stages, by first producing the word's syllable structure and stress, along with the most noticeable phonetic features. A more precise pronunciation would come later, after this phonetic 'outline' had been mastered.

Learning intonation

Most children have begun to make some use of their language's intonation patterns (§12) before the end of the first year. Different tones of voice are used to express such meanings as questioning, demanding, calling, greeting, warning, recognition, and surprise. Once a child learns a word, intonation can be used to vary its use as a sentence. At fourteen months, one child was recorded saying *dada*, with a high rising tone, when she heard footsteps on the gravel path outside the door ('Is that daddy?'). As her father entered the room, she said *dada*, with a falling tone ('It is daddy!'). Then she said *dada* with an insistent mid-level tone, with arms outstretched ('Pick me up, daddy!'). Later, such distinctions will be expressed by grammar – statement vs. question vs. command. But at fourteen months, there is only intonation to rely upon.

During the second year, as simple sentences develop, a wider range of attitudes is expressed, and prosody begins to signal differences in emphasis. At this point, it becomes possible to distinguish such general sentences as *Daddy gone* from the contrastive *Daddy gone* (i.e. not someone else). As the child's grammatical and social abilities develop, so new uses of intonation emerge. For example, the contrast between rising and falling tones differentiates the two functions of a tag question in English – 'asking', as in *She's outside, isn't she?*, and 'telling', as in *She's outside, isn't she!* This is learned during the third year, along with the grammar.

What is surprising is that the learning of intonation goes on for so long. Children seem to master the formal patterns of intonation quite early on, but their awareness of the range of meanings that these patterns convey is still developing as they approach their teens. This was first shown in a study of the way British radio and TV announcers read out football results (e.g. *Everton 3, Liverpool 3*). By listening to the intonation of the first part of the result, it is possible for adults to predict whether the score is going to be a draw, a home win, or an away win. When this task was given to children aged seven to eleven, it was found that the youngest children were hardly able to do it, and even the oldest children did not reach the level of competence shown by the adults. In fact, only one child out of twenty-eight got all the results right.

The implications of this experiment go well beyond the world of football, for the intonation patterns used are to be found in everyday speech also. And quite a wide range of grammatical structures are distinguished by differences in intonation. Even young teenagers have been shown to have difficulty understanding the way intonation distinguishes some sentences. For example, they have difficulty hearing the difference, signalled by intonation and pause (and shown here in punctuation), between the sentences *She dressed, and fed the baby* (i.e. the person dressed herself, and then fed the baby) and *She dressed and fed the baby* (i.e. the baby is both dressed and fed). It seems that aspects of the intonation system are not only the first pronunciation features to be learned, but also some of the last.

15
How speech can go wrong

If all goes well, we learn to control the phonetic parameters involved in speech early in the first year, and develop most of our pronunciation ability between the ages of two and five (§§13–14). By the time we reach our teens, we have acquired all the pronunciation features we need in everyday speech. All that remains is to develop our expressive repertoire further, if we so choose, either for artistic reasons, such as in acting or singing, or because our profession makes further demands upon our voice, as in the case of auctioneers and preachers. We also have the option of changing our accent without having to start all over again. Once acquired, our pronunciation ability remains with us for the rest of our lives.

But something can interfere with this process, so that we end up with an immature or abnormal pronunciation. The interference can be present at birth, so that the dice are loaded against the development of a normal pronunciation at the outset. It can appear gradually as the child grows, or suddenly as the result of some accident or disease. There is no age limit. Accidents and diseases affecting our speech can happen to us at any time. And any of the factors involved in speaking can be the focus of the interference.

Losing our voice

In popular usage, this phrase means being unable to speak at all. In fact, when we lose the ability to control the vibration of the vocal folds – which is what is technically meant by *voice* (p. 26) – we can still make some sort of sound, but it is markedly abnormal. When we whisper, we are speaking without voice. If we have the ability to turn the whisper on and off at will, we are in control. But people who suffer from a *voice disorder* may no longer have this ability. The whispery quality is there all the time.

It is not only whisper. Many develop an expressive disability in which the pitch, loudness, and timbre of the voice (§12) is so inefficient that the message carried by the spoken language may be unintelligible. Even if the speech can be understood, the voice quality interferes with communication by calling attention to itself. The sound can be highly unpleasant – harshly hoarse or stridently nasal. Alternatively, the voice quality may simply be inappropriate to the speaker – as when an older male teenager retains the high-pitched voice of a younger child.

We can classify voice problems into two types. *Disorders of phonation* refer to an abnormal kind of vibration in the vocal tract, as when the vocal folds fail to function normally. *Disorders of resonance* refer to abnormal modifications of the sound vibration as it passes through the cavities of the vocal tract (§4). The first type manifests itself mainly in abnormal qualities of pitch and loudness – such as very monotonous, high-pitched, or weak voices – and in a range of breathy, husky, and hoarse effects that are cumulatively labelled *dysphonia*. The second type is best illustrated from the many abnormal nasal resonances that can affect the voice – some excessively nasal (or 'twangy'), some with reduced nasality ('blocked nose' effects).

About a third of all voice disabilities have a clearly physical cause: there is some sort of abnormality in the vocal tract. Excessive friction between the vocal folds can cause *nodules* or *nodes* to form at their margins. Other interfering formations include polyps, contact ulcers, and various kinds of cancerous growth. Vocal-fold movement may become weak because of disease affecting the main nerve leading to the larynx.

External damage, such as a blow to the neck, can easily affect the functioning of the larynx.

Probably the most dramatic consequence for the voice results from malignant growths in the region of the vocal folds. This condition can be treated with radiotherapy, but if this fails, it may be necessary to remove the larynx surgically, in an operation known as a *laryngectomy*. After this operation, the windpipe cannot be rejoined to the pharynx (p. 18), as food would spill into the lungs. The defect in the pharynx is therefore closed during the operation, and an alternative opening to the trachea is made at the front of the neck (a *tracheostomy*). This is the laryngectomy operation. Patients are no longer able to speak normally, using lung air, so they have to learn to use the upper part of their pharynx and oesophagus to initiate vibration. If they are successful, they can speak again, but with a throaty *oesophageal* voice quality. Alternatively, they can use an *artificial larynx* – a device that emits a buzzing sound – to provide a source of vibration. They place this against their neck while they are 'mouthing' speech, and it provides a source of phonation.

Most voice disorders, however, are not like this, for they have a non-physical cause. Emotional stress can itself be sufficient for people to 'lose their voice', resulting in a range of psychological conditions that require lengthy and sympathetic investigation and therapy if they are to be resolved. Factors of this kind may also have physical consequences. Nodules and ulcers can result from *vocal abuse* – an excessive use of the voice, which in time causes chronic dysphonia. In cases such as these, the reasons for the abuse arise out of the life-style of the speakers. In particular, it is very common for nodules to form in those who live by their voice, such as singers and teachers, and who are regularly faced with vocally demanding situations.

Losing our fluency

A disorder of *fluency*, in the context of language, refers to a major lack of ability to communicate easily, rapidly, and continuously. The problem is most noticeable when people have difficulty in controlling the rhythm and timing of their speech, to produce the phenomenon of *stuttering* or (as it is more widely known in Britain) *stammering*.

Stuttering involves several kinds of non-fluency which vary considerably from speaker to speaker.

- The most widely recognized symptom is the abnormal amount of repetition of sounds, syllables, words, or phrases, e.g. *p-p-p-please*, *he's got a – got a – got a – car*.
- Sounds may be abnormally lengthened, e.g. *ssssay*, where the initial [s] can last several seconds, often with an uncertain rhythm.
- The speaker prepares to articulate a sound, but is unable to release it. In severe cases, facial spasms and sudden body movements may be used in an effort to get over the *block*.
- Words show erratic stress patterns, and there is an abnormal intonation and speed of speech.
- Words and phrases may be left unfinished.
- Speakers may avoid words and phrases that contain the sounds they find difficult, and replace these by circumlocutions. One stutterer, who had great difficulty with [d], would always replace *dog* by 'barking animal'.

A certain amount of 'normal non-fluency' is found in young children (especially around the age of three), and indeed everyone is prone to hesitation, especially in situations where they have to speak under pressure. Stutterers too vary greatly in the control they have over their speech, and clinicians therefore look closely at the contexts that most promote a stutter when they are investigating the problem. It is very difficult to draw a clear line between normal speech and stuttering, though there is no mistaking the disability in its severe form, with its uncontrolled, tense, and irregular speech, and the anxiety and embarrassment (for listener as well as speaker) that is invariably present.

Many theories of stuttering have been proposed, and there are several contributing causative factors. Physical factors may be involved, such as a defect in the feedback mechanism between ear and brain, so that a person would be unable to monitor output efficiently. The speaker's personality or emotional state may be important. And adverse listener reactions can play a part in promoting a stutter. A typical example is when parents prematurely correct their children for non-fluency, or become impatient when their child is non-fluent; this causes insecurity and anxiety, which in turn causes further growth in the non-fluency.

Many treatment methods and programmes are now available. Some methods focus on the feedback problem, such as by taking stutterers' attention away from their non-fluent speech (by playing specially generated noise into their ears while they speak). Others focus on altering the stutterer's breath control, or develop techniques in which speech comes more slowly or evenly than normal. Learning to relax is an essential feature of many methods, as is learning to interact with others (especially in the situations that cause particular tension). These days, particular attention is paid to helping stutterers develop a style of behaviour which more closely resembles that of fluent people. Many stutterers have become so isolated and withdrawn, on account of their stutter, that they may need to be taught a new way of life (or at least, way of looking at life) as therapy proceeds.

Losing our articulation

A problem of articulation appears if someone is unable to pronounce vowels and consonants properly. But this definition covers a multitude of conditions. At one extreme, there are slight difficulties with pronunciation which hardly interfere with communication, but which can cause some anxiety to the speaker, such as the effects we hear as a lisp or a 'weak' r. At the other, there are sound systems which are so misarticulated or disorganized that the person is largely unintelligible.

In children, many of the pronunciation problems that cause parental concern are due to a general delay in the ability to control movements of the vocal organs. Some children at age four or five are still pronouncing words in ways typical of a child of two or three – making immature omissions, substitutions, additions, or transpositions of sounds. (The children's hearing may be perfectly normal in such cases.) Others have more serious problems of incoordination, such as being unable to control the speed and direction of their tongue movements, or to maintain consistent pressure between the articulating organs (§10). It takes only a slight lack of control to turn a plosive into an affricate or fricative (e.g. [p] becoming [pf] or [f]), or a fricative into a plosive (e.g. [s] becoming [t]).

An example of a severe kind of articulation problem is the speech of children who are born with a cleft of the lip or palate. This has very serious consequences because the condition affects not only the development of speech, but also the child's ability to eat. It is also extremely disfiguring, and a source of great emotional trauma to parents. Early surgical intervention is thus normal (lip operations are usually within the first three months). Special prosthetic devices are sometimes used to cover the palatal gap, until the operation is performed, to aid the development of normal movement within the mouth. Because of the early intervention, many cleft palate children develop fairly normal speech. However, problems of voice quality (often very nasal) and articulation can persist for several years. A child who is making poor progress can still be largely unintelligible to all but the immediate family at the age of three or four. The availability of intensive speech therapy is a crucial factor.

At the opposite extreme, we find articulation problems that cannot be explained by such factors as deficient anatomy or poor motor coordination. Most of the children seen in a speech therapy clinic show some kind of delay in their development of spoken language. Their speech displays poor rhythmical ability and immature sound formation, and they have difficulty in discriminating sounds. Delays range from a barely noticeable few months to one of several years. In severe conditions, teenage children may still be using a kind of spoken language equivalent to that found in pre-school children. One twelve-year-old was still pronouncing *car* as /ta:/, *spoon* as /pu:n/, and *feather* as /teda/ – all features which would be expected in a child around the age of two.

In about a third of cases, the reason for the delayed language development is known. Mentally disabled children, for example, display some of the most marked delays. Other groups where the language delay is part of a more general problem include those who are deaf, psychologically disturbed, autistic, or physically disabled. In the majority of cases, however, there is no clear physical reason for the language delay. The children have no relevant medical history, are of normal intelligence, and are not socially deprived or emotionally disturbed. Nonetheless, their speech is well behind that of their peers. In several instances, there are accompanying difficulties of a cognitive or social kind – such as poor memory or concentration, or a reluctance to cooperate with others. However, not all delayed children display such problems: for many, the speech difficulty is the primary or only symptom. Doubtless something is wrong in the areas of the brain involved in the control of pronunciation skills, but research has not yet been able to demonstrate what this might be.

16

How we write

In normal circumstances, speech is something which develops naturally. There is only one way to speak, and that is by using the vocal apparatus (§4). By contrast, there are several ways in which we can communicate using the medium of writing. Language study always distinguishes *spoken* from *written* language; but the latter term does not capture the range of expression that the visual medium makes available. *Written* implies, first and foremost, *handwritten*, but plainly there are many other ways of presenting written language, using such technologies as the printing press, the typewriter, the computer, and the mobile phone. I shall use the term *graphic expression* to include all these modes. I shall not, however, use the phrase *graphic language*, as found in such fields as typography, because it applies to much more than language in the sense of this book – such as pictures, graphs, and musical notation.

The written medium of a language can be studied from two points of view, which relate to each other in the same way that phonetics and phonology do for the study of speech (§11). First of all, we can study the physical properties of the marks on a surface out of which we make writing systems, and this branch of the subject I call *graphics*, on analogy with *phonetics*. If phonetics can be briefly defined as 'human sound-making' – how we speak – then graphics is, correspondingly, 'human mark-making' – how we write. The other dimension is the study of the linguistic contrasts that different writing systems convey, and this branch of the subject is widely known as *graphology*, on analogy with *phonology*. Under this heading we study the letters, symbols, punctuation marks, and other features that distinguish one writing system from another.

When we examine writing from a graphetic point of view, we deal with the range of implements and associated human skills required when we produce and receive (read) linguistic marks on surfaces, screens, and other backgrounds, in any language. It involves the study of the motor control and coordination of hands and eyes, and of the psychological processes involved when these marks are perceived and processed by the reader.

There is a huge range of variation in graphetic practice displayed by modern languages and throughout the history of writing. Most noticeably, languages vary in the direction in which they are written – left-to-right, right-to-left (e.g. Arabic), top-to-bottom (e.g. traditional Japanese), and the uncommon bottom-to-top (e.g. some forms of Ancient Greek). More than one direction may be involved, as in the *boustrophedon* method of writing lines in alternate directions, used in several early systems. The Greek name means 'ox-turning', referring to the way the ox would pull a plough, moving first in one direction, then the other. A language may use several different conventions simultaneously – such as the common use in English of vertical arrangement in neon signs and on book spines.

The nature of the writing implement and surface will have some influence on the kind of system that develops. The history of graphic expression shows a variety of implements, including the use of reeds, quills, brushes, steel points, fountain pens, pencils, ball-point pens, fibre-tipped pens, chalks, crayons, typewriters, laser printers, photocomposing systems, and everything that modern computation makes available. The implements rely on a range of natural and synthetic products, from the early use of blood and plant juices to the modern range of coloured inks, photochemicals, lights, and electrical charges. Many surfaces have been involved, such as animal bone, rock, clay, wax, pottery, cloth, papyrus, parchment, paper, film, and electronic display screens. Often, techniques have to be devised for special functions, such as architectural drawing, record keeping, laundry marking, security coding, writing on glass, wood, or film, and writing that can be read electronically, as in department store check-outs and libraries.

The three main eras of graphic expression – handwriting, printing, and the electronic medium – share many graphetic properties, but they have developed separate traditions and disciplines of study. The study of the oldest tradition, the many forms and styles of handwriting, is known as *chirography*. Each of the main families of writing systems has its own complex history of handwriting styles, and several professional disciplines have evolved to study them.

- *Palaeography* is the investigation of ancient and medieval handwriting in order to establish the provenance, date, and correct form of a text. The subject principally involves the study of writing on papyrus, parchment (vellum), or paper, though it does not exclude other forms (such as graffiti). It is detective work which is much assisted by a detailed knowledge of the language, the historical events of the period, the contemporary use of writing materials, the mannerisms of the scribes, and especially the history of handwriting styles. In modern times, such techniques as the use of ultraviolet light (to bring out faded handwriting) have proved invaluable.

- *Epigraphy* is the study of ancient inscriptions – texts that have been written on hard, durable material, such as stone, marble, metal, clay, pottery, wood, and wax, using such techniques as engraving, carving, embossing, and painting. Its aim is to ascertain the nature of the original records of ancient civilizations, thereby providing the primary data for historical and philological enquiry. In this process, it provides considerable insight into the early development of writing systems.

- *Diplomatics*, from the Greek *diploma* ('folded'), is the study of legal and administrative documents of all kinds. Most attention has been paid to the public documents of monarchs, emperors, and popes, which are usually classified separately from the many varieties of private document that exist. One of the main aims of the subject is the identification of genuine documents as distinct from drafts, copies, or forgeries.

- *Calligraphy* is the art of penmanship, or handwriting at its most formal. It is a major art form in eastern Asia, China, Korea, Japan, and in Arabic-speaking countries. The artistic effect depends on a combination of factors – good-quality materials, the selection of an appropriate and effective writing instrument, the correct formation of the symbols according to an accepted style of writing, the placing of these symbols in an elegant sequence, and the harmonious layout of the text upon the page.

An evolving system

We are so used to the writing system we learn in school that it can come as a surprise to realize that other systems do not work in the same way. For example, we are used to a system which makes use of both large (*capital*) and small letters – a *dual alphabet*. However, if we look at the original Greek and Latin alphabets, we find that they did not use this distinction. Those alphabets consisted of capital letters, broadly contained within a single pair of horizontal lines, and the writing is usually referred to as *majuscule*. The Latin form used throughout the Roman Empire from the 1st century AD is known as *rustic* capitals (in contrast with the great square capitals chiselled on stone in Roman inscriptions).

Minuscule writing consisted of small letters whose parts extend above and below a pair of horizontal lines. It was a gradual development, in regular use for Greek by the 7th–8th century AD. A form of writing known as *uncial* was especially used in Greek and Latin manuscripts from the 4th–8th century AD. It consisted of large (the term meant 'inch-high') rounded letters. A later development, *half uncial*, prepared the way for modern small letters. Another development was *cursive* writing, where the characters are joined in a series of rounded, flowing strokes, which promotes ease and speed. It is found in general use from around the 4th century BC, and in time replaced uncial and half-uncial writing as a handwriting norm.

The dual alphabet – the combination of capital letters and small letters in a single system – is first found in a form of writing named after Emperor Charlemagne (742–814), *Carolingian minuscule*. It was widely acclaimed for its clarity and attractiveness, and exercised great influence on subsequent handwriting styles throughout Europe. *Black-letter* writing, for example, is one development of Carolingian minuscule, widely used in many variations between the 11th and 15th centuries. The rounded strokes became straighter, bolder, and more pointed. Often referred to as *Gothic* script, it became the earliest model for printer's type in Germany. Another derivative of Carolingian was devised in Italy by Poggio (1380–1459) as an alternative to black-letter writing. It was originally known as Antiqua, reflecting the concern of the humanist movement of the period to return to ancient Latín sources. It subsequently became the basis for roman letters in printing. And, as a third example, the Italian scribe Niccolò Niccoli (1364–1437) developed a form of sloped cursive lettering, which in due course led to the development of italic letters in printing.

Analysing handwriting

A person's handwritten mark or signature holds a special place in society. It is required for legal agreements, and its forgery can be illegal. Likewise, a person's general handwriting conveys identity: no two people's writing is the same in every respect. Any orthographic system will display handwriting variations, and these can be analysed into a set of separate factors. The variables can be illustrated from the way we use the Roman (or Latin) alphabet, but several of the points apply equally to other alphabets, and indeed to other writing systems.

- *Layout*: We can vary the way we arrange our writing on the page, such as the size of margins and the distance between lines (narrow or wide, constant or varying).
- *Lines*: We can vary the direction of the lines, making them straight or curved, slope upwards or downwards.
- *Connection*: We can join a sequence of symbols together or leave

them separate. If we join them, then we can vary the way in which the upstrokes and downstrokes interconnect (curved or angular, with various flourishes).

- *Speed*: We can write rapidly or slowly, and the result is apparent in a number of ways. In rapid writing, the cross stroke of a *t* may be misplaced or a dot may be separated from its *i*. Strokes may even appear between adjacent words.
- *Regularity*: We can vary the consistency of the size, angle of writing, and distance between strokes. Stretches of writing can appear even or disjointed.
- *Letter-forms*: We can opt for a simplified symbol or (as in calligraphy) we can elaborate it. Signatures often show extremes of simplicity or elaboration.
- *Size*: We can make our symbols large or small, wide or broad, constant or varying. Individual symbols can vary in size, as can symbol elements, such as the length of the cross stroke of a *t*.
- *Angle*: We can vary the verticality of our symbols, keeping them upright or slanting them to the left or right. This is one of the most noticeable identifying features of a person's handwriting. It may be constant or varying.
- *Shading*: Depending on the implement we use, we can alter the thickness or thinness of different strokes.

Handwriting characteristics have been studied professionally with reference to all kinds of normal and pathological psychological and physiological states. Most of the early publications dealt with the writing of monarchs, criminals, authors, politicians, and other professionals, but more recent works have examined the writing of the general population, sometimes from quite specific points of view (such as to determine someone's suitability for employment). Professional handwriting analysts are often called *graphologists* – but this is a different use of the term *graphology* from the one found in linguistics (§17).

Later systems

The selection and organization of letter-forms and other graphic features of the printed page is the concern of *typography*. It deals with all matters which affect the appearance of the page, and which contribute to the effectiveness of a printed message: the shapes and sizes of letters, diacritics, punctuation marks, and special symbols; the distances between letters and words; the length of lines; the space between lines; the size of margins; the extent and location of illustrations; the use of colour; the selection of headings and sub-headings; and all other matters of spatial organization, or *configuration*. In addition, typographers need to be involved in such matters as the kind of ink used, the choice of paper, and the method of printing. Each of these components has to be evaluated in its own right, as part of an overall judgement about the *weight*, *colour*, or *atmosphere* of the page as a whole.

There are two main dimensions to printing: the use of a device to make copies of an image, and the availability of movable type. The first of these is known to have been used in China from at least around the 7th century AD: the earliest known book, *The Diamond Sutra*, was printed using inked wooden blocks, in 868. The second dimension emerged during the 11th century, when movable blocks, carved with individual characters, came to be used. However, these discoveries did not become known in the West, and they had no influence on the subsequent history of printing.

In Europe, the main step forward came in the mid-15th century, with the invention in Germany of movable metal type in association with the hand-operated printing press – developments that are generally credited to Johannes Gutenberg (1390–1468). Metal type was set by hand until the introduction of various systems of mechanized typesetting in the 19th century. The linotype machine was introduced towards the end of the century, and became standard in newspaper offices. Techniques of photocomposition became a commercial reality in the 1950s. Computerized typesetting began to be used from the late 1960s. The prototype of the typewriter was built in 1867 by the American inventor Christopher Latham

Sholes (1819–90), and rapidly achieved popularity. Modern developments include the electronic typewriter, the word processor, the use of the telephone keypad to send messages, and the computer keyboard – now the preferred mode of graphic expression for most young people.

17
How we make writing systems: early times

Graphology, in its linguistic sense, is the study of the systems of symbols that have been devised to communicate language in written form. We need to see it in contrast with *graphetics*, the study of the physical properties of manuscript, print, and other forms of graphic expression (§16). Linguistic graphology deals with the kind of elements used in a language's writing system, the number of elements there are and how they interrelate, and the rules governing the way these elements combine in written texts.

Graphemes

The term *graphology* was coined on analogy with *phonology*, and several of the phonological notions used in the study of speech have also been applied to the study of written language. In particular, analysts have developed the idea of a *grapheme*, analogous to a *phoneme* (p. 68). Graphemes are the smallest units in a writing system capable of causing a contrast in meaning. In the English alphabet, the switch from *cat* to *bat* introduces a meaning change; therefore, *c* and *b* represent different graphemes. It is usual to transcribe graphemes within angle brackets, to show their special status: <c>, <b>. The main graphemes of English are the twenty-six units that make up the alphabet. Other graphemes include the various marks of punctuation: <.>, <;>, etc., and such special symbols as <@>, <&>, and <£>.

Graphemes are abstract units, which may adopt a variety of forms. The grapheme <a>, for example, may appear as A, *a*, *A*, or in other forms, depending on the handwriting style or typeface chosen. Each of these possible forms is known as a *graph*. There is a vast amount of physical variation in the shapes of graphs that does not affect the underlying identity of the grapheme. Whether a word is printed *cat*, *CAT*, *Cat*, *caT*, or *cAt*, we still recognize it as a sequence of three graphemes <c>, <a>, <t>.

Graphemes have several functions, in addition to the way they represent individual sounds. They may signal whole words or word parts – as with the numerals, where each grapheme <1>, <2>, etc. is spoken as a word that varies from language to language (a *logogram* – see below). Graphemes of punctuation show links and boundaries between units of grammar that may have nothing to do with the sound of speech (notably, the use of the hyphen (§18)). And several of the relationships between words are conveyed by graphology more clearly than by phonology: for example, the link between *sign* and *signature* is very clear in writing, but it is less obvious in speech, because the *g* is pronounced in the second word, but not in the first.

When graphs are analysed as variants of a grapheme, they are known as *allographs* (analogous to *allophones*, p. 68). It is sometimes possible to work out the rules governing the use of particular allographs: in English, for example, we find *capital* letters (*upper case* letters) at the beginning of a sentence or proper name and in a few other contexts; otherwise we use small letters (*lower case* letters). However, the choice of most allographs seems to be dictated by factors that are little understood, such as fashion, prominence, elegance, or personality.

Graphology also makes use of the notion of *distinctive features* (p. 69). We perceive a grapheme as a single configuration, and not as a set of lines and dots; but it is nonetheless possible to analyse the shapes into their components, to determine what the salient parameters of contrast are – curve vs. straight line, presence vs. absence of dot, left-facing vs. right-facing curve, and so on. In French, accents are contrastive (as in <é>, <ê>, and <è>). In Chinese and Japanese, the contrasts are carried by the strokes that constitute the characters.

How writing began

Myths and legends of the supernatural surround the early history of writing, as they do of speech (§54). Archaeological discoveries provide enthralling pinholes of illumination along with frustrating problems of interpretation. An account of the early history of writing has gradually emerged, but it contains many gaps and ambiguities.

The matter is complicated by the fact that, in this early period, it is by no means easy to decide whether a piece of graphic expression should be counted as an artistic image or as a symbol of primitive writing. In principle, the difference is clear: artistic images convey personal and subjective meanings, and do not combine into a system of recurring symbols with accepted values; by contrast, written symbols are conventional and institutionalized, capable of being understood in the same way by all who are using the system. When the product is a rock carving or painting of an animal, there is little doubt that its purpose is non-linguistic (though whether it has an aesthetic, religious, or other function is debatable). However, when the product is a series of apparent geometrical shapes or tiny characters, the distinction between art and writing becomes less obvious.

The earliest examples of a conventional use of written symbols are on clay tablets discovered in various parts of the Middle East and south-east Europe from around 3500 BC. Large numbers of tablets made by the Sumerians have been found in sites around the Rivers Tigris and Euphrates in present-day Iraq and Iran. For example, on tablets from the city-state of Uruk, about 1,500 symbols have been listed, most of them abstract in character. They seem to have recorded such matters as land sales, business transactions, and tax accounts. Several correspondences have been noted between the symbols used on these tablets and the clay tokens that were used throughout the area for several thousand years before the advent of writing. These tokens, of several distinctive shapes, seem to have been used as a system of accounting from at least the 9th millennium BC.

It now seems most likely that writing systems evolved independently of each other at different times in several parts of the world – in Mesopotamia, China, Meso-America, and elsewhere. There is nothing to support a theory of common origin. There are of course similarities between these systems, but these are not altogether surprising, given the limited ways of devising a system of written communication.

Types of writing system

It is possible to talk about writing systems on the basis of such graphetic factors (§16) as the size, style, and configuration of the symbols, or the direction in which they are written; but this does not help us understand what the graphemes are and how they are used. In principle, any of the systems described below could be written in almost any set of graphetic conventions. For example, several directions might be used during the history of a language: at different periods, early Greek was written right-to-left, left-to-right, and even using alternate directions (in boustrophedon writing, p. 98).

A useful approach to writing systems is to classify them into cases that show a clear relationship between the symbols and sounds of the language (*phonological* systems) and those that do not (*non-phonological* systems). The vast majority of present-day systems are phonological in character (see §18). The non-phonological systems are mainly found in the early history of writing.

Pictographic writing

In pictographic writing, the graphemes (often referred to as *pictographs* or *pictograms*) provide a recognizable picture of entities as they exist in the world. For example, a set of wavy lines might represent the sea or a river, and outlines of people and animals represent their living counterparts. There is no intention to draw the reality artistically or exactly, but the symbols must be sufficiently clear and simple to enable them to be immediately recognized and reproduced, as occasion demands, as part of a narrative.

To 'read' such a script, it is enough only to recognize the symbols, and the sequence may then be verbally described in a variety of ways, in whatever language one happens to speak. There is thus a great deal of possible ambiguity when it comes to reading sequences of pictograms, and many of these scripts have proved difficult or impossible to decipher.

Pictograms constitute the earliest systems of writing and are found in many parts of the world where the remains of early people have been discovered. They have been discovered in Egypt and Mesopotamia from around 3000 BC, and in China from around 1500 BC. The most famous is probably the Egyptian form which came to be called *hieroglyphic* (from the Greek 'sacred carving'), because of its prominent use in temples, tombs, and other special places. The term has also come to be used for scripts of a similar character from other cultures, such as the Hittite, Mayan, or Indus Valley.

The units of the Egyptian system are known as *hieroglyphs*. They tend to be written from right to left, with the symbols generally facing the beginning of a row; but vertical rows are also found, following the line of a building. The script gives the general impression of being pictorial, but in fact it contains three types of symbol that together represent words.

- Some symbols are used as ideograms (see below), representing real-world entities or notions.
- Some symbols stand for consonants, in much the same way as the *rebus* system is used in present-day children's games. For example, in English we might use a picture of a bee followed by the letter *R* to represent the word *beer*, or followed by *K* to represent the word *beak*. In hieroglyphic, this convention was used to express two-consonant sequences as well as single consonants.
- Hieroglyphic also used signs that had no phonetic value but were placed next to other symbols to tell the reader what kind of meaning a word has. Words that would otherwise appear to be identical could thus be differentiated. An analogy might again be drawn with a word game in English that could distinguish the two senses of the word *table* by adding a chair (for the item of furniture) and an eye (for the typographical arrangement).

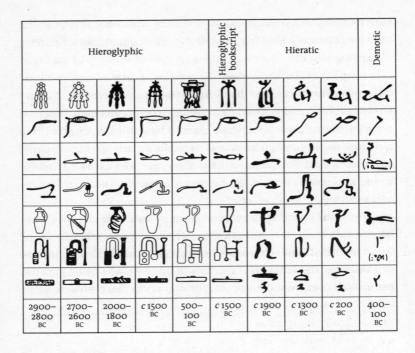

	Hieroglyphic					Hieroglyphic bookscript	Hieratic			Demotic
2900–2800 BC	2700–2600 BC	2000–1800 BC	c 1500 BC	500–100 BC	c 1500 BC	c 1900 BC	c 1300 BC	c 200 BC	400–100 BC

Fig. 10. Egyptian hieroglyphs over time

Ideographic writing

Ideographic writing is usually distinguished as a later development of pictographic. *Ideograms*, or *ideographs*, have an abstract or conventional meaning, no longer displaying a clear pictorial link with external reality. The shape of an ideogram may so alter that it is no longer recognizable as a pictorial representation of an object; or its original meaning may extend to include notions that lack any clear pictorial form. In early Sumerian writing, for example, the picture of a starry sky came to mean 'night', 'dark', or 'black', and other such notions.

It is rare to find a 'pure' ideographic writing system – that is, one in which the symbols refer directly to notions or things. Most systems that have been called ideographic in fact contain linguistic elements. The symbols stand for words in the language, or parts of the symbols represent sounds. The Sumerian, Egyptian, Hittite, and other scripts of the early period were all mixtures of pictographic, ideographic, and linguistic elements.

Cuneiform writing

The cuneiform method of writing dates from the 4th millennium BC. The name derives from the Latin, meaning 'wedge-shaped', and refers to the technique used to make the symbols. A stylus was pressed into a tablet of soft clay to make a sequence of short straight strokes. In later periods, harder materials were used. The strokes are thickest at the top and to the left, reflecting the direction of writing: at first, symbols were written from top to bottom; later, they were turned onto their sides, and written from left to right.

The earliest cuneiform was a development of pictographic symbols. Subsequently, the script was used to write words and syllables, and to mark phonetic elements. It was used for over 3,000 years throughout the Near East by such cultures as the Sumerians, Babylonians, Assyrians, and Hittites, finally dying out as the Christian era approached. The script could not be read until the 19th century, when several of the languages it represented were finally deciphered.

Logographic writing

Logographic writing systems are those where the graphemes represent words. The best-known cases are Chinese, and its derivative script, Japanese *kanji*. The symbols are variously referred to as *logographs*, *logograms*, or – in the case of oriental languages – *characters*. Because Chinese writing derives from an ideographic script, with several pictographic elements, the characters are also commonly referred to as *ideographs*. However, this term is really not appropriate, as the characters refer to linguistic units, and not directly to concepts or things. Also, the characters in fact often represent parts of words as well as whole words, so that even the term *logographic* is somewhat misleading.

Several thousand graphemes are involved in a full logographic system. In modern Chinese, basic literacy requires knowledge of some

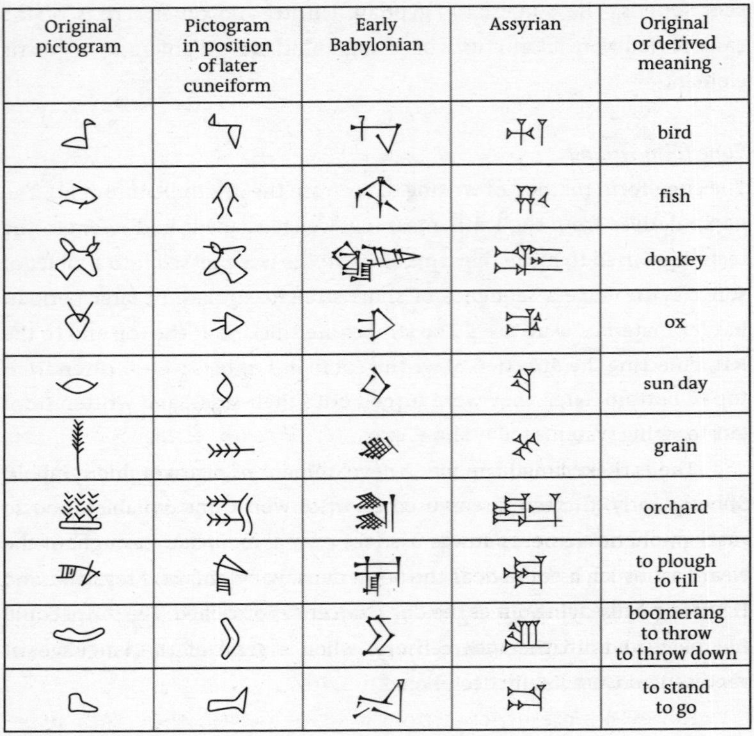

Original pictogram	Pictogram in position of later cuneiform	Early Babylonian	Assyrian	Original or derived meaning
				bird
				fish
				donkey
				ox
				sun day
				grain
				orchard
				to plough to till
				boomerang to throw to throw down
				to stand to go

Fig. 11. Sumerian pictograms related to cuneiform

2,000 characters. In Japanese, 1,945 characters are prescribed by the Ministry of Education and adopted by law as those most essential for everyday use. Of these, 1,006 are taught during the six years of elementary school. But probably all written languages today make use of some logograms. English, for example, has &, 2, +, £, =, as well as the most famous logogram of the electronic age – @.

18
How we make writing systems: modern times

Most writing systems today show a clear relationship between the symbols and sounds of the language, and they are therefore known as *phonological* systems (p. 108). There are two types. In a *syllabic* system, or *syllabary*, each grapheme corresponds to a spoken syllable, usually a consonant–vowel pair, such as *ka* or *do*. These systems have been found from earliest times (e.g. Mycenaean Greek), and in modern times can be seen in Amharic, Cherokee, and Japanese *kana*. The number of graphemes in a syllabary varies – from around fifty to several hundred.

However, most modern writing systems are *alphabetic*. With alphabetic writing, there is a direct correspondence between graphemes and phonemes, and this makes it the most economic and adaptable of all the writing systems. Instead of several thousand logograms, or several hundred syllables, the system needs only a relatively small number of units, which it then proves easy to adapt to a wide range of languages. Most alphabets contain twenty to thirty symbols, but the total number depends on the complexity of the sound system. The smallest alphabet seems to be Rotokas, used in the Solomon Islands, with eleven letters. The largest is Khmer, with seventy-four letters. English, of course, has twenty-six.

In a perfectly regular system, as in some of the alphabets that have been devised by linguists to record previously unwritten languages, there is one grapheme for each phoneme. However, most alphabets in

Phoenician	Old Hebrew	Early Greek	Classical Greek	Etruscan	Early Latin	Modern Roman
						Aa
						Bb
						Cc
						Dd
						Ee
						Ff
						Gg
						Hh
						Ii
						Jj
						Kk
						Ll
						Mm
						Nn
						Oo
						Pp
						Qq
						Rr
						Ss
						Tt
						Uu
						Vv
						Ww
						Xx
						Yy
						Zz

Fig. 12. Some alphabetic systems

present-day use fail to meet this criterion, to some degree, either because the writing system has not kept place with changes in pronunciation, or because the language is using an alphabet not originally designed for it. Languages vary greatly in their graphemic/phonemic regularity. At one extreme we find such languages as Spanish and Finnish, which have a very regular system; at the other, we find such cases as English and Gaelic, where there is a marked degree of irregularity. The extent to which there is a lack of correspondence between graphemes and phonemes is inevitably reflected in the number of arbitrary 'spelling rules' that children have to learn (§20).

Greek form	Greek name	Cyrillic	Hebrew form	Hebrew name	Arabic form	Arabic name
Αα	alpha	Аа	א	'aleph, 'alef	ا	'alif
Ββ	beta	Бб	ב	bēth	ـب	bā
Γγ	gamma	Вв	ג	gimel	ـت	tā
Δδ	delta	Гг	ד	dāleth	ـث	thā
Εε	epsilon	Дд	ה	hē	ح	jīm
Ζζ	zēta	Ее	ו	vav, waw	ح	hā
Ηη	ēta	Ёё	ז	zayin	ح	khā
Θθ	thēta	Жж	ח	ḥeth	د	dāi
Ιι	iota	Зз	ט	ṭeth	ذ	dhāi
Κκ	kappa	Ии Йй	י	yod, yodh	ر	rā
Λλ	lambda	Кк	ךכ	kāph	ز	zāy
Μμ	mu	Лл	ל	lāmedh	س	sin
Νν	nu	Мм	םמ	mēm	ش	shin
Ξξ	xi	Нн	ןנ	nūn	ص	ṣād
Οο	omicron	Оо	ס	samekh	ض	ḍād
Ππ	pi	Пп	ע	'ayin	ط	ṭā
Ρρ	rho	Рр	ףפ	pē	ظ	ẓā
Σσς	sigma	Сс	ץצ	sade, ṣadhe	ع	'ayn
Ττ	tau	Тт	ק	qōph	غ	ghayn
Υυ	upsilon	Уу	ר	rēsh	ف	fā
Φφ	phi	Фф	שׂ	sin	ق	qāf
Χχ	chi, khi	Хх	שׁ	shin	ك	kaf
Ψψ	psi	Цц	ת	tāv, tāw	ل	lam
Ωω	omega	Чч			م	mim
		Шш			ن	nun
		Щщ			ه	hā
		Ъъ			و	wāw
		Ьь			ي	yā
		Ыы				
		Ээ				
		Юю				
		Яя				

There are also many alphabets where only certain phonemes are represented graphemically. These are the *consonantal* alphabets, such as Aramaic, Hebrew, and Arabic, where the marking of vowels (using diacritics) is optional. There are also cases, such as the alphabets of India, where diacritics are used for vowels, but the marking is obligatory, with the diacritics being attached to the consonantal letters.

The earliest known alphabet was the North Semitic, which developed around 1700 BC in Palestine and Syria. It consisted of twenty-two consonant letters. The Hebrew, Arabic, and Phoenician alphabets were based on this model. Then, around 1000 BC, the Phoenician alphabet was itself used as a model by the Greeks, who added letters for vowels. Greek in turn became the model for Etruscan (*c.* 800 BC), and from this came the letters of the ancient Roman alphabet, and ultimately all western alphabets.

Graphological contrasts

Once a writing system has been devised, it can be used to convey a wide range of graphological contrasts. These are most conveniently illustrated from the range of possibilities available in alphabetic systems.

Spelling

The essential identity of written words is conveyed by the correct selection and sequence of graphemes – the spelling rules of the language. This is the main component of any graphological description. It is a study that needs to include, not only the 'normal' rules that have to be learned in order to read and write, but any dialectal, stylistic, or 'free' variations.

- Dialect variation is illustrated by American–British differences such as *color/colour* or the use of *thru* for *through*.
- Stylistic variation can be illustrated by the way authors adapt the spelling system to reflect or suggest the pronunciation of non-standard speech. An example is the use of *sez* for *says*: the two forms reflect identical pronunciations, but the former conveys the impression of a non-standard accent.
- Free variations include those cases where more than one spelling can be used in a particular dialect, such as the alternative spellings of *judgment/judgement* or words ending in *-ise/-ize*. Although it is sometimes possible to explain the variation – for example, in terms of the spelling preference of a particular publishing house – a writer can use either form without it being considered a mistake.

Capital letters

Initial capitals mark both lexical units and grammatical units. Capitalized lexical units are the set of proper names, such as *David*, *Tuesday*, and *London Bridge*, and most abbreviations (see below). In English, the first-person pronoun (*I*) is also capitalized – a feature that most other languages do not share. (However, some languages do capitalize other pronouns, such as the 'you' forms seen in German *Sie* and Spanish *Vd* 'usted'.) The chief grammatical use is to identify the beginning of a sentence. Capitals are also available to add semantic nuance, as in *Out of the train stepped a Very Important Person*. And a stretch of discourse can be capitalized, for emphasis, as in newspaper headlines. There are also some sociolinguistic restrictions: in Internet interaction, for example, capitalized text is widely interpreted as 'shouting', and considered bad netiquette.

A single graphic contrast is involved: large vs. small. The graphic contrast between different sizes of capital letter (*A* vs. the *A*, for example) conveys no conventional meaning difference, though it is widely used by publishers to identify certain kinds of information, as when *AD* and *BC* are printed in small capitals. There are also certain restrictions – numerals, for example, do not capitalize.

Abbreviations

Shortened forms of words are a major feature of written language, as in the use of titular contractions and abbreviations such as *Mr*, *Dr*, *Ms*, *Lt*, and *Capt*, or the use of acronyms, such as *COD*, *VIP*, and *UNESCO*. The abbreviations may even come from a different language, and the full form may not be known, as in the case of *e.g.* (= Latin *exempli gratia*) or *i.e.* (= Latin *id est*). Some abbreviations are spoken as words (e.g. *UNESCO* is usually /juːˈneskəʊ/); some are spelled out (e.g. *VIP* is always /ˈviː ˈaɪ ˈpiː/); some are automatically expanded (e.g. Mr is /ˈmɪstə/); and some permit a choice (e.g. *viz.* spoken as /vɪz/ or as *namely*).

Special symbols

Several symbols are available to express frequently occurring meanings in an economical way. Most of these are logograms (p. 111), such as +, @, and £; but some do not relate to individual words, such as the dagger (†) showing that a person is dead. Special symbols may also be used to help organize a written text, such as asterisks or superscript numbers relating to footnotes. Other symbols draw attention to part of a text, as when a large star is used before a name in an advertisement. An important use of the asterisk is to show omitted letters, especially in taboo words, as with f**k.

Punctuation

The punctuation system of a language has two functions. Its primary purpose is to enable stretches of written language to be read in a coherent way. Its secondary role is to give an indication of the rhythm and colour of speech (though no language's punctuation does this consistently). It roughly corresponds to the use of suprasegmental features (§12), but it differs from speech in that its contrasts are to some extent taught in schools, and norms of punctuation are conventionally laid down by publishing houses in their style manuals.

Features that separate

Punctuation is mainly used to separate units of grammar and discourse (paragraphs, sentences, clauses, phrases, and words) from each other (§36). The various marks are organized in a broadly hierarchical manner: some identify large units of writing, such as paragraphs; others identify small units of intermediate size or complexity. The main English-language conventions are as follows:

- *space*: separates words; identifies paragraphs – the first sentence begins a new line, with the first word usually indented; extra space may also be inserted between paragraphs, especially to mark a break in the discourse.

- *period (full stop)*: identifies the end of a sentence, along with question and exclamation marks; sometimes followed by a wider space than is usual between words (printing and typing conventions differ); also traditionally used to mark abbreviations (though modern practice usually omits them); a sequence of (usually three) periods indicates that the text is incomplete.
- *semi-colon*: identifies the coordinate parts of a complex sentence, or separates complex points in a list (as in the previous paragraph).
- *colon*: used mainly to show that what follows it is an amplification or explanation of what precedes it – as in the present sentence.
- *comma*: a wide range of uses, such as marking a sequence of grammatical units, or a unit used inside another; displays a great deal of personal variation (such as whether it should be used before *and* in such lists as *apples, pears, and plums*).
- *parentheses* ( ) and *brackets* [ ]: used as an alternative to commas to mark the inclusion of a grammatical unit in the middle or at the end of a sentence.
- *dash*: used in pairs with the same function as parentheses or brackets; used singly to separate a comment or afterthought occurring at the end of a sentence or to express an incomplete utterance; in informal writing, often replaces other punctuation marks.
- *quotation marks (inverted commas)*: identify the beginning and end of an extract of speech, a title, a citation, or the 'special' use of a word. The choice of single vs. double quotes is variable: the latter are more common in handwritten and typed material, and in American printing.
- *hyphen*: marks two kinds of divisions within a word – to show that a word has been split in two because of the end of a line (a feature that has no spoken counterpart), and to relate the parts of a phrase or compound word to each other (as in *pickled-herring merchant* – vs. *pickled herring-merchant* – and *washing-machine*); practice varies greatly in the latter use, with British English using hyphens in many contexts where American English would omit them.

Features that convey meaning

Some punctuation features express a meaning in their own right, regardless of the grammatical context in which they occur.

- *Question mark*: usually expresses a question, but occasionally found with other functions, such as marking silence or uncertainty (e.g. *this is an interesting (?) point*).
- *Exclamation mark*: shows varying degrees of exclamatory force (e.g. *!!!*); also, some special uses (e.g. *John (!) was there*).
- *Apostrophe*: most commonly used to mark the genitive singular or plural (*cat's, cats'*), and grammatical contractions (*I'm, won't*); found also in certain words (*o'clock, fish 'n' chips*); subject to a great deal of usage variation (*St Johns* or *St John's? Harrods* or *Harrod's?*) and uncertainty (*Ice cream cone's, Todays bargains*).

Graphic contrasts

Italic, boldface, colour, and other graphic variations are major ways of expressing semantic contrasts. The size of the graphemes, for example, conveys the relative importance of parts of a message, as in advertisements or invitations. The switch from Roman to Gothic type may convey an 'old world' connotation, as in many Christmas cards and shop signs. Colour has become a major means of textual organization on the Web, and is highly functional in its use as a marker of a hypertext link.

Spatial organization

The general disposition of written symbols on a page or other format can itself convey semantic contrasts. This is something newspaper editors are very much aware of when they juxtapose stories, place headlines or captions, and lay out headings and sub-headings. Spatial organization can be a critical feature of some genres, such as poetry. But any text will rely on spatial configuration as part of its graphic accessibility – as illustrated by the present page.

19

How we read

We began the study of speaking and listening with an account of the *vocal organs* (§4), but it does not make sense to begin the study of reading and writing in the same way. The eyes and hands are not analogous 'visual organs' – organs which have been adapted to enable human beings to process written language. Written language, only some 10,000 years old (§54), is too recent a development in human history. As a consequence, research into the way we write devotes little time to the structure and function of the eyes and hands, focusing instead on the way the brain works when it processes written language.

Eye movements

One physiological topic has attracted considerable attention, however: the nature of eye movements. These movements can be recorded using various techniques, such as by attaching a mirror to a contact lens placed on the cornea; it is then possible to film a beam of light reflected off the mirror. Using such methods, researchers have shown that the eyes work together, and that when searching for an object they move in a series of rapid jerks, known as *saccades* (from French, 'the flick of a sail'). Between each movement there is a period of relative stability, known as a *fixation*. During reading, the eyes do not follow lines of print in a smooth linear manner, but proceed in a series of saccades and fixations. We usually make three-to-four fixations a second, though rate and duration can be affected by the content of what is read, and there are some variations between languages.

What happens during a fixation is of particular importance in studying the process of reading. The nerve cells that convert light into electrical pulses are located in the retina, at the back of the eye. The central region of the retina, where these receptor cells are packed closely together, is known as the *fovea*. This is the area that gives the best visual detail, such

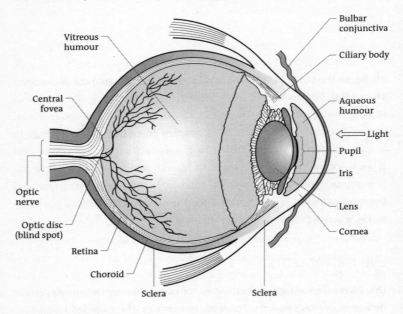

Fig. 13. Anatomy of the eye

as is required for identifying graphic forms. The further a stimulus is from the fovea, the poorer our ability to discriminate. The *parafoveal* area surrounds the fovea, and this in turn is surrounded by the *periphery*. These areas are less involved in the act of reading, but they do have some relevance in the detection of larger visual patterns in a text.

Following a fixation during reading, a visual pattern of graphic features is conveyed to the retina, and then transmitted via the optic nerve for interpretation by the brain. The stages involved in this process are not well understood, and several different theories have been proposed to explain what happens when fluent readers read. One reason why the field is so controversial is that it is extremely difficult to obtain precise information about the events that take place when people read. In fact, very little actually seems to happen, apart from the eye movements – and these do not begin to explain how the reader is managing to draw meaning out of the graphic symbols. Similarly, if people are tested after they have read something, we may find out something about what they have read, but not about how they read it.

Reading in all of this does not mean simply *reading aloud*, which might be done by a suitably equipped automatic machine that would not know what it was saying. Reading crucially involves appreciating the sense of what is written: we read for meaning. It is this link – between graphology and semantics – that has to be explained by any theory of reading.

Reading by ear or by eye?

Most people have encountered the struggle that takes place as a child is learning to read. A major feature of this task is that words and letters are 'sounded out'. It is as if reading is possible only if the symbols are heard – *reading by ear*. One theory of reading therefore argues that a phonic or phonological step is an essential feature of the process – a theory of *phonic mediation*. The view implies that reading is a serial or linear process, taking place letter-by-letter, with larger units gradually being built up.

The alternative view argues that there is a direct relationship between the graphology and the semantics, and that a phonological bridge is unnecessary (though it is available for use when reading aloud). Words are read as wholes, without being broken down into a linear sequence of letters and sounded out – *reading by eye*. Readers use their peripheral vision to guide the eye to the most likely informative part of the page. Their knowledge of the language and general experience helps them to identify critical letters or words in a section of text. This initial sampling gives them an expectation about the way the text should be read, and they use their background knowledge to 'guess' the remainder of the text and fill in the gaps. In this view, a text is like a problem that has to be solved using hypotheses about its meaning and structure.

The arguments for and against these views are complex and multi-faceted, deriving from the results of a vast number of experiments on aspects of reading behaviour. Some of the points that have been raised are summarized below.

Support for the ear

Associating graphemes and phonemes is a natural process, which cannot be avoided when first learning to read.

- Letter recognition is very rapid – about 10–20 msec per letter – which is enough to account for average reading speeds (around 250 words per minute). These speeds are similar for both silent and oral reading (though the latter is slightly slower, presumably for articulatory reasons), and are close to the norms for spontaneous speech (p. 21).
- Statistical studies of word frequency show that most words in a text are of very low frequency, several occurring only once over long periods; some will be completely new to a reader. Readers can therefore have few expectancies about such material and will need to decode it phonologically. It is an everyday experience to break new long words up into phonemes or (more usually) syllables: try the nonsense word *picomalesefeso*, and see.
- When people read difficult material, they often move their lips, as if the phonology is needed in order to help comprehension. There may be other sub-vocal movements not so far observed.
- It is difficult to see how the 'eye' theory can handle the many variations in type and handwriting. Yet we are able to read these variations quite rapidly, even in experimental situations (using such forms as *BoAt*).
- Reading by eye would be a very complex matter. Each word would

have to be given a separate orthographic representation in the brain, along with a separate retrieval process. This is not a parsimonious explanation.

Support for the eye

- Fluent readers are not confused by such homophones as *two* and *too*. Phonology cannot help in such cases. Moreover in words like *tear*, there is no way of deciding which pronunciation is involved (/tiə/ or /tɛə/) until after the reader has selected a meaning.
- In one type of reading disorder (phonological dyslexia, p. 143), people lose the ability to convert isolated letters into sounds; they are unable to pronounce even simple nonsense words, e.g. *pob*). But they are able to read real words, showing that a non-phonological route from print to meaning must exist.
- The 'ear' theory does not explain how some people can read at very rapid speeds, which can be in excess of 500 words per minute. The eyes can take in only so many letters at a time. Rapid reading poses less of a problem for the 'eye' theory, as it simply requires that readers increase their sampling as they speed up.
- In brief exposure experiments, people identify whole words more rapidly than isolated letters. For example, if subjects are shown *BAG*, *BIG*, *A*, *I*, *IBG*, etc., and asked whether they have just seen *A* or *I*, they perform best with the familiar words. This is the *word superiority* effect.
- The fact that different sounds are written identically, and different letters can have the same pronunciation, complicates a phonological view. Also, some orthographic rules seem totally unrelated to the phonology, e.g. *skr-* is acceptable in English speech, but does not occur in normal writing.
- Some higher-order processing must be involved in reading, because of several observed effects. Experiments have shown that it is easier to recognize letters in real words than in nonsense words. Typo-

graphic errors are often not noticed when reading through a text (the proof-corrector's problem). Errors made by fluent readers while reading aloud are usually syntactically or semantically appropriate; they make few phonologically induced errors.

It is evident that neither approach explains all aspects of reading behaviour; it is likely that people make use of both strategies at various stages in learning and in handling different kinds of reading problem. The 'ear' approach (sometimes referred to as a *bottom-up* or *Phoenician* theory, because of its reliance on basic letter units) is evidently very important during the initial stages. Perhaps after several exposures to a word, a direct print-meaning pathway comes to be built up. But the 'eye' approach (sometimes referred to as a *top-down* or *Chinese* theory, because of its reliance on whole-word units) is certainly needed in order to explain most of what goes on in fluent adult reading.

20
How we write and spell

It is extremely difficult to discover what goes on when people write. Direct observation of someone engaged in writing or typing tells us little about what is happening 'beneath the surface'. And direct observation of the written product gives very limited information, for it fails to preserve the order in which revisions are made, or the amount of time devoted to producing any part of it.

All writing involves a planning stage, during which we organize our thoughts and prepare an outline of what we want to say. Even the shortest of messages requires a moment or two of planning. At the very least, we need to work out what our readers need to know, in order for our message to be understood. We also need to anticipate the effect our words could have.

Much more is involved when we write more complex messages. In particular, we have to supplement the notion of 'writing' with that of 'rewriting'. Any model of what happens when we write must take into account the act of revision – from the first stages of making notes, jottings, and headings, through various drafts, to the final version. All writers introduce errors and make self-corrections while composing.

Writers also pause a great deal – stopping the movement of their pen or of their fingers while they type. During these pauses, other kinds of body activity take place. The eyes may scan the text or look away. The hands may stay close to the page or keyboard (suggesting that the writer expects to resolve the problem quickly) or move away (suggesting that a more serious process of reflection is taking place). Pauses reflect the occurrence of mental planning and provide clues to the difficulty of the writing task.

A model of written composition must also allow for the fact that what people see when they write may affect the way they think. Authors' comments are illuminating: 'It doesn't look right now I've written it down', 'That's not what I'm trying to say.' Full meaning does not always exist prior to writing; often the process operates in reverse. A typical comment is Edward Albee's: 'I write to find out what I'm thinking about'. Such remarks emphasize the main lesson to be learned from the study of the process of writing: it is not a merely mechanical task, a simple matter of putting speech down on paper. It is an exploration in the use of the graphic potential of a language – a creative process, an act of discovery.

Spelling

Reading and writing have long been thought of as complementary skills: to read is to recognize and interpret language that has been written; to write is to plan and produce language so that it can be read. It is therefore widely assumed that being able to read implies being able to write – or, at least, being able to spell. Often, children are taught to read but given no formal tuition in spelling; it is felt that spelling will be 'picked up'.

Matters are not so simple. There is no necessary link between reading and writing: good readers do not always make good writers. Nor is there any necessary link between reading and spelling: there are many people who have no difficulty in reading, but who have a major persistent handicap in spelling – this may be as many as 2% of the population. There seems moreover to be a neuro-anatomical basis for the distinction, for there are brain-damaged adults who can read but not spell, and vice versa.

With children, too, there is evidence that knowledge of reading does not automatically transfer to spelling. If there were a close relationship, children should be able to read and spell the same words; but this is not so. It is commonplace to find children who can read far better than they can spell. More surprisingly, the reverse happens with some children in the early stages of reading. One study gave children the same list of words to read and to spell: several actually spelled more words correctly than they were able to read correctly.

Why so difficult?

Why should reading and spelling be so different? It is partly a matter of active production skills being more difficult than passive, receptive ones. Spelling is a more conscious, deliberate process, which requires awareness of linguistic structure, and a good visual memory, to handle the exceptions to the regular patterns. It is possible to read by attending selectively to the cues in a text, recognizing just a few letters, and guessing the rest. It is not possible to spell in this way: spellers have to reproduce all the letters.

Also, more things can go wrong while spelling: there are far more graphemic alternatives for a phoneme (p. 68) than there are phonemic alternatives for a grapheme (p. 105). For example, *beat* has really only one possible pronunciation, /biːt/; whereas the form /biːt/ could be written in several different ways – *beet, beete, beat, beate, biet* . . . One study worked out that in English there are 13.7 spellings per sound, but only 3.5 sounds per letter.

However, the differences between reading and spelling cannot be explained simply by arguing that spelling is 'more difficult', for this would not explain those children who can spell better than they read. Rather, the two skills seem to involve different learning strategies. Whereas reading is largely a matter of developing direct links between graphic expression and meaning, spelling seems to involve an obligatory phonological component (§11) from the very outset. These signs of phonological activity can be very noticeable – as when we see beginners painfully writing *C-A-T* and saying the letter names of sounds as they write, or adult writers sounding out words (especially long words) while writing them down.

To be a good speller, we need to have both good phonological awareness (to cope with the regular spelling patterns) and good visual awareness (to cope with the exceptions). Poor spellers, it seems, lack this double skill.

Irregular spelling

The task is not helped when a language has a spelling system containing a great deal of irregularity – as in the case of English, which is often said to be 'chaotic' and 'unpredictable' in its spelling. But just how irregular is English? The impression of fundamental irregularity is based on such famous sentences as *Though the rough cough and hiccough plough me through, I ought to cross the lough*. But this kind of thing is the exception rather than the rule.

It is difficult to arrive at a firm figure for the amount of spelling irregularity in a language, because people differ over which words to include in the study. Should proper names be included, for example? In one study, a computer analysis of 17,000 English words showed that 84% were spelled according to a regular pattern, and that only 3% were so unpredictable that they would have to be learned totally by rote. A widely cited figure is that English is about 75% regular. On the other hand, many of the 400 or so irregular spellings are among the most frequently used words in the language, so this promotes a strong impression of irregularity.

The spelling irregularities in a language are always explained by its history. In the case of English, the causes go back to Anglo-Saxon times.

- In the Anglo-Saxon period, an alphabet of twenty-four graphemes (the Latin alphabet, plus four new symbols) had to cope with a sound system of nearly forty phonemes, which meant that many sounds had to be signalled by combinations of letters.
- After the Norman conquest, French scribes re-spelled a great deal of the language, introducing such conventions as *qu* for *cw* (*queen*), *gh* for *h* (*night*), and *c* instead of *s* before *e* or *i* in such words as *circle* and *cell*.
- The printing process caused complications. Many early printers were foreign, and they used their own spelling norms.
- Especially after printing, the writing system did not keep pace with the sound changes that were affecting the language. During the

Middle Ages, letters that were sounded in Anglo-Saxon became 'silent', e.g. the *k* of *know* and *knight*, or the final *e* in *stone*, *love*, etc. There was also a major shift in the pronunciation of vowels during the 15th century.

- In the 16th century, there was a fashion to make spellings reflect word history. If a word originated in Latin or Greek, letters might be added to show the relationship. For example, a *g* was added in *reign*, to show that it came from Latin *regno*, and a *b* was added to *debt*, to show it came from *debitum*.

- In the late 16th and early 17th centuries, many new loan words entered English from such languages as French, Latin, Greek, Spanish, Italian, and Portuguese, resulting in words which contained such alien spellings as *-que* and *-zz-*, as in *grotesque* and *piazza*.

- Later centuries saw further periods of lexical borrowing, with Chinese, Japanese, Arabic, Indian languages, and African languages all contributing words of unfamiliar sound, requiring decisions to be made about how they were to be spelled. Sometimes no agreement was reached, and alternative spellings exist – as in the case of *yogurt*, *yoghourt*, and *yoghurt*.

The result is a 'system' that is an amalgam of Anglo-Saxon, French, Classical, and other sources. The system is basically a phonemic one, but the phonemes are represented by letter patterns as well as by single letters. As a result, the task facing the child learner is much greater than in the case of a system (such as Spanish and Welsh) where for the most part there is a regular one sound–one spelling relationship throughout.

Spelling reformers

People have tried to eradicate irregular spellings in English for centuries. As early as 1551, John Hart was complaining of the 'vices' of English writing which cause it to be 'learned hard and evil to read'. In the following centuries, several experimental orthographies were published. In 1876, the Spelling Reform Association was founded in the USA, followed by the

Simplified Spelling Board (1906) and (in Britain) the Simplified Spelling Society (1908). A system of *Nue Spelling* was devised and widely promulgated, and this was followed by many other proposals in the first half of the 20th century.

The advantages of spelling reform are clear. Children would save an enormous amount of time and emotional effort in learning to read, and there would be considerable benefits to foreign learners of English. Because fewer letters would be used (an estimated saving of 15%), there would be a great saving in writers' time, and in the time and costs of typing, printing, and associated matters (paper, ink, storage, transport, etc).

But the disadvantages are also clear. There would be a major break in continuity between old and new spelling, especially in the more radical schemes. The problem of inertia and conservatism would make a transition difficult: all who have learned old spelling have a vested interest in it, and few would be willing to learn an alternative system, or wish to have their children learn one. And the saving in costs might be outweighed by the need to reprint important works in new spelling.

The history of the spelling-reform movement indicates that the disadvantages are generally felt to outweigh the advantages. Probably the biggest problem is that there has never been any agreement among the various groups of spelling reformers about an optimum system. It is difficult to see how a programme of spelling reform could be implemented in a practical or realistic way. But the enthusiasm of spelling-reform bodies all over the world continues unabated.

21

How we learn to read and write

Listening and speaking are natural behaviours. Unless there is something wrong with the child (§15) or something lacking in the child's environment, speech will emerge towards the end of the first year and develop steadily thereafter. Reading and writing, however, are quite different. They have to be taught and painstakingly learned.

Literacy has long been considered the main evidence of a child's educational progress. As a result, more attention has been paid to the nature of the task facing children as they learn to read than to any other area of the curriculum. Hundreds of reading schemes and philosophies have been devised in the past 200 years, and many have achieved a degree of success. However, it is usually an open question whether success is due to the properties of an approach or to the enthusiasm with which it is promoted by its adherents.

Various positions are advocated. Some recommend the initial use of a particular scheme or method to all children; others argue that there is no 'right way', and that a range of approaches should be available to suit the needs of individual children. For some, reading is essentially the skill of decoding written symbols; for others, it is a means of discovering the meaning 'behind' the symbols. In this deeper view, reading plays a fundamental role in promoting children's critical and imaginative think-ing, and thus their intellectual and emotional development. A similar concern motivates the view that the teaching of reading should not be restricted to the classroom. Several studies have suggested that regular reading aloud to children by their caretakers, accompanied by informal discussion of what is being read, may be the single most important factor in promoting reading ability.

Since the early 19th century, the relative merits of two main approaches have dominated educational debate about the teaching of reading. Schemes have been devised based largely on one principle or the other, and there have been several 'mixed' schemes, which attempt to integrate the strengths of each.

- *Phonic* approaches are based on the principle of identifying the regular sound–letter relationships in a writing system, and teaching the child to use these to construct or decode words. Phonic schemes are now thought to be absolutely fundamental, because they give children a rationale for 'sounding out' new words. On the other hand, phonic skills have to be taught carefully. The task of blending isolated sounds into whole words is not easy: to get from *c* [kə] + *a* [a] + *t* [tə] to *cat* [kat], an actual change of pronunciation is involved, as the phonetic transcription shows. And first books have severe restrictions on their permitted vocabulary, which often results in artificial or bizarre sentences (e.g. *Pat and Dad ran*).
- *Whole-word* or *look-and-say* approaches are based on the principle of recognizing individual words as wholes, without breaking them down into constituent letters or sounds. The main aim is to avoid the use of strings of meaningless phonic syllables, and to permit access to longer and more meaningful sentences, through the use of frequently occurring words (*the, go, saw, little, my,* etc.) – and even much longer words, such as *aeroplane* and *doctor*. Whole-word approaches in early readers have been criticized for their lack of clear grading principles, and for the way words are often arbitrarily selected, unrelated to the child's experience. But eventually whole-word reading skills have to be acquired, as they are the only means whereby we achieve a rapid reading ability. We 'see' most words and read them, without needing to phonically decode them (§19).

But even if a combination of phonic and whole-word approaches are used, this is not all there is to reading.

Learning to read: active skills

Children need to be motivated by having materials and activities that are interesting. It is often pointed out that the content of traditional reading-scheme books is singularly uninspiring: children view such reading as a dull decoding task, and choose very different kinds of books ('real books') when they read by themselves for enjoyment. Today, this contrast is much less apparent, with new schemes placing a greater emphasis on story-telling and more appealing visual design. The world of the child's own experience is also increasingly represented, through the use of familiar social situations and everyday visual language contexts, such as road signs and shop names.

Children also need to foster their cognitive skills in order to read efficiently. Research has shown the relevance of such abilities as classifying, sequencing, and pattern matching; and *pre-reading* materials can provide practice in these areas, along with opportunities to draw, cut out, colour in, and so on. Many children find their first encounter with the world of print confusing, so that a great deal of attention is now being paid to ways of providing them with opportunities to think about what is involved in reading and writing (e.g. how are books made? what is writing for?), and giving them a metalanguage for talking about these activities (e.g. *page, line, beginning, space*).

All of this is part of an active approach to reading. When children encounter a word they cannot read, emphasis is laid on helping them to work out for themselves what it must be, by using such techniques as reading on to the end of the sentence, reading back to the sentence beginning, and checking any illustrations. The intention is to make them rely less on the mechanical task of decoding letters, and to capitalize more on their linguistic experience and awareness of context so that they can guess what a word might be. This is not to say that accuracy in word decoding is unimportant. Rather, 'getting the words right' is a gradual process – as indeed it is in spoken language acquisition.

We should also note the many different kinds of activity that are found under the heading of *fluent reading*. At one extreme, there is the careful, complete, and vocal technique known as *reading aloud*; at the other, there is the rapid, selective, and silent technique known as *scanning* or *skimming* – something widely practised by time-pressed adults as they work quickly through a report or read the morning newspaper. In between there are many other activities, such as *critical reading* (e.g. underlining sections of text, or adding marginal notes), *proof-reading* (checking our own or someone else's text for errors), and *reading for learning* (if you suddenly discovered that as soon as you had read the next page you would be asked questions on it, your reading strategy would alter immediately). Current thinking about reading draws attention to the importance of all these real-world skills.

Learning to write: motor skills

Many people think of learning to write as just a matter of forming and sequencing letters in a fluent, automatic manner, and positioning them clearly on a page. But far more is involved than the correct formation of letter shapes: letter sizes, word spaces, spaces between lines, margins, and other matters of layout also need to be consistent, if a writing style is to be acceptable.

Most attention has been paid to the question of *writing posture* – the optimum position of the body for writing. We need to consider such factors as hand position, finger grip, the angle of the body towards the paper, and the height of the writer's chair. Too low a chair, for example, can cause a twisted hand position, which inhibits finger movement, and thus prevents the formation of a free cursive (p. 100) style. In addition, the child needs to learn simple management strategies – such as the need to move the writing paper upwards as one nears the bottom of a page (rather than to move oneself, which is what some children do).

The type of writing implement and the kind of paper need to be considered. A child may be unwilling to write with a certain kind of pen, or find it difficult. The question of when to introduce lined paper needs careful thought: lines help the child to control the direction and size of script, but they also constrain the spontaneity of a natural writing style. There may also be difficulty in transferring letter shapes from one visual plane (e.g. on a blackboard) to another (the page). And there may be problems of coordination between eye and hand movements, especially if there has been little experience of scribbling and drawing. It is easy to see why it can take children three years or more to develop a reasonably smooth, automatic writing technique.

Learning to write: functional skills

There is far more to writing than the automatic exercise of a motor skill. Writing gives children a unique way of formulating their thoughts to themselves, and of reflecting on what they mean. It is seen as an integral part of the process of learning, and not simply as an ancillary function – something to be used as a way of checking that learning has actually taken place (as in the traditional subject essay). This view requires an appreciation that writing is used for a wide range of purposes and a variety of audiences.

Writing is used for an indefinitely large number of purposes – to express feelings, tell stories, report events, complete forms, keep records, and much more. Children have to learn about these purposes, and how the functional differences affect the nature of the language that is used. The style and content of written language is much affected by the nature of the recipient, and an important goal in working with children is thus to develop their 'sense of audience'. There are several possible audiences.

- Children may address themselves, as in diaries, notes, and first drafts.
- They may address their peers, as in writing an account of an event for their class, or writing a letter to a friend.
- They may address a trusted adult, using a very personal style of writing.
- They may address their teacher, seen as a partner in dialogue, in the expectation that they will receive help.

- They may address examiners, whether in routine class assessments or in formal examinations.
- They may address an unknown audience, as when they have to produce work for a public occasion, or write a letter of application for a job.

Some studies have shown that half of all school writing has an examiner in mind. In other words, writing seems to be used more as a means of testing than as a means of learning. It is not being seen as part of the learning process, but as something that happens after learning is supposed to have taken place. It is therefore very important to give children the opportunity of writing for a wide range of audiences, in view of the demands that will be placed upon them once they leave school. There needs to be a balanced writing curriculum.

Based upon this thinking, several ways of fostering children's ability and enjoyment of writing have been suggested. New writing programmes encourage teachers to provide a variety of real audiences and functions for their pupils' work, so that children can see that their writing has a genuine purpose, and that it is not being done solely to be 'marked'. In addition to essays and experimental reports, there are now increasing opportunities to write in other styles for other audiences – such as magazine articles, or letters to the press. And more attention is now paid to discussing samples of writing with the children, both in groups and individually. It has long been appreciated that writing arises out of talk, in the early years; perhaps the most important aspect of current thinking is the realization that the reverse process is just as important – to give children the opportunity to talk about what they write.

Learning to write: linguistic skills

In addition to motor ability and functional awareness, young writers need to develop the ability to use the structures of language in an appropriate and mature manner. This ability takes several years to emerge.

A speech-dependent stage emerges at around the seventh year, when children begin to use the writing system to express what they talk about. Writing at this stage closely reflects the patterns of the spoken language. There may be many colloquialisms, strings of clauses linked by *and*, unfinished sentences, and other features of the child's conversational experience.

From around the ninth year, writing begins to diverge from speech, and develops its own patterns and organization. Errors are common at first, as children learn new standards, and experiment with new structures found in their reading. Their written work becomes fuller and more diverse, as they encounter the need to produce different kinds of writing for different audiences and situations.

It is at this point that children most need guidance about the structures and functions of written language. In particular, they need to learn that writing aids thinking in ways that speech cannot perform (§23). Writing is a medium where there is time to reflect, to re-think, to use language as a way of shaping thought. They therefore need to see the importance of drafting, revising, and editing as essential ways of obtaining the best expression. From this point of view, such activities as crossing out have to be seen not simply as 'mistakes', to be criticized on grounds of haste or carelessness, but as an indispensable step in the search for the best expression of what children are trying to say.

The end of the process is a stage when writers have such a good command of language that they can vary their stylistic choices at will and develop a personal 'voice'. This skill is rare before the middle teenage years, and it continues to develop throughout adult life.

22
How reading and writing can go wrong

Since the early years of the 20th century, it has come to be widely recognized that there are children who, after a few years at school, are consistently seen to fail at the tasks of reading, writing, and spelling, despite normal intelligence, instruction, and opportunity to learn. No medical, cultural, or emotional reason is available to explain the discrepancy between their general intellectual and linguistic abilities and their level of achievement in handling written language. There is often a history of early language delay, but by age nine or so, spoken language ability is apparently normal, whereas written language skills may remain at the level of a five- or six-year-old.

These are the children who have been called *dyslexic*, though alternative labels have been devised for the condition in an attempt to escape the originally medical connotations of this term (notably *specific reading disability* and *learning disability*). In fact there are around forty different terms used for problems in this area, some of which retain a medical bias, such as *minimal brain dysfunction* and (in parts of Europe) *legasthenia*. Because the disability is viewed as a problem with *written* language in all its forms, the term *dyslexia* usually subsumes the kind of difficulties sometimes separately referred to as *dysgraphia*.

The blighted school career of such children, when no one recognizes their disability, has been well documented. Their inability to read, whether for information or pleasure, and their daily failure in their attempts at written work, have a devastating effect upon their ability and motivation to learn. There are often associated problems in coping with number symbols (in arithmetic), and in tasks requiring short-term memory, such as following instructions. Their poor writing and spelling tends to be viewed as a symptom of educational subnormality or lack of intelligence – or, if the child is known to be intelligent, leads to a charge of laziness or 'not trying', with subsequent punishment in school and increased family tension at home. As a result, it is not surprising to find that many such children become anxious, withdrawn, or aggressive – with deteriorating behaviour in some cases leading to them being described as maladjusted. Career prospects, in such cases, are poor.

From a time – not so long ago – when dyslexia was dismissed out of hand as parental imaginings, the problem has become widely recognized, with organizations now existing in many countries to draw attention to the disability and to provide special help. In a very few countries, this help is guaranteed by legislation. It is, however, extremely difficult to arrive at an accurate estimate of incidence because there are no internationally accepted reading tests and criteria of disability.

The uncertainty derives from the fact that reading difficulty is a continuum from normal to abnormal, with the only criterion of disability being that the children's ability is well below their age and intelligence. Everything therefore depends on how intelligence and reading achievement is measured, and what is considered to be 'well' below normal. For example, if the definition of dyslexia includes only those children who are retarded by at least two years in reading ability, the numbers affected will be appreciably greater than one which requires that they be retarded by at least three years. Such differences of method, even within a single country, make it virtually impossible to arrive at an agreed statement of incidence.

The question of causation has also promoted great controversy. Until recently, there was a widespread assumption that all dyslexics were fundamentally alike, and that a single cause of the disability could be found. A large number of candidate 'causes' were therefore proposed, postulating any of several medical or psychological factors, such as problems of visual perception, intersensory integration, memory, attention, eye movement, verbal processing, or hemispheric dominance in the brain (p. 173). There could be several possible approaches within any one of these headings. For example, under dominance it has been argued that dyslexia is the result of (a) a lack of dominance, (b) a lag in dominance development, (c) a specific left-hemisphere deficit, (d) right-hemisphere interference, or (e) a disintegration of functioning between the two hemispheres (see §27). The role of the brain's left hemisphere is strongly implicated (as is suggested by associated spoken-language delays and errors, and problems of motor coordination), but its exact influence is unclear.

Recent reviews of what is now a vast experimental literature indicate that a unitary explanation for dyslexia is illusory. The modern focus on individual case studies (as opposed to the traditional use of group studies) is bringing to light the existence of a variety of dyslexic syndromes, reflecting several possible causes. A popular contemporary view is that there is a large set of factors implicated in dyslexia, some of which turn up in individual cases. For example, in one group of children, there was clear evidence of an unstable eye dominance: the children had not established a stable *leading eye* in their reading. Another group showed difficulties with making perceptual distinctions (e.g. distinguishing same/different letters). A further group displayed problems with short-term memory. Genetic factors are now known to exist.

The main methodological problem in such research is to determine whether the weakness shown by dyslexics is the cause or the result of the disability. For example, many of these children have faulty eye movements (shorter saccades, longer fixations, more regressions, §19), but it is an open question whether these form a constitutional problem that made it difficult for them to learn to read, or whether the poor movements began as a result of their difficulties with reading, or whether there is no functional relationship between them at all. If information is not available on what the children were like before they began to read, and on how they perform with non-reading tasks, it is difficult to interpret the results of such experiments.

The conflicting and ambiguous research findings, linked with ambitious claims about 'the' cause of dyslexia, have led to a great deal of scepticism about the condition, especially when the possibility of an underlying medical cause is being stressed. These doubts are slowly being resolved, but there is still a need for new research initiatives – in particular, devising individual development profiles, and relating findings more to the nature of reading development in normal children, in order to establish what counts as an 'abnormal' error. In such ways, it will be possible to devise better developmental classifications based on behavioural symptoms.

Adult problems

The onset of brain damage in adult life frequently leads to a disorder of reading or writing in people who have previously been literate. The disability is usually accompanied by other symptoms affecting spoken language (*dysphasia* or *aphasia*); occasionally, it is the only, or predominant, symptom. In all cases, the reading disorder is referred to as (*acquired*) *dyslexia* and the writing disorder as (*acquired*) *dysgraphia*. In an alternative terminology, the *a-* prefix is used, especially in continental Europe and North America (*alexia*, *agraphia*). The label *acquired* distinguishes the disability from the more widely known *developmental* kinds of dyslexia and dysgraphia that occur in children where there is no evidence of any brain damage.

Neuropsychological studies of these disabilities have generally proceeded by classifying patients into types, based on a detailed description of the kinds of errors made. The process is a slow and difficult one, partly because of the large amounts of vocabulary that have to be analysed before an error pattern emerges, and partly because there are usually associated language symptoms that also need to be taken into account. Nonetheless, since the 1970s several types of acquired dyslexia and dysgraphia have been proposed, based on a small number of case studies.

- *Phonological dyslexia*: People with this problem are unable to read on the basis of the *phonic* rules that relate graphemes to phonemes

(§21). This means that they can manage to read familiar words, but they have great difficulty with new words (such as technical terms) or with simple nonsense words (such as *lak*).

- *Deep dyslexia*: Here too people are unable to read new or nonsense words, but in addition they make many semantic errors (e.g. reading *forest* as 'trees'). There are also several other types of difficulty, including visual errors (e.g. reading *signal* as 'single'), and errors that combine visual and semantic properties (e.g. reading *sympathy* as 'orchestra', presumably because of the link via *symphony*). Words with concrete (as opposed to abstract) meanings are easier to read.

- *Surface dyslexia*: People with this problem are very poor at recognizing words as wholes, and rely greatly on a process of 'sounding out' the possible relationship between graphemes and phonemes. Irregular words (such as *yacht*) pose particular difficulty. A wrongly pronounced word will be given a meaning on the basis of how it sounds, not how it looks (e.g. one person read *begin* as 'beggin', then added 'collecting money'). There is a problem with homophones (e.g. one person understood *bury* as 'a kind of hat').

Several other types have been proposed. There is, for example, a visually based dyslexia, in which people fail to read the parts of a word correctly (e.g. one person read 'night' when shown *near + light*), or confuse words of similar appearance (as when *met* was misread by one patient as 'meat', and *rib* as 'ride'). In such cases, the reader can often name the letters of the word correctly, but remains unable to identify the whole word. There are also several disorders of a neurologically more 'peripheral' kind, such as letter-by-letter reading, in which patients find it necessary to name all the letters of a word (aloud or sub-vocally) before they can identify it. The search for 'pure' types of dyslexia is complicated by the occurrence of individual differences between patients, and by the existence of cases where symptoms are 'mixed'.

A similar set of syndromes can be seen in adult problems with writing – which mainly seem to affect spelling.

- *Phonological dysgraphia*: People with this problem can spell real words but not nonsense words (though they can sometimes read many of them, and speak them aloud).
- *Deep dysgraphia*: Here too there is no ability to spell on a phonetic basis; asked to write a dictated nonsense word, for example, it is often replaced by a real word that is similar in sound (e.g. *blom* is written *flower*, presumably because of the word *bloom*). Errors seem to be semantically related (e.g. one person, asked to write *bun*, wrote *cake*). The spelling of words with concrete meaning is better than that of words with abstract meaning. The relationship to reading ability is unclear: one patient studied had normal reading ability, but most seem to have some deep dyslexic symptoms also.
- *Surface dysgraphia*: People with this problem can spell spoken nonsense words in a plausible way, but cannot spell irregular real words (e.g. one person wrote *biscuit* as *bisket*) – and even regular words may be affected. They seem dependent on using grapheme–phoneme conversion rules (p. 143); whole-word spelling is impaired, though not entirely lost (e.g. one person spelled *yacht* as *yhagt*, showing some visual recall).

Acquired dysgraphic patients are usually also dyslexic to some degree. Moreover, classification must allow for cases where there are specific motor or sensory impairments. For example, there are people who can speak, read, spell aloud, and type, yet who cannot produce the letter shapes or movements required for writing by hand. Letters are badly formed, misplaced, repeated, or omitted. In such cases, it is graphetic rather than graphological ability that is affected (p. 97).

Child and adult: same or different?

The several similarities between the symptoms presented by child and adult dyslexia have led some researchers to argue that there is an underlying identity. They have proposed parallels between developmental dyslexics and acquired deep dyslexics – for example, both groups have trouble reading nonsense words, and are better at reading concrete words. However, so far there is little clear evidence that children display the kinds of semantic error that are crucial to the identity of the deep dyslexia syndrome.

Similarly, there have been proposals that developmental dyslexia displays a parallel with acquired surface dyslexia – for example, because there are similarities in phonic reading ability. Another suggestion is that there are parallels with phonological dyslexia – for example, because there are similarities in direct visual word recognition. None of these positions has yet produced a substantial child database, however, and several differences between the adult and child populations remain – in particular, the greater variability of children's performance.

There is, moreover, always the possibility that the brain mechanisms that underlie reading acquisition in children are different from those used to maintain reading skills in later life. The unity view thus provides us with a set of intriguing but at present largely speculative hypotheses.

23

How writing and
speech differ

The history of language study illustrates widely divergent attitudes concerning the relationship between writing and speech. For several centuries, the written language held a preeminent place. It was the medium of literature, and, thus, a source of standards of linguistic excellence. It was felt to provide language with permanence and authority. The rules of grammar were, accordingly, illustrated exclusively from written texts.

The everyday spoken language, by contrast, was ignored or condemned as an object unworthy of study, demonstrating only lack of care and organization. It was said to have no rules, and speakers were left under no illusion that, in order to 'speak properly', it was necessary to follow the 'correct' norms, as laid down in the recognized grammar books and manuals of written style. Even pronunciation could be made to follow the standard written form, as in recommendations to 'say your h's' and not to 'drop your g's'. The written language, in short, was the main plank on which the prescriptive tradition rested (§69).

There was sporadic criticism of this viewpoint throughout the 19th century, but it was not until the 20th century that an alternative approach became widespread. This approach pointed out that speech is many thousands of years older than writing; that it develops naturally in children (whereas writing has to be artificially taught); and that writing systems are derivative – mostly based on the sounds of speech. 'Writing is not language', insisted the American linguist Leonard Bloomfield

(1887–1949), 'but merely a way of recording language by means of visible marks.'

It was also argued that, as speech is the primary medium of communication among all peoples, it should therefore be the primary object of linguistic study. In the majority of the world's cultures, in fact, there would be no choice in the matter, as the languages have never been written down. Early linguistics and anthropology therefore stressed the urgency of providing techniques for the analysis of spoken language – especially in cases where the cultures were fast disappearing and languages were dying out.

Because of this emphasis on the spoken language, it was now the turn of writing to fall into disrepute. Many linguists came to think of written language as a tool of secondary importance – an optional, special skill, used only for sophisticated purposes (as in scientific and literary expression) by a minority of communities. It was needed in order to have access to the early history of language (philology, §55), but this was felt to be a woefully inadequate substitute for the study of the 'real' thing, speech. Writing, seen as a mere 'reflection' of spoken language, thus came to be excluded from the primary subject matter of linguistic science. The pendulum swung to the opposite extreme in the new generation of grammars, many of which presented an account of speech alone.

Writing and speech should never have been allowed to confront each other in this way. There is no sense in the view that one medium of communication is intrinsically 'better' than the other. Whatever their historical relationship, the fact remains that modern society makes available to its members two very different systems of communication, each of which has developed to fulfil a particular set of communicative needs, and now offers capabilities of expression denied to the other. Writing cannot substitute for speech, nor speech for writing, without serious disservice being done to each.

The differences

Writing and speech are now seen as alternative, 'equal' systems of linguistic expression, and research has begun to investigate the nature and extent of the differences between them. Most obviously, they contrast in physical form: speech uses *phonic substance*, typically in the form of air-pressure movements (§6); writing uses *graphic substance*, typically in the form of marks on a surface. But of far greater interest are the differences in structure and function that follow from this basic observation.

These differences are much greater than people usually think. The contrast is greatest when written texts are compared with informal conversation; but even in fairly formal and prepared speech settings, such as a teacher addressing a class, the structure of the language that is spoken bears very little similarity to that found in writing. It is something that is immediately apparent if a stretch of speech is recorded and transcribed. Even a fluent speaker produces utterances that do not read well when written down.

The differences of structure and use between spoken and written language are inevitable, because they are the product of radically different kinds of communicative situation. Speech is time-bound, dynamic, transient – part of an interaction in which, typically, both participants are present, and the speaker has a specific addressee (or group of addressees) in mind. Writing is space-bound, static, permanent – the result of a situation in which, typically, the producer is distant from the recipient, and, often, may not even know who the recipient is (as with most literature). Such differences have many consequences.

• The permanence of writing allows repeated reading and close analysis. It promotes the development of careful organization and more compact, intricately structured expression. Units of discourse, such as sentences and paragraphs, are clearly identified through layout and punctuation. By contrast, the spontaneity and rapidity of speech minimizes the chance of complex preplanning, and promotes features that assist speakers to 'think standing up' – looser construction, repetition, rephrasing, filler phrases (such as *you know*, *you see*), and the use of intonation and pause to divide utterances into manageable chunks (§12).

- The participants in written interaction cannot usually see each other, and they thus cannot rely on the context to help make clear what they mean, as they would when speaking. As a consequence, writing avoids words where the meaning relies on the situation (*deictic* expressions, such as *this one*, *over there*). Writers also have to anticipate the effects of the time-lag between production and reception, and the problems posed by having their language read and interpreted by many recipients in a diversity of settings. In the absence of immediate feedback, available in most speech interaction, care needs to be taken to minimize the effects of vagueness and ambiguity.

- Written language displays several unique features, such as punctuation, capitalization, spatial organization, colour, and other graphic effects (§18). There is little in speech that corresponds, apart from the occasional prosodic feature (§12): for example, question marks may be expressed by rising intonation; exclamation marks or underlining may increase loudness; and parentheses may lower tempo, loudness, and pitch. But the majority of graphic features present a system of contrasts that has no spoken-language equivalent. As a result, there are many genres of written language whose structure cannot in any way be conveyed by reading aloud, such as timetables, graphs, and complex formulae.

- Grammatical and lexical differences are also important. Some constructions may be found only in writing, as in the case of the French simple past tense. Certain items of vocabulary are rarely or never spoken, such as many polysyllabic chemical terms, or the more arcane legal terms. Conversely, certain items of spoken vocabulary are not normally written, such as *whatchamacallit* (with no standard spelling), and certain slang or obscene expressions.

- Written language tends to be more formal than spoken language and is more likely to provide the standard that society values. It also has a special status, mainly deriving from its permanence. Written formulations, such as contracts, are usually required to make agreements legally binding. Sacred writings are used as part of the identity and authority of a religious tradition.

Despite these differences, there are many respects in which the two mediums can influence each other. Soon after learning to read, children use the written medium as a means of extending their spoken vocabulary – as indeed do many adults. Some words may be known only in written form. Loan words may come into a spoken language through the written medium. Sometimes the whole of a language may be known only from writing (as with Latin, or certain cases of foreign language learning). And an old written language can be the source of a modern spoken one (as in Hebrew). Writing systems may derive from speech, in a historical sense, but in modern society the dependence is mutual.

The differences between speech and writing are most clearly displayed when people attempt to portray the sound of the former using the graphic properties of the latter. The most complex and ingenious ways of doing this are to be found in written literature, where authors are continually battling to put sounds into words. Different languages do not display the same range of written language conventions for the portrayal of speech.

In English, for example, emphatic speech is not usually printed in a heavy typeface, but this is common in Chinese fiction. And the use of repeated letters (as in *ye-e-es*) can have a range of interpretations, such as emphasis and hesitation, in different languages. This can lead to ambiguity, especially when texts are translated. For example, a character in the English translation of Alexander Solzhenitsyn's *Cancer Ward* is recorded as saying *No-o*. The use of this convention in the original Russian would convey an emphatic negative; but the English version is far more likely to signal a hesitant one. Italics, likewise, can be ambiguous, both within and between languages, being used variously as a marker of foreign words, technical terms, book titles, emphasis, and several other effects.

Writing – or speaking?

The functions of speech and writing are usually said to complement each other. We do not write to each other when we have the opportunity to speak – apart from such exceptional cases as secretive children in class and partners who are 'not talking'. Nor can we speak to each other at a distance – except in special cases involving technical equipment.

On the other hand, there are many functional parallels which ought not to be ignored, especially as these are on the increase in modern society.

- The relative permanence of written language makes it ideally suited for such functions as recording facts and communicating ideas. But these days, talking books for blind people, libraries of recorded sound, and other facilities are providing alternatives.
- Letters and messages for distant contacts used only to be written. Nowadays, they can also be spoken – thanks to tape cassettes, telephone answering machines, radio phone-ins, and other such developments.
- The immediacy of speech makes it ideal for social (or *phatic*) functions (p. 464). But writing also has its phatic functions, and these seem to be increasing, as suggested by the expanding business of producing cards to mark special occasions – birthdays, Christmas, anniversaries, examination results, passing (or failing) a driving test, and many more.

However, when it comes to tasks of memory and learning, speech is no substitute for writing. Written records are easier to keep and scan. Written tables and figures readily demonstrate relationships between things. Written notes and lists provide an immediate mnemonic. Written explanations can be read often, at individual speeds, until they are understood.

For centuries, linguistic communication has for most educated people been a question of choosing between speech and writing. In our lifetime, however, this choice has been extended by the arrival of a further means of communication – the electronic medium – which is neither clearly speech nor clearly writing.

24

How the electronic medium differs

The electronic medium is neither exactly like speech nor exactly like writing. Commentators have struggled to describe it. When Homer Simpson asks his friends 'What's an e-mail?', they are confused. Lenny replies, 'It's a computer thing, like, er, an electric letter.' Carl adds, 'Or a quiet phone call.' To see why Homer and his friends are having trouble, we need to consider all the functions that the medium is capable of performing.

The Internet is an association of computer networks with common standards which enables messages to be sent from any central computer (or *host*) on one network to any host on any other. It enables us to perform three main functions: to link the sites comprising the World Wide Web, to send electronic mail between private mailboxes, and to permit groups of people to engage in continuous discussion in chatrooms or by instant messaging. These functions facilitate and constrain our ability to communicate in ways that are fundamentally different from those found in other linguistic situations. Many of the expectations and practices which we associate with spoken and written language no longer obtain.

Not like speech

Computer-mediated communication is not like speech, even in those electronic situations which are most speech-like, such as e-mailing or messaging. There is, to begin with, a lack of the simultaneous feedback which is an essential part of a successful spoken conversation (§42). While A speaks to B, B does not stay unmoved and silent: B's face and voice provide an ongoing commentary on what A is saying. Nods and smiles work along with a wide range of vocalizations, such as *uh-huh*, *yeah*, *sure*, and *ooh*. Without these, a conversation quickly breaks down, or becomes extremely stilted and artificial.

In e-mail and chatroom interaction, there is no simultaneous feedback, for the obvious reason that the messages sent via a computer are complete and unidirectional. Our message does not leave our computer until we *send* it, and that means the whole of a message is transmitted at once, and arrives on the recipient's screen at once. There is no way that a recipient can react to our message while it is being typed, because recipients do not know they are getting any messages at all until the text arrives on their screens. Correspondingly, there is no way for a sender to get a sense of how successful a message is, while it is being written – whether it has been understood, or whether it needs repair. This factor alone makes e-conversations totally unlike those which take place in 'real world' speech.

Another difference can be illustrated from real-time chatrooms. If we are in a chatroom, talking around a particular theme, we see on our screen messages coming in from all over the world. We can attend to all of these, and respond to as many as we wish, governed only by our interests and our ability to type rapidly. By contrast, the traditional speech situation has never allowed us to 'listen' to multiple conversations at once, and to participate in them.

A third difference results from the limitations of the technology: the rhythm of an Internet interaction is very much slower than that found in a speech situation, and disallows some of conversation's most salient properties. A response to a message may be anything from seconds to months, the rhythm of the exchange depending on such factors as the recipient's computer (e.g. whether it announces the instant arrival of a message), the user's personality and habits (e.g. whether messages are replied to at regular times or randomly), and the circumstances of the interlocutors (e.g. their computer access). This interferes with another core feature of traditional face-to-face interaction, the conversational *turn* (p. 268).

Turn-taking is so fundamental to conversation that most people are not conscious of its significance as a means of enabling interactions to be successful. But it is a conversational fact of life that people follow the routine of taking turns, when they talk, and avoid talking at once or interrupting each other randomly or excessively. Moreover, they expect certain *adjacency-pairs* to take place: questions to be followed by answers, and not the other way round; similarly, a piece of information to be followed by an acknowledgement, or a complaint to be followed by an excuse or apology. These elementary strategies, learned at a very early age, provide a normal conversation with its skeleton.

On the Internet, the turn-taking can become so unusual that its ability to cope with a topic can be destroyed. This is because turn-taking, as seen on a screen, is dictated by the software, and not by the participants. In a chatroom or instant-messaging environment, for instance, even if we did start to send a reaction to someone else's utterance before it was finished, the reaction would take its turn in a non-overlapping series of utterances on the screen, dependent only on the point at which the send signal was received at the host server. Messages are posted to a receiver's screen linearly, in the order in which they are received by the system. In a multi-user environment, messages are coming in from various sources all the time, and with different lags. Because of the way packets of information are sent electronically through different global routes, between sender and receiver, it is even possible for turn-taking reversals to take place, and all kinds of unpredictable overlaps.

This medium is also unlike speech with respect to the formal properties of the medium – properties that are so basic that it becomes extremely difficult for people to live up to the recommendation that they should 'write as they talk'. Chief among these is the domain of tone of voice (§12). There have been somewhat desperate efforts to replace tone of voice on screen in the form of an exaggerated use of spelling and punctuation, and the use of capitals, spacing, and special symbols for emphasis. Examples include repeated letters (*aaaaahhhhh*, *soooo*), repeated punctuation marks (*whohe????*, *hey!!!*), and conventions for expressing emphasis, such as *the *real* point*. These features are capable of a certain expressiveness, but the range of meanings they signal is few, and restricted to gross notions such as extra emphasis, surprise, and puzzlement. Less exaggerated nuances are not capable of being handled in this way, even through the use of *smileys* (*emoticons*) such as :-).

Not like writing

Computer-mediated communication does not display the properties we would expect of speech, but neither does it display the properties we expect of writing. To begin with, it lacks the space-bound character of traditional writing – the fact that a piece of text is static and permanent on the page. If something is written down, repeated reference to it will be an encounter with an unchanged text. We would be surprised if, upon returning to a particular page, it had altered its graphic character in some way. Putting it like this, we can see immediately that computer-mediated communication is not by any means like conventional writing.

A 'page' on the Web often varies from encounter to encounter (and all have the option of varying, even if page-owners choose not to take it) for several possible reasons – for instance, its factual content might have been updated, its advertising sponsor might have changed, or its graphic designer might have added new features. Nor is the writing that we see necessarily static, given the technical options available which allow text to move around the screen, disappear/reappear, change colour, and so on. From a user point of view, there are also opportunities to 'interfere' with the text in all kinds of ways that are not possible in traditional writing. A page, once downloaded to the user's screen, may have its text cut, added to, revised, annotated, even totally restructured, in ways that make the result seem to come from the same source as the original.

The other Internet situations also display differences from traditional writing, with respect to their space-bound presence. E-mails are in principle static and permanent, but routine textual deletion is commonplace, and it is possible to alter messages electronically with an ease and undetectability which is not possible when people try to alter a traditionally written text.

What is especially revolutionary about e-mails is the way the medium permits what is called *framing*. We receive a message from X which contains, say, three different points in a single paragraph. We can, if we want, reply to each of these points by taking the paragraph, splitting it up into three parts, and then responding to each part separately, so that the message we send back to X then looks a bit like a play dialogue. Then, X can do the same thing to our responses, and when we get the message back, we see X's replies to what we sent. We can then send the lot on to Y for further comments, and when it comes back, there are now three voices framed on the screen. And so it can go on – replies within replies within replies – and all unified within the same screen typography. Traditional writing practice never permitted anything like this.

Another feature of computer-mediated communication takes us even further away from traditional writing. This is the *hypertext link*, the jump that users can make if they want to move from one page or site to another. It is the most fundamental structural property of the Web, without which the medium would not exist. There are some parallels with traditional written text. For example, the use of footnotes is a sort of primitive hypertext link, moving the eye from one part of a page to another, or from one page of a text to another (if the footnotes are collected at the back of a book, for example). But footnotes are marginal to traditional written language; we can easily think of texts which have no footnotes at all. The Web, by contrast, could not exist without its hypertext links.

Finally, e-mails, messaging, and chatgroup interactions lack the carefully planned, elaborate construction which is characteristic of so much writing, because there is so much pressure to communicate rapidly. Some people are happy to send messages with no revision at all, not caring if typing errors, erratic capitalization, lack of punctuation, and other anomalies are included. This is actually a rather minor effect, which rarely interferes with intelligibility. It is patently a special style arising out of the pressures operating on users of the medium, plus a natural desire (especially among younger – or younger-minded – users) to be idiosyncratic and daring. It is by no means universal. There are many e-mailers who take as many pains to revise their messages as they would in non-Internet settings.

On the whole, computer-mediated communication – often referred to as CMC, or Netspeak – is better seen as written language which has been pulled some way in the direction of speech than as spoken language which has been written down. However, expressing the question in terms of the traditional dichotomy is itself misleading. CMC is identical to neither speech nor writing, but selectively and adaptively displays properties of both. It also does things which neither of the other mediums do, presenting us with novel problems of information management.

CMC is more than an aggregate of spoken and written features. Because it does things that the other mediums do not do, it has to be seen as a new species of communication. It is more than just a hybrid of speech and writing, or the result of contact between two long-standing mediums. Electronic texts, of whatever kind, are simply not the same as other kinds of texts. They display fluidity, simultaneity (being available on an indefinite number of machines), and non-degradability in copying; they transcend the traditional limitations on textual dissemination; and they have permeable boundaries (because of the way one text may be integrated within others or display links to others). Several of these properties have consequences for language, and these combine with those associated with speech and writing to make electronic communication a genuine 'new medium'.

25
How sign language works

Speech, writing, and computer-mediated communication are the three mediums available to everyone, but they do not exhaust the possibilities of human language. There is a fourth medium, used by deaf people: sign language.

Probably no topic in linguistics has been subject to so many misconceptions as sign language. In the popular mind, there is a widespread belief that signing is no more than a system of sophisticated gesturing, and not a real language at all. Signs are also thought to be simply pictorial representations of external reality; and because of this, people assume there is just one sign language, which can be understood all over the world. All of this is wrong.

Guessing the meaning?

When non-signers see a sign language in operation, they often try to guess the meaning of some of the hand movements – and they may occasionally get them right. This is because a few of the signs in any system are indeed *iconic* – that is, they reflect properties of the external world – and therefore people have a chance of recognizing what they refer to. However, the vast majority of signs do not fall into this category. They are arbitrary, just as the words of spoken language are. There is nothing in the spoken word *car* which physically resembles the object 'car', and it is the same with the sign for *car* in a sign language.

It is of course possible that some signs were iconic when they were first devised, but the iconicity has been lost because of linguistic change, which affects sign as it does spoken and written language (§17). It is no longer possible to see the originally iconic basis of most Chinese characters, for example, and it is the same with signs. We do not know how old most signs are, but even if a sign language has a history of only a few hundred years, this is more than enough time for signs to change their form. In addition, the speed at which signers express themselves – one or two signs a second – also makes it difficult to see any underlying iconicity.

Many signs are deceptively iconic. A sign may appear 'obvious' after its meaning has been revealed, but it proves not so easy to predict the meaning from the shape of the sign alone. The reason is that there are so many properties in a real-world entity that a sign could reflect. A sign for an animal, for example, could be based on its physical shape or its movement, and within the former category on its head or legs or any other distinctive piece of its anatomy. The sign might have nothing to do with physical appearance at all, but relate to the animal's behaviour or uses in society. When we consider the range of animals that exist, it is evident that there could be no simple way of expressing the required set of discriminations. We might notice hand shapes which represent, say, ears, but without further knowledge of the sign as a whole it would be impossible to say which animal the ears belonged to.

The point emerges again if we compare signs in different languages. There are signs which have the same form in two languages but different meanings. For example, in American Sign Language (ASL), the sign for *push* looks the same as one in Chinese Sign Language (CSL), but the CSL sign means *help*. Or again: ASL signers recognize the CSL sign for *father*, but interpret it as the ASL sign for *secret*. This is analogous to the situation in spoken language where, for example, *demander* in French reminds us of *demand* in English, so we assume the French word means 'demand'. We are wrong, of course: *demander* means 'ask'. There are many such 'false friends' between sign languages too.

As a result of linguistic change, and because of the way new sign languages seem to have independently emerged in different parts of the world, no single sign language exists. Rather, there are many independent languages – French Sign Language, Danish Sign Language, and so on – and they are not mutually intelligible. Even within an area that uses the same spoken language, the differences may be so great as to preclude mutual comprehension. It sometimes surprises people to learn that British Sign Language (BSL) and ASL are not mutually intelligible. When Mark Medoff's play about deafness, *Children of a Lesser God*, was first shown in London, the actors used ASL. BSL members of the audience had to have the signs interpreted.

Lacking structure?

Sign languages have a structure of comparable complexity to spoken and written language and perform a similar range of functions. Each language uses its own rules governing the way signs are formed and how they are sequenced – rules that have to be learned either as children (from deaf parents, or in a school for deaf children) or as adults (such as when working with deaf people). Thousands of signs are available within a sign language, and they are used to convey a considerable range of meaning. Fluent signing operates at a rate comparable to that of fluent speech. It usually takes longer to make a sign than to pronounce a word, but many signs express a meaning far more succinctly than the corresponding spoken output. When two fluent signers communicate, they provide clear evidence of the creative potential of sign, and of its social and psychological reality as a language.

Just as spoken languages differ in the types of sound they use, so sign languages differ in the way they make hand configurations. For example, in Chinese Sign Language (CSL) there are sign shapes and movements which are not possible formations in ASL. And there are signs which combine elements in different ways: elements of the CSL sign for *distracted* are like the ASL signs for *yellow* and *separate*, but the particular CSL combination is not an ASL sign.

The chief characteristic of signing is the way it uses a three-dimensional *sign space*. Vertically, this consists of the distance just below the waist to the top of the head – signs are rarely made above the head, below the waist, or towards the back of the head or body. Laterally, the space forms a 'bubble' which extends outwards in front of the signer from extreme right to extreme left. Within this space, there is room to make an indefinitely large number of signs, and it is possible to see several organizational principles operating. The whole spatial area can be enlarged or confined to express 'louder' or 'quieter' signing. *Locations* can be established that identify different sentence elements or semantic functions.

An example of a location is the one used for the expression of time, corresponding chiefly to the use of tenses in spoken and written language. Time relationships can be expressed by dividing the sign space into neutral (present), further forward (future), and further back (past) areas. These areas can then be used both for tense forms and for time adverbs (*then*, *now*, *next*, *last*, etc.). Another location is for the expression of persons (the 'pronouns' of traditional grammar), which can be distinguished using different spatial areas: *you* is front-centre; one third-person form (*he*, *she*, *it*, *they*) is signed to the right; another to the left; and others divide up the intervening space. Once a space is established for a given person, it is normally 'reserved' for that person for the remainder of the conversation.

Visual means are available to distinguish a wide range of grammatical functions. Questions can be signalled by an appropriate accompanying facial expression, such as raised eyebrows and a backward movement of the head. Great use is made of repeated actions (*reduplication*) to express such notions as plurality, aspect, degree, or emphasis; for example, such verbal meanings as continuity or habituality can all be signed by repeating a verb sign with varying speed. The use of pause between signs or sign sequences marks grammatical boundaries, as it does in speech, and as punctuation does in writing.

Studying sign

An important stage in the history of sign language analysis took place in the 1960s, when the term *cherology* was coined on analogy with phonology (§11) to refer to the study of the contrastive units (*cheremes*) that occur in a sign language. The structural analyses subsequently made provided a valuable indication of the difficulty researchers face as they try to 'capture' the dynamic, multidimensional properties of sign.

In this approach, three classes of cheremes are identified: the *location* in the sign space where a sign is made; the active hand *configuration* used to make the sign; and the *action* of the active hand. Signs are described as simultaneously occurring combinations of these parameters. Not all possible combinations occur. Some, indeed, are physically impossible. There is a strong tendency towards hand symmetry: if a sign requires two active hands, both hands will have identical shapes and orientations. Several such constraints govern the structure of a sign language, and a major focus of research has been to discover the rules governing sign formation, and the contexts (such as poetry, irony, or humour) where departures from these rules are tolerated.

Sign language, in short, is not like the kind of everyday gesturing which we discussed in §2, where none of this structure is present. Everyone can gesture; but few have learned to sign. When people sign, they use the hands in a conscious, 'verbal' way, to express the same kind of meaning as would be achieved by using speech or writing. Ordinary gesturing is far less systematic and comprehensive. There are in fact very few everyday hand gestures and facial expressions, and these are used to express a very small number of basic notions. It is not possible to tell a complicated story using everyday gestures. In sign language, it is routine.

26
How sign languages vary

Very little information is available about the early history of sign languages. References to deaf signing are found in Greek and Roman writings, but there are no details. In recent times, we can date the study of signing from the work of the French educator Abbé Charles Michel de l'Epée (1712–89), who in 1775 developed a sign language for use in a school for deaf people in Paris. The origins of his system are obscure. Several of his signs were modifications of those used by the French native deaf population, but he also made some use of a Spanish manual alphabet, and he may have incorporated some of the signs used by Spanish Benedictine monks.

Several foreign educators studied at his school, and the influence of his system spread to many parts of the world, including Russia, Ireland, and America. For example, the American educator Thomas Gallaudet (1787–1851), together with Laurent Clerc (1785–1869), a teacher of deaf people, brought the signs to the USA, where they came to be used alongside those already in use by the American deaf population. Modern American Sign Language (ASL) derives from this system.

When a sign language becomes widely used, it develops the same kind of dialects and varieties as occur in spoken language, and eventually can evolve into different languages, in much the same way as French, Spanish, and Italian and the other Romance languages have evolved from Latin. When a sign language is used by large numbers, it may contain a great deal of variation. This can be seen in ASL, which is now used by over half a million deaf people – by many, as a native language. Some varieties are regional in origin, but others are due to the age at which the sign language is learned, and to social factors, such as the home environment (whether the parents are deaf) and the educational background of the signer.

A further important variable is the extent to which the sign language has been influenced by the spoken language of the surrounding community. A dialect *continuum* often exists among the members of a deaf community, just as it does with spoken language (§51). At one end of the continuum there are varieties that show no influence of speech at all; at the other, there are varieties that have been markedly shaped by properties of the spoken or written languages used in the wider community – in particular, by their word order. Several pidgin varieties of signing also exist along this continuum (§53).

Types of sign language

Several kinds of sign system exist, based on very different principles. The most widely used are the concept-based systems that have developed naturally among the deaf communities, and it is these that are most commonly referred to as *sign language* – ASL, British Sign Language (BSL), Spanish Sign Language, etc. In addition, some educators and linguists have devised alternative kinds of signing system. They are sometimes called *contrived* sign languages, to distinguish them from those that are used as a matter of course in deaf families and social communities. Contrived languages are mainly taught to deaf children or adults, but they are also sometimes found used with other populations, such as children with learning difficulties.

The greatest proliferation of new signing systems has been within the English speech community. One set of approaches involves making modifications to ASL or BSL, with the aim of bringing the signing closer to spoken English. Several of these systems emerged in the late 1960s in the USA, notably Seeing Essential English (1966), and its two derivatives,

Linguistics of Visual English (1971) and Signing Exact English (1972). Other systems were devised that closely followed the structure of speech, such as Signed English (1969) and Manual English (1972). Given the urgent need for progress in the educational domain, and the sincerity and enthusiasm of the creators, all of the systems have found homes in a range of teaching situations.

Each of these systems aims to reflect the structure of English, but they do this in different ways. All follow English word order, but they differ in the way they form signs, and in how much finger spelling (see below) they use. Many arbitrary decisions have to be made by the system's creators; for example, it is not obvious how to allocate signs to such forms as irregular nouns, verbs, or adjectives. Should past tense forms (*took*, *gone*, etc.) be signed with the same sign as past participle forms (*taken*, *went*, etc.) or with different signs? Should *took* be signed as '*take* + *PAST*', '*take* + *-ed*', '*take* + *e* + *d*', or '*t* + *o* + *o* + *k*'? There are many such possibilities, and different systems go in different directions, with varying degrees of consistency.

Paget–Gorman Sign System (PGSS)

The earliest proposal to be widely adopted in modern times was based on Richard Paget's *A Systematic Sign Language* (1951). After his death in 1955, this system was developed in Britain by his widow, Grace Paget, and Pierre Gorman, at that time librarian of the Royal National Institute for the Deaf. It contains some 3,000 signs, representing the words and word-elements of spoken English. Sentences are signed following English word order.

The system makes use of a set of *basic* signs – semantic fields such as 'action', 'animal', 'colour', 'container', and 'food'. Different words belonging to each field are identified with reference to the same basic sign, plus an identifying sign. The different colour words, for example, are all derived from a single basic sign. To sign *blue*, one hand is held as for *colour*, while the first finger of the other hand is held pointing up, back outwards, in line with the signer's side (i.e. the colour of the sky). To sign *red*, the same basic sign is used, while the other hand makes the sign for *blood*.

Amer-Ind

Over the centuries, Native North Americans have spoken hundreds of languages from several different families (§62). It is not surprising, then, that they developed a form of signing as a means of communication between different tribes. Following early descriptions of this 'hand talk', an adaptation was made for use with disabled people by Madge Skelly (b. 1903), an Indian-born speech pathologist. The system is conceived as a gestural code, rather than a language. It contains a limited number of signs, representing concrete meanings, and it has no grammatical structure apart from sequence. The signs are chosen so as to be immediately recognizable, so that the viewer can interpret without formal instruction, and regardless of language background.

Finger-spelling

Finger-spelling, or *dactylology*, is a signing system in which each letter of the ordinary alphabet is given its own sign. The principle can be applied to any language which has developed an alphabetic writing system. However, there are conventional differences: in particular, the British manual alphabet is formed using two hands, whereas the American and Swedish systems, for example, use only one.

The main strength of finger-spelling is its great scope and flexibility. It is quick to learn, and can then be used to sign an indefinite number of words. It is a particularly useful system for signing proper names, which do not have their own signs. Sign languages have signs for *woman* and *country*, but none for *Greta Garbo* and *Birmingham* – these would have to be finger-spelled. However, it is a slow system to use, rarely exceeding 300 letters per minute (about 60 words). Moreover, it cannot be used at all unless the signer is able to spell – a problem for young children, who also have difficulty controlling the hand shapes required. From the receiver's point of view, it is difficult to distinguish the hand shapes at a distance, and, even close to, intelligibility can be a problem if the rate of signing speeds up, and the signer begins to omit letters.

Despite the difficulties, signers cannot do without finger-spelling. It is best thought of as an auxiliary signing system, a convenient bridge

How sign languages vary

between spoken or written language and sign language proper. The use of the method has been documented from the 17th century. The philosopher George Dalgarno (c. 1626–87), for example, recommended its use by all members of a family whenever it contained a deaf child, arguing that the acquisition of spelled language would thereby be as natural as the acquisition of spoken language. In modern times, some educational approaches make a great deal of use of it. The Rochester method in the USA, for example, is based on a combination of finger-spelling and speech.

Cued speech

Normal lip-reading techniques allow only certain sounds – those towards the front of the mouth – to be easily distinguished; and there are many sentences which lip readers find difficult to make out, especially when the context is unclear – such as *It is in the tin*, where the lip position is almost identical throughout. Cued speech aims to eliminate such difficulties by making it possible for a deaf person to 'see' the sounds of speech as they are spoken. It is a system of hand cues that are used alongside lip movements to draw attention to the phonemic (§11) contrasts of speech. The system was devised in 1966 by the American educator R. Orin Cornett (1913–2002), and it has since been adapted for use in well over fifty languages.

The system uses thirty-six cues for the forty-four English phonemes. Vowel cues are shown by the position of the hand. Four positions are recognized: at the side, throat, chin, and mouth. Each position signals a group of three vowels of different lip shapes; vowels with the same lip shape can then be readily distinguished by noting the accompanying sign. Consonant cues are shown by the shape of the hand. There are eight hand shapes, each of which is associated with a group of consonants of different lip shapes; as with vowels, consonants with the same lip shape can then be distinguished by noting the accompanying sign.

It is evident that the 'family' of sign languages is very large and diverse. It contains both natural and artificially constructed kinds of communication, some of which are language-like in character, some of which are more

British

American

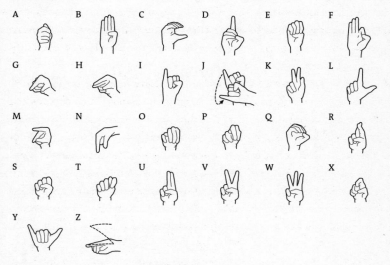

Fig. 14. Two-handed and one-handed finger-spelling

like codes. Finger-spelling, for example, is exactly like Morse Code or semaphore in its letter-by-letter composition. The question of whether a contrived approach can be called a 'language' at all is itself contentious. When the PGSS was being developed, there was much debate among its authors as to whether it should be called a 'sign language' or a 'sign system'; in the end, they settled for the latter – hence it is now known as PGSS not PGSL.

However, we must not allow questions of definition to obscure the most important observation about deaf signing – that here we have a distinct medium of communication, operating in its own terms as an alternative to spoken and written language. It is a medium which by its nature needs appropriate exposition, using film, video, or other forms of animation. A book presentation is inadequate, for it cannot convey the dynamic and multidimensional character of sign discourse. Internet and mobile phone technology will help enormously in presenting sign languages to a wider population, as well as providing a way of enhancing communicative opportunities among signers themselves.

27

How the brain
handles language

The human brain consists of several anatomically distinct regions. The largest part is the cerebrum, which is divided into two great lobes of similar size – the left and right cerebral *hemispheres*. The hemispheres are connected to the spinal cord by the *brain stem*, which consists of the *mid-brain*, the *pons*, and the *medulla oblongata*. At the back of the pons is the *cerebellum*, which is responsible for the maintenance of body posture and the smooth coordination of all movements. These features are shown in Figure 15.

Most research has focused on the structure and function of the cerebrum, especially on its surface layer of *grey matter* (nerve cells), the *cerebral cortex*, which is the area primarily involved in the control of voluntary movement and intellectual functions, and in the decoding of information from the senses. Beneath the cortex is a body of *white matter* (fibre tracts), which transmits signals between the different parts of each hemisphere, and between the cortex and the brain stem. A notable feature is that the surface of the cortex is not smooth, but has folded in on itself to produce a series of convolutions, or *gyri*, which are separated by fissures, or *sulci*.

Seen from above, the main feature of the brain is the *median longitudinal fissure* separating the hemispheres. It does not extend the whole way through the cerebrum: lower down, the hemispheres are joined by a thick bundle of nerve fibres, the *corpus callosum*. This is the means whereby information can be transmitted from one hemisphere to the

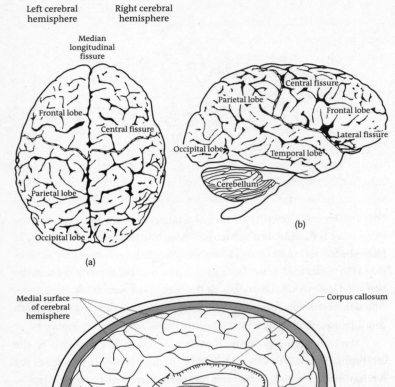

Left cerebral hemisphere

Right cerebral hemisphere

Median longitudinal fissure

Frontal lobe

Central fissure

Parietal lobe

Occipital lobe

(a)

Central fissure

Parietal lobe

Frontal lobe

Lateral fissure

Occipital lobe

Temporal lobe

Cerebellum

(b)

Medial surface of cerebral hemisphere

Corpus callosum

Pons

Mid brain

Cerebellum

Spinal cord

Medulla oblongata

(c)

Fig. 15. Different views of the brain

other. Seen from the side, the main features are the central sulcus (the *fissure of Rolando*) and the lateral sulcus (the *Sylvian fissure*), which are used as criteria for dividing the brain into its four main lobes: *frontal*, *temporal*, *parietal*, and *occipital*.

Each hemisphere controls movement in and receives sensory input from the opposite side of the body. Many nerve fibres from the two hemispheres cross each other as they descend through the brain stem, so that the left hemisphere controls the movement of the right side of the body, and vice versa. That is why brain damage to one hemisphere is usually correlated with bodily effects (such as paralysis) on the opposite side. In the case of the ears, signals from each ear go to both hemispheres, but most information is transmitted to the opposite side. In the case of the eyes, the situation is yet more complex: the left half of the visual field of each eye transmits information to the right hemisphere, and vice versa. Such sophisticated 'wiring', it has been suggested, enables us to make many more qualitative judgements about sounds and images (e.g. about their distance and location) than might otherwise be possible.

Dominance

The functional relationship between the brain's two hemispheres has been a major focus of research for over a century. Each has its own role, being more involved in the performance of some activities and less involved in others. A hemisphere is thus said to be the *dominant* or *leading* one for certain mental functions, and the development of these functions within one or the other hemisphere is known as *lateralization*.

Language and handedness have long been the two major factors in any discussion of cerebral dominance. The left hemisphere is dominant for language in most right-handed people (estimates are usually over 95%). However, the relationship is not a symmetrical one: it does not automatically follow that the right hemisphere is dominant for language in left-handed people. Left-handers are by no means a homogeneous group, and in over 60% of cases the left hemisphere is either dominant for language or very much involved (*mixed* dominance).

The specialized intellectual functions of each hemisphere are only partly understood, but tentative generalizations have been made. With right-handed people, the left hemisphere is found to be dominant in such activities as analytical tasks, categorization, calculation, logical organization, information sequencing, complex motor functions, and language. The right is said to be dominant for the perception and matching of global patterns, part–whole relationships, spatial orientation, creative sensibility, musical patterns, and emotional expression or recognition.

These identifications must be made cautiously, avoiding an over-simplified contrast – such as is found when people talk about the left hemisphere as the 'analytic' or 'intellectual' part of the brain, and the right as the 'creative' or 'emotional' part. It is now known, for example, that the right hemisphere can handle certain nonverbal tasks that require intellectual capacity (such as spatial judgement), and that it has a limited capability for auditory analysis and comprehension. Moreover, several activities usually involve both hemispheres (such as face recognition).

Localization

The idea that a single area of the brain can be related to a single be-havioural ability, such as vision or speech, is known as the theory of cerebral *localization*. Support for the theory came from the work of such neurologists as Paul Pierre Broca (1824–80) and Carl Wernicke (1848–1905), who had found that damage to specific areas of the cortex correlated with the loss of certain kinds of linguistic ability in their patients. Damage to *Broca's area* resulted in a reduced ability to speak, though comprehension remained relatively unimpaired. Damage to *Wernicke's area* resulted in a reduced ability to comprehend speech, though the ability to speak was relatively unaffected. Other areas involved in the processing of speaking, listening, reading, writing, and signing were later identified, and these are locatable in Figure 16.

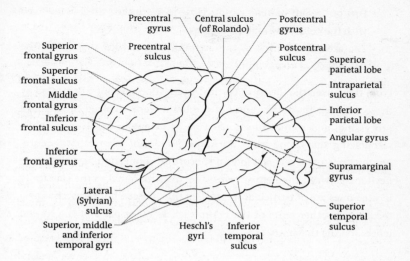

Fig. 16. Surface areas of the cortex

- The front part of the parietal lobe, along the fissure of Rolando, is primarily involved in the processing of sensation, and may be connected with the speech and auditory areas at a deeper level.
- The area in front of the fissure of Rolando is mainly involved in motor functioning, and is thus relevant to the study of speaking and writing.
- An area in the upper back part of the temporal lobe, extending upwards into the parietal lobe, plays a major part in the comprehension of speech. This is Wernicke's area.
- In the upper part of the temporal lobe is the main area involved in auditory reception, known as *Heschl's gyri*, after the Austrian pathologist R. L. Heschl (1824–81).
- The lower back part of the frontal lobe is primarily involved in the encoding of speech. This is Broca's area.
- Another area towards the back of the frontal lobe may be involved in the motor control of writing. It is known as *Exner's centre*, after the German neurologist Sigmund Exner (1846–1926).

- Part of the left parietal region, close to Wernicke's area, is involved with the control of manual signing.
- The area at the back of the occipital lobe is used mainly for the processing of visual input.

From the outset, the theory of cortical localization was hotly contested by those who felt that other areas of the brain were involved in language processing; and a multifunctional view is generally held today. While recognizing that some areas are more important than others, neurolinguists postulate several kinds of subcortical connection, as well as connections between the hemispheres. The areas marginal to the classically located ones are of particular interest, in this respect; but research is also focusing on other parts of the brain, such as other parts of the frontal lobes, and the thalamus.

Neurolinguistic processing

In real life, a snatch of dialogue (*How are you?*, *Fine, thanks*) takes place so quickly that it is easy to forget the complexity of the neurological planning and execution involved in the process. Any model of the production and comprehension of language – whether spoken, written, or signed – involves several steps, each of which must have some kind of neural representation. Neurolinguistic models attempt to delineate what these steps are and how they interrelate.

- In speech production, for example, an initial intention to communicate is followed (or perhaps accompanied) by some kind of conceptualization of the message.
- There has also to be a point at which this conceptualization is encoded into the semantic and syntactic structure of the language used by the speaker (though it is not clear how far this stage can be separated from the preceding one).
- If the structure is to be spoken, it must first be given some sort of phonological representation (e.g. as syllables, phonemes, or distinctive features, §11).

- A motor-control programme must then be used, to coordinate the multiplicity of signals that have to be sent to the appropriate muscles controlling the different parts of the vocal tract (§4).
- While this activity takes place, it is being constantly self-monitored: *feedback* is being received from the ear, from the sense of touch, and from the internal sensations generated by the movement of parts of the body (*proprioceptive* feedback).

Other kinds of internal monitoring, at 'higher' levels, may also take place. An analogous sequence of events would be involved if the structure were to be written or signed.

The nature of neurolinguistic programmes has attracted a great deal of research in recent years, especially in relation to speech production. It is evident, for example, that the brain does not issue motor commands one segment at a time. A word such as *soup* is not neurologically transmitted as three separate steps – [s] + [u] + [p]. The articulation of [s] is lip-rounded, under the influence of the following vowel, which shows that the brain must be 'scanning ahead' while issuing commands for particular segments (coarticulation, p. 52).

When we consider the whole range of factors that affect the timing of speech events (such as breathing rate, the movement and coordination of the articulators, the onset of vocal-fold vibration, the location of stress, and the placement and duration of pauses), it is evident that a highly sophisticated control system must be employed, otherwise speech would degenerate into an erratic, disorganized set of noises. It is now recognized that many areas of the brain are involved: in particular, the cerebellum and thalamus are known to assist the cortex in exercising this control.

No detailed model of neurolinguistic operation yet exists that takes all the variables into account, but it is possible to construct general models of linguistic processing which can be tested experimentally.

- For speech production, the basic structure of the utterance is thought to be generated in Wernicke's area and sent to Broca's area for encoding. The motor programme is then passed on to the adjacent motor area, which governs the articulatory organs (§4).

- For speech comprehension, the signals arrive in the auditory cortex from the ear (§7), and are transferred to the adjacent Wernicke's area, where they are interpreted.
- For reading aloud, the written form is first received by the visual cortex (§19), then transmitted via the angular gyrus to Wernicke's area, where it is thought to be associated with an auditory representation. The utterance structure is then sent on to Broca's area, for processing there.

One kind of evidence

One type of detailed evidence which throws light on how the brain works comes from the analysis of *slips of the tongue*. Tongue slips are involuntary departures from the speaker's intended production of a sequence of language units. A speaker intends to say *I baked a cake* and instead says *I caked a bake*, or something similar. They are very common: sounds, syllables, words, and sometimes other units of grammar can be affected.

The main linguistic finding is that tongue slips are not random, but are largely explicable by reference to certain basic constraints. For example, the two words involved in a tongue slip (the word containing the slip and the word that influences it) are often found within the same grammatical construction or rhythm unit (§§12, 39). Moreover, the influencing word is often the most strongly stressed word within the rhythm unit. And most tongue slips involve the symmetrical substitution within a syllable of one sound by another: for example, an initial segment in the influencing word replaces the initial segment in the slipped word (as in **c**aked a **b**ake).

Combining such constraints, it is possible to make predictions about the form tongue slips are likely to take when they occur. Given the intended sentence *The car missed the bike / but hit the wall* (where / marks a rhythm boundary, and the strongly stressed words are underlined), the likely slips are going to include *bar* for *car* or *wit* for *hit*. Most unlikely would be *har* for *car* (showing the influence of a less prominent word in the second rhythm unit) or *lit* for *hit* (showing a final consonant replacing an initial one).

Tongue slips tell us a great deal about the more detailed neurological processes that underlie speech. The different kinds of errors provide indirect evidence for some of the stages recognized by models of speech production, and suggest the kinds of linguistic unit that these models need to take into account.

28
How to investigate language structure

Whether we are speaking, writing, or signing, there is too much going on when we use language to enable us to describe its characteristics in a single, simple statement. Even in a short spoken sentence such as *Where's the station?*, several things are taking place at once.

- Some of the words convey a particular meaning, telling us what the sentence is about. *Where's the station?* contrasts with *Where's the beach?*, *There's the station*, and much more. This is the area of vocabulary (§30).

- There is a likely order in which the words may appear. We would not say *The station where's?* or *Where's station the?* These are issues to do with grammar (§36).

- Each word is composed of a specific sequence of sounds, which may alter when used together in connected speech: *Where's the station?* is a more colloquial form of *Where is the station?* This is part of the subject of phonology (§11).

- The sentence as a whole is uttered in a particular tone of voice, one feature of which is signalled in writing through the question mark. There is a difference between *Where's the station?* and *Where's the station!* (suggesting 'What a silly question!'), or the way a novelist might express it: *'Where's the station?' Mike asked abruptly/pleadingly/urgently* . . . This is another part of the subject of phonology (§12).

While we say or hear an utterance, we are not consciously aware of all these facets of its structure, but once our attention is drawn to them, we easily recognize their existence. We could even concentrate on the study of one of these facets largely to the exclusion of the others – something that takes place routinely in language teaching, for instance, where we may learn about aspects of grammar one day, and of vocabulary or phonology the next.

Selective focusing of this kind in fact takes place in all linguistic studies. It is an essential part of the business of discovering how language works, and also a helpful way of simplifying the task of description. The different facets are usually referred to as *levels* of linguistic organization, though other terms are also used, such as *components*, *strata*, or *branches*. Each level is studied using its own terminology and techniques, enabling us to obtain information about one aspect of language structure while temporarily disregarding the involvement of others.

The field of phonology, for example, is analysed using a set of phonetic procedures that are quite distinct from anything encountered at other linguistic levels (§9). When we do phonological research, we try to disassociate ourselves from the problems and practices we would encounter if we were carrying out a study at the level of, say, vocabulary. Similarly, vocabulary study takes place using approaches that are in principle independent of what goes on in phonology. Grammar is different again. Each level provides us with a distinct 'slant' on the workings of language structure.

The notion of levels is widely used. It enables us to see and state patterns of organization more clearly and succinctly than any other way that has so far been devised. In a word, levels help us to *focus*. They are more than just a linguist's construct: there is evidence that they are represented differently in the brain. For example, following certain kinds of brain damage, a person may retain the ability to control the structures operating at one level of language, but lose the ability to control them at another.

At the same time, we must never forget that, when we isolate a level for independent study, we are introducing an artificial element into our enquiry. The sounds of speech that we study via phonetics are, after all, the substance through which the patterns of grammar and vocabulary are conveyed. There will therefore be interrelationships between levels that need to be taken into account if we wish to understand the way language as a whole is organized. As with any structure, the whole cannot be broken down into its constituent parts without some loss; and we must always recollect the need to place our study of individual levels within a more general structural perspective.

How many levels are there?

It is not difficult to sense the complexity of language structure, but it is not so easy to say how many levels should be set up in order to explain the way this structure is organized. Some simple models of language recognize only two basic levels: the set of physical *forms* (the sounds, letters, signs, constructions, words) contained in a language, and the range of abstract *meanings* conveyed by these forms. More commonly, the notion of forms is subdivided, to distinguish different kinds of organization.

In speech, for example, the physical facts of pronunciation, as defined by the processes of articulation, acoustic transmission, and audition, are considered to be the subject matter of the level of *phonetics* (§9). The way different languages organize sounds to convey differences of meaning is studied at the level of *phonology* (§11). And the study of the way meaningful units are brought into sequence to convey wider and more varied patterns of meaning is the province of *grammar* (§36). The term *semantics* is then used for the study of the patterns of meaning themselves (§29).

Four-level models of language (phonetics/phonology/grammar/semantics) are among the most widely used, in the study of speech, but further divisions within and between these levels are often made. For example, within the level of grammar, it is common to recognize a distinction between the study of word structure (*morphology*) and the study of word order within sentences (*syntax*) (§39). Within phonology, the study of vowels, consonants, and syllables (*segmental phonology*) is usually distinguished from the study of prosody and other tones of voice (*non-segmental phonology*) (§12). Within semantics, the study of vocabulary is sometimes taken separately from the study of larger patterns of meaning (under such headings as *text* or *discourse*) (§41). All of these are regularly referred to as *levels* of structure.

We could continue, making divisions within divisions, and recognizing more subtle kinds of structural organization within language. We could extend the notion to include other aspects of language functioning apart from structure – as when some scholars talk of a *pragmatic* level (§43). But there comes a point when the notion ceases to be helpful. When a theory sets up a large number of levels, it becomes difficult to plot the relationships between them, and to retain a sense of how they integrate into a single system.

In this book

For this book, I have organized the topic of language structure by setting up three main levels of enquiry:

- Under *semantics*, I examine how meaning is expressed and understood within a language. An important distinction is drawn between the meaning of individual words and idioms (*vocabulary*, or *lexicon*) and the meaning of larger stretches of *discourse*.
- Under *grammar*, I examine how sentences are used to structure meaningful expression. An important distinction is drawn here too, between the study of the way sentences are constructed (*syntax*) and the study of the way words are constructed (*morphology*).
- Under *medium of linguistic transmission*, I examine the way in which meaningful sentences can be conveyed between the participants in an act of communication. The three chief means are speech, writing, and sign (§§23, 25). Further distinctions are routinely made within these headings – notably, the distinction between phonetics and phonology used in the study of speech (§11).

When we have completed the investigation of how the structure of language is organized, we proceed to the corresponding study of how language is used. This part of the enquiry is taken up in §42.

Where to start?

Is there a 'best' direction for the study of a language, using the framework of levels? I have already begun this book by exploring the different mediums of transmission (beginning in §§4, 16, 24, 25). Where should we go next? Should the next chapter be about grammar or semantics? The American linguist Leonard Bloomfield (1887–1949) recommended an approach in which one worked through the various levels in a particular order, beginning with a phonetic description, proceeding through phonology, morphology, and syntax, and concluding with semantics. In this view, the analysis at each level apart from the first is dependent on what has gone before. On this basis, grammar would have to come next.

The opposite approach is also possible. We can begin by analysing the semantics of a language – chiefly through the vocabulary it possesses – then see how that vocabulary is put to grammatical use within sentences. Following that, we examine how in spoken language these sentences are structured phonologically and expressed phonetically. An analogous procedure operates for the realizations of sentences in writing and in sign language. On this basis, a study of semantics would always precede a study of grammar.

Neither approach actually represents the complex reality of analysing a language. It is possible to carry out an analysis at one level only if we make certain assumptions about other levels. Our choice of sounds to describe phonetically depends to some extent on our awareness of which sounds play an important role in a language (phonology), which in turn depends on our awareness of the way sounds distinguish words and word sequences (grammar) enabling them to convey differences in meaning (semantics). Similarly, when we study grammatical patterns, such as sentence structure, we need to be aware of both semantic factors (such as the relationships of meaning that bring the patterns together) and phonological factors (such as the features of intonation that help to identify sentence units in speech). When we work with levels, we need to be able to think of all directions at once.

But this cannot be done in a book. A direction has to be chosen. And I have chosen to make semantics the next step in the present exposition. This is because I find it much easier to discuss what grammar is all about after having laid a foundation in the study of meaning. The aim of grammar, I shall be arguing, is to give structure to meaning. So meaning is where we must begin.

29
How we mean

The observation that 'language is used to convey meaning' seems so obvious and straightforward that it hardly seems to warrant a chapter to explicate it. And yet it is one of the most difficult topics of all, as the work of generations of philosophers, logicians, and linguists illustrates. The technical term for the study of meaning in language is *semantics*. But as soon as this term is used, a word of warning is in order.

Any scientific approach to semantics has to be clearly distinguished from a pejorative sense of the term that has developed in popular use, when people talk about the way language can be manipulated in order to mislead the public. A newspaper headline might read, 'Tax increases reduced to semantics' – referring to the way a government was trying to hide a proposed increase behind some carefully chosen words. Or someone might say in an argument, 'That's just semantics', implying that the point is purely a verbal quibble, bearing no relationship to anything in the real world. This kind of nuance is absent when we talk about semantics from the objective viewpoint of linguistic research. The linguistic approach studies the properties of meaning in a systematic and objective way, with reference to as wide a range of utterances and languages as possible.

One of the first problems it encounters is the many ways in which the term *mean* is itself used. Here is a small selection of them:

'intend' – *I mean to visit Jane next week.*
'indicate' – *A red signal means stop.*
'refer to' – *What does 'telemetry' mean?*
'have significance' – *What does global warning mean?*
'convey' – *What does the name McGough mean to you?*

Any large dictionary will distinguish at least twenty different 'meanings of meaning'. Faced with such diversity of usage, it is unlikely we will be able to find a wholly satisfactory answer to the question 'What is meaning?'. But certain important clarifications are now well recognized.

Distinguishing natural and conventional

An early distinction emerged when the Greek philosophers debated the nature of meaning by examining the relationship between words and things. Two main views emerged. The *naturalist* view, deriving largely from Plato, maintained that there was an intrinsic connection between the sound of a word and the thing it referred to. The *conventionalist* view, largely Aristotelian, held that there was no such connection: the relationship was wholly arbitrary.

In their extreme forms, both views are untenable. If the naturalist view were valid, we would be able to tell the meaning of words just by hearing them. Only onomatopoeic words, such as *bow wow* and *splash*, come close to this, and even they change greatly from language to language. But naturalistic thinking is still widely encountered, especially in the concern many people have over the use of certain words – as when they introduce euphemisms to avoid mentioning words to do with death.

The conventionalist position emphasizes the arbitrary relationship between words and things, and this is a principle accepted by modern semanticists. There is nothing in the form of the word *table* that bears any direct relationship to the 'thing'. At the same time, we have to recognize that many words do exist containing some element of real-world symbolism in the sounds they use – as in *splash, jiggle, quack, teeny-weeny*, and *slime*.

Distinguishing sense and reference

A basic principle in semantics is the need to analyse the *senses* of words, not their *reference*. *Sense* is the meaning of a word within a language. *Reference* is what a word refers to in the world outside language – the 'real world', as it is often described. Other people than linguists study the real world – physicists, biologists, geographers, and so on. Linguists study only how we talk about this world. And it turns out that the relationship between the two is never simple. Different languages talk about the world in different ways.

It is crucial to look at different languages. If we restrict our view to just one language – our own – we will never truly understand the distinction between sense and reference, because it is natural to think that 'our' way of talking about the world is the only one, or the most natural one. It is only when we study or learn a foreign language, and realize that other people see things differently, that we become aware of how arbitrary the relationship is between words and entities or concepts.

Different languages 'parcel out' the world in different ways. In the 'real' world, mothers and fathers have brothers and sisters, but languages talk about them differently. In English, there are no single words expressing the notions 'mother's brother', 'father's brother' (we have to use *uncle* for both), 'mother's sister', or 'father's sister' (we have to use *aunt* for both). In the Australian language Pitjanjatjara, however, we have a different situation: *ngunytju* = 'mother's sister', *kamuru* = 'mother's brother', *kurntili* = 'father's sister', and *mama* = 'father's brother'. The same biological relationships are given a different lexical treatment. Family photographs would look the same, but the words would have different senses.

These examples are not isolated cases. They are typical. Just within the field of kinship there are hundreds of instances where terminology changes across languages. In English, *cousins* can be male or female; in French, male *cousin* is distinguished from female *cousine*. There is no single term for 'grandfather' or 'grandmother' in Swedish: *farfar* = 'father's father', *morfar* = 'mother's father', *farmor* = 'father's mother', and *mormor* = 'mother's mother'. In Njamal (Australia), some terms express generation distance; the same word *maili* can refer to either 'father's father' or 'daughter's son's wife's sister' – both are two generations away.

Even within a single language, we need to distinguish sense from reference, to explain the way language makes divisions where there are none in reality. The neat scientific classifications of fauna and flora, where each name has its place in a system of terms, are not typical of language. In everyday life, we use such words as *hill* and *mountain* or *stream* and *river*, where the real-world notions are quite indeterminate. When does a hill become a mountain, or a stream a river? There is an inherent fuzziness in reality, which individual words can never capture.

There is also the problem of how we explain what a word's meaning is. Let us imagine someone who had encountered the word *chair* and did not know what it meant. One procedure would be to explain its reference: we could take the person to a chair and point to it. But this would be of limited help, for how would the person know from that experience which *other* objects in the world should also be called chairs? The wrong deduction might also be made, that what we were pointing at was the quality 'wooden', or the concept of 'furniture' – the kind of error children make when they learn vocabulary (§31). And with many words, it is difficult to know what to point to at all – *noise, help, language* . . .

A better procedure is to explain the sense of the word, in the case of *chair* using a rough definition such as a 'seat with four legs and a back'. Such a definition would enable the person to look out for other objects with similar properties, and thus use the word appropriately. The definition could then be sharpened, as related words were met (e.g. *armchair, stool*). But this whole process of vocabulary learning continues without any direct reference to the objects in the real world: there is total reliance on the use of words to explain the sense of other words – a process that reaches its logical conclusion in a dictionary (§33).

Identifying linguistic resources

We can make some progress if we replace the question 'What is meaning?' by 'How do we express meaning?', for there is a limited number of ways in which we can organize the resources of a language to do the job. The chief means are words, sentences, patterns of discourse, and certain aspects of phonology and graphology (§§11, 17). The traditional focus has been on words – vocabulary – but the relevance of other factors is plain when we consider the following examples, each of which introduces a change into the meaning of a sentence.

- We change a word: *I see the starship* vs. *I see the alien*.
- We change the grammatical structure: *I see the alien* vs. *The alien sees me*.
- We change the sound – such as the intonation: *The alien is friendly, isn't it!* vs. *The alien is friendly, isn't it?*
- We change the spelling: *Look – a tea shop* vs. *Look – a tea shoppe*.
- We change the capitalization: *This is a really big issue* vs. *This is a Really Big Issue*.
- We change the way we expect the discourse to work: *Can you tell me the time? It's three o'clock* vs. the jocular or less cooperative *Can you tell me the time? I can*.

Of all these, it is vocabulary which most people immediately associate with the notion of sense. This is partly because of the quantities involved. In English, for example, we have just a few dozen sounds to learn, a few hundred sound combinations in syllables, and around 3,000 grammatical constructions – but there are hundreds of thousands of units of vocabulary. So the focus of any semantic approach must lie here, in vocabulary, and that is how it has always been.

But vocabulary within sentences, always. It is the interaction between words and sentence structure which actually conveys our 'sense of sense'. Words by themselves do not actually 'make sense'. Only when they are used within a sentence do they 'make sense'. Sentences exist to enable us to 'make sense' of words. That is why sentence study is the foundation of grammar (§39).

Dictionaries, of course, tend to give the opposite impression. Indeed, if we do not know the meaning of a word, we say to ourselves that we will 'look it up in a dictionary'. But it is easy to show that most everyday words, by themselves, convey little sense – or perhaps it should be that they convey too much sense. It is not possible to work out the sense of a word (e.g. *table*, *charge*) by seeing the word alone. In the case of *table*, the word could mean the item of furniture, or a graphic display in a book, or any of its other senses. The ambiguity can be resolved only by putting the word into a sentence: *I am sitting on a table*. *There's a misprint in the table*. That is why it is essential for dictionaries to provide several real, clear, sentence-based examples (§33).

Undoubtedly there are many cases where it is possible to ask what the meaning of a word is, and get a sensible answer. This happens when the word has just a single use in a language, as is the case with many scientific or technical terms – *otology*, *semiconductor*, *phycocyanin*. These words are *monosemic*. Some everyday words are monosemic too – *handkerchief*, *gaudy*, *crybaby*. And we are also used to thinking of some proper names in this way, where the word refers to one place, one person, one company, and so on: *Reykjavik*, *Lithuania*, *Microsoft*.

But most everyday words are not like this. They are *polysemic* – expressing several meanings. The word *charge* could be something to do with money, crime, soldiering, electricity, or explosives – to take just five possibilities. It does not make much sense to ask 'What does *charge* mean?'. The only way in which we can find out is by using the word in relation to other words – typically, by putting it into a sentence, so that we can distinguish, for example, *The battery was charged with special chemicals* and *He was charged with homicide*.

Isolated words do not lack meaning. Rather, they have the potential for conveying too much meaning. Many everyday words have a dozen or more senses. A common word like *take* may have fifty or more. Plainly, we need to analyse the relationships between words so that we can distinguish these senses clearly. This is what a good dictionary does, and it is what the science of words, *lexicology*, does too.

30
How we analyse meaning

Words have been the traditional focus of enquiry in the study of meaning, as §29 illustrates, and one of the most fruitful approaches to the semantic analysis of vocabulary has come from the application of structuralist ideas. From this viewpoint, language is seen as a network of systematic relationships between units of meaning. The analogy is with other areas of language, such as phonology and graphology. Phonology can be seen as a system of sound units, the phonemes (§11). Graphology can be seen as a system of graphic units, the graphemes (§17). What are the equivalent units in semantics?

In the previous chapter I used the term *word* to discuss semantic units, and this is the traditional use. People readily talk about the 'meaning of words'. However, if we wish to enquire precisely into semantic matters, this term will not do, and an alternative must be found. There are three main reasons.

- The term *word* is used in ways that obscure the study of meaning. The forms *walk*, *walks*, *walking*, and *walked* are all 'different words', yet from a semantic point of view they are all variants of the same underlying unit, *WALK*. If the variants are referred to as *words*, though, what should the underlying unit be called? It would not be particularly clear to say that 'these four words are different forms of the same word'.

- The term *word* is useless for the study of idioms, which are also units of meaning. A much-used example is *kick the bucket* (= 'die'). Here we have a single unit of meaning, which happens to consist of three words. Again, it would hardly be clear to talk of this unit as a 'word', if we then go on to say that this word consists of three words.
- The term *word* has in any case been appropriated for use elsewhere in linguistic study – in the field of grammar, where it is an important concept in both syntax and morphology (§36).

For such reasons, many linguists employ other terminology to talk about the basic units of semantic analysis, and both *lexeme* and *lexical item* are widely used. We may now avoid the lack of clarity referred to above, and say that the 'lexeme' *WALK* occurs in several variant forms – the 'words' *walk*, *walks*, etc. Similarly, we can say that the 'lexeme' *KICK THE BUCKET* contains three 'words'. It is lexemes that are usually listed as headwords in a dictionary. Accordingly, we shall put this term to use in the remainder of this chapter.

The distinction between *word* and *lexeme* can make a big difference – for example, in estimating the size of someone's vocabulary. If we count all the different words in Shakespeare, we reach a total of around 30,000. If we count all the different lexemes, the total is less than 20,000.

Semantic fields

One way of imposing some order on vocabulary is to organize lexemes into *fields* of meaning. Within each field, the lexemes interrelate, defining each other in specific ways. For example, the various lexemes for 'parts of the body' (*head*, *neck*, *shoulders*, etc.) form a semantic field, as do the different lexemes for 'vehicles', 'fruit', 'tools', or 'colour'. It has been argued that the whole of a language's vocabulary is structured into fields; but there is a great deal of fuzziness as we move from one part of the language to another. It is not difficult to gather together all the English lexemes for 'body parts'; but it is very difficult to do the same job for 'noise' or 'ornaments'.

There have been many philosophical and linguistic attempts to organize the concepts or words in a language – notably in thesauruses. In the famous *Thesaurus* of Peter Mark Roget (1779–1869), first published in 1852, we find vocabulary divided into six main areas: abstract relations, space, matter, intellect, volition, and affections. Each area is then given a detailed sub-classification, producing a thousand semantic categories in all.

Thesauruses have now been produced for several languages, and prove to be a useful adjunct to many practical linguistic activities, such as professional writing, translating, and setting or solving crosswords. For the semanticist, however, their value is limited, as they contain no information about the way the lexemes relate to each other. They leave open the question of how the lexemes of a language are organized.

To think of lexemes as a long list, such as we might find in a dictionary, is highly misleading. There is no semantic reality in alphabetical order. On the contrary, alphabetical order destroys semantic structure, keeping apart lexemes that should belong together, such as *aunt* and *uncle*, or *big* and *little*. Rather, we need to develop an alternative conception, based on our intuitions that small groups of lexemes are related in sense. And modern accounts of semantic structure recognize two main kinds of relationship between lexemes.

Collocations

One relationship results from the way lexemes occur in sequences. For example, in the sentence *It was a very auspicious –*, fluent speakers of English 'know' that the omitted item will be one of a very small set of lexemes, such as *occasion* or *event* – unless, of course, a literary or humorous point is being made, as in *It was a very auspicious bottle of wine*. The tendency of lexemes to work together in predictable ways is known as *collocation*. The British linguist J. R. Firth (1890–1960) put it this way: 'You shall know a word by the company it keeps'.

Every lexeme has collocations, but some are much more predictable than others. *Blond* collocates strongly with *hair*, *flock* with *sheep*, *neigh* with *horse*. Some collocations are totally predictable, such as *spick* with *span*, or *addled* with *brains* or *eggs*. Others are much less so: *letter* collocates with a wide range of lexemes, such as *alphabet* and *spelling*, and (in another sense) *box*, *post*, and *write*. Yet other lexemes are so widely used that they have no predictable collocates at all, such as *have* and *get*.

Collocations differ greatly between languages, and provide a major difficulty in mastering foreign languages. In English, we 'face' problems and 'interpret' dreams; but in modern Hebrew, we have to 'stand in front of' problems and 'solve' dreams. In Japanese the verb for 'drink' collocates with water and soup, but also with tablets and smoking.

Collocation should not be confused with 'association of ideas'. The way lexemes work together may have nothing to do with 'ideas'. We say in English *green with jealousy* (not *blue* or *red*), though there is nothing literally 'green' about 'jealousy'. *Coffee* can be *white*, though the colour is brown, in the real world. Both *lads* and *lasses* may be well rounded enough to be called *buxom*, but this lexeme is used only with the latter.

Collocations are also quite different from the idiosyncratic links between ideas that we express in words. On a psychiatrist's couch, we may 'free associate', responding to *farm* with *Easter*, or *jam* with *mother*. This is not collocation, but personal word association. Collocations are links between lexemes made by *all* who speak a language.

Sense relations

The second kind of semantic relationship results from the way lexemes can substitute for each other in a sentence. For example, in the exchange *Is that a new radio? No, it's an old radio*, the substitution of *old* for *new* results in a change of meaning that we recognize as an *opposite*. Several types of substitution have been recognized.

The most familiar relationship is *synonymy*, the relationship of *sameness* or *similarity* of meaning. In *I've bought a new car/I've bought a new automobile*, *car* and *automobile* are synonyms. The search for synonyms is a well-established classroom exercise, but it is as well to remember that lexemes rarely (if ever) have exactly the same meaning. There are usually stylistic, regional, emotional, or other differences to consider – British and American usage, in the above example. And context must always be taken into account. Two lexemes might be synonymous in one sentence but different in another: *range* and *selection* are synonyms in *What a nice – of furnishings*, but not in *There's the mountain –*.

Another relationship refers to the notion of *inclusion*, whereby we can say that 'an X is a kind of Y'. This relation is called *hyponymy*. For example, *rose* is a hyponym of *flower*, and *car* of *vehicle*. From the other direction, we may also say that *flower* is a *hypernym* of *rose*, and *vehicle* of *car*. It follows from this that several lexemes will be *co-hyponyms* of the same superordinate term: *rose, pansy, tulip* . . . are all hyponyms of *flower*.

Once again, it must be stressed that this is a linguistic, and not a real-world, classification. Languages differ in their superordinate terms and in the hyponyms they accept under one such term. For instance in classical Greek the lexemes for 'carpenter', 'doctor', 'flautist', and other occupations are all hyponyms of *demiourgos*; but there is no equivalent superordinate term in English. We simply do not have a single 'occupational' term that would allow us to say 'A carpenter/doctor/flautist, etc. is a kind of –'.

The third kind of sense relationship is *antonymy* – *oppositeness* of meaning. Antonyms are often thought of in the same breath as synonyms, but they are in fact very different. There may be no true synonyms, but there are several kinds of antonyms. Three types are especially important.

- *Gradable* antonyms, such as *big/small*, *good/bad*, permit the expression of degrees. We can say *very big*, *quite small*, *bigger than me*, and so on.
- *Nongradable* antonyms, such as *single/married*, *male/female*, do not permit degrees of contrast. It is not possible to talk of *very male*, *quite married*, *more married than me*, and so on, except in jest. Opposites like this are often called *complementary terms*.
- *Converse terms* are two-way contrasts that are interdependent, such as *buy/sell* or *parent/child*; one member presupposes the existence of the other.

A fourth kind of sense relationship is called *incompatibility*. Under this heading are grouped sets of lexemes that are mutually exclusive members of the same superordinate category. For example, *red*, *blue*, *green*, etc. are incompatible lexemes within the category *colour*. It would not be possible to say 'I am thinking of a single colour, and it is green and red.' On the other hand, *red* is not incompatible with such lexemes as *round* or *dirty* (something can be simultaneously 'red and round'). Terms for fruit, flowers, and musical instruments illustrate other incompatible sets.

This may seem obvious, but we must be prepared for some unexpected usages. In English, *black*, *white*, and *grey* are not always included within the category of colour: for example, we can talk about *black-and-white films* (as opposed to films *in technicolour*). And in snooker, the term *red* is excluded from the category of colour: we may proceed to play the *coloured* balls only after all the red balls have been potted.

These are not the only sense relationships in language. Another one is the relationship between *parts* and *wholes*, such as the relationship between *wheel* and *car* or *shin* and *leg*. A further example is the *cyclical* relationship that relates sets of lexemes, such as the days of the week or the months of the year. It is plain that the lexemes of a language are interrelated in many intricate ways.

31
How we learn vocabulary

When we acquire a new lexical item, we do not simply tack it on to the end of a list of already-learned items. Rather, the new item has to find its place within the lexicon we have already acquired. Let us imagine we encounter the item *sponsorship* for the first time: this becomes part of the set of items we already have for types of money-giving, such as *donation*, *award*, *grant*, *fee*, *endowment*, *gift*, *scholarship*, *honorarium*, *subsidy*, and *annuity*. It does not become part of the items we already know for types of fruit or types of vehicle. And in joining the relevant set, it has to elbow its way in: we may have to change our mind about the sense of other items already there. *They're offering us a sponsorship*, we might say, then learn that what we have been offered is really a *donation*, because of the different tax implications, and thereafter the meaning of *donation* is narrower for us than it was before we learned *sponsorship*. When we learn a new lexeme, we always make at least two gains in precision, not one.

Increasing the range of vocabulary inevitably increases precision, as long as the acquisition of the new item is properly integrated into the existing lexicon, and this requires that we recognize the crucial role of semantic structure. In the terms of §30, learning a new lexeme is a matter of showing how it fits into a semantic field. And this is how it is from the very outset of lexical learning. *There dog*, says the child, pointing to a cat. *No darling*, says the mother, *that's a cat, not a dog*. But few mothers would stop there. *Cats go miaow, dogs go woof,* one mother might say. Another might draw attention to the differences in shape, or touch, or size. And when other animals come into view, yet other distinguishing features will be mentioned – whether they can be eaten, whether they live on the farm or in the jungle, and whether they are dangerous.

To learn a set of lexical items is to learn the features which distinguish or relate the items, thereby building up primitive *definitions*: 'a cow is a thing that goes moo, gives milk, lives on a farm', and so on. Later, children learn the name of the semantic field that cows are part of: *animals*. And gradually they learn how to define: 'an X is a Y which has the features A,B,C . . .' It is not done all at once. To build up a solid definition can take years, and mistakes can be made along the way. For a long time, Sue, aged six, misunderstood the word *factory*. 'It's a place where you make things', she had been told. So the kitchen in her house, for example, she would call a factory, because she had seen her mother making things there. Only in school did she learn the truth – that factories involve mass production for selling. And in adult life we might have to refine the definition still further – in relation to a planning application, for example.

Learning vocabulary is learning to make the best lexical choice for the needs of the moment. Students therefore need to have an array of lexemes available, so that they can see the contrasts between them. It is like supermarkets: a local store has limited choice, so many people travel out of town to a place where there is more choice. But if there is too much choice people get confused, as they try to work out what the differences are between competing products. They find they need to consult consumer magazines. It is the same with language. The consumer magazines are there, telling us exactly what all the differences are: they are called dictionaries. Dictionaries are the most important intermediary between the developing lexical intuition of the student and the target lexical world of the language. If the dictionary is well structured, it gives the student a basis for choice.

How do we make a lexical choice? When we choose an item from all those belonging to a semantic field we are trying to find the best one to suit what we want to express, and this presupposes that we can tell the difference between them. Telling the difference – identifying what two items have in common and what makes them different – is what we call a *definition*. It is commonplace in language classes to be given guidance about definitions. Two types of sense relation are often mentioned: synonyms and antonyms (§30). However, these are not the most useful types of sense relation when it comes to defining lexemes.

- Synonyms are not very useful because they are so unusual. In fact it may be impossible to find in a language two words with exactly the same meaning. Why should a language waste its resources in this way? Invariably there is some difference – regional use (*tap* vs. *faucet*), stylistic level (*house* vs. *domicile*), and so on. Items may seem the same on first encounter (*kingly, royal, regal*), but on closer examination display many individual nuances (we say *royal mail*, not *kingly/regal mail*; *the queen looks very regal*, not *kingly*).
- And antonyms are also unusual. Most of the lexical items in the language do not have opposites. There are indeed several types of oppositeness, such as *big* vs. *small*, *single* vs. *married*, and *employer* vs. *employee*; but most items are not like this. What is the opposite of *furniture, oboe, compete, Tuesday, however, horizon, fax*? Knowing about opposites is important, but it tells only a tiny part of the lexical story of a language.

Far more important are the sense relations of hyponymy and incompatibility (§30). When introducing students to a new lexical item, we would automatically use both. What's a *pterodactyl*? Answer: *It's a kind of prehistoric reptile, which could fly*. This sentence illustrates hyponymy, the relationship of inclusion, and the basic principle of dictionary definition. *Flying* and *prehistoric* tell us in which respects this particular reptile is different from ('is incompatible with') others. A more everyday example would be *clarinet*, which is a type of *woodwind* instrument: it is incompatible with the other woodwind instruments – *oboe, bassoon, flute*, etc. If pressed, we could define the exact features which make these instruments incompatible – their size, tone, how they are played, and so on. That would be to amplify their definitions.

In the real, psycholinguistic world, a definition is not learned all at once; it is learned bit by bit, by adding features of meaning to the account. We must not expect total accuracy first time. To say that a factory is a place where you make things is actually a half-truth. To be precise, according to one dictionary, it is 'a building or group of buildings in which goods are produced in large quantities, using machines' (*The Longman Dictionary of Contemporary English*). That would be too much to take in all at once. Half-truths are best, if we want people to learn. We build up to the total reality gradually, as need requires. In many cases, we stop well short of reality.

Of course, the best semantic explanations give more information than the bare minimum about a new lexical item, showing how it relates to other items within a semantic field. What does *engrossing* mean? All four of the sense relations discussed so far can be helpful, as these informal conversational responses illustrate:

hyponymy: 'it's a kind of feeling . . .'
incompatibility: 'it's like when you're interested in something, only more so . . .'
synonymy: 'it means fascinating, gripping, enthralling . . .'
antonymy: 'it's when you're not bored . . .'

One dictionary definition runs: 'if something engrosses you, it interests you so much that you do not notice anything else', bringing together aspects of all four structural relations.

In studying definitions it is also possible to work the other way round, taking a set of defining attributes (often called semantic *features* or *components*) and seeing which lexeme best captures them. The approach can be briefly illustrated from the lexeme *man*, which can be analysed into the attributes ADULT, HUMAN, and MALE. It is a procedure which was originally devised by anthropologists as a means of comparing vocabulary from different cultures, and many semanticists use it as a general framework for the analysis of meaning. Whole systems of relationships can be established, using a small set of attributes.

Here, for instance, is the opening of a matrix of attributes for some verbs of human motion.

	NATURAL	HURRIED	FORWARD	ONE FOOT ALWAYS ON GROUND	etc.
walk	+	−	+	+	
march	−	+	+	+	
run	−	+	+	−	
limp	−	−	+	+	
etc.					

It is easy, using a system of this kind, to see what *lexical gaps* there are in a language. For example, this matrix suggests there is no single English lexeme expressing the notion of 'limp hurriedly'. Nor does there seem to be a single lexeme to express the notion of 'hurried movement backwards with one foot always on the ground'. Maybe that's a good thing.

The approach can also be used in language teaching. Using the above dictionary, we find the definition of *walk* as: 'to move forward by putting one foot in front of the other'. What might a teacher do with this, to develop a student's sense of the English semantic system? The first step would be to identify the attributes which make up the sense. There are three, as the above diagram suggests: MOVE, FORWARD DIRECTION, and FOOT IN FRONT OF OTHER. Each of these can now be contrasted to point in the direction of other lexemes (all definitions are from the same dictionary):

- MOVE: there is one contrast with 'not move' (*stop*), and others by varying speed or manner:
    'to move very quickly, by moving your legs more quickly than when you walk' – *run*
    'to move very quickly, especially because you need to be somewhere very soon' – *rush*
    'to move by jumping on one foot' – *hop*

- FORWARDS: the contrasts are all with direction – sideways, backwards, upwards, etc:

'to move up, down, or across something using your feet and hands, especially when this is difficult to do' – *climb*

'to walk or move unsteadily from side to side as if you are going to fall over' – *totter*

- ON FOOT: the contrasts here include movement on the ground or in some other medium, or adding another attribute (another part of the body, or another feature of foot-movement, such as the sound it makes):

  'to move yourself through water using your arms and legs' – *swim*

  'to move along on your hands and knees with your body close to the ground' – *crawl*

  'to walk very slowly and noisily, without lifting your feet off the ground' – *shuffle*

Many other lexemes can be interrelated in this way.

This chapter illustrates some of the ways in which system can be introduced into the study of the lexicon. And system is certainly needed. Vocabulary has – by comparison with pronunciation and grammar – received far less attention, in the methodology of language teaching. From my bookshelves I pull down at random a language-teaching text, and open it at random, and find the following list of words to be learned at the end of a particular lesson: *grandmother, attentive, foreign, handkerchief, smooth, pure, tasty, tired, grass* – a list which, from a semantic point of view, is equally random. No such randomness applies to the way sounds and grammatical patterns are introduced in this text. Vocabulary is still something of a poor relation, in language teaching.

32
How children learn to mean

The learning of vocabulary is the most noticeable feature of the early months of language acquisition. From the point when a child's 'first word' ('first lexeme', in the terminology of §30) is identified, there is a steady lexical growth in both comprehension and production. An indication of the scope and speed of progress can be obtained from a study of American one-year-olds: the average time it took eight children to get from ten to fifty words in production was 4.8 months – about ten new words a month. In comprehension, the children understood an average of over twenty new words each month. By eighteen months, it is thought that most children can speak about fifty words and understand about four to five times as many.

Lexical meanings

Young children talk about what is going on around them – the 'here and now' – and rapidly build a vocabulary in several semantic fields (§30). At around eighteen months, most of their words can be grouped into a dozen categories:

- *People*: mainly relatives and house visitors – *daddy, baba, grandma, man, postman*.
- *Actions*: the way things move (*jump, kiss, gone, give*), and routine activities in the child's day (*bye-bye, hello*).

- *Food*: occasions as well as products – *din-din, milk, juice, drink, apple*.
- *Body parts*: usually facial words first (*mouth, nose*), then other areas (*toes, handie(s)*) and body functions (*wee-wee*).
- *Clothing*: of all kinds – *nappy/diaper, shoes, coat*.
- *Animals*: whether real, in pictures, or on TV – *doggie, cat, horse, lion*.
- *Vehicles*: objects and their noises – *car, choo-choo, brrm*.
- *Toys and games*: any possibilities – *ball, bricks, book, dolly, peep-bo*.
- *Household objects*: all to do with daily routine – *cup, spoon, brush, clock, light*.
- *Locations*: several general words – *there, look, in, up*.
- *Describing words*: early adjectives – *hot, pretty, big*.
- *Situational words*: several 'pointing' words – *that, mine, them*.

In addition, they use a number of 'social' words or vocalizations, such as the response utterances *mm, yes, no*, and *ta*.

By age two, spoken vocabulary usually exceeds 200 words. But after this, estimates become extremely vague. A dramatic increase in the size and diversity of the lexicon takes place during the third year, so much so that researchers have not yet been able to make accurate calculations (especially about vocabulary comprehension), or work out any norms of spoken lexical frequency. Three-year-olds have an active vocabulary of at least 2,000 words, and some have far more. By five, the figure is well over 4,000. The suggestion is that they are learning, on average, three or four new words a day. Once they get to school, they are exposed to a huge number of new words. Learning to read also greatly increases vocabulary. A child reading Roald Dahl stories at age nine is being exposed to over 10,000 different words.

We can get a sense of the range of a five-year-old's lexicon from this extract taken from the beginning of a survey made in the 1980s:

> able, about, above, absolutely, accident, accidentally, ache, achy, acorns, acres, across, action, actually, address, advert, advertise, aerial, aeroplane, afraid . . .

The presence of several 'long words' should not be surprising, especially when we reflect on the reading (*beanstalk*, *stepmother*), television programmes (*commercials*, *lottery*), and other experiences (*frankincense*, *myrrh*) many children of that age have experienced. Here are some others, from the same survey:

> *apparatus, beanstalk, blackcurrant, calculator, cardigan, charmingly, chrysalid, crockery, emergency, helicopter, medicine, microphone, parachute, sarcastic, suspension bridge, tonsilitis, truthfully, wallpaper*

Children do not learn such words with their meaning 'ready made'. They have to work out for themselves what words must mean, and in so doing they make errors. It is possible to see their strategies of deduction emerging very early on, during the second and third year. Three types of error have been noticed.

- *Overextension*: They make a word apply to other objects that share a certain feature, such as a common property of shape, colour, or size. *Dog*: might be applied to other animals, or *moon* to other round objects.
- *Underextension*: They use a word more narrowly than its meaning in the adult language. *Dog* might be applied only to the family dog, or *shoes* only to a child's own shoes.
- *Mismatch*: They misapply a word, for no apparent reason, as when in one case a telephone was referred to as a *tractor*. There is usually no way of tracing back the association of ideas that has caused such misidentifications.

These processes are not, of course, restricted to children. Adults learning new words make similar errors (§31).

In the middle of the third year, there is a significant shift in procedure. Children start asking lots of questions about the names of things: *What's that?*, *What's that called?* Parents usually do quite well in replying to these opening questions, but they tend not to be so good in answering the follow-up ones, many of which begin with 'Why?': *Why is it a jackdaw?* Most people cannot answer, other than wearily and emptily:

Because that's its name, Because it is. We find it difficult to say such things as *Because it's a bird and it's black,* as that is not how we are used to using the word *because.* But it is precisely such details that the child is hoping to hear.

The three-year-old period of intense questioning has an important purpose. It is a way in which children find out how words relate to each other. And it is important that adults help in this process, by juxtaposing the new word with familiar ones, as in this parental response: *That's not a horse, that's a zebra. Look, it's got stripes.* Replies of this kind are doing more than teaching about the world; they are teaching the rudiments of definition. The strategy is similar to the procedures that teachers use when they are introducing children to new concepts. Nor does it stop with children. Anyone learning a new subject finds it important to have their new vocabulary related to their old.

Sentence meanings

The study of semantic development in children involves far more than vocabulary. Their learning of grammatical constructions also needs to be studied from a semantic point of view – for example, the way in which they master the complex conditional meaning of *if* constructions, or the causal meaning of *because, so,* or *since.* That there are problems here can be readily shown from the errors they make. Here are some typical sentences from young primary-school children grappling with the meaning of *because.*

- The second part of the sentence says more about the first part:

  We got a new cat, because it was called Katie.

- One event follows the other in time, but does not cause it:

  I hurt my leg because I had to go to the doctor's.

- The second part of the sentence explains how someone knew what happened in the first part:

  There was an awful crash because my dad saw it.

The children have evidently mastered the grammar of such constructions very well, but they are still having difficulty with the meanings they encode.

Several other areas of grammar cause semantic difficulty, even after children arrive in school. The difference between active and passive constructions (*the panda chased the rabbit, the panda was chased by the rabbit*) is not fully mastered by many children until around eight or nine. They have trouble with the meanings of such auxiliary verbs as *ought, must,* and *should.* And there are subtle verb contrasts to be learned, such as the difference between *ask* and *tell, say* and *promise,* or *lend* and *borrow.*

The ability to use figurative expressions, and to see double meanings in language, also develops largely after the age of six. Asked to complete a comparison: *The bus was as big as –*, very young children do little more than repeat themselves: many say *as big as big.* Pre-school children do somewhat better, but most keep their comparisons short and conventional: *as big as a giant, as big as you.* Seven-year-olds remain quite literal-minded, preferring concrete comparisons: *as big as a mountain, as big as a tree.* Occasionally, though, we encounter some quite poetic or dramatic comparisons: *as big as a rainbow, as big as a spaceship.* These more imaginative comparisons become increasingly evident at older ages.

Learning to define

Semantic development continues throughout the school years – and, indeed, throughout adult life. Unlike phonology and grammar, it is not largely over by the time children enter their teens. There is always new vocabulary to be learned, and new worlds of meaning to explore. And some of the semantic strategies learned in the school years will be repeatedly used. One of the most significant developments of this kind is the ability to integrate several features of semantic knowledge into a single defining statement. It is a process that takes several years to complete.

Young children, around age three, cannot define. In response to such questions as *What's X?*, they give empty, ambiguous, or idiosyncratic replies. 'What's a shoe?' asked an adult. *That*, replied one young child, pointing. *And a sock*, replied another. *Mummy got a shoe*, replied a third.

Gradually, definitions become more sophisticated – as we would expect if they have assimilated the parental efforts to respond effectively to their *Why?* questions. A more mature stage involves the children introducing an example from their own experience. 'What's a bicycle?' *I ride on and fall off*, replied one four-year-old – a response which may be true for that particular child, but hardly a defining feature of bicycles in general. Another strategy at this age is for single attributes to be used as if they were sufficient explanations. 'What's an umbrella?' *It's black.*

Before long, the feature which children single out becomes the critical one or its primary function is specified. They say such things as *A knife is sharp* or *A knife is when you cut with it.* The development in definitional phrasing is important. If children say *when you . . .* or *you could . . .* they are demonstrating their awareness that word meanings are shared by others. It shows a developing sense that definitions are generalizations.

Around age eight or nine, statements begin to be produced with something resembling an adult definitional form, with hyponyms (p. 196) and attributes: *An apple is a sort of fruit, and it's round and red, and we eat it.* But it is not until the early teens that we find definitions phrased in a truly adult way: *A bus is a vehicle which has lots of seats and carries passengers for money.* By this time, of course, schooling has exposed children to the world of the dictionary.

33
How dictionaries work

A dictionary is a reference book that lists the words of one or more languages, usually in alphabetical order, along with information about their spelling, pronunciation, grammatical status, meaning, history, and use. The process of compiling dictionaries is known as *lexicography*, and the people who carry out this task are *lexicographers*.

In literate societies, most homes have a dictionary, but there is enormous variation in the way this is used. Some people constantly use them as a serious educational tool, aiming to improve their own or their children's 'word power'. Others use them only for fun – as the arbiter in a game of Scrabble, for instance. Others do not use them at all and do not replace them when they fall badly out of date. The continued use of ten- or twenty-year-old dictionaries is by no means uncommon.

For a book that is viewed with a level of respect normally accorded only to the Bible, it is remarkable how casually dictionary-users treat their dictionaries. A few years ago, a survey asked people what factors governed their choice of dictionary. Most cited linguistically irrelevant matters, such as price, pictorial content, and size – not in terms of number of entries, but whether it would fit on a shelf, or in a pocket. Most admitted they had never bothered to read the Preface to their dictionary – the place where the layout and conventions of the book are systematically explained. As a consequence they were unable to say what the various abbreviations and symbols meant, or why they were there. The general conclusion is inescapable: most people who would check out every tiny feature of their new car before buying it are unaware of the power that lies under the bonnet of their dictionary.

Evaluating dictionaries

Dictionaries are as diverse as cars, compiled to respond to the demands of all kinds of linguistic terrains. They can be classified in many ways. One dimension is whether they are monolingual, bilingual, or multilingual. Another is whether they are dictionaries of the contemporary language or whether they have a historical dimension. Another is whether they include encyclopedic information (such as about people, places, and historical events), as traditional American dictionaries do, or whether they restrict their coverage to purely linguistic entities – the nouns, verbs, adjectives, and other word classes of a language – as traditional British dictionaries do.

The distinction between coverage and treatment is fundamental. Advertisements for dictionaries usually focus on their size – defined in terms of the number of words (or *lexemes*, as described in §30) they include. But these claims have to be viewed with caution, because '50,000 words', for example, can mean several different things. It might refer just to the number of *headwords* in the dictionary – that is, the bold-face items that occur at the beginning of each entry. Or it might include in addition all the subsidiary bold-face items that occur within an entry: under *sad*, for example, there will be -*ly* and -*ness*. Different word classes might be counted separately (e.g. *play* noun vs. *play* verb), as might idioms, and irregular grammatical forms (e.g. *go, went*). Depending on what you decide to count, you can end up with two very different totals for the same dictionary.

The best way to evaluate the coverage of a dictionary is to compare the words and senses it includes with another dictionary of about the same size. It is notable how even the largest dictionaries present great differences in their coverage – the variation being particularly noticeable in the way they treat world regional vocabulary, local dialect words, abbreviations, slang and sub-standard forms, new coinages and borrow-ings. How many Australian, South African, or West Indian forms does an English dictionary include, for example? It has been estimated that the lack of correspondence in large English dictionaries can be as great as 50% – indicating that a truly comprehensive dictionary of the language has yet to be compiled.

There are many variables to be considered under the heading of treatment. First and foremost is the kind of information provided about each entry. Obviously there is a certain basic minimum of information to be included if a work is to count as a dictionary at all. It must contain a list of words, organized alphabetically, and it must contain a list of the senses of each word. But both of these criteria can be amplified in various ways, and these variables can be used as criteria for evaluating dictionaries.

How sophisticated is the word-list? Does it include variations in spelling (such as British and American) and capitalization? Does it indicate how the word is to be split at the end of a line (where to hyphenate)? Does it include abbreviations? Does it give the word's grammatical status – its word class, or part of speech? Does it show the word's inflectional endings? Does it give the word's pronunciation, along with any variations? If so, what sort of representation is used – a phonetic transcription, such as IPA (p. 53) or a re-spelling convention (e.g. *essential* as *isenshul*).

How sophisticated are the definitions? Are they easy to understand? Do they use a defining vocabulary (that is, a 'pool' of basic words on which all definitions draw)? Do they provide helpful alternatives, so that vicious circularity is avoided (as when X is defined as Y, and Y is then defined as X)? Do they show how words work by illustrating their use in sentences – and, if so, are the sentences artificially composed by the editors or are they real examples taken from a specially collected corpus?

Most modern dictionaries do not restrict themselves to basic words and definitions. They add information about how words are used in society. There will be stylistic labels, such as *formal*, *slang*, *medical*, or *archaic*. They will include idioms and perhaps longer lexical units, such as proverbs, catch-phrases, and aphorisms. There may be usage essays, focusing on points of uncertainty, such as the distinction between *disin-*

terested and *uninterested*. The words may be placed in a historical perspective, showing their origins and development – their *etymology*.

The best dictionaries these days try to get to grips with semantic structure (§30). They show how words are related to each other in meaning, by listing synonyms and antonyms, grouping words into semantic sets, identifying important collocations (p. 194), and so on. There can be tables of related words, such as military ranks, or appendices dealing with such matters as weights and measures. There may be pictures, illustrating the words identifying the parts of an entity (such as a car engine) or simply illustrating a concept which a definition finds difficult to capture (such as a spiral staircase).

Lexicographical history

The earliest dictionaries had a practical aim. They were often bilingual or polyglot word-lists aimed at the traveller and the missionary, or glossaries written to help people understand words which were dialectal, technical, or rare. The history of lexicography in fact goes back over 2,000 years, to ancient China, Greece, and Rome. From as early as the 5th century BC, the Greeks were compiling *glossai*, explaining difficult words in such authors as Homer. The first vocabulary lists in English were similar: these were 8th-century Anglo-Saxon glosses, in which English words were written between the Latin lines. Later, these glosses were collected together as lists. But random collections of words or glosses are not dictionaries: to count as a dictionary, the words need to be organized in a systematic way – such as through the use of the alphabetical principle.

There has never been a historical period when some kind of lexicographical work was not in progress. Hsu Shen compiled the first systematic Chinese dictionary in the 2nd century AD. The Hindu grammarian Amarasimha compiled a Sanskrit dictionary in the 6th century. Arabic dictionaries flourished from around the 8th century onwards. There was a flurry of activity in several languages following the invention of printing. The *Vocabolista italiano-tedesco,* printed in Venice in 1477, was the earliest printed bilingual dictionary. The Accademia della Crusca, in Italy, produced its dictionary in 1612 (the first to be compiled by a team of people), and prompted several other national dictionary projects.

Polyglot dictionaries were particularly numerous in the 17th century, with the development of trade and missionary activities around the world. The 18th century saw a fresh direction in lexicography, following the discoveries of the comparative philologists (§55), and the first major historical dictionaries began to be compiled. The 19th century saw many large-scale dictionary projects, produced by teams of compilers, and several specialized dictionaries (such as of dialect or technical words). The 20th century saw the development of lexicography as a scholarly subject, largely under the influence of linguistics, and promoted especially by the growth of academic societies, such as the European Association for Lexicography (EURALEX, 1983).

Leading lexicographers

In the history of English lexicographers, some writers hold a special place. Credit for the first monolingual English dictionary is usually given to Robert Cawdrey, whose *A Table Alphabeticall...*, a work of around 2,500 entries, was printed in 1604. In 1755, Samuel Johnson (1709–84) published his great dictionary in two volumes, a work whose influence on subsequent lexicography was unequalled. That dictionary was very different from previous English works:

- It aimed to be a scholarly record of the whole of a language – a marked contrast with the haphazard dictionaries of 'hard words' previously compiled.
- It was based on a corpus of examples of usage, largely from the period 1560 to 1660.
- It introduced a literary dimension, departing from the previous concentration on technical language. Half of all Johnson's quotations come from Shakespeare, Dryden, Milton, Addison, Bacon, Pope, and the Bible. The dictionary is very much the language of the 'best' authors.

Dictionaries became more authoritative – and authoritarian – as a consequence. They were increasingly used in a normative way, as guides to good usage – a bias which did not begin to be corrected until the 20th century.

The works of Noah Webster (1758–1843) on spelling, grammar, and lexicon constituted the first major account of American English, and gave that variety a clear identity and status. *An American Dictionary of the English Language*, published in two volumes in 1828, consisted of around 70,000 entries. Particular attention was paid to the inclusion of scientific terms, and to etymological background. The latest revision is the *Third New International Dictionary* (Merriam, 1961), containing over 450,000 entries, which took 757 editor-years to complete. Supplements appeared in 1976, 1983, and 1986.

James Murray (1837–1915) was the editor of what was originally called the *New English Dictionary*. He planned the whole of the dictionary, and he edited more than half of its first edition himself. The first instalment was published in 1884. It took 44 years to complete the dictionary, in 125 instalments – four times longer than had been expected. The complete work, totalling 424,825 entries, was then published as the *Oxford English Dictionary* (*OED*) from 1933 onwards, with four supplements issued from 1972. An integrated edition appeared in 1989, and was later released on CD.

Since the 1970s, the flow of dictionaries has been unabated, as publishers try to meet the needs of an increasingly language-conscious age. In English, for example, new editions and supplements to the well-known dictionaries have appeared, and several publishers have launched new general series. Prominent also have been the dictionaries for special purposes (foreign language teaching, linguistics, medicine, chemistry, etc.). For the first time, spoken vocabulary has begun to find its way into dictionaries (though by no means all are yet willing to include the more colloquial words and uses).

The 1980s was the decade in which computer applications began to radically alter the methods and the potential of lexicography. The future is online, in the form of vast lexical databases, continuously updated, that can generate a dictionary of a given size and scope in a fraction of the time it used to take. We can now interrogate lexical databases in ways unimaginable a generation ago, finding all the words that entered the language in a particular year, or all words containing a particular ending or letter-sequence. Databanks of examples enable us to see how words are used in real-world contexts. Multimedia technology allows us to hear pronunciations and see colourful encyclopedic links. The emphasis today is on presentation and accessibility. Lexicography has moved into a new world of dynamic design.

34

How names work

In traditional British (but not American) reference publishing, dictionaries and encyclopedias show very little overlap in their coverage. Common nouns, verbs, and so on are dealt with in dictionaries: the 'proper names' of people, places, and things are dealt with in encyclopedias. It is a distinction which is slowly breaking down, as publishers come to realize that, in the popular mind, the difference is not at all clear. Words cross the divide – *Whitehall* and *The White House*, for example, have both a particular meaning (locations in London and Washington, respectively) and a general meaning (the voice of the respective governments). A new generation of hybrid 'lexicopedic' works (combining lexicographical and encyclopedic information) is a likely outcome.

From a linguistic point of view, names have idiosyncratic properties, reflecting the fact that they refer to entities as individuals, and not as members of a class. *Everest*, for example, is a unique name (a *proper noun*), whereas *mountain* applies to a whole class of objects (a *common noun*). In the written language, European languages generally recognize the distinction by writing names with an initial capital letter. But many writing systems do not distinguish upper- and lower-case letters, and even in Europe there are several arbitrary conventions and points of uncertainty. English, for example, is idiosyncratic in its use of capitals for days of the week and proper adjectives (as in *the Chinese language*). And decisions have to be made over whether one writes *the moon* or *the Moon*, *the church* or *the Church*, *bible* or *Bible*.

The science that studies names is known as *onomastics*. It is usually divided into the study of personal names (*anthroponomastics*) and place names (*toponomastics*). In more popular usage, however, the term *onomastics* is used for the former, and *toponymy* for the latter. The division is ultimately an arbitrary one, as places are often named after people (e.g. *Washington*) and vice versa (e.g. *Israel* is sometimes used as a first name). Other categories of name (such as ships, trains, yachts, domestic pets, race horses, and commercial products) also need to be taken into account. But most name studies fall under one of the two major headings.

Personal names

Most people are familiar with only one personal naming system, and are surprised to learn that practices differ greatly from language to language. Even such a basic distinction as *given name* (or *Christian name*) and *family name* (or *surname*) is not universal. In Europe, it began to be used only in the late Middle Ages, reaching some areas only as recently as the 19th century. These names are also often referred to as 'first' and 'last' names; but this nomenclature is ambiguous when comparing languages, as there is considerable variation in the order in which such names occur. In most European languages, the family name follows the given name; but the reverse is the case in, say, Hungarian and Chinese (e.g. *Mao Ze-Dong*).

In some societies, a middle name is also regularly used. This is the case in America, for instance, where an initial is especially favoured (e.g. *John H. Smith*). In Europe, middle names are less common, unless acquired at a special occasion (such as the Catholic ceremony of Confirmation). Where there is a sequence of names, there may also be variation in levels of importance. In Britain, for example, the first name is the important one – *David Michael Smith* would usually be referred to as *David*; in Germany, the name nearest to the surname is more important – *Johann Wolfgang Schmidt* would usually be referred to as *Wolfgang*.

Some languages make use of *patronymics* – a name derived from the father's given name: in Russian, Ivan's son would be known as *Ivanovich*, and his daughter as *Ivanovna*. The opposite practice of naming a parent after a child (*teknonymy*) is less common, but is widespread in the Arab world, for example, where a parent is often called 'father of' or 'mother of' the eldest son. In Russian, the patronymic is placed between the child's given and family names. In Icelandic, the patronymic serves as the surname, which then changes with each generation. Amharic names consist simply of the child's given name plus the father's given name. In English, patronymic prefixes and suffixes are used only in family names (e.g. *Robertson*), and this is common throughout Europe (e.g. 'son of' appears in Scots *Mac/Mc-*, Irish *O'*, Welsh *Ap*, Polish *-ski*, Russian *-ovich*).

There are some impressive similarities in naming practice across different languages, such as the use of names based on professions. *Smith*, and its foreign-language equivalents, is the best-known case, being the most common surname in many parts of Europe: Arabic *Haddad*, Hungarian *Kovács*, Russian *Kuznetsov*, Portuguese *Ferreiro*, German *Schmidt*, Spanish *Hernández/Fernández*, French *Le Fèvre/La Forge*, and so on. But the differences in naming practices are far more striking.

The possibilities of variation seem endless. We find the tripartite personal names of the Romans (e.g. *Gaius Julius Caesar*), the compound names of early Germans and Celts (e.g. *Orgetorix* 'king of killers'), and the use of *by-names* to distinguish people who have the same name (e.g. Welsh *Dai Jones-the-milk* vs. *Dai Jones-the-post*). In Europe, there is a great diversity of given and family names. By contrast, in several oriental societies the possibilities are highly restricted – for example, just three family names, *Kim*, *Pak*, and *Yi*, are used by most of the people of Korea.

We find children named after saints, events, places, omens, personal traits – even animals (as with Native North Americans, e.g. *Little Bear*). In some societies, divine names can be used (*theophoric* names, such as Greek *Herodotus* 'given by Hera' or Arabic *Abd Allah* 'slave of Allah'). At the opposite extreme, children might be named after unpleasant notions to make them undesirable to evil spirits (*apotropaic* names, such as 'cripple' or 'ugly'). Where personal names are concerned, there seems to be no limit to parental idiosyncrasy and invention, two fine examples being the

Puritan given name *Kill Sin*, and the Russian concoction *Mels* – an acronym for 'Marx-Engels-Lenin-Stalin'.

First names

In 1623, the historian and antiquary William Camden (1551–1623) published an appendix to his guide book to Britain, in which he included a long list of the most popular given names and surnames of his time. Since then, there have been several academic studies of given names in a wide range of European languages, and many popular accounts, aimed especially at providing information for parents who do not know what to call their baby.

The studies are both etymological and statistical. The former have universal appeal. People are fascinated by the history of names – in particular, where their own name comes from and how its usage has changed over the centuries. For example, *Hilary* is from Latin *hilarius*, meaning 'cheerful'. It has been used by three male saints (including one Pope), and it has continued as a male name in Europe. However, in Britain, it fell out of use in the 17th century, and when it revived in the 1890s, it was usually as a female name. Its peak British usage was during the 1950s and 1960s.

Interesting though the origin of a name may be, it exercises very little influence on most parental choice and is of little value in the study of naming trends. Far more important is the recent history of the name in a society – whether it has been used by parents or near relatives, or by famous individuals such as film stars, pop stars, or members of a royal family. Nations have different traditions in this respect. Britain and America permit all possible names, whereas in France and Germany there are approved lists of names that must be used if a child is to be legally recognized. The influence of a religious tradition (as in the Catholic use of saints' names) is often of particular significance.

Information about name use over the years comes from a variety of sources such as parish records, national censuses, newspaper birth announcements, and special surveys by name scholars and enthusiasts. There has, for example, been a survey of every first name used by the Smiths in England and Wales since 1837. In the case of English, it is also important to consider all parts of the English-speaking world to discover whether there have been directions of influence.

Place names

The names people give to their surroundings provide a unique source of information about a society's history, beliefs, and values. There are so many aspects of a country's development that achieve linguistic recognition in its place names. The various steps in the exploration of America, for example, can be seen reflected in the 'layers' of Spanish, French, Dutch, Indian, and English names introduced by different groups of explorers; and Celtic, Roman, Anglo-Saxon, Scandinavian, and Norman names provide a similar insight into British history. Often, a place name is the only record of a historical event or of a person's existence. The name of *Reada*, 'the red', lives on in the town of *Reading*, in Berkshire, UK ('the people of Reada'); but of his life and deeds, nothing else is known.

The study of place names includes the 'small' places and institutions (such as names of streets, houses, inns, and fields) as well as the main geographical features of the world (such as seas, rivers, mountains, cities, and towns); but most academic study has been in relation to the latter. Place names are sometimes fanciful and idiosyncratic (e.g. USA *Rabbit Hash*, Britain *Thertheoxlaydede* 'there the ox lay dead', or jocular house names such as *Webiltit* and *Noname*), but the vast majority can be explained with reference to a small set of creative processes. With geographical names, some of the most widespread types of derivation include the following:

- natural features, such as hills, rivers, and coast-lines, e.g. *Dover* (water), *Staines* (stones), *Honolulu* (safe harbour), *Rotorua* (two lakes), Kalgoorlie (a native shrub), *Twin Forks*, *South Bend*;
- special sites, such as camps and forts, e.g. *Doncaster* (camp on the Don), *Barrow* (burial mound);
- religious significance, such as gods, saints, and churches, e.g. *Providence*, *Godshill*, *Axminster*, *St Neots*, *Sacramento*, *Santa Cruz*, *Thorsley* (from *Thor*);

- royalty, e.g. *Queensland, Victoria Falls, Carolina, Kingston, Louisiana, Maryland, Fredericksburg*;
- explorers, e.g. *America, Cookstown, Columbus, Flinders*;
- famous local people, such as presidents, politicians, tribesmen, e.g. *Delaware, Baltimore, Washington, Everest, Reading, London* (town of *Londinos* – 'the bold one');
- memorable incidents or famous events, such as a battle, e.g. *Waterloo, Crimea, Blenheim, Cape Catastrophe, Anxious Bay, Manhattan* ('the place of great drunkenness'); and
- other place names, such as a famous city, or a town from an immigrant's home-land, e.g. in the USA *Paris, Memphis, Troy, Hertford, London*.

Many other factors have been recognized. There are the appealing names introduced by explorers as they encountered good and bad fortune on their travels (e.g. *Cape Tribulation* and *Weary Bay* in Australia). Animal names are sometimes used (e.g. *Beaver City, Buffalo*). And there are many names of a purely descriptive type, such as *North Sea, South Island*, and – perhaps the most common place name of all – the 'new town' (*Newtown, Neuville, Naples, Villanueva, Novgorod, Neustadt*, and – less obviously, because of its Phoenician origin – *Carthage*). By contrast, there seem to be few names derived from famous writers and artists: there is a distinct paucity of towns called *Shakespeare, Voltaire*, or *Tolstoy*.

Place names have an intrinsic fascination, and many specialized studies have been undertaken. But it must not be forgotten that many thousands of names have an unclear or unknown etymology, and it is this which provides a continuing motivation for place-name study, such as is carried on by the English Place-Name Society, the American Name Society, and similar bodies. These studies also relate to matters of practical import. To facilitate international communication by post, telex, and telephone, the various problems posed by linguistic place-name variation need to be anticipated. Place names can vary greatly between languages (e.g. *Munich* vs. *München*) and be unrecognizable in different scripts. Names can change along with governments, as in the switching between *St Petersburg* and

Leningrad during different political systems in Russia. New systems of naming may need to be introduced for special purposes, such as with domain names on the Internet, or as a means of designating stellar objects (e.g. *NGC 4565*, *M101*). There is thus a pressing need for international cooperation in the coining and use of place names – a need that can only become more urgent as the Internet grows and the exploration of space proceeds.

35
How vocabulary grows

Vocabulary never stands still. New words continually arrive in a language, and old words disappear. We tend to notice the former and not the latter. The arrival of a new word may even attract newspaper coverage. Each time a new edition of a major dictionary is published, several of the new words it has included are circulated as a press release, and the items regularly make the front pages. By contrast, no obituaries of dying words are ever published – for the simple reason that it is impossible to say when a word has died out until well after it has happened. We know now that words like *leman* ('sweetheart'), and *hie* ('hasten'), found in Shakespeare, are no longer used. But what was the last year in which somebody used *leman*? We shall never know.

Borrowing

In most languages, the vast majority of new words are in fact *borrowings* from other languages – though this term is not especially appropriate, as the words are not given back at a later stage! Borrowing proceeds in all directions. *Weekend* and *parking* have been borrowed by French from English; *chic* and *savoir-faire* have been borrowed by English from French. Some languages have borrowed so extensively that native words are in a minority. English is a case in point, as it has sucked in words from over 350 other languages, and less than a quarter of its word-stock actually reflects its Germanic origins. English has always been a vacuum-cleaner of a language.

Loan words are especially in evidence as a language becomes international in its usage, because it comes into increasing contact with other languages, and exchanges words with them. English, as a global language, had its vocabulary hugely increased during the 20th century, for that reason. A dictionary of South African English, for example, contains thousands of words from Afrikaans, Zulu, Xhosa, and the other indigenous languages of southern Africa. A short selection from the opening pages of one such dictionary contains the entries on *aandag*, *aandblom*, *aap*, *aar*, *aardpyp*, *aardvark*, *aardwolf*, *aas*, and *aasvoël* (all from Afrikaans) as well as *abadala*, *abafazi*, *abakhaya*, *abakwetha*, *abantu*, *abaphansi*, *abathagathi*, and *abelungu* (all from Nguni languages). These are all words used, it should be noted, in published *English* sources. They are for the most part unintelligible outside of South Africa.

South Africa has ten official languages from which English can borrow words (or vice versa). In Nigeria, where over 400 languages are spoken, the potential for loan-word exchange is very much greater. Words from many of these languages are now heard in the local varieties of English spoken throughout the area as a lingua franca. Quite a few enter the written language, such as in menus, where the names of local foods and recipes are widely in evidence: examples include *agidi*, *gari*, *eba*, *iyan*, *edikagong*, *suya*, *dodo*, *foofoo*, *moinmoin*, and *efo elegusi* – all found on the *English*-language menu of one Nigerian restaurant.

A special type of borrowing is known as a *loan translation* or *calque*. In this process, a word is not borrowed whole, but its parts are translated separately and a new word formed – as when German produced the equivalent of English *telephone* in *Fernsprecher* (literally, *fern* 'distant' + *sprecher* 'speaker'). The South African situation has resulted in many such examples, such as *afterclap* and *after-ox*, from Afrikaans *agter* + *klap* 'flap' and *agter* + *os*, respectively. There are also many hybrid forms where a foreign root is given an English affix, as in *Afrikanerdom* and *Afrikanerism*, or where two languages are involved in a blend, as in *Anglikaans*.

Changing structures

Another common process of word creation is the formation of new words out of old ones, or out of the parts of old ones. In the case of *compounds*, two or more whole words are combined to function as a single item. So, *scarecrow* does not refer to two independent notions, of *scaring* and *crows*, but to an object whose purpose is to scare crows. Such words are pronounced as single units, with a single stress, and they are used grammatically as a single unit: the plural is *scarecrows*. Thousands of compounds exist in English, written either solid (*flowerpot*) or with a hyphen (*flower-pot*), and sometimes printed as separate words (*flower pot*). The latter possibility makes them more difficult to identify, of course: a *hot dog* is just a warm animal, but a *hot dog* as a compound word is something you can eat.

Very similar to compounds are formations where one of the elements is a whole word and the other is not, as in *agriculture*, *biotechnology*, *Eurodollar*, *technophobia*, and *workaholic*. They are traditionally found in the domains of science and scholarship, but in recent years some have become productive in everyday contexts too, especially in advertising and commerce.

Most formations of this kind involve additional elements called *affixes*, which in English are of two types: *prefixes*, occurring before the stem of a word, and *suffixes*, occurring after (§37). English does not have affixes in large numbers – about fifty common prefixes and somewhat fewer common suffixes. Prefixes include, *dis-*, *mal-*, *ex-*, and *semi-*, as in *disinterested*, *malformed*, *ex-husband*, and *semi-detached*. Suffixes include *-ship*, *-ness*, *-ette*, and *-let*, as in *hardship*, *goodness*, *kitchenette*, and *booklet*. Clusters of affixes can be used to build up complex words:

> nation, national, nationalize, nationalization
> denationalization, antidenationalization

Over half the words in English are there because of processes of this kind. And this is one reason why children's vocabulary grows so quickly (p. 205), once they learn some prefixes and suffixes.

It is also possible to make new words by changing the function of old words in a sentence: for example, a noun used as a verb, or vice versa. The process is called *conversion* or *functional shift*, and it has been an important process in the history of English (less so in languages which make use of many inflectional endings). Verbs have become nouns in such cases as *a swim*, *a cheat*, and *a bore*. Nouns have become verbs in *to bottle* and *to referee*, and adjectives in *reproduction furniture* and *brick wall*. Adjectives have become nouns in *a regular* and *a monthly*, and verbs in *to dirty* and *to empty*. Other word-classes are sometimes found, as in *to down tools* (preposition becomes verb) and *ifs and buts* (conjunctions become nouns).

Several other types of word formation exist. *Reduplicated* words are those like *goody-goody* and *flip-flop*, where the constituents are the same or very similar in sound. We also make many new words by abbreviating others. *Abbreviations* are of several kinds. *Initialisms* are spoken as individual letters, as with *BBC* and *MP*. *Acronyms* are pronounced as single words, such as *NATO* and *UNESCO*. *Clippings* are shortened words, where a part is used for the whole, as in *exam* and *ad*. *Blends* join the shortened forms of two words together, as in *brunch* and *smog*.

Changing meaning

When a word or sense ceases to be used, it is said to be *obsolescent* or *obsolete*. This often happens because an object or concept is no longer of value to a community, other than to the historian or literary scholar. But a word or sense may become obsolescent if it develops unpleasant associations, or is replaced by another word which is felt to be more modern. *Wight* ('person'), *leman* ('sweetheart'), and *hie* ('hasten'), are examples from Elizabethan English which are now no longer used; *humour* (= 'temperament') and *conceit* (= 'idea') illustrate obsolete senses from the same period.

There are several types of semantic change. In *extension* or *generalization*, a word widens its meaning: in Latin, for example, *virtue* was a male quality (*vir* is Latin for 'man'); today, it applies to both sexes. *Office* and *novice* were originally restricted to religious domains in English. The opposite process is *narrowing* or *specialization*, where a word becomes more specialized in meaning. In Old English, *mete* referred to food in general (a sense which is retained in *sweetmeat*); today, it refers to only one kind of food (*meat*). *Art* originally had some very general meanings, mostly connected to 'skill'; today, it refers just to certain kinds of skill, chiefly in relation to aesthetic skill – 'the arts'.

A more radical kind of change occurs in *semantic shift*, where a word moves from one set of circumstances to another. *Navigator* once applied only to ships, but it now applies to planes, and even to cars. Quite often, the shift is based upon an analogy or likeness between things; for example, a *crane*, a bird with a long neck, has led to the use of *crane* as a piece of equipment for lifting weights.

Attitudinal nuances are an important part of semantic change. In the case of *amelioration*, a word loses an original sense of disapproval. *Mischievous*, for example, has lost its strong sense of 'disastrous', and now means the milder 'playfully annoying'. The opposite effect is *pejoration*, where a word develops a sense of disapproval. An example here is *notorious*, which once meant 'widely known', and which now means 'widely and unfavourably known'.

Lexical change exercises a continual fascination, because it is profoundly connected with the life, literature, and culture of a community. Innumerable examples can be found in the pages of old books, or simply by careful watching and listening to everyday usage. But plotting the history of the changes in the form, meaning, and use of words and morphemes is difficult work, because the evidence is often lacking. To find out about lexical history, or *etymology*, the best source of information is a dictionary which has been written on historical principles, such as the *Oxford English Dictionary*. Many languages also have specialized etymological dictionaries.

Tracing the history of words can result in some surprising etymologies. Only by a careful exploration of older usage can we see why, for example, *treacle* once had the meaning of 'wild animal', *villain* was once 'farm labourer', or *cheater* once meant 'rent collector'. *Grammar* and *glamour* share a common origin, as do *salary* and *sausage*, and *sly* and *slay*. In these etymologies, the senses have evolved naturally and gradually over time. Many abstract words are continually changing their meaning, as people apply new interpretations to them. The varied history of the word *culture* is a well-known case in point.

Rather different are *folk etymologies*, also called *popular etymologies*, where people hear a foreign or unfamiliar word and try to make sense of it by relating it to words they know well. They guess what it must mean – but guess wrongly. However, if enough people make the same guess, the error becomes part of the language. This is how *sparrow-grass* has come to be a colloquial way of referring to *asparagus* – even though the vegetable has nothing to do with sparrows.

One thing to avoid is the *etymological fallacy* – the view that an earlier meaning of a word, or its original meaning, is the true or correct one. It is commonly heard in arguments, when people appeal to what a word once meant in order to justify their position. When Sigmund Freud was investigating hysteria, he encountered resistance from his colleagues, who argued that, because the term *hysteria* derived from the Greek word for 'womb', the concept of male hysteria was a contradiction in terms. The argument is fallacious because it ignores semantic change. Most words have experienced several changes in meaning throughout their history, so that it is impossible to say which stage in their meaning is the 'true' meaning. And if we attempt to go back to 'the beginning', we find it is impossible, for the original history of most words is quite lost.

36

How we study grammar

No other subject in this book elicits so many different reactions and attitudes as grammar. This is partly because it has been the focus of scholarly attention over the past fifty years, resulting in a remarkable range of widely differing approaches. But it is also because this subject, like no other in the field of language study, has been substantially affected by generational change. The dates below are those which defined the situation in Britain, but the same trend emerged in most parts of the English-speaking world, and was apparent in relation to several other languages as well.

- If you went to school before the 1960s, you would have been taught about your language using *traditional grammar* – an approach which for English dates from the end of the 18th century. This would have given you a set of techniques for analysing sentences (*parsing*) and a *prescriptive* conception of grammar which would have instilled in your mind a firm set of opinions about correct and incorrect usage (§69).

- If you went to school between the 1960s and mid-1990s, you would have been taught little or no grammar at all. Instead, you would have been introduced to ways of investigating aspects of selected uses of language in society. As a result, you would now have only a vague and unsystematic appreciation of sentence structure and little understanding of grammatical terminology.

- If you went to school after the mid-1990s, you would have found a resurgence of interest in grammar, as part of the new National Curriculum, in which techniques of grammatical enquiry were re-introduced, underpinned by a concern to explain their meanings and effects in communication, and avoiding the old prescriptive biases. This has introduced a new momentum into the study of grammar, and given a new generation of young adults a fresh sense of its importance.

Under these circumstances, it is plain that people will have different expectations about the subject, and approach the question of 'How grammar works' in different ways.

Many types of grammar

Grammars can be written for several reasons, and the mention of 'school' above illustrates one of them. Grammars used in schools are *pedagogical grammars* – designed specifically for teaching a foreign language, or for developing an awareness of the mother tongue. Such 'teaching grammars' are widely used, so much so that many people have only one meaning for the term *grammar*: a grammar book. However, it is possible to write a 'teaching grammar' in two very different ways.

- *By prescribing*: A prescriptive grammar is essentially a manual that focuses on constructions where usage is divided, and lays down rules governing the socially correct use of language. These grammars were a formative influence on language attitudes in Europe and America during the 18th and 19th centuries. Their influence lives on in the handbooks of usage widely found today, such as *A Dictionary of Modern English Usage* (1926) by Henry Watson Fowler (1858–1933), though such books include recommendations about the use of pronunciation, spelling, and vocabulary, as well as grammar.
- *By describing*: A descriptive grammar describes the form, meaning, and use of grammatical units and constructions in a language, without making any evaluative judgements about their standing in society.

These grammars became commonplace in 20th-century linguistics, where it was standard practice to investigate a *corpus* of spoken or written material, and to describe in detail the patterns it contains.

- When a descriptive grammar acts as a reference guide to all patterns of usage in a language, it is often called a *reference grammar*. An example is *A Comprehensive Grammar of the English Language* (1985) by Randolph Quirk (1920–) and his associates. Such grammars are not primarily pedagogical in intent, as their aim – like that of a 'reference lexicon', or unabridged dictionary – is to be as comprehensive as possible. They provide a sourcebook of data from which writers of pedagogical grammars can draw their material.

All these approaches have one thing in common: they are grammars of a particular language. By contrast, much of 20th-century linguistics has been devoted to an approach usually called *theoretical grammar*. Here, investigators are not interested in the study of an individual language, such as English or Chinese, but in the grammatical properties of language in general. The aim is to establish what constructs and principles are needed in order to do any kind of grammatical analysis, and to determine how these apply in the investigation of any human language.

Two steps can usually be distinguished in the linguistic study of grammar. The first is to identify meaningful units or patterns in the stream of speech (or writing, or signing) and to name them – units such as *word*, *sentence*, *adjective*, and *passive*. The second step is to analyse the meanings and effects that these units and patterns convey. Depending upon which units we recognize at the beginning of the study, so the definition of grammar alters. Most approaches begin by recognizing the *sentence*, and grammar is thus most widely defined as 'the study of sentence structure'. Some approaches take the *word* as the starting point, and sometimes other units (e.g. *clauses*) are proposed.

In the opening pages of the most influential grammatical treatise of recent times, *Syntactic Structures* (1957), the American linguist Noam Chomsky (1928–) writes that a grammar is a 'device of some sort for producing the sentences of the language under analysis', to which is added the rider that the sentences produced must be grammatical ones, acceptable to the native speaker. A grammar of a language, from this point of view, is an account of the language's possible sentence structures, organized according to certain general principles.

Within this general perspective there is room for many different positions. In particular, there are two quite distinct applications of the term *grammar*, yielding both a general and a specific sense. The general sense, popularized by Chomsky, subsumes all aspects of sentence patterning under the heading of grammar, including considerations of phonology (§11) and semantics (§29). The specific sense is the more traditional: here, grammar is presented as just one branch of language structure, distinct from phonology and semantics. This is the approach used in the present book.

Old and new approaches

Traditional grammars taught people to *parse*, or analyse, a sentence, by making a series of divisions within it. *The foreign tourists visited the museum and the castle*, for example, would be divided into a *subject* (*the foreign tourists*), and a *predicate* (*visited the museum and the castle*). The predicate would then be divided into its *verb* (*visited*) and the *object* (*the museum and the castle*). Other divisions would be made (such as distinguishing the two *coordinated* elements in *the museum and the castle*) until all the features of the sentence had been identified.

All grammars parse sentences. It is an essential first step – in the same way that all doctors have to learn anatomy to identify the parts of the human body. But if the study of grammar stops there, presenting only the anatomy of sentences, the result is an approach to language study that many people recall with distaste. It is an approach particularly associated with traditional grammar.

All too often, in the traditional grammars, insufficient reasons were given for making a particular sentence analysis. As a consequence, it was common to find children learning analyses and definitions off by heart, without any real understanding of what was going on. In particular, they had to master the cumbersome, Latin-based grammatical terminology as an end in itself (terms such as *accusative*, *complement*, *apposition*), and apply it to examples of language that were either artificially constructed, or taken from abstruse literature.

It was all at a considerable remove from the child's real language world, as found in conversation or the media. Little attempt was made to demonstrate the practical usefulness of grammatical analysis in the child's daily life, whether in school or outside. And there was no interest shown in relating this analysis to the broader principles of grammatical patterning in the language as a whole. It is not surprising, then, that most people who were taught parsing in school ended up unable to see the point of the exercise, and left remembering grammar only as a dead, irrelevant subject – the morbid anatomy of language.

The reality is quite the opposite. The techniques of grammatical analysis can be used to demonstrate the enormous creative power of language – how, from a finite set of grammatical patterns, even a young child can express an infinite set of sentences. They can help us all to identify the fascinating 'edges' of language, where we find the many kinds of humorous and dramatic effects, both in literature and in everyday language. As we discover more about the way we each use grammar as part of our daily linguistic survival, we inevitably sharpen our individual sense of style, and thus promote our abilities to handle more complex constructions, both in speaking/listening and in reading/writing. We become more likely to spot ambiguities and loose constructions, and to do something about it.

Moreover, the principles of grammatical analysis are general ones, applicable to the study of any language, so that we find ourselves developing a keener sense of the similarities and differences between languages. In addition, many kinds of specialized problems can be illuminated through the study of grammar – such as the difficulties facing the language-disabled, the foreign-language learner, or the translator. Grammar need not be dry, arcane, pointless; it can be alive, entertaining, relevant. As with so many subjects, it depends only on how it is put across.

An analogy is often drawn with the way in which other school subjects are taught. Imagine teaching a child about the structure of a flower in the following way. A hypothetical plant is drawn on the board, and its parts labelled: stamen, pistil, stalk, and so on. Each term is defined, and the children write them in their books. They have to learn them off by heart, and until they do – the teacher insists – they will not be allowed to see or work with any real plant!

It is unlikely that anyone in a modern biology class would be taught this topic through such an approach. In one class I observed, the teacher arrived armed with real plants, and gave them out; the children examined them thoroughly, and asked for help with the 'naming of parts' as they went along. Later, the teacher got them to write up their project in a book, and at that point asked for some terms to be learned.

That is the modern way: discovery first, definitions of terms last. But grammar always suffered, in many schools, by being taught the other way round. A hypothetical sentence would be put on the board, and the required grammatical terminology would be learned, before any attempt would be made to grapple with real sentences in a real world. Often, even, no attempt at all would be made to go searching for interesting, real sentence specimens. It is as if the children's knowledge of plants were to remain forever solely on the blackboard. No one would tolerate such a bizarre pedagogical approach for biology. But for over 200 years, just such an approach was actively practised for grammar. The only thing that surprises me is why it took so long for educational practice to get rid of it.

37
How words work

The range of construction that is studied by grammar is very large, and grammarians have often divided it into sub-fields. The oldest and most widely used division is that between the study of the grammatical structure of words (*morphology*) and the study of the grammatical structure of sentences (*syntax*, §39). This chapter discusses the first of these domains.

The term *morphology* dates from the early 19th century, where it was first used in biology, referring to the form and structure of animals and plants. Later, it was extended to other sciences, such as geology (*geomorphology*), where there was a corresponding emphasis on the constituent parts of an entity. It is most generally defined as 'the science of form', and when it was first used in philology (its earliest recorded use is 1869) it was applied to the study of the form and structure of words.

Two main fields are traditionally recognized within morphology.

- *Inflectional morphology* studies the way in which words vary (or *inflect*) in order to express grammatical contrasts in sentences, such as singular/plural or past/present tense. In an older grammatical terminology, dating from the early 16th century, this was the subject of *accidence*. *Boy* and *boys*, for example, are two forms of the 'same' word; the choice between them, singular vs. plural, is a matter of grammar, and thus the business of inflectional morphology.

- *Derivational morphology* studies the principles governing the construction of new words, without reference to the specific grammatical role a word might play in a sentence. In the formation of *drinkable* from *drink*, or *disinfect* from *infect*, for example, we see the formation of new words, each with its own grammatical properties.

Analysing words

In the sentence *The results of the meeting shocked the campaigners*, most of the words can be analysed into further parts, each of which has some kind of independent meaning.

- *results* – *result* + an ending, *-s*, which turns a singular noun into a plural
- *meeting* – *meet* + an ending, *-ing*, which turns a verb into a noun
- *shocked* – *shock* + an ending, *-ed*, which turns the present tense of a verb into a past tense
- *campaigners* – *campaign* + an ending, *-er*, which turns an abstract noun into an agentive noun ('someone who campaigns'), and another plural ending

Words like *the* and *of* have no internal structure capable of carrying meaning. We can analyse them into their constituent sounds, of course, such as the [ə] + [v] in *of*, but these sounds have no meaning – they are simply phonemes (p. 68). Nor, of course, can we find any further meaningful elements inside such words as *meet* and *shock*. We have reached a bottom limit, from a grammatical point of view, when we analyse the sentence into the following string of elements:

The + result + s + of + the + meet + ing + shock +ed + the + campaign + er + s

The smallest meaningful elements into which words can be analysed are known as *morphemes*; and the way morphemes operate in language provides the subject matter of *morphology*. In this approach, the morphemes which can occur on their own as separate words (such as *meet* and *shock*) are called *free* morphemes; those which are dependent on other morphemes for their occurrence (such as *-s* and *-ing*) are called *bound* morphemes. The morpheme which forms the structural core of a word is referred to variously, as the word's *root*, *base*, or *stem*.

In another terminological tradition, dating from the 17th century, the bound elements of a word are referred to as *affixes* (see also §35). Those affixes occurring before the root are known as *prefixes*; those following the root are known as *suffixes*. *Infixes* are also possible, where an affix is inserted within a stem. The nearest we get to this in English is emphatic forms such as *abso-blooming-lutely*; but in many languages, infixation is a normal morphological process.

It is an easy matter to analyse the above words into morphemes, because a clear sequence of elements is involved. Even an unlikely word such as *anti-dis-establish-ment-arian-ism* would also be easy to analyse, for the same reason, as the hyphens show. In many languages (the so-called *agglutinating* languages, p. 369), it is quite normal to have long sequences of morphemes occur within a word, and these would be analysed in the same way. For example, in Eskimo the word *angyaghllangyugtuq* has the meaning 'he wants to acquire a big boat'. Speakers of English find such words very complex at first sight; but things become much clearer when we analyse them into their constituent morphemes:

angya-	'boat'
-ghlla-	an element expressing size
-ng-	'acquire'
-yug-	an element expressing desire
-tuq-	an element expressing third person singular

English has relatively few word structures of this type, and it is the lack of a complex morphology in English which accounts for the widespread impression (among native speakers of English) that English 'doesn't have much grammar'. It is a view most commonly expressed by people who learned such languages as Latin, German, Spanish, or French in school, and who remember the difficulties they encountered in committing to memory the systems of word endings (the *inflections*) involved. It is true that English has little inflectional morphology. But what it lacks in morphology, it more than makes up for in syntax (§39).

Some morphology problems

Not all words can be analysed into morphemes so easily. In English, for example, it is difficult to know how to analyse irregular nouns and verbs: *feet* is the plural of *foot*, but it is not obvious how to identify a plural morpheme in the word, analogous to the *-s* ending of *hands*. In the word *children*, an unexpected *r* turns up as part of the plural of *child – child + r + en*. The problem does not appear in the corresponding words *oxen* and *brethren*: there is no *r* in *oxen* and the *r* in *brethren* is already present in the word *brother*.

All irregular words present problems of this kind – indeed, that is why they are called irregular in the first place, because they do not conform to the standard morphological pattern. English has only a few irregular nouns (*feet*, *mice*, *geese*, etc.) but has several hundred irregular verbs, where the normal past tense ending (*-ed*, as in *I walked*) is replaced by something unpredictable (*I took*, *went*, *saw*, etc.). Effects of this kind complicate morphological analysis – and add to its fascination. To those with a linguistic bent, there is nothing more intriguing than the search for regularities in a mass of apparently irregular morphological data.

Another complication is that morphemes sometimes have several phonetic forms, depending on the context in which they occur. In English, for example, the past tense morpheme usually written as *-ed* is pronounced in three different ways, depending on the nature of the sounds that precede it. If the preceding sound is /t/ or /d/, the ending is pronounced /ɪd/, as in *spotted*; if the preceding sound is a voiceless consonant (p. 26) other than /t/, the ending is pronounced /t/, as in *walked*; and if the preceding sound is a voiced consonant other than /d/ or a vowel, the ending is pronounced /d/, as in *rolled*. Variant forms of a morpheme are known as *allomorphs* (just as variants of phonemes are called *allophones*, p. 68).

Identifying words

Words sit uneasily at the boundary between morphology and syntax. In some languages – *isolating* languages, such as Vietnamese – they are plainly low-level units, with little or no internal structure. In others – *polysynthetic* languages, such as Eskimo – word-like units are highly complex forms, equivalent to whole sentences. The concept of *word* thus ranges from such single sounds as English *a* to *palyamunurringkutjamunurtu* ('he/she definitely did not become bad') in the Western Desert language of Australia.

Words are usually the easiest units to identify, in the written language. In most writing systems, they are the entities that have spaces on either side. (A few systems use word dividers (e.g. Amharic), and some do not separate words at all (e.g. Sanskrit).) Because a literate society exposes its members to these units from early childhood, we all know where to put the spaces – apart from a small number of problems, mainly to do with hyphenation. Should we write *flower pot* or should it be *flower-pot*? *Well known* or *well-known*? *No one* or *no-one*?

It is more difficult to decide how to identify words in the stream of speech, especially in a language that has never been written down. But there are problems, even in languages like English or French. Certainly, it is possible to read a sentence aloud slowly, so that we can 'hear' the spaces between the words; but this is an artificial exercise. In natural speech, pauses do not occur between each word, as can be seen from any acoustic record of the way people talk. Even in very hesitant speech, pauses come at intervals – usually between major grammatical units, such as phrases or clauses (p. 250). So if there are no audible 'spaces', how do we know what the words are? Linguists have spent a great deal of time trying to devise criteria for word identification.

- *Adding pauses*: Say a sentence out loud, and ask someone to 'repeat it very slowly, with pauses'. The pause will tend to fall between words, and not within words. For example, *the/three/little/pigs/went/to/market*. But the criterion is not foolproof, for some people will break up words containing more than one syllable, e.g. *mar/ket*.

- *Adding extra words*: Say a sentence out loud, and ask someone to 'add extra words' to it. The extra items will be added between the words and not within them. For example, *the pig went to market* might become *the big pig once went straight to the market*, but we would not have such forms as *pi-big-g* or *mar-the-ket*. However, this criterion is not perfect either, in the light of such forms as *abso-blooming-lutely*.

- *Minimal free forms*: The American linguist Leonard Bloomfield (1887–1949) thought of words as *minimal free forms* – that is, the smallest units of speech that can meaningfully stand on their own. This definition does handle the majority of words, but it cannot cope with several items which are treated as words in writing, but which never stand on their own in natural speech, such as English *the* and *of*, or French *je* ('I') and *de* ('of').

- *Listening for phonetic boundaries*: It is sometimes possible to tell from the sound of a word where it begins or ends. In Welsh, for example, long words generally have their stress on the penultimate syllable, e.g. **car**tref 'home', car**trefi** 'homes'. In Turkish, the vowels within a word harmonize in quality (p. 86), so that if there is a marked change in vowel quality in the stream of speech, a new word must have begun. But there are many exceptions to such rules.

- *Identifying semantic units*: In the sentence *Spurs defeat Rangers*, there are plainly three units of meaning, and each unit corresponds to a word. But language is usually not as neat as this. In *I switched on the light*, *the* has little clear 'meaning', and the single action of *switching on* involves two words (p. 193).

Most of the time we have no problem recognizing words when we see or hear them, and we use the notion of 'word' so often in everyday circumstances that it hardly seems to be a technical term at all. But it does have to be used with caution at times, as an earlier chapter has suggested (p. 192).

38
How we classify words

Since the early days of grammatical study, words have been grouped into classes, traditionally labelled the *parts of speech*. In most grammars, eight such classes were recognized, illustrated here from English:

nouns	*cup, happiness, giant*
pronouns	*she, them, who*
adjectives	*splendid, three, soft*
verbs	*arrive, say, have*
adverbs	*fortunately, soon, often*
prepositions	*in, of, with*
conjunctions	*and, as, if*
interjections	*ah, alas, wow*

In some systems, participles (*looking, taken*) and articles (*a, the*) were also listed as separate classes.

Modern approaches classify words too, but the use of the label *word class* rather than *part of speech* represents a change in emphasis. Modern linguists are reluctant to use the notional definitions found in traditional grammar – such as a noun being the 'name of something'. The vagueness of these definitions has often been criticized: is *beauty* a 'thing'? Is not the adjective *red* also a 'name' of a colour? To supplement definitions based on meaning, there is now a focus on the structural features that signal the way in which groups of words behave in a language. In English, for example, the definite or indefinite article is one criterion that can be used to signal the presence of a following noun (*the car*); similarly, in Romanian, the article (*ul*) signals the presence of a preceding noun (*avionul* 'the plane').

In languages which have a complex morphology (p. 238), it is often possible to tell which class a word belongs to just by looking at its shape. A particular kind of prefix might identify verbs; a particular kind of suffix might identify nouns. English has only a few endings which are strongly associated with word classes in this way: *-ness*, for example, is a noun suffix; *-ize* is a verb suffix. Most of the time, you cannot tell what class a word belongs to simply by listening to it or looking at it.

When there is no word-class marker, everything depends on how the word 'behaves' in a sentence. *Round* is a good illustration of this principle in action, for it can belong to any of five word classes, depending on the grammatical context.

- In the sentence *Mary bought a round table*, it functions as an adjective, like *red*, *big*, *ugly*, and many more.
- In the sentence *The car skidded round the corner*, it functions as a preposition, like *into*, *past*, *near*, and many more.
- In the sentence *The yacht will round the buoy soon*, it functions as a verb, like *pass*, *reach*, *hit*, and many more.
- In the sentence *We walked round to the shop*, it functions as an adverb, like *quickly*, *happily*, *regularly*, along with many more.
- In the sentence *It's your round*, it functions as a noun, like *turn*, *chance*, *decision*, and many more.

Most words are not like this: they belong to a single class. But the opportunity is always there for a word to take on additional functions. This is the phenomenon of *conversion* (p. 227), widely encountered in the history of English, as in these cases of nouns becoming verbs:

Tut, tut, grace me no grace, nor uncle me no uncle (Shakespeare, *Richard II*)
Petition me no petitions (Henry Fielding, *Tom Thumb*)
Diamond me no diamonds (Tennyson, *Idylls of the King*)

Poem Me No Poems (website poetry collection, 2002)

But Me No Buts (name of a punk rock group, 2001)

Grouping words

Above all, the modern aim is to establish word classes that are coherent: all the words placed within a class should behave in the same way. For instance, *jump, walk,* and *ask* form a coherent class, because all the grammatical operations that apply to one of these words apply to the others also. They all take a third person singular form in the present tense (*she jumps/walks/asks*), they all have a past tense ending in *-ed* (*jumped/walked/asked*), and so on. Many other words display the same (or closely similar) behaviour, and this would lead us to establish the important class of *verbs* in English. Similar reasoning would lead to an analogous class being set up in other languages, and ultimately to the hypothesis that this class is required for the analysis of all languages.

Several of the traditional parts of speech lacked the coherence required of a well-defined word class – notably, the adverb. Some have likened this class to a dustbin, into which grammarians would place any word whose grammatical status was unclear. Certainly, the following words have very little structurally in common, yet all have been labelled *adverb* in traditional grammars:

tomorrow	very	no
however	quickly	when
not	just	the (in such contexts as *the more the merrier*)

Modern grammars avoid heterogeneous classes of this kind, preferring to establish smaller classes, based on their distinctive behaviour, and calling them by different names, such as *disjunct* and *conjunct*.

Word classes should be coherent, indeed; but if we do not want to set up hundreds of classes, we have to let some irregular forms into each one. For example, for many speakers *house* is the only English noun ending in /s/, where the /s/ becomes /z/ when the plural ending is added (*houses*). Although in theory it is 'in a class of its own', in practice it is grouped with other nouns, with which it has a great deal in common. The alternative would be to set up virtually every irregular word as its own word class.

Because of the irregularities in a language, word classes are thus not as neatly homogeneous as the theory implies. Each class has a core of words that behave identically, from a grammatical point of view. But at the 'edges' of a class are the more irregular words, some of which may behave like words from other classes. For example, some adjectives have a function similar to nouns: for instance, *rich*, usually an adjective, is used like a noun in *the rich*. Some nouns behave similarly to adjectives: for instance, *railway*, usually a noun, is used like an adjective before *station*.

The movement from a central core of stable grammatical behaviour to a more irregular periphery has been called *gradience*, because the sub-classes of words gradually become less and less like each other. Adjectives display this phenomenon very clearly. Let us review the five main criteria usually used to identify the central class of adjectives in English:

(A) they occur after forms of *to be*, as in *he's sad*;
(B) they occur after articles and before nouns, as in *the big car*;
(C) they occur after *very*, as in *very nice*;
(D) they occur in the comparative or superlative form as in *sadder/saddest*, *more/most impressive*; and
(E) they occur before *-ly* to form adverbs, as in *quickly*.

We can now use these criteria to test how much like an adjective a word is.

A word like *happy* is clearly an adjective, because it behaves according to all five of these criteria. We can say:

he's happy, the happy girl, very happy, happier/happiest, happily

By contrast, a word like *jump* is plainly nothing like an adjective. We cannot say:

he's jump, the jump girl, very jump, jumper/jumpest, jumply

In between, there are several words which behave in some ways like adjectives and in other ways not like them. The numerals are a case in point. Words like *two*, *three*, and *twenty* are similar to adjectives in some respects:

> he's twenty, the twenty girls

but they are not like adjectives in others:

> very twenty, twentier / twentiest, twentily

And words like *abroad*, *ablaze*, and *asleep*, beginning with *a-*, which are sometimes grouped along with adjectives, are in fact very different indeed, as they are similar only in respect of the first criterion. We can say:

> they are abroad

but we cannot say:

> the abroad girl, very abroad, abroader / abroadest, abroadly

Some adjectives, it seems, are much more adjective-like than others.

The idea of grouping words into classes is logical and necessary, and proves its worth when we are teaching a language or using a dictionary, where it is helpful to distinguish different uses of words. But we must not expect all words to fit easily into the word-class approach. Words like *yes* and *no* have a clear function in making responses, but few other words work like them. Words like *well* at the beginning of a sentence express hesitation, among other discourse functions; again, few other words behave similarly.

The most difficult cases to handle are the emotional noises – what were once uncomfortably called *interjections*, because they could 'interject' themselves into any part of a sentence. These are hardly like conventional words at all – not least because they often break the pronunciation rules of the language. A 'word' like *shhh* has no vowel in it. The various sounds expressed by the *yuk* of disgust, some alien to the English sound system, are poorly captured by its conventional spelling.

There are more important things to say about such words as *yes*, *well*, and *yuk* than to try to set them up with an identity as word classes. It is more sensible to think of other ways – syntactic ways – of describing their grammatical behaviour.

39

How sentences work

Syntax is the way in which words are arranged to show relationships of meaning within (and sometimes between) sentences. The term comes from *syntaxis*, the Greek word for 'arrangement'. Syntactic studies focus on sentence structure because this is where the most important grammatical relationships are expressed.

Traditionally, grammars define a sentence in such terms as 'the complete expression of a single thought'. Modern studies avoid this emphasis, because of the difficulties involved in saying what 'thoughts' are. *An egg* can be the expression of a thought, but it would not be considered a complete sentence. *I shut the door, as it was cold* is one sentence, but it could easily be analysed as two thoughts. The notion of 'completeness' is plainly central to any definition, but it needs to be given some formal identity if it is to be useful.

Some grammars give a logical definition to the sentence. The most common approach proposes that a sentence has a *subject* (= the topic) and a *predicate* (= what is being said about the topic). This approach works quite well for some sentences, such as *The book is on the table*, where we can argue that *the book* is what the sentence is talking about and *is on the table* adds some further information. But in many sentences it is not so easy to make this distinction. *It's raining* is a sentence, but what is the topic? And in *Michael asked Mary for a pen*, it is difficult to decide which of Michael, Mary, or the pen is the topic – or whether we have three topics.

In each case, though, there is a feeling of completeness as these sentences are said.

In some written languages, it is possible to capture this feeling of completeness and arrive at a working definition of *sentence* by referring to the punctuation we are taught to use in school. Thus, an English sentence for many people 'begins with a capital letter and ends with a full stop' (or some other mark of 'final' punctuation). The problem is that many languages (e.g. in Asia) do not make use of such features; and even in those that do, punctuation is not always a clear guide. It may be omitted (in notices and legal documents, for example); and it proves difficult to prescribe rules governing its use other than 'good practice'. People therefore often disagree about the best way to punctuate a text. In some manuals of style, it is recommended that we should not end a sentence before a coordinating conjunction (*and, or, but*). But there are often cases where an author might feel it necessary – for reasons of emphasis, perhaps – to do the opposite.

It is even more difficult to identify sentences in speech, where the units of rhythm and intonation often do not coincide with the places where full stops would occur in writing. In informal speech, in particular, constructions can lack the careful organization we associate with the written language (p. 149). It is not that conversation lacks grammar: it is just that the grammar is of a rather different kind, with sentences being particularly difficult to demarcate. In the following extract, it is not easy to decide whether a sentence ends at the points marked by pauses (–), or whether this is all one loosely constructed sentence:

> when the children fed the pigs/they all had to stand well back/ – and they were allowed to take the buckets – but they weren't allowed to get near they pigs/you see/ – so they weren't happy . . .

Here, our sense of completeness is not so certain.

Linguistic approaches

Despite all the difficulties, we continue to employ the notion of *sentence*, and modern syntacticians try to make sense of it. But they do not search for a satisfactory definition of *sentence* at the outset. Rather, they aim to analyse the linguistic constructions that occur, recognizing the most independent of them as sentences. This is how our feeling of completeness is captured – by identifying utterances (in speech or writing) which are constructed according to certain rules and which can 'stand on their own', making sense at the point where they are used in a discourse.

The following utterances can all stand on their own as utterances in a discourse, and they can all be analysed as having a particular syntactic structure. They would therefore be recognized as sentences in a grammar of English. (Note that our sense of their completeness does not depend on their spelling and punctuation – omitted here, to make the point.)

> she asked for a book/
> come in/
> the horse ran away because the train was noisy/

The following utterances, however, would not be called sentences, because although constructed according to some grammatical rules of English they cannot stand on their own:

> car at 3 o'clock
> will be here
> the car

And an utterance like this is not constructed according to any predictable rules, so it does not 'make sense':

> at car the will here be

We cannot use the term *sentence* for random locutions where there are no rules governing the order of the words.

In linguistics, a sentence is commonly defined as the largest unit to which syntactic rules apply. The emphasis is important, because it allows us to include as grammatical such cases as the following, where a sentence is allowed to omit part of its structure:

A: Where are you going?
B: To town.

To town would normally not count as a sentence, because it cannot stand on its own and make sense. But in the context of the preceding utterance, it is perfectly natural. Cases where the syntactic rules that complete this sentence are to be found in a preceding or following utterance are usually called *elliptical sentences*.

Finding hierarchy

One of the first things to do in analysing a sentence is to look for groupings within it – sets of words (or morphemes, p. 237) that hang together. In the following example, we might make an initial division as follows:

The agent/couldn't sell/the houses.

Units such as *the agent*, *the houses*, and *couldn't sell* are called *phrases*. The first two of these would be called *noun phrases*, because their central word (or *head*) is a noun – *agent* and *houses*. The second would be called a *verb phrase*, because its head is a verb, *sell*. Other types of phrase also exist – *adjective phrases*, for example, such as *very good*, where the head word is an adjective, *good*.

Phrases may in turn be divided into their constituent words (p. 236):

couldn't + sell   the + houses

And words may be divided into their constituent morphemes, if there are any:

could + n't   house + s

This conception of sentence structure as a hierarchy of levels, or ranks, may be extended 'upwards'. The sentence can be made larger by linking several units of the same type:

The agent couldn't sell the houses, but she did sell the farm.

Here, too, we have a sentence, but now we have to recognize two major units within it – each of which has a structure closely resembling that of an independent sentence. These units are traditionally referred to as *clauses*. In the above example, the clauses have been *coordinated* through the use of the conjunction *but*. An indefinite number of clauses can be linked within the same sentence.

A five-level hierarchy is a widely used model of syntactic investigation:

sentences	morphemes
which are analysed into	which are used to build
clauses	words
which are analysed into	which are used to build
phrases	phrases
which are analysed into	which are used to build
words	clauses
which are analysed into	which are used to build
morphemes	sentences

Morphemes are the 'lower' limit of grammatical enquiry, for they have no grammatical structure (p. 237). Similarly, sentences form the 'upper' limit of grammatical study, because they do not usually form a part of any larger grammatical unit. This is not to deny that there are some interesting grammatical relationships which operate above the sentence, in paragraphs and dialogues. But these relationships are far less systematic and predictable than those which operate within the construction we call a sentence.

Displaying sentence structure

One of the most widely used techniques for displaying sentence structure is the use of *immediate constituent* (IC) analysis. This approach works through the different levels of structure within a sentence in a series of steps. At each level, a construction is divided into its major constituents, and the process continues until no further divisions can be made. For example, to make an IC analysis of the sentence *the agent couldn't sell the houses*, we carry out the following steps:

1 Identify the major constituents: *the agent* and *couldn't sell the houses*.
2 Divide the next-biggest constituent into two, viz. *couldn't sell the houses* into *couldn't sell* and *the houses*.
3 Continue dividing constituents into two until we can go no further, viz.
   the agent and *the houses* into *the + agent, the + houses*;
   couldn't sell into *couldn't + sell*
   couldn't into *could + n't*, *houses* into *house + s*

The order of segmentation can be summarized using lines or brackets. If the first cut is symbolized by a single vertical line, the second cut by two lines, and so on, the sentence would look like this:

The /// agent / could //// n't // sell /// the house //// s

However, a much clearer way of representing constituent structure is through the use of *tree diagrams*, such as the following, and this kind of representation is widespread in modern linguistics, with labels identifying the different analysis points within the tree. The divisions, labels, and associated abbreviations of course, reflect the theoretical viewpoint and conventional practice of the analyst.

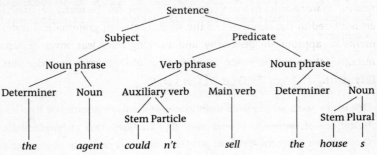

This is just one possible representation of the internal structure of this sentence. An alternative analysis might dispense with the binary division into 'Subject – Predicate'. An alternative nomenclature, such as the one introduced by Noam Chomsky in the 1950s, might retain this binary division but use different labels, such as NP + VP.

The representations become more complex as more awkward sentences are processed. It is sometimes not clear where the cuts should be made. For instance, should we divide *the two old detached houses* into:

the + two old detached houses
the two + old detached houses
the + two old detached + houses

or in some other way? And, whichever way we choose, what are we to call the constituents? Plainly, the answer will depend on how exactly we see the relationship between these words, and how this particular construction relates to others in the language.

More important, the process of segmenting individual sentences takes us only a short way into understanding the grammar of a language. We need more than an analysis of an individual sentence. We also need to devise a way of showing how sentences relate to each other grammatically – as with *statements* and *questions*, *actives* and *passives*. And, in general linguistics, we need to devise representations which can be used to analyse the grammar of any language, not just English. Noun phrases, for example, may have the article preceding the noun or following the noun, and in many languages there are no articles at all. Statements relating to word order in a sentence have to allow for the many variations encountered in the languages of the world. Devising grammatical statements of appropriate generality and working out clear ways of representing them has been the primary focus of linguistics over the past fifty years.

The earliest stage of grammatical development hardly seems like grammar at all, since only single words are involved – utterances such as *Gone*, *More*, *Dada*, and *Bye-bye*. Sometimes longer-sounding utterances are heard (such as *Allgone* or *All-fall-down*), but these are deceptive: they have been learned as whole phrases, and children use them as if they were single units.

Over half of the words used at this stage (p. 204) seem to have a naming function and will develop into nouns. About a fifth express actions. Many of these will develop into verbs, though not all. When a child says *In!*, holding a brick and gesturing violently at a container, we have to interpret this as an action utterance, even though the word class (p. 242) is a preposition. Other word classes are also found at this stage (such as adjectives and adverbs), along with several words that it is difficult to assign to any word class (such as *Bye-bye*).

The 'one-word' stage is usually most noticeable between twelve and eighteen months. But to talk about it solely in terms of 'words' is misleading. In many respects, these early utterances function as if they were sentences (and I have given them capital letters above, to represent this interpretation). For example, one child used the word *dada* in three differ-ent ways (§14): as she heard someone approach outside, she said *Dada?*, with a rising intonation; as she saw that it was indeed daddy, she said *Dada*, with a triumphant, falling intonation; and then she said *Da-da!*, with an insistent, level, intonation, with her arms outstretched. At a later stage in development, these three functions would be called *question*, *statement*, and *command*. At this stage, these utterances do not have a distinctive grammatical form, but the use of prosody and gesture (§§2, 12) conveys the force of these sentence types nonetheless. In such cases, many scholars describe them as *one-word sentences*, or *holophrases*.

Joining words together

Most people think of 'real' grammar as beginning when children string two or more words together, which takes place at around eighteen months. This tends not to happen abruptly. There is usually a transitional period, in which words are brought together, but the sequence is not uttered as a single, rhythmical unit, as in *Daddy. Gone.* Lengthy sequences of such words can often be heard: one child said *Daddy. Garden. See. Daddy. Daddy. Garden* in quick succession. But soon two-word sentences emerge with great confidence – and increasing frequency.

Several studies have been made of the meanings expressed by these two-word sentences. They include such sequences as the following:

an Actor performs an Action	*Daddy kick.*
an Action affects an Entity	*Shut door.*
an Entity is given a Location	*There teddy.*

These sentences could also be described in more traditional grammatical terms. *Daddy kick*, for example, has the clause structure (p. 251) Subject + Verb. However, not all sentences uttered by children at this stage are capable of a clear grammatical or semantic analysis. One child looked at a photograph of her father and said *Daddy Mummy*; another put a car in a garage and said *Car want*. We may hazard plausible meanings to such sequences, but definite interpretations are often out of the question.

At around two years of age, many children produce sentences that are three or four words in length, and combine these words in several different ways to produce a variety of grammatical constructions. Typical sentences at this stage include *Man kick ball*, *Him got car*, *Where mummy going?*, and *Put that on there.* Questions and commands are being used as well as statements, and different clause patterns are now evident. By the end of the third year, structures of four or five elements can be heard, as in *You give me my car now*.

The *telegraphic* character of early sentences has often been noted in many children – an impression which derives from the omission of grammatical words (such as *the* and *is*) and word endings (such as *-ing*). By the end of the third year, this character has largely disappeared, and children's sentences more closely resemble their adult counterparts.

Towards the age of three, there is a major grammatical advance, with the appearance of sentences containing more than one clause. A large proportion of these sentences are coordinate clauses (p. 251), linked mainly by *and* – a pattern which, once learned, produces utterances that can go on and on:

> Daddy have breaked the spade all up and – and – and it broken – and – he did hurt his hand on it and – and – and – it's gone all sore and . . .

Sentences involving subordinate clauses are also increasingly found at this age, using such words as *'cos, so, if, after, what*, and *when*:

> I let go 'cos it hurted me.
> Tell me what it's called.

A great deal of grammatical knowledge is required before these constructions are used correctly, and it is common to find errors and non-fluency as children attempt to handle longer sequences. For example, this child of three years, nine months gets into trouble with his sequence of tenses, as he tries to express a complicated thought:

> If Father Christmas come down the chimney, and he will have presents when he came down, can I stay up to see him?

The sorting out of grammatical errors is a particular feature of four-year-old speech. Many of the irregularities of syntax and morphology (§§37, 39) are being mastered around this age, though it can take several years before such errors as the following are eliminated:

You bettern't do that.

That's more better.

Are there much toys in the cupboard?

It just got brokened.

Are we going on the bus home?

The study of errors is important, because they show children breaking fresh grammatical ground. They provide the main evidence of how children go about actively learning new constructions.

More advanced grammatical constructions continue to be acquired throughout the early school years. Around the age of seven, more sophisticated forms of sentence connection begin to emerge, using such words as *really, though, anyway,* and later *for instance, actually,* and *of course.* Children begin to distinguish different underlying meanings for sentences that look the same (e.g. *Ask John what time it is* vs. *Tell John what time it is*). And they consolidate their awareness of the way sentences may have the same meaning even though they look very different – for example, the relationship between active and passive sentences (*The girl chased the boy – The boy was chased by the girl*), which is not thoroughly sorted out until the ninth year. A popular impression of grammatical learning is that it is complete by age five; but developmental studies have shown that the acquisition of several types of construction is still taking place as children approach ten or eleven.

Coping with complexity

The beauty of child language acquisition lies in the detail, as we observe an individual child getting to grips with the great range and complexity of a grammar and efficiently sorting it out in just a few years. It might take several months, or even years, to master all the uses of a particular type of grammatical construction. For example, the apparently simple process of 'asking questions' in English breaks down into three major stages:

- The earliest stage makes use of intonation (§12), e.g. *Daddy there?*, spoken with a high rising tone, in effect asks 'Is Daddy there?'
- During the second year, children start to use question words. *What* and *where* are usually the first to be acquired, with *why, how,* and *who* coming later. These questions become more complex as the third year approaches, e.g. *Where Katie going?, What you doing in there?*
- A major advance comes with the learning of the verb *to be*, and such auxiliary verbs as *have* and *do*. Children discover the apparently simple rule that turns statements into questions by changing the order of the Subject and Verb (e.g. *That is a car – Is that a car?*), and then learn that it is not so simple after all (e.g. it cannot be *Went she to town?*, but *Did she go to town?*). Sentences that use question words pose particular problems: *Where is Katie going?* has in fact two forms indicating its status as a question – the word *where* and the inversion *is Katie*. Children often rely on the first alone, and for a while produce such sentences as *Where Katie is going?*

The complexity of question formation can be seen from the following selection of errors, all made by two-year-olds:

Whose is that is?
What are you did?
What did you brought?
Is it's my car?
Don't he wanted it?

Despite this complexity, most of these difficulties are overcome before the age of three.

Another set of stages can be seen in the way children learn to 'say no'.

- The first negative words emerge in the second year – usually *no* or *not* as a one-word sentence.
- The negative words combine with other words to make two-word sentences: *No sit, Gone no, Not there*. Several different meanings can

be expressed at this stage – in particular, non-existence, e.g. *No car* (while looking for a toy); rejection, e.g. *No drink* (while pushing a drink away); and denial, e.g. *Not mine* (pointing to someone else's coat).

- During the third year, negative words come to be used within constructions, e.g. *You no do that, Mummy not got it.* At the same time, such verbs as *can't* and *won't* appear.

- The negative words and endings come to be used more accurately: *not* replaces *no*, and *n't* is used with more verbs, e.g. *You've not got one, She isn't going.* 'Double' negatives for emphasis are a normal development, e.g. *Nobody don't like to go in.*

- A few advanced negative constructions are not acquired until the early school years, e.g. the use of *some* vs. *any* (cf. *I've not got any* and not *I've got any*), or the use of *hardly* and *scarcely*.

In learning such detail, of course, the child is not alone. Parents, siblings, and other acquaintances are constantly providing input which contains more mature forms. There is a routine and largely unconscious strategy of rephrasing or expanding a learner's efforts, as can be seen in this exchange with a four-year-old which focuses on the irregular plural of *mouse*:

Child: Me not like them mouses.
Parent: Don't you like the mice, darling?
Child: No, don't like the mices.
Parent: Why don't you like the mice?
Child: Cos – cos mice are scary.

It would have been perfectly possible for the mother, in her second response, to have asked simply *Why not?* The fact that she spelled it out again suggests that she is attuned to the child's emerging grammar and is, probably without realizing it, adopting the role of teacher.

41
How we discourse

The traditional concern of linguistic analysis has been the construction of sentences (§39); but in recent years there has been an increasing interest in analysing the way sentences work in sequence to produce coherent stretches of language. Two main approaches have developed.

- *Discourse analysis* focuses on the structure of naturally occurring spoken language, as found in such *discourses* as conversations, interviews, commentaries, and speeches.
- *Text analysis* focuses on the structure of written language, as found in such *texts* as essays, notices, road signs, and chapters.

However, this distinction is not clear-cut, and there have been many other uses of these labels. In particular, both *discourse* and *text* can be used in a much broader sense to include all language units with a definable communicative function, whether spoken or written. Some scholars talk about *spoken and written discourse*; others about *spoken and written text*. In Europe, the term *text linguistics* is often used for the study of the linguistic principles governing the structure of all forms of text.

The approaches have a common concern: they stress the need to see language as a dynamic, social, interactive phenomenon – whether between speaker and listener, or writer and reader. We convey meaning not by single sentences but by more complex exchanges, in which the participants' beliefs and expectations, the knowledge they share about each

How Language Works

other and about the world, and the situation in which they interact, play a crucial part.

Structuring a text

To call a sequence of sentences a *text* is to imply that the sentences display some kind of mutual dependence; they are not occurring at random. Sometimes the internal structure of a text is immediately apparent, as in the headings of a restaurant menu; sometimes it has to be carefully demonstrated, as in the network of relationships that enter into a literary work. In all cases, the task of textual analysis is to identify the linguistic features that cause the sentence sequence to *cohere* – something that happens whenever the interpretation of one feature is dependent upon another elsewhere in the sequence. The ties that bind a text together are often referred to under the heading of *cohesion*, and several types have been recognized:

- *Conjunctive relations*: What is about to be said is explicitly related to what has been said before, through such notions as contrast, result, and time:

  I left early. *However*, Jean stayed till the end.

  Lastly, there's the question of cost.

- *Coreference*: Features that cannot be semantically interpreted without referring to some other feature in the text. Two types of relationship are recognized: *anaphoric* relations look backwards for their interpretation, and *cataphoric* relations look forwards:

  Several people approached. They seemed angry.

  Listen to this: Dan's getting married.

- *Substitution*: One feature replaces a previous expression:

  I've got a pencil. Do you have one?

  Will we get there on time? I think *so*.

- *Ellipsis*: A piece of structure is omitted, and can be recovered only from the preceding discourse (p. 250):

  Where *did you see the car*? In the street.

- *Repeated forms*: An expression is repeated in whole or in part:

    Canon Brown arrived. Canon Brown was cross.

- *Lexical relationships*: One lexical item enters into a structural relationship with another (p. 195):

    The *flowers* were lovely. She liked the *tulips* best.

- *Comparison*: A compared expression is presupposed in the previous discourse:

    That house was *bad*. This one's far *worse*.

Cohesive links go a long way towards explaining how the sentences of a text hang together, but they do not tell the whole story. It is possible to invent a sentence sequence that is highly cohesive but nonetheless incoherent, as in this coinage by Nils-Erik Enkvist:

A week has seven days. Every day I feed my cat. Cats have four legs. The cat is on the mat. Mat has three letters.

A text plainly has to be coherent as well as cohesive. The concepts and relationships expressed should be relevant to each other, thus enabling us to make plausible inferences about the underlying meaning. Both factors underlie a successful conversation (§42).

Monologues and dialogues

There are so many kinds of text that no single system of classification is yet capable of handling all the variations involved. Texts, after all, range from a single-word, such as *STOP* in a road sign, to a novel of indefinite length. They have to include the loosely structured interactions that constitute a spoken conversation as well as the tightly constrained divisions used in a scientific report. Each subject domain has its own discourse history which conditions present-day usage: the conventions governing religious discourse, for example, can go back hundreds or thousands of years. The language of the law displays the influence of innumerable generations of lawyers.

The broadest distinctions are well recognized. The number of participants involved in an activity has led to a major division of texts into *monologues* and *dialogues*. A monologue, as its name suggests, has only one person involved in the production of a linguistic act; a dialogue has more than one. But the distinction is more subtle than it seems. A monologue does not mean that a person is alone; there may well be an audience present, physically or virtually. Rather, a monologue is a use of language where the speaker or writer does not expect an immediate response. It is language conceived as a self-contained presentation. By contrast, it is the essence of dialogue that the participants expect each other to respond, and it contains many features which enable this to happen, such as question forms. Typically, speech has an audience present and writing does not. But the focus on audience enables us to notice many interesting cases that seem to fall between the two types.

Monologues without an audience present are common enough in writing – I am engaged in one now – but they are unusual in speech. Indeed, why should we say anything at all if there is no-one present to hear it? The answer, of course, is that we use ourselves as the audience – as when we remark aloud about a situation even when there is no one else around, or vocally rehearse the steps in a solution, such as finding our way through a maze of streets. Other types of 'pseudo-audience' include inanimate objects, such as plants and cars. We talk to them, coax them, cajole them, curse them. Virtually any object can be addressed as if it were a person, even though we know it cannot respond. 'Aren't you lovely!' said a man outside the window of a car showroom, unaware that a linguist was passing him at the time.

We might call these 'pseudo-dialogues' rather than monologues. And there are pseudo-dialogues even when someone else is present. Once again, the point is that the second participant is unable to respond, or in no position to respond. Talking to a prelinguistic baby, or a baby in the womb, is one example. And most of us have experienced the pseudo-dialogue when the dentist, having filled your mouth with teeth-seeking equipment, asks you whether you enjoyed your holiday.

There are pseudo-dialogues in written language too. Written

examination answers are a clear case. It is a dialogue of a sort: the examiner has asked a question. But the answer is effectively a monologue, for the student has no expectation of a response (except indirectly, in the form of a grade). We can also address ourselves, as when we write ourselves notes when preparing a speech, or compile a daily diary. Writing online also blurs the monologue/dialogue distinction. Many people who write Internet diaries in the form of blogs (weblogs) are evidently writing monologues; but in putting them online they are plainly intending them to be in public view, and that allows for the possibility of a response. The software may even invite responses, though the number of blogs where the writers are gratified by a reaction are far outnumbered by those where the text is ignored. With millions of blogs now 'out there', this is hardly surprising.

The more we explore the distinction between monologue and dialogue, the more intermediate cases we find. Dialogues can be imagined as monologues. In speech, actors rehearsing their lines can pretend an audience is present. In writing, similarly, someone preparing a lecture handout anticipates the way the points will eventually be presented to the audience. By contrast, monologues can be imagined as dialogues. A politician may prepare a speech, planning the points at which an audience response is likely. The three-point climax ('We have fought before – we are fighting now – and we will go on fighting!' – cheers) is a well-established case. Speech-writers often mark in their texts the points where they expect to elicit audience reactions. And even if the reactions are unplanned, as in political heckling or the 'Amens' which accompany some church sermons, the fact that the writer knows they are likely to be given alters the dynamic of the text. These are monologues masquerading as dialogues.

How we dialogue

Thanks to a lifetime of experience of reading written dialogues in the form of play scripts, language teaching courses, and questionnaires, there is a widespread impression that spoken dialogue is the same. A speaks and B replies, then A speaks again, and so the interaction continues, in a neatly organized way, until the dialogue ends. Listen to a conversation taking place, around a table in a restaurant, say, and it soon becomes apparent that dialogues are only occasionally like this. People talk at the same time, interrupt, and overlap in their speech in all kinds of ways. The more people engaged in the conversation, and the more informal the occasion, the more this happens. Nor is it restricted to domestic situations, as any broadcast dialogue between a politician and radio or TV presenter will illustrate.

The stereotype is that people speak in complete sentences, taking well-defined turns (p. 155), carefully listening to each other, and producing balanced amounts of speech. The reality is that people often share in the sentences they produce, interrupt each other, do not pay attention to everything that is said, and produce a discourse where the contributions of the parties are wildly asymmetrical. Yet such dialogues work.

Take this extract from a recorded conversation, where the four members of a family are engaged in dialogue around a dinner table.

> David (to Lucy): Are you going out this evening?
> Lucy (to anyone): Where did I put my green skirt?
> Ben (to Lucy): Pass the salt, Luce.
> Hilary (to David, mainly): She can never find that skirt.
> Lucy (to herself, mainly): I think I put it in the wash.
> David (to Ben, passing the salt): There you are.

In textbooks, we are taught that a question is followed immediately by an answer. Here we have a question followed by a question, a question being self-answered, and a stimulus being separated from its response by other observations. It is, of course, all part of a perfectly normal conversation.

Or take this example. It is from a humorous dialogue written to illustrate the way in which people complete other people's sentences. The phenomenon is sometimes called 'sentences in progress'.

> Jules: . . . so he was talking about sentences in progress.
> Jim: Sentences in?
> Jules: Progress. It's where one person starts, and another

Jim: Chips in and finishes it off. I know what you mean. I've got a friend who's always doing it. Uncanny sometimes, how he's able to antici-pate exactly

Jules: What you're going to say. I know, some people are almost – almost –

Jim: Obsessive

Jules: Yes, obsessive about it . . .

The practice is universal, and not usually noticed. It only draws attention to itself when someone overuses it as a strategy. It can be very irritating to be talking to someone who persistently tries to finish off your sentences, even though you are perfectly capable of finishing them yourself. And this makes another point, which requires separate attention. There are rules lurking underneath the surface of all conversations, and respecting these rules is a critical factor if we want a conversation to succeed.

42
How conversation
works

Of the many types of communicative act, most study has been devoted to conversation, seen as the most fundamental and pervasive means of conducting human affairs. It turns out, upon analysis, to be a highly structured activity, in which people tacitly operate with a set of basic conventions. A comparison has even been drawn with games such as chess: conversations, it seems, can be thought of as having an opening, a middle, and an end game. The participants make their moves and often seem to follow certain rules as the dialogue proceeds. But the analogy ends there. A successful conversation is not a game: it is no more than a mutually satisfying linguistic exchange. Few rules are ever stated explicitly (some exceptions are *Don't interrupt!*, and *Look at me when I'm talking to you*). Furthermore, apart from in certain types of argument and debate, there are no winners.

For a conversation to be successful, in most social contexts, the participants need to feel they are contributing something to it and are getting something out of it. For this to happen, certain conditions must apply. Everyone must have an opportunity to speak: no one should be monopolizing or constantly interrupting. The participants need to make their roles clear, especially if there are several possibilities (e.g. *Speaking as a mother/linguist/Catholic . . .*). They need to have a sense of when to speak or stay silent; when to proffer information or hold it back; when to stay aloof or become involved. They need to develop a mutual tolerance, to allow for speaker unclarity and listener inattention: perfect expression and comprehension are rare, and the success of a dialogue largely depends on people recognizing their communicative weaknesses, through the use of rephrasing (e.g. *Let me put that another way*) and clarification (e.g. *Are you with me?*).

There is a great deal of ritual in conversation, especially at the beginning and end, and when topics change. For example, people cannot simply leave a conversation at any random point, unless they wish to be considered socially inept or ill-mannered. They have to choose their point of departure (such as the moment when a topic changes) or construct a special reason for leaving. Routines for concluding a conversation are particularly complex, and cooperation is crucial if it is not to end abruptly, or in an embarrassed silence. The parties may prepare for their departure a long way in advance, such as by looking at their watches or giving a verbal early warning. A widespread convention is for visitors to say they must leave some time before they actually intend to depart, and for the hosts to ignore the remark. The second mention then permits both parties to act.

The topic of the conversation is also an important variable. In general it should be one with which everyone feels at ease: 'safe' topics between strangers in English situations usually include the weather, pets, children, and the local context (e.g. while waiting in a room or queue); 'unsafe' topics include religious and political beliefs and problems of health. There are some arbitrary divisions: asking what someone does for a living is generally safe: asking how much they earn is not. Cultural variations can cause problems: commenting about the cost of the furniture or the taste of a meal may be acceptable in one society but not in another.

Taking conversational turns

Probably the most widely recognized conversational convention is that people take turns to speak. But how do people know when it is their turn? Some rules must be present, otherwise conversations would be continually breaking down into a disorganized jumble of interruptions and simultaneous talk. In many formal situations, such as committee meetings and debates, there are often explicit markers showing that a speaker is about to yield the floor, and indicating who should speak next (*I think Mr Smith will know the answer to that question*). This can happen in informal situations too (*What do you think, John?*), but there the turn-taking cues are usually more subtle.

People do not simply stop talking when they are ready to yield the floor. They usually signal some way in advance that they are about to conclude. The clues may be semantic (*So anyway . . ., Last but not least . . .*); but more commonly the speech itself can be modified to show that a turn is about to end – typically, by lowering its pitch, loudness, or speed (§12). Body movements and patterns of eye contact are especially important (§2). While speaking, we look at and away from our listener in about equal proportions; but as we approach the end of a turn, we look at the listener more steadily. Similarly, when talking to a group of people, we often look more steadily at a particular person, to indicate that in our view this should be the next speaker.

Listeners are not passive in all of this. Here too there are several ways of signalling that someone wants to talk next. Most obviously, the first person in a group actually to start speaking, after the completion of a turn, will usually be allowed to hold the floor. More subtly, we can signal that we want to speak next by an observable increase in body tension – by leaning forward, or producing an audible intake of breath. Less subtly, we can simply interrupt – a strategy which may be tolerated, if the purpose is to clarify what the speaker is saying, but which more usually leads to social sanctions.

Because conversational discourse varies so much in length and complexity, analysis generally begins by breaking an interaction down into the smallest possible units, then examining the way these units are used in sequences. The units have been called *exchanges* or *interchanges*, and in their minimal form consist simply of an initiating utterance (I) followed by a response utterance (R), as in:

I: What's the time?
R: Two o'clock.

Two-part exchanges (sometimes called *adjacency pairs*) are common-place, being used in such contexts as questioning/answering, informing/acknowledging, and complaining/excusing. Three-part exchanges are also important, where the response is followed by an element of feedback (F). Such reactions are especially found in teaching situations and are common in child language acquisition (p. 477):

> Teacher: Where were the arrows kept? (I)
> Pupil: In a special kind of box. (R)
> Teacher: Yes, that's right, in a box. (F)

What is of particular interest is to work out the constraints that apply to sequences of this kind. The teacher-feedback sequence would be inappropriate in many everyday situations (the asterisk shows the inappropriate sentence):

> A: Did you have a good journey?
> B: Apart from a jam on the M25.
> A: *Yes, that's right, a jam on the M25.

Unacceptable sequences are easy to invent:

> A: Where do you keep the jam?
> B: *It's raining again.

On the other hand, with ingenuity it is often possible to imagine situations where such a sequence could occur (e.g. if B were staring out of the window at the time). And discourse analysts are always on the lookout for unexpected, but perfectly acceptable, sequences in context, such as:

> A: Goodbye.
> B: Hello.

used, for example, as A is leaving an office, passing B on his way in.

An important aim of discourse analysis is to find out why conversations are not always successful. Misunderstanding and mutual recrimination is unfortunately fairly common. Participants often operate with different rules and expectations about the way in which the conversation should proceed – something that is particularly evident when people of different cultural backgrounds interact. But even within a culture, different rules of interpretation may exist.

It has been suggested, for example, that there are different rules governing the way in which men and women participate in a conversation. A common source of misunderstanding is the way both parties use head nods and *mhm* noises while the other is speaking – something that women do much more frequently than men. Some analysts have suggested that the two sexes mean different things by this behaviour. When a woman does it, she is simply indicating that she is listening, and encouraging the speaker to continue, but the male interprets it to mean that she is agreeing with everything he is saying. By contrast, when a man does it, he is signalling that he does not necessarily agree, whereas the woman interprets it to mean that he is not always listening. Such interpretations are plausible, it is argued, because they explain two of the most widely reported reactions from participants in cross-sex conversations – the male reaction of 'It's impossible to say what a woman really thinks', and the female reaction of 'You never listen to a word I say.'

How we learn conversation

The origins of turn-taking have been traced to the earliest months of life. Primitive conversations (§41) have been observed between mother and child during feeding. While the mother brings the baby to the food-source, she speaks to it in pseudo-dialogue ('You are hungry, aren't you . . . What a noise! . . .'); while the baby feeds, she remains silent; and when there is a pause in the feeding she speaks again, inviting a response ('Wasn't that nice . . ., Where's that wind? . . .'). When the baby 'replies', by producing a burp, it is interpreted as a vocal response and given a further reaction ('What a good girl! . . .'). Nor is it only feeding. All rituals, such as nappy-changing, bathing, tickling games, and bed-time, are accompanied by caretaker speech.

In the second year, conversation gets a bit more structured. A widely used strategy is for the caretaker to expand the child's efforts at sentence construction. A typical dialogue begins with the child noticing something and spontaneously naming it: *Dog*. The adult then responds by taking the child's word and putting it into a bigger sentence, such as:

Yes, darling, that's a dog.

But the response does not usually stop there. Other sentences are added on, such as:

It's a lovely dog, isn't it. Look at its big tail.

It is easy to see what is happening. It is a piece of instinctive teaching by the caretaker, who is 'showing the way' as far as more complex language is concerned. The responses, in effect, say to the child: 'Your sentence was fine, as far as it went, but there are other ways of saying it, more complex ways, offering more opportunities for expression in due course – and, by the way, there are other things to be said about dogs too, such as the fact that they have tails . . .' The child is being taught a lot, without realizing it.

Parents generally appreciate these opportunities instinctively, and make use of them. To react to spontaneous utterances at this stage of development by saying nothing, or just *yes*, or some other monosyllabic response, is reducing the child's opportunities to learn language. Of course, we mustn't overdo it. We mustn't spend *all* our conversational time expanding children's utterances, otherwise they will have little motivation to take the more advanced initiatives themselves. But a regular expanding and amplification of primitive sentences is an essential part of learning in the early years.

By the end of the third year, a great deal of grammatical learning has taken place (§40). Children are now producing quite complex sentences, and dialogues are much more like adult conversations, as this exchange between a mother and her three-year-old illustrates:

Child: Hester be fast asleep, mummy.
Mother: She was tired.
Child: And why did her have two sweets, mummy?
Mother: Because you each had two, that's why. She had the same as you.
    Ooh, dear, now what?

Child: Daddy didn't give me two in the end.
Mother: Yes, he did.
Child: He didn't.

But there is still a great deal to learn about how conversation works.

In particular, during the fourth year children begin to learn that not everything they can say is acceptable. They are introduced to the rules of conversational politeness – what we describe as part of pragmatics (§43). This is the time when they will receive such instructions as:

Don't talk with your mouth full.
I haven't heard that little word yet. (i.e. please)
That's rude.
Don't shout. I'm not deaf.

And around the age of four, they will learn a Great Truth of conversational life, that you have to interpret the underlying meaning behind what people say. This dialogue illustrates:

Child: Can I have a biscuit, mummy?
Mother: You've just had one.

Note that, from the child's point of view, this is not a refusal. No negative word is in the response. So it is not surprising, then, to find children repeating the request. But the second time will produce a more explicit answer:

Mother: No, I've just told you, you've already had one.

If we were to model the child's process of reasoning, it might be something like this: 'So, the sentence "You've just had one" means "no", even though there is no negative word in it. Hmmm. This language-learning business is going to be more complicated than I thought . . .'

Nonetheless, the basic rules governing conversation have been acquired by children by the time they go to school (§73). There is, of course, still quite a bit left to do. Rules have to be learned about how to converse in more structured situations, talking to a wider range of people than would have been encountered at home. The rules of engagement for very formal occasions (such as job interviews) have to be acquired, as well as those needed in sensitive settings, such as funerals. It will take several more years to become a competent conversationalist, capable of participating in the myriad situations that define adult life. But the basis of good conversational practice is well established by the age of five.

43
How we choose
what to say

In theory, we can say or write anything we like. In practice, we follow a large number of social rules (most of them unconsciously) that constrain the way we speak and write. There are norms of formality and politeness which we have intuitively assimilated, and which we follow when talking to people who are older, of the opposite sex, and so on. Signing behaviour is constrained in similar ways. *Pragmatics* is the branch of linguistics which studies the factors that govern our choice of language in social interaction and the effects of our choice on others.

Pragmatic factors always influence our selection of sounds, grammatical constructions, and vocabulary from the resources of the language. Some of the constraints are taught to us at a very early age – in British English, for example, the importance of saying *please* and *thank you*, or (in some families) of not referring to an adult female in her presence as *she*. In many languages, pragmatic distinctions of formality, politeness, and intimacy are spread throughout the grammatical, lexical, and phonological systems, ultimately reflecting matters of social class, status, and role. A well-studied example is the pronoun system, which frequently presents distinctions that convey pragmatic force – such as the choice between *tu* and *vous* in French, or the use of pronouns of respect in several oriental languages.

Languages differ greatly in these respects. Politeness expressions, for instance, may vary in frequency and meaning. Many European languages do not use their word for *please* as frequently as English does; and the function and force of *thank you* may also alter. For example, following the question *Would you like some more cake?*, English *thank you* means 'yes', whereas French *merci* would mean 'no'. Conventions of greeting, leave-taking, and dining also differ greatly from language to language. In some countries it is polite to remark to a host that we are enjoying the food; in others it is polite to stay silent (§41).

Pragmatic errors break no rules of phonology, syntax, or semantics. The elements of *How's tricks, your majesty?* will all be found in English language textbooks and dictionaries, but for most of us the sequence is not permissible from a pragmatic viewpoint. Pragmatics has therefore to be seen as separate from the *levels* of language structure represented in linguistic models of analysis (§28). Pragmatic rules govern the way the linguistic features made available at these levels are put to use in actual situations of speaking, writing, and signing.

The field of pragmatics is very broad, and it has been studied by scholars coming from a variety of intellectual perspectives. One approach focuses on the factors formally encoded in the structure of a language (such as the choice between *tu* and *vous*). Another relates it to a particular view of semantics: here, pragmatics is seen as the study of all aspects of meaning other than those involved in the analysis of sentences in terms of truth conditions. Other approaches adopt a much broader perspective. The broadest sees pragmatics as the study of the principles and practice underlying all interactive linguistic performance – including all aspects of language usage, understanding, and appropriateness, and thus incorporating subject matter which might otherwise be thought of as belonging to sociolinguistics or stylistics (§§48, 49). Textbooks on pragmatics to date, accordingly, present a diversity of subject matter, orientations, and methodologies.

Using speech acts

The British philosopher J. L. Austin (1911–60) was the first to draw attention to the many functions performed by utterances as part of interpersonal communication. In particular, he pointed out that many utterances do not communicate information, but are equivalent to actions. When someone says *I apologize . . .*, *I promise . . .*, *I will* (at a wedding), or *I name this ship . . .*, the utterance immediately conveys a new psychological or social reality. An apology takes place when someone apologizes, and not before. A ship is named only when the act of naming is complete. In such cases, to say is to perform. Austin thus called these utterances *performatives*, seeing them as very different from statements that convey information (*constatives*). In particular, performatives are not true or false. If A says *I name this ship . . .*, B cannot then say *That's not true!*

In *speech act* analysis, we study the effect of utterances on the behaviour of speaker and hearer, using a threefold distinction. First, we recognize the bare fact that a communicative act takes place: the *locutionary act*. Secondly, we look at the act that is performed as a result of the speaker making an utterance – the cases where 'saying = doing', such as betting, promising, welcoming, and warning: these, known as *illocutionary acts*, are the core of any theory of speech acts. Thirdly, we look at the particular effect the speaker's utterance has on the listener, who may feel amused, persuaded, warned, etc., as a consequence: the *perlocutionary effect*. It is important to appreciate that the illocutionary force of an utterance and its perlocutionary effect may not coincide. If I warn you against a particular course of action, you may or may not heed my warning.

There are thousands of possible illocutionary acts, illustrated by a wide range of verbs in a language. Many of them can be grouped into basic types, such as the following:

- *Representatives*: The speaker is committed, in varying degrees, to the truth of a proposition, e.g. *affirm*, *believe*, *conclude*, *deny*, *report*.
- *Directives*: The speaker tries to get the hearer to do something, e.g. *ask*, *challenge*, *command*, *insist*, *request*.
- *Commissives*: The speaker is committed, in varying degrees, to a certain course of action, e.g. *guarantee*, *pledge*, *promise*, *swear*, *vow*.

- *Expressives*: The speaker expresses an attitude about a state of affairs, e.g. *apologize, deplore, congratulate, thank, welcome*.
- *Declarations*: The speaker alters the external status or condition of an object or situation solely by making the utterance, e.g. *I resign, I baptize, You're fired, War is hereby declared*.

Such classifications are difficult, because verb meanings are often not easy to distinguish, and speakers' intentions are not always clear.

Making satisfactory speech acts

Speech acts are successful only if they satisfy several criteria, known as *felicity conditions*. For example, the *preparatory* conditions have to be right: the person performing the speech act has to have the authority to do so. This is hardly an issue with such verbs as *apologize, promise*, or *thank*, where anyone can perform these actions, but it is an important constraint on the use of such verbs as *fine, baptize, arrest*, and *declare war*, where only certain people are qualified to use these utterances.

The speech act has to be executed in the correct manner: in certain cases there is a procedure to be followed exactly and completely, as in the activity of *baptizing*. In others, certain expectations have to be met: we should only *welcome* someone with a pleasant demeanour.

Certain *sincerity* conditions also have to be present: the speech act must be performed in a sincere manner. Verbs such as *apologize, guarantee*, and *vow* are effective only if speakers mean what they say; *believe* and *affirm* are valid only if the speakers are not lying.

Ordinary people automatically accept these conditions when they communicate, and they depart from them only for very special reasons. For example, the request *Will you shut the door?* is appropriate only if (a) the door is open, (b) the speaker has a reason for asking, and (c) the hearer is in a position to perform the action. If any of these conditions does not obtain, then a special interpretation of the speech act has to apply. It may be intended as a joke, or as a piece of sarcasm. Alternatively, of course, there may be doubt about the speaker's visual acuity, or even sanity!

Making speech acts indirectly

Some speech acts directly address a listener, but the majority of acts in everyday conversation are indirect. For example, there are a very large number of ways of asking someone to perform an action. The most direct way is to use the imperative construction (*Shut the door*), but it is easy to sense that this would be inappropriate in many everyday situations – too abrupt or rude, perhaps. Alternatives stress such factors as the hearer's ability or desire to perform the action, or the speaker's reasons for having the action done. These include the following:

> I'd be grateful if you'd shut the door.
> Could you shut the door?
> Would you mind shutting the door?
> It'd help to have the door shut.
> It's getting cold in here.
> Shall we keep out the draught?
> Now, Jane, what have you forgotten to do?
> Brrr!

Any of these could, in the right situation, function as a request for action, despite the fact that none has the clear form of an imperative. But of course, it is always open to the hearer to misunderstand an indirect request – either accidentally or deliberately.

> Teacher: Johnny, there's some chalk on the floor.
> Johnny: Yes, there is, sir.
> Teacher: Well, pick it up, then!

Understanding why

Pragmatic perspectives for language have become popular in recent years because they add a satisfying explanatory perspective for the way we use language. A descriptive account of a particular type of construction – the use of a clause in the passive voice, for example – can take us only so far.

A *grammatical* analysis of passive clauses would describe how they are constructed and how they relate to active clauses – the changes in word order and in the form of certain words:

The dog chased the cat – The cat was chased by the dog

A *semantic* analysis would draw attention to the way the meaning stays the same between the two clauses, allowing for differences in emphasis as the position of the agent (*the dog*, in this example) changes. It would also note that in the 'short' form of the passive (*The cat was chased*), the omission of the agent makes the clause sound distant or impersonal. But neither grammatical nor semantic observation answers the question: who would use passives in the first place – and in what circumstances and for what reasons?

These reasons would be at the heart of any pragmatic investigation of the use of the passive. Why would we ever want to omit the agent? Here are some of the circumstances.

- We may have no choice in the matter, either because we do not know the performer of the action, or it is impossible to say who or what it is:

  Order is being restored in the capital.

  The pictures have been stolen.

- We may not want to identify the performer of the action – especially if we don't want to draw attention to ourselves:

  Teacher: What was that noise?

  Pupil: The window's been smashed, sir.

- We may decide there is no need to identify the performer of the action, because it is obvious from the context. We usually say the first of these sentences, not the second:

  Mary's had her hair done.

  Mary's had her hair done by a hairdresser.

- We may want to avoid particularizing – something very common when trying to be objective, as in science:

When the jug is emptied, it should be cleaned and disinfected, so that it can be used again.

- We may want to avoid a personal tone, as when officials send letters to members of the public:

    The delay is regretted.

In each case, we see a pragmatic perspective operating – identifying the factors that govern our choice of the passive when we engage in social interaction. And every choice we make in language – of pronunciation, orthography, grammar, and vocabulary – no matter how minute, can be studied from a pragmatic point of view.

44
How we can't choose what to say

When we speak, write, or sign, we are never in total control. In particular, certain features of what we communicate are beyond our conscious choice because they are a reflection of our physical being. They give our addressees information about our physical identity – especially about our age, sex, and physical condition. They are there in everything we communicate, acting as a set of permanently present, background, identifying characteristics.

That there must be some kind of relationship between physical condition and language is plain from the way language can be affected in cases of physical disability. Several disorders of constitutional origin have a direct effect on a person's ability to use language, variously affecting the ability to comprehend and produce speech, writing, and sign. Temporary disabilities may have minor but quite noticeable effects – such as the change in voice quality that accompanies a cold or a sore throat, or the alterations in pronunciation that may follow a visit to the dentist. At a much more serious level, there are such cases as the child with cleft palate, or the adult with myasthenia gravis, where speech can be fundamentally and dramatically affected. Here, it is often possible to make deductions about the nature of the person's disability solely from a tape recording. Voice quality, individual sounds, grammar, vocabulary, and other features of language can all be affected.

Telling a person's age

Age is one of the most noticeable features in speech. We have little difficulty identifying a baby, a young child, a teenager, a middle-aged person, or a very old person from a tape recording. With children, it is possible for specialists in language development, and people experienced in child care, to make very detailed predictions about how language correlates with age in the early years. Our voice quality, vocabulary, and style alter as we grow older.

One of the earliest signs of maturation is the phenomenon of *voice mutation*, which accompanies the development of secondary sex characteristics during puberty. At this time, the child voice differentiates into male and female types, due mainly to the rapid growth of the larynx. The development is far more noticeable in boys: male vocal folds become about 1 cm longer, whereas with girls the increase is only around 3–4 mm. As a consequence, in boys, the entire vocal range is both broadened and lowered by about one octave. In girls, there is no such *octave shift*, and the increase in voice range is much less marked: the lower limit of their range extends by only one-third of an octave, and the upper limit by only a few tones.

As well as the pitch change, certain other vocal features usually mark the onset of puberty. The voice is often husky and weak, with poorly controlled vocal-fold vibration (§§4, 5). Subsequently, in males, the voice depth is the most noticeable feature; in females, the voice becomes louder, and it changes in timbre – the thin childlike voice becomes fuller and more vibrant.

The phenomenon is usually described as the voice 'breaking', but this is not always an accurate way of describing the changes that take place. The change from infantile to adult voice is often a gradual transition, rather than a sudden shift, especially in females. Moreover, the speaking voice and the singing voice may be differently affected. The mutational change of the former usually takes between three and six months, whereas the latter may take much longer. For this reason, it is generally felt to be wise to delay adult singing instruction until well after the change in speaking voice has taken place, to avoid the risk of vocal strain.

There is no predictable rule relating adult singing registers to child voices. Whether a boy is soprano or alto, he will develop a bass or baritone singing voice in about two-thirds of cases – a phenomenon that accounts for the common complaint among conductors about the shortage of tenors, and the fact that operatic tenors receive the higher salaries! Analogously, sopranos are far more common than other female voices.

There are also some very noticeable developments at the opposite end of the age scale. In old age, speech is likely to be affected by reductions in the efficiency of the vocal organs. The muscles of the chest weaken, the lungs become less elastic, the ribs less mobile: as a result, respiratory efficiency at age seventy-five is only about half that at age thirty, and this has consequences for the ability to speak loudly, rhythmically, and with good tone. The cartilages, joints, muscles, and tissues of the larynx also deteriorate, especially in men; and this affects the range and quality of voice produced by the vocal folds, which is often rougher, breathier, and characterized by tremor. In addition, speech is affected by poorer movement of the soft palate and changes in the facial skeleton, especially around the mouth and jaw.

There are other, more general signs of age. Speech rate slows, and fluency may be more erratic. Hearing deteriorates, especially after the early fifties. Weakening faculties of memory and attention may affect the ability to comprehend complex speech patterns. But it is not all bad news: vocabulary awareness may continue to grow, as may stylistic ability – skills in narration, for example. And grammatical ability seems to be little affected.

Telling a person's sex

The phonetic contrast between male and female is also a very noticeable difference – though it is not totally predictable. We can be surprised, after hearing a low-pitched voice, to see that it is a female speaker, or after hearing a high-pitched voice to see that it is a male. And differences of timbre (p. 35) overlap between the sexes. There are also non-phonetic differences. In several languages of the world, such as Japanese, Thai, and

Carib, males and females speak in very different ways, making different choices in phonology, grammar, and vocabulary. A female might use a distinctive set of pronouns, for example, or a distinctive set of endings on nouns or verbs.

In a language like English, the situation is less clear. There are no grammatical forms, lexical items, or patterns of pronunciation that are used exclusively by one sex. But there are several differences in frequency. For example, among the words and phrases that women are supposed to use more often are such emotive adjectives as *super* and *lovely*, exclamations such as *Goodness me* and *Oh dear*, and intensifiers such as *so* or *such* (e.g. *It was so busy*). This use of intensifiers has been noted in several languages, including German, French, and Russian.

More important are the strategies adopted by the two sexes in cross-sex conversation (§42). Women have been found to ask more questions, make more use of positive and encouraging 'noises' (such as *mhm*), use a wider intonational range and a more marked rhythmical stress (§12), and make greater use of the pronouns *you* and *we*. By contrast, men are much more likely to interrupt (more than three times as much, in some studies), to dispute what has been said, to ignore or respond poorly to what has been said, to introduce more new topics into the conversation, and to make more declarations of fact or opinion.

However, these differences are not a reflex of physical characteristics. They are usually interpreted as a consequence of the contrasting social roles of the sexes in modern society. Men are seen to reflect in their conversational dominance the power they have traditionally received from society; women, likewise, exercise the supporting role that they have been taught to adopt – in this case, helping the conversation along and providing men with opportunities to express this dominance. The situation is undoubtedly more complex than this, as neither sex is linguistically homogeneous, and considerable variation exists when real contexts of use are studied.

Telling anything else?

Although age and sex are strongly identifiable, there is no simple relationship between speech and other physical characteristics such as height, weight, head size, and shape. That there is some correlation is evident from our surprise when we hear a large person come out with a thin, high-pitched voice. There is a general expectation that size relates to loudness and pitch depth. However, there is no conclusive way of predicting from physical appearance alone whether a person's vocal range is going to be soprano, contralto, tenor, or bass.

There is also little in the anatomy of the human vocal tract to account for the linguistic differences between people and groups. The proportions of the various vocal organs (§4) seem to be very similar in all human beings. Individual variations of course exist in size and shape: for example, the height of the palate varies a great deal, as does the length and flexibility of the tongue. Some people can make the tip of their tongue touch their uvula; others can hardly make their tongue touch their hard palate. More men than women can make the edges of their tongue curl upwards. But, pathological cases aside, these differences do not seem to add up to much, as far as spoken language is concerned. There is no evidence to suggest that anatomical variations have any effect on the ability of a person to learn or use speech.

We have to reach a similar conclusion when we consider the kinds of anatomical variation that distinguish the world's racial groups. Certainly several differences could be relevant for speech – for example, there is considerable variation in the length of the tongue between some races, and people have speculated whether this factor would make it more difficult for someone to speak a language of a racially different group. Everyday experience suggests that this is not the case. One indication of this is the language-learning ability of second-generation immigrants, whose accents may be indistinguishable on tape from those of the indigenous population. A widely recognized experience is for London bus passengers to hear behind them a perfectly articulated Cockney *Any more fares please?*, only to find a conductor who is plainly West Indian or African in racial origin.

Similarly, it is not possible to make strong connections between linguistic features and such psychological attributes as intelligence, concentration, personality, memory, and so on. There is no simple relationship between language and intelligence, for example, and nothing in the voice which would unequivocally identify a particular level of intelligence. Studies with mentally disabled children have shown that a certain minimum level of intelligence, as measured on conventional tests, is a prerequisite for language development. However, this need not be very high, and there is no clear relationship between intelligence and the ability to use particular language structures. Attempts have been made to relate intelligence to quantity of infant babbling, amount of vocabulary, grammatical complexity, the prosodic features of speech, the use of figurative expressions, and other variables. In no case is there a neat correlation, though stereotypes of performance undoubtedly exist.

Similarly, there is no easy relationship between language and personality traits and types. *Traits* are styles of behaviour that an individual displays, whatever the stimulus, in many different circumstances. *Types* involve the identification of a salient feature that is then used as a label for the whole personality. There are thousands of trait labels in a language, describing people as honest, tidy, shy, thoughtful, stupid, and so on. Several approaches group traits into much smaller sets of basic dimensions, such as dominance, extraversion, or likeability. But there is no simple correlation between these judgements and any set of linguistic features – despite the fact that people are very ready to make such correlations.

People do form stereotyped impressions about personality on the basis of linguistic features, especially the prosody of the voice (§12). Comments such as *You can tell he's anxious from his voice* or *She sounds very strong minded* are often to be heard. All accents, dialects, and languages seem to be affected by evaluations of this kind. If speakers use a standard accent, speak quickly and fluently, and use few hesitations, they are likely to be rated as more competent, dominant, and dynamic. The use of regional, ethnic, or lower-class varieties, on the other hand, is associated with greater speaker integrity and attractiveness. Even national personalities can be perceived: British speakers rate French as a more romantic language, it seems, and German as a more businesslike one.

Stereotypes of this sort markedly colour interpersonal and inter-group relationships, and are encountered in all kinds of contexts. For example, it has been established that the character of a person's voice can affect the way in which a jury judges the credibility of what is said. In education, teachers' evaluations of a pupil's capabilities can be more influenced by speech style than by written composition, artistic work, or personal appearance. Our impressions of a person's guilt, innocence, intelligence, or stupidity are, it seems, much affected by phonetic and linguistic factors. It is an area of behaviour where we need to be very much on our guard, to prevent inappropriate decisions being made.

45

How we know where someone is from

The most widely recognized features of linguistic identity are those that point to the geographical origins of the speakers – features of *regional dialect*. But there are several levels of response to the question *Where are you from?* We might have a single person in mind, yet all of the following answers would be correct: *Britain*, *the east of England*, *East Anglia*, *Norfolk*, *Norwich*. People belong to regional communities of varying extent, and the dialect they speak changes its name as we 'place' them in relation to these communities.

It is sometimes thought that only a few people speak regional dialects. Many restrict the term to rural forms of speech – as when they say that 'dialects are dying out these days'. But dialects are not dying out. Country dialects are not as widespread as they once were, indeed, but urban dialects are now on the increase, as cities grow and large numbers of immigrants take up residence.

People often hold negative views about dialects, because of the traditional social associations of the term. Languages in isolated parts of the world, which may not have been written down, are sometimes referred to pejoratively as 'dialects', as when someone talks of a tribe speaking 'a primitive kind of dialect'. But this fails to recognize the true complexity of the world's languages. There is no such thing as a 'primitive language'. All languages have complex phonologies, grammars, and lexicons. And all languages can be analysed into a range of dialects which reflect the regional and social background of their speakers.

Some people think of dialects as sub-standard varieties of a language, spoken only by low-status groups – illustrated by such comments as 'He speaks correct English, without a trace of dialect'. Comments of this kind fail to recognize that standard English is as much a dialect as any other variety – though a dialect of a rather special kind, because it is one to which society has given extra prestige. Everyone speaks a dialect – whether urban or rural, standard or non-standard, upper class or lower class.

It is important to distinguish *dialect* and *accent*, when discussing someone's linguistic origins. Both notions are important. Accent refers just to distinctive pronunciation, whereas dialect refers to spoken grammar and vocabulary as well. The difference between *bath* with a 'short *a*' [a] and *bath* with a 'long *a*' [ɑː] is to do with accent, as this is solely a matter of pronunciation. But if we heard one person say *He done it* and another say *He did it*, we would refer to them as using different dialects, because a grammatical difference is involved. Similarly, the choice between *wee bairn* and *small child* is dialectal, because this is a contrast in vocabulary.

Usually, speakers of different dialects have different accents; but speakers of the same dialect may have different accents too. The most famous case is the dialect known as *standard English*, which is used by educated people throughout the world, but it is spoken in a vast range of regional accents.

Probably no two people are identical in the way they use language or react to the usage of others. Minor differences in phonology, grammar, and vocabulary are normal, so that everyone has, to a limited extent, a 'personal dialect', technically known as an *idiolect*. In fact, when we investigate a language, we have no alternative but to begin with the speech habits of individual speakers: idiolects are the first objects of study. Dialects can thus be seen as an abstraction, deriving from an analysis of a number of idiolects; and languages, in turn, are an abstraction deriving from a number of dialects.

Distinguishing dialects and languages

At first sight, there may appear to be no problem. If two people speak differently, then, it might be thought, there are really only two possibilities. Either they are not able to understand each other, in which case they can be said to speak different languages; or they do understand each other, in which case they must be speaking different dialects of the same language. This criterion of *mutual intelligibility* works much of the time; but matters are not always so simple, as is discussed in §51.

An interesting problem arises in cases where there is a geographical *dialect continuum*. There is often a *chain* of dialects spoken throughout an area. At any point in the chain, speakers of a dialect can understand the speakers of other dialects who live in adjacent areas to them; but they find it difficult to understand people who live further along the chain; and they may find the people who live furthest away completely unintelligible. The speakers of the dialects at the two ends of the chain will not understand each other; but they are nonetheless linked by a chain of mutual intelligibility.

This kind of situation is very common. An extensive continuum links all the dialects of the languages known as German, Dutch, and Flemish. Speakers in eastern Switzerland cannot understand speakers in eastern Belgium; but they are linked by a chain of mutually intelligible dialects throughout the Netherlands, Germany, and Austria. There is a West Romance continuum, which links rural dialects of Portuguese, Spanish, Catalan, French, and Italian. We are used to thinking of these languages as quite different from each other, but this is only because we are usually exposed to their standard varieties, which are not mutually intelligible. At the local level, it is not possible to make a clear decision on linguistic grounds.

But decisions are of course made on other grounds. As we cross a well-established national boundary, the variety of speech will change its name: 'Dutch' will become 'German', 'Spanish' will become 'Portuguese', 'Swedish' will become 'Norwegian'. It is important to appreciate that the reasons are political and historical, not linguistic. Arguments over language names often reduce to arguments of a political nature, especially when there is a dispute over national boundaries (p. 334).

Establishing linguistic areas

Geographical identity can sometimes be established within a broader context than that provided by rural or urban dialectology. Certain features of speech can identify someone as coming from a particular part of the world, but the area involved may extend over several countries, languages, or even language families. The study of *areal features* of this kind is sometimes referred to as *areal linguistics*.

Features of pronunciation are often shared by adjacent, but historically unrelated languages. In the indigenous languages of southern Africa, the use of click sounds in speech (p. 21) identifies speakers of the Khoisan languages as well as of local Bantu languages, such as Zulu and Xhosa. In the Indian subcontinent, languages that belong to different families (such as Indo-European and Dravidian) have several important phonological features in common, such as the use of retroflex consonants (p. 59).

Grammatical features can also cross linguistic and national boundaries. In Europe, the Balkans constitutes a particularly well-defined linguistic area. For example, Albanian, Romanian, Bulgarian, and Macedonian all place the definite article after the noun, as in Romanian *lup* ('wolf') and *lupul* ('the wolf'), whereas historically related languages outside of the Balkans area (such as Italian) do not.

How do areal features develop? In some areas, dialect chains have probably helped to diffuse a linguistic feature throughout an area. Concentrations of bilingual speakers along lines of communication have also played a part, and political factors have exercised their influence. Sometimes, the progress of an areal feature can be traced – an example being the uvular pronunciation of /r/. Originally, speakers of European languages pronounced /r/ with the front of their tongue; but, in the 17th century, Parisians began to use a uvular variant. The variant caught on, spreading first throughout most of France, then to parts of Italy, Switzerland, Luxembourg, Belgium, Holland, Germany, Denmark, and (by the end of the 19th century) to southern Norway and Sweden. Spain, Austria, England, and other countries were not affected.

Guessing where someone is from

How easy is it to tell where someone is from? In Britain a few decades ago, it would have been relatively straightforward for a specialist to work out from a sample of speech the features that identified someone's regional background. Many people lived all their lives in the same place, so that their speech was readily identifiable. Some dialect experts used to run radio shows in which they were able to identify the general regional background of members of their audience with considerable success. But it is doubtful whether anyone ever developed the abilities of George Bernard Shaw's Professor Henry Higgins: 'I can place any man within six miles. I can place him within two miles of London. Sometimes within two streets' (*Pygmalion*, Act 1).

These days, dialect identification has become much more difficult, mainly because of increased social mobility. In many countries, it is less common for people to live their whole lives in one place, and 'mixed' dialects are more the norm. Also, as towns and cities grow, once-distinct communities merge, with a consequent blurring of speech patterns. And nowadays, through radio and television, there is much more exposure to a wide range of dialects, which can influence the speech of listeners or viewers even within their own homes. A radio dialect show would be much less impressive today. On the other hand, meticulous analysis can bring results, and there have been several notable successes in the field of forensic linguistics, where the accurate identification of the regional background of a voice (on a tape recording, for example) can provide important evidence.

Although accents and dialects are changing in character, there is no evidence to suggest that they are losing their role as markers of identity in society. There is, after all, nothing quite like speech in its potential for expressing who we are. If we want to display to others where we are from, we can use clothing or badges or wave a flag. But these behaviours are of no use round corners, where they cannot be seen, and they are useless for several hours each day, when it is dark. Speech, however, can be perceived round corners and in the dark. It is the most universal way of expressing our regional identity – and also the cheapest, for no clothes, badges, or flags need to be bought.

It seems totally natural to speak like the other members of our own group and not to speak like the members of other groups. The tendency, well recognized in modern sociolinguistics, is called *accommodation*. It is an ability which probably emerged early on in the evolution of the human race, because it had considerable survival value. When primitive people heard voices outside a cave, did they go outside to greet them with a smile or proceed cautiously with a club? Recognizing the Cro-Magnon equivalent of an accent would have made all the difference.

The systematic study of regional dialects is known variously as *dialectology*, *dialect geography*, or *linguistic geography*; but these terms are not exact equivalents. In particular, the latter terms suggest a much wider regional scope for the subject. Dialect specialists who spend their lives researching the local usage of a single Yorkshire village are not usually called *linguistic geographers*, though they are certainly *dialectologists*. By contrast, the *geographer* designation would be quite appropriate for anyone involved in plotting the distribution of forms over a large area, such as Scotland, or the eastern United States.

There is another difference between these terms. Traditionally, *dialectology* has been the study of regional dialects, and for many people that is still its main focus. But in recent decades, dialectologists have been paying more attention to social as well as geographical space, in order to explain the extent of language variation. Factors such as age, sex, social class, and ethnic group are now seen as critical, alongside factors of a purely regional kind.

But whatever the approach, the contemporary fascination with dialects seems no less than that shown by previous generations. Radio programmes on dialect variations are popular in several countries, and compilations of dialect data continue to be produced in the form of grammars, dictionaries, folklore collections, and guides to usage. Local dialect societies thrive in many parts of the world. Dialects continue to be seen as a major source of information about contemporary popular culture and its historical background. In 2005 the BBC launched its recording project *Voices*, the most ambitious attempt ever to provide an auditory snapshot of accents and dialects in a country (*www.bbc.co.uk/voices*).

Probably the most important application of dialectology these days is in education, where the development of dialect *awareness* in children is widely recognized as a way of getting them to see the heterogeneity of contemporary society and their place within it. Teachers are often faced with a conflict between the child's spontaneous use of dialect forms and the need to instil a command of the standard language, especially in writing. The conflict can be resolved only by developing in children a sense of the relationships between the two kinds of language, so that the value of both can be better appreciated. There needs to be an awareness of the history, structure, and function of present-day dialects – and this is what dialectology can provide.

The origins of dialectology

While there has been sporadic interest in regional dialects for centuries, the first large-scale systematic studies, in Germany and France, did not take place until the end of the 19th century. In 1876, Georg Wenker (1852–1911) began sending out questionnaires to all the school districts in the German Empire. It took him ten years to contact nearly 50,000 local teachers, who were asked to provide equivalents for forty sentences in the local dialect. An enormous amount of data was received, and this led to the publication in 1881 of the first linguistic atlas, *Sprachatlas des Deutschen Reichs*.

The postal questionnaire method enables a large amount of data to be accumulated in a relatively short time, but it has several limitations – chiefly that dialect pronunciations cannot be accurately recorded. The alternative, to send out trained field workers to observe and record the dialect forms, was first used in the linguistic survey of France, which began in 1896. The director, Jules Gilliéron (1854–1926), appointed Edmond Edmont (1849–1926) – a grocer with a very sharp ear for phonetic differences – to do the field work. For four years, Edmont went around France on a bicycle, conducting interviews with 700 informants using a specially devised questionnaire of nearly 2,000 items. The *Atlas linguistique de la France* was subsequently published in thirteen volumes between 1902 and 1910. It stands as the most influential work in the history of dialectology.

In the first half of the 20th century, major projects were initiated in many parts of Europe, such as Romania, Italy, the Netherlands, Spain, and Denmark, and there were several impressive publications. In due course large-scale dialect surveys of the United States and England began. In some countries, surveys leading to a 'second generation' of linguistic atlases have begun. Direct interviewing and postal questionnaires continue to be used today, as does the tradition of presenting the linguistic material in the form of maps; and in recent years, dialectology has benefited enormously from the development of techniques using tape recorders. The field is also now being influenced by the electronic revolution, with computers helping to 'crunch' the data provided by questionnaires, and making large databases of regional variants more available, accessible, and analysable – and even more visible and audible, using computer techniques. The potential of the Internet has still to be explored.

Once the speech of dialect informants has been collected, it is analysed, and the important features are marked on a map of the area in which the informants live. When several points on the map have been located, it is then possible to see whether there is a pattern in the way these features are used. The usual way of identifying dialect patterns is to draw lines around the places where the people use a linguistic feature in the same way. These boundary lines are known as *isoglosses*. For example, one famous isogloss runs across England, from the Severn to the Wash: it distinguishes northern speakers who pronounce a rounded *u* /ʊ/ in words like *cup* from southern speakers who keep the vowel open and unrounded, /ʌ/. The map on p. 298 shows another example, identifying locations in England where *r* is pronounced after vowels.

When isoglosses were first introduced, at the end of the 19th century, it was expected that they would provide a clear method for identifying dialect areas. Because people from a particular part of a country 'speak in

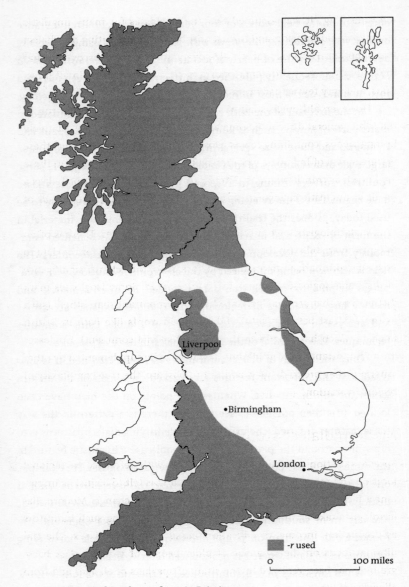

Fig. 17. Lexical isoglosses for -r in Britain

the same way', it was assumed that the isoglosses for many linguistic features would coincide, and form a neat *bundle*, demarcating one dialect from another. However, early dialectology studies soon discovered that the reality was very different. Isoglosses criss-crossed maps in all directions, and very few actually coincided.

However, although isoglosses rarely coincide, they do often run in the same general direction. Some areas, called *focal areas*, are relatively homogeneous, containing few isoglosses. Where focal areas merge, there is a great deal of linguistic variation, with many isoglosses present: these are known as *transition areas*. Often, a feature might be left isolated, as a result of linguistic change affecting the areas around it: these *islands* of more conservative usage are called *relic areas*.

Dialectologists have mixed feelings about isoglosses. There is often too much variability in the way a linguistic feature is used for the data to be easily summarized in a single isogloss. Also, the relative significance of different isoglosses remains to be interpreted. Some isoglosses mark distinctions that are considered to be more important than others (such as the contrast between short and long *a* in words like *bath* in British English, which has long been the focus of special comment). Isoglosses are an important visual guide, but they need to be supplemented by other criteria if they are to display, and not to obscure, the true complexity of regional variation.

Modern dialect studies

Speech variation can be partly understood with reference to regional location and movement, but social background is felt to be just as important a factor in explaining linguistic diversity and change. Modern dialectologists take account of socioeconomic status, using such indicators as occupation, income, or education, along with age and sex. The traditional focus on the language of older people of working-class backgrounds has been replaced by the study of speakers of all ages and from all walks of life.

Dialect studies have moved from the country to the city. The description of rural dialects yielded fascinating results, but only a small proportion of a country's population was represented in such studies. In many countries, over 80% of the population live in towns and cities, and their speech patterns need to be described too – especially as linguistic change so often begins when people from the country imitate those from urban areas. This change of focus, accordingly, has led to the emergence of *urban dialectology*.

In the older studies, small numbers of speakers were carefully chosen to represent what were thought of as 'pure' forms of dialect. Today, larger numbers of people are chosen from the whole population of a city – perhaps using the electoral register or a telephone directory. Also, the earlier approach generally asked for one-word responses to a range of carefully chosen questions. This produced useful data, but these speech patterns were unlikely to have been typical. When people have their attention drawn to the way they speak, they usually adopt a more careful and unnatural style. Attempts are therefore now made to elicit speech that is more spontaneous in character by engaging informants in topics of conversation that they find interesting or emotionally involving. The questionnaire has been largely replaced by the tape recorder.

In the 1970s, the notion of the *linguistic variable* was developed, as a means of describing this variation. A linguistic variable is a unit with at least two variant forms, the choice of which depends on other factors, such as sex, age, social status, and situation. For example, in New York City, speakers sometimes pronounce /r/ in words like *car* and sometimes they do not. This unit can thus be seen as a variable, (r), with two variant forms, /r/ and zero. (It is usual to transcribe linguistic variables in parentheses.) It is then possible to calculate the extent to which individual speakers, or groups of speakers, use /r/, and to determine whether there is a correlation between their preferences and their backgrounds.

Individuals vary in their pronunciation, grammar, and vocabulary. Is there a reason for this variation, or is it random – *free* variation, as it is often called? The current belief is that most of the variation is systematic, the result of the interplay between linguistic and social factors. Traditional dialectology studied the fact that different people do not speak in the same way. Contemporary dialectology adds to this study the fact that the same person does not speak in the same way all the time.

47
How we know
what someone is:
the ethnic issue

Regional dialects (§45) provide us with the most familiar index of community belonging, but in many parts of society other forms of linguistic identity take priority. The issue is no longer one of deciding where people are from, in terms of some geographical location, but of what they are, in terms of their ethnicity, religion, social status, or social role.

Linguistic markers of ethnic identity are especially powerful. Ethnicity is allegiance to a group with which we have ancestral links. It is a general notion, which applies to everyone, and not just to those who practise a traditional rural culture (a current usage of the term *ethnic*). However, questions of ethnolinguistic identity in fact arise most often in relation to the demands and needs of those who are in an ethnic minority within a community, such as the many groups of immigrants, exiles, and foreign workers in Europe and the USA, or the tribal divisions that characterize several African countries. Both languages and dialects are involved.

Respecting languages

Questions of ethnicity are closely related to those of national identity. Once a group becomes aware of its ethnic identity, it will wish to preserve and strengthen its status, and this often takes the form of a desire for some sort of political recognition, often self-government. Political commentators have stressed the subjective element in the idea of a 'nation' – the difficulty of defining the psychological bond that motivates a nationalistic movement, or predicting which elements will contribute most to a group's sense of identity. Religious practices, long-standing institutions, and traditional customs are all important in this respect; but perhaps the most widely encountered symbol of emerging nationhood is language. In the 18th and 19th centuries in particular, linguistic nationalism was a dominant European movement, with language seen as the primary outward sign of a group's identity. Today, a comparable concern can be observed in many areas of the world, as part of separatist political demands.

Linguistic conflicts due to divided ethnic and national loyalties are often bitter and violent. In recent years, there have been major incidents in several countries, such as India, Spain, Canada (Quebec), Belgium, the USA, South Africa, and the Celtic-speaking areas of Britain. The reasons for conflict vary greatly. In some cases, the use of a language is declining, and the reaction is a desperate attempt to keep it, and the community it represents, alive. In others, a minority group may be rapidly growing in numbers, so that its language begins to compete with the established languages of the country for educational, media, and other resources. In still others, the number of speakers may be stable, but there has been an awakening (or reawakening) of cultural identity, with a subsequent demand for recognition and (usually) territorial independence.

Why should language be such a significant index of ethnic or nationalistic movements? One reason is undoubtedly that it is such a widespread and evident feature of community life. To choose one language over another provides an immediate and universally recognized badge of identity. Another reason is that language provides a particularly clear link with the past – often the only detailed link, in the form of literature. There is also a tendency for language to act as a natural barrier between cultural groups, promoting conflict rather than cooperation – as has often been seen in political meetings between opposed groups, when the question of which language to use in the discussion has become a major procedural decision. In bilingual communities, or areas where there is a recognized lingua franca, this factor is less important; but even here, language can focus the sense of political grievance in a clearer way than any other factor. There is no more awesome testimonial to the power of language than the fact that there have been so many people ready to die if their demands for linguistic recognition were not met.

The way language can become a symbol of national identity is very clearly seen in the history of Basque (*Euskera*), and the attitude towards it of the Spanish government under Franco, from 1937 until the mid-1950s. The teaching of the language in schools was forbidden, as was its use in the media, church ceremonies, and all public places. Books in the language were publicly burnt. Basque names were no longer allowed in baptism, and all names in the language on official documents were translated into Spanish. Inscriptions on public buildings and tombstones were removed.

By the early 1960s, official policy had changed. Basque came to be permitted in church services, and then in church schools and broadcasts. In 1968, a government decree authorized the teaching of regional languages at the primary level in Spain. By 1979, the Ministry of Education had accepted responsibility for Basque teaching programmes at all levels of education. In March 1980, the first Basque Parliament was elected, with Euskera recognized as an official language along with Spanish in the Basque provinces. Current discontent, as a consequence, is focused more on the region's future socioeconomic development, associated with persistent demands for political autonomy. But the language issue is never far away.

Issues of ethnolinguistic identity have long been noticeable in northwest Europe, raised by the presence of large numbers of migrant workers (sometimes called *Gastarbeiter*, 'guest workers') and their dependants. They came from several countries, such as Turkey, Greece, Italy, Japan, the Balkan states, and the Arabic-speaking countries. The demands of their new life required a level of adaptation that transcends language frontiers, and these workers often did not make an issue of their linguistic identity. On the other hand, their communication skills were usually limited, and the social and educational problems for the receiving country were considerable.

In the early 1990s, for example, there were over 750,000 foreign pupils in German schools, and about 1 million in French schools. In 1995, minority languages being taught in French schools included German, English, Spanish, Italian, Portuguese, Arabic, Hebrew, Russian, Japanese, Dutch, Chinese, and Turkish. Even in a small country, significant minority language problems exist: in Denmark, for example, migrants from the Balkan States, Turkey, and the Nordic countries have to be catered for. In Britain, there are over 300 minority languages in the London area alone.

The situation is becoming more complex with increasing international mobility within the European Union – already very noticeable before the expansion to twenty-five member states in 2004. At least the problem is now officially recognized. As early as 1977, the Council of the European Economic Community issued a directive on the education of children of migrant workers in Europe. The directive applied only to member states, but the Council resolved to extend the measures to include all immigrant children within the Community. The aim of the exercise was to adapt school structures and curricula to the specific educational needs of these children without losing sight of their cultural and linguistic identity.

> Article 2 Member States shall, in accordance with their national circumstances and legal systems, take appropriate measures to ensure that free tuition to facilitate initial reception is offered in their territory to the children . . . including, in particular, the teaching – adapted to the specific needs of such children – of the official language or one of the official languages of the host State.
>
> Article 3 Member States shall, in accordance with their national circumstances and legal systems, and in cooperation with States of origin, take appropriate measures to promote, in coordination with normal education, teaching of the mother tongue and culture of the country of origin for the children . . .

Brave words, but expensive ones. And in the new millennium we are a long way from achieving this educational ideal.

Respecting dialects

Ethnic identity is also often signalled through dialects. In fact, probably the most distinctive feature of ethnicity in immigrant groups is not their mother tongue (which may rarely be heard outside the home), but the foreign accent and dialect that characterizes their use of the majority language. In the course of time, many of these features become established, resulting in new varieties of the majority language. Well-known cases include the range of English accents and dialects associated in Britain with speakers from the Indian subcontinent or from the West Indies, and in the USA with speakers from Mexico or Puerto Rico. A non-regional example would be people with a Jewish background, whose speech has had a distinctive influence on many European languages.

One of the clearest examples of ethnic linguistic variety is provided by the contrast between the speech of black and white Americans. There is no simple correlation between colour and language, because there is considerable linguistic variation within both racial groups, and it is perfectly possible for black speakers to 'sound' white, and vice versa, depending on educational, social, and regional factors. The term *Black English* has been criticized, therefore, because of its suggestion that all blacks use the same variety, and has been replaced in academic study by *African-American English Vernacular* (AAEV), referring to the speech of the group most often studied in this context – the non-standard English spoken by lower-class African-Americans in urban communities.

The dialect has several distinctive features, as these examples illustrate:

- No final *s* in the third-person singular present tense, e.g. *he walk*, *she go*.
- No use of forms of the verb *be* in the present tense, when it is used as a copula, or *linking* verb, within a sentence, e.g. *They real fine*, *If you interested*.
- Use of the verb *be* to mark habitual meaning, but without changing its grammatical form ('invariant' *be*), e.g. *Sometimes they be walking round here*.

- Use of *been* to express a meaning of past activity with current relevance, e.g. *I been known your name*.
- Use of *be done* in the sense of 'will have', e.g. *We be done washed all those cars soon*.
- Use of *it* to express existential meaning (cf. standard English *there*), e.g. *It's a boy in my class name Mike*.
- Use of double negatives involving the auxiliary verb at the beginning of a sentence, e.g. *Won't nobody do nothing about that*.

It is not clear just how widespread these features are amongst the black community; nor is it immediately obvious where they come from. In one view, all AAEV features can be found in white English dialects (especially those of the southern USA), suggesting that black English historically derived from white. The association with blacks is then explained as a result of their emigration to the northern cities, where these features were perceived as a distinctive marker of ethnic, as opposed to regional, identity. With the development of urban ghettos, the contrast became more marked over time.

An alternative view argues that the origins of AAEV lie in the use of a creole English (§53) by the first blacks in America. This language, originally very different from English as a result of its African linguistic background, has been progressively influenced by white English so that it now retains only a few creole features. Most contemporary linguists who have studied this topic accept a version of the creole hypothesis, because of the striking phonological and grammatical similarities between AAEV and other creoles, such as those of the West Indies; but they allow for the probability that some features of AAEV may have arisen partly or wholly as the result of white dialects.

There is a continuing need to disseminate the facts about the relationship between standard English and non-standard varieties, such as AAEV, because the principle of mutual recognition and respect is constantly being challenged. In particular we have to anticipate the severe linguistic disadvantage that affects children from these dialect backgrounds when they go to school, where the medium of instruction and criterion of successful performance is standard English. These days there is an increasing understanding of the educational issues in the USA; but an enlightened approach to the problem is by no means universal.

48

How we know
what someone is:
the social issue

The question 'What are you?' can also be answered with reference to our place in society. We acquire varying status as we participate in social structure; we belong to many social groups; and we perform a large variety of social roles.

Social class

One of the chief forms of sociolinguistic identity derives from the way in which people are organized into hierarchically ordered social groups, or classes. Classes are aggregates of people with similar social or economic characteristics. They are complex notions, in which factors such as family lineage, rank, occupation, education, and material possessions are all taken into account. And the way people talk (and, to a lesser extent, write) reflects this background to a considerable extent. Both accent and dialect (§45) are implicated.

Everyone has developed a sense of values that make some accents seem 'posh' and others 'low', some features of vocabulary and grammar 'refined' and others 'uneducated'. The distinctive features have been a long-standing source of comment, as this conversation illustrates. It is between Clare and Dinny Cherrel, in John Galsworthy's *Maid in Waiting* (1931, Ch. 31), and it illustrates a famous linguistic signal of social class in Britain – the two pronunciations of final *ng* in such words as *running*, [n] and [ŋ].

'Where on earth did Aunt Em learn to drop her g's?'

'Father told me once that she was at a school where an undropped "g" was worse than a dropped "h". They were bringin' in a country fashion then, huntin' people, you know.'

This example illustrates very well the arbitrary way in which linguistic class markers work. The [n] variant is typical of much working-class speech today, but a century ago this pronunciation was a desirable feature of speech in the upper middle class and above – and may still occasionally be heard there. The change to [ŋ] came about under the influence of the written form: there was a *g* in the spelling, and it was felt (in the late 19th century) that it was more 'correct' to pronounce it. As a result, 'dropping the *g*' in due course became stigmatized.

Probably the clearest examples of social dialects are those associated with a caste system. Castes are social divisions based solely on birth, which totally restrict a person's way of life – for example, allowing only certain kinds of job, or certain marriage partners. A well-known system is that of Hindu society in India, which has four main divisions, and many sub-divisions – though in recent years, the caste barriers have been less rigidly enforced. The Brahmins (priests) constitute the highest class; below them, in descending order, are the Kshatriyas (warriors), Vaisyas (farmers and merchants), and Sudras (servants). The so-called 'untouchables', whose contact with the other castes is highly restricted, are the lowest level of the Sudra caste. Phonology, grammar, and vocabulary all combine to produce linguistic correlates of caste.

Social standing

Status is the position a person holds in the social structure of a community – such as a priest, an official, a wife, or a husband. *Roles* are the conventional modes of behaviour that society expects a person to adopt when holding a particular status. Public roles often have formal markers associated with them, such as uniforms; but among the chief markers of social position is undoubtedly language. People exercise several roles: they have a particular status in their family (head of family, first-born, etc.), and another in their place of work (supervisor, apprentice, etc.); they may have a third in their church, a fourth in a local sports centre, and so on. Each position will carry with it certain linguistic conventions, such as a distinctive mode of address, an 'official' manner of speech, or a specialized vocabulary. During the average lifetime, people learn many such linguistic behaviours.

It is only occasionally that the adoption of a social role requires the learning of a completely different language. For instance, a knowledge of Latin is required in official Roman Catholic practice; a restricted Latin vocabulary was once prerequisite for doctors in the writing out of prescriptions; students in some schools and colleges still have to speak a Latin grace at meal-times; and Latin may still be heard in some degree ceremonies. More usually, a person learns a new variety of language when taking up a social role – for example, performing an activity of special significance in a culture (such as at a marriage ceremony or council meeting), or presenting a professional image (as in the case of barristers, the police, and drill sergeants). One of the most distinctive indications of professional role is the intonation, loudness, tempo, rhythm, and tone of voice in which things are said (§12).

The use of a different language is often a sign of a distinct religious or political group – as in the cases of French and English in Quebec, French and Flemish in Belgium, Latin, or the many official languages of the Indian subcontinent. Switching from one language to another may also be a signal of distance or solidarity in everyday circumstances, as can be seen in strongly bilingual areas, such as Paraguay. Here, the choice of Spanish or Guaraní is governed by a range of geographical and social factors, among which intimacy and formality are particularly important. In one study, bilingual people were asked which language they would use in a variety of circumstances – for example, with their spouse, sweetheart, children, boss, doctor, or priest. For most, Guaraní was the language of intimacy, indicating solidarity with the addressee. The use of Spanish would indicate that the speaker was addressing a mere acquaintance or a stranger. Spanish was also the language to use in more formal situations, such as patient–doctor, or student–teacher. Jokes would tend to be in Guaraní. Courtship often began in Spanish, and ended in Guaraní.

In monolingual communities, a major way of marking factors such as solidarity, distance, intimacy, and formality is to switch from one language variety to another. A Berlin business manager may use standard German at the office and lapse into local dialect on returning home. A conference lecturer in Paris may give a talk in formal French, and then discuss the same points with colleagues in an informal variety. A London priest may give a sermon in an archaic, poetic style, and talk colloquially to the parishioners as they leave. During the service, the priest might have used a modern English translation of the Bible, or one which derives from the English of the 16th century.

Languages have developed a wide range of varieties for handling the different kinds and levels of relationship which identify the social structure of a community. In English, for example, forms such as *liveth and reigneth, givest, vouchsafe*, and *thine* have long been distinctive in one variety of religious language; but in the 1960s, as proposals for the modernization of Christian liturgical language were debated, this variety came to be seen as a symbol of traditional practice with which people chose to identify or from which they dissociated themselves. The case is worth citing because the world-wide status of Christianity meant that many speech communities were involved, and over a quarter of the world's population was affected. No other linguistic change can ever have raised such personal questions of linguistic identity on such a global scale.

Perhaps the clearest use of varieties as markers of social structure is in the case of *diglossia* – a language situation in which two markedly divergent varieties, each with its own set of social functions, coexist as standards throughout a community. One of these varieties is used (in many localized variant forms) in ordinary conversations; the other variety is used for special purposes, primarily in formal speech and writing. It has become conventional in linguistics to refer to the former variety as *low* (L), and the latter as *high* (H).

Diglossic situations are widespread, some of the better-known ones including the distinction between Classical and Colloquial Arabic and between High German (*Hochdeutsch*) and Swiss German (*Schweitzer-deutsch*). The functional distinction between H and L is generally clear-cut. H is used in such contexts as sermons, lectures, speeches, news broadcasts, proverbs, newspaper editorials, and traditional poetry. It is a language that has to be learned in school. L is used in everyday conversation and discussion, radio 'soap operas', cartoon captions, folk literature, and other informal contexts. H and L varieties can display differences in phonology, grammar, and vocabulary.

In diglossic situations, the choice of H vs. L can easily become an index of social solidarity. A Swiss German speaker who used Hochdeutsch in everyday conversation would be considered snobbish or artificial – and if the context were a political discussion, it could even raise questions of national loyalty, as Hochdeutsch is used as the everyday language by people outside the country. Religious as well as political attitudes may be involved. The H form is often believed to be the more beautiful and logical, and thus the more appropriate for religious expression – even if it is less intelligible. And strong views are always expressed by Arabic speakers about Classical Arabic, which, as the language of the Qur'an, belongs to God and heaven.

Gender

The relationship between language and gender has attracted considerable attention in recent years, largely as a consequence of public concern over male and female equality. In many countries, there is now an awareness, which was lacking a generation ago, of the way in which language can reflect and help to maintain social attitudes towards men and women. The criticisms have been directed almost exclusively at the linguistic biases that constitute a male-orientated view of the world, fostering unfair sexual discrimination, and, it is argued, leading to a denigration of the role of women in society. English has received more discussion than any other language, largely because of the impact of early American feminism.

Several areas of grammar and vocabulary have been cited. In grammar, the issue that has attracted most attention is the lack of a sex-neutral, third-person singular pronoun in English, especially in its use after indefinite pronouns, e.g. *If anyone wants a copy, he can have one*. (In the plural, there is no problem, for *they* is available.) No natural-sounding option exists: *one* is considered very formal, and forms such as *he or she* are stylistically awkward. As a result, there have been many proposals for the introduction of a new English sex-neutral pronoun – including *tey*, *co*, *E*, *ne*, *thon*, *mon*, *heesh*, *ho*, *hesh*, *et*, *hir*, *jhe*, *na*, *per*, *xe*, *po*, and *person*. None of these proposals has attracted widespread support, but *co*, for example, has been used in some American communes, and *na* and *per* have been used by some novelists. Less radical alternatives include advice to restructure sentences to avoid the use of *he*-forms.

Many other examples of linguistic bias have been given. In the lexicon, particular attention has been paid to the use of male items in sex-neutral contexts, such as *man* in generic phrases (*the man in the street*, *stone-age man*, etc.), and the potential for replacing it by genuinely neutral terms (*chairman – chairperson, salesman – sales assistant*, etc.). Another lexical field that is considered problematic is marital status, where bias is seen in such phrases as *X's widow* (but not usually *Y's widower*), the practice of changing the woman's surname at marriage, and the use of *Mrs* and *Miss* (hence the introduction of *Ms* as a neutral alternative). The extent of the bias is often remarked upon. In one computer analysis of child school books, male pronouns were four times as common as female pronouns. In another study, 220 terms were found in English for sexually promiscuous women, and only 22 for sexually promiscuous men. It is easy to see how sexual stereotypes would be reinforced by differences of this kind.

What has happened to sexist language, as a result of this criticism? So far, the effect has been far more noticeable in writing than in speech. Several publishing companies have issued guidelines about ways of avoiding its use, and many writers and editors now make a conscious effort to avoid unintentional biases. Legal changes, such as the Sex Discrimination Act in Britain (1975), have caused job titles and much of the associated language to be altered. The written language has been most affected, but there have been signs of change in speech behaviour too. Plainly, the last quarter of the 20th century saw a general raising of consciousness about the issue of linguistic sexism, and this is likely to have a permanent effect upon the language.

49
How we know who someone is: the stylistic issue

The way people use language gives us information about the regional or social group they belong to (§§46–48). But there is more to identity than group involvement. We are individuals, and the uniqueness each of us feels is reflected in a unique use of language – a personal dialect, or *idiolect* (p. 290). For most people, the idiosyncratic properties of their idiolect give rise to no comment. Some people, however, make a living out of their idiolect, spoken or written. They go by such names as 'orators' and 'authors', and the result of their labours is usually described in terms of *style*.

Style has had hundreds of definitions. To Samuel Wesley, it was 'the dress of thought'; to Jonathan Swift, it was 'proper words in proper places'; to W. B. Yeats, it was 'high breeding in words and in argument'. The many nuances can be classified into two broad types: the evaluative, and the descriptive.

- Under the first heading, style is thought of in a critical way: the features that make someone or something stand out from an 'undistinguished' background. In this sense, it implies a degree of excellence in performance or a desired standard of production, as when someone is complimented for 'having style', or condemned for writing 'without style'.
- The second sense lacks these value judgements and simply describes

the set of distinctive characteristics that identify objects, persons, periods, or places. In this sense, we talk of 'Shakespearean style', the 'house style' of an institution, and all the variations in expression that relate to psychological or social states – 'informal style', 'legal style', and so on.

Both senses are widely used in language study. Evaluative notions are an essential part of aesthetic approaches to language, and are implicit in such areas as elocution, oratory, and literary criticism. Descriptive approaches are found more in scientific studies, such as the various branches of linguistics, where there is a concern for objective identification without evaluation.

How to analyse individual style

A common strand runs through both notions: style always involves an appreciation of contrast between alternative locations, periods, appearances, or behaviour. As language observers, we distinguish 'Shakespearean' from 'not Shakespearean', 'formal' from 'informal', 'scientific' from 'religious'. And as producers of language ourselves, we can to a large extent *choose* the linguistic 'guise' in which we wish to appear.

This concept of *choice* is central to stylistic study. Style is seen as the (conscious or unconscious) selection of a set of linguistic features from all the possibilities in a language. The effects these features convey can be understood only by intuitively sensing the choices that have been made, as when we react to the linguistic impact of a religious archaism or a poetic rhyme scheme, and it is usually enough simply to respond to the effect in this way. But there are often occasions when we have to develop a more analytical approach, such as when we are asked our opinion about a particular use of language. Here, when we need to explain our responses to others, or even advise others how to respond (as in the teaching of literature), our intuition needs to be supplemented by a more objective account of style. It is this approach which is known as *stylistics*.

The recognition and analysis of all forms of linguistic variation depends on the making of comparisons. We intuitively sense that individuals and groups differ and develop, and we seek to explain our intuition by systematically comparing the way in which they make use of specific linguistic features. If we wish to make our account objective, sooner or later we need to count the frequency of these features, plot their distribution in controlled samples, and quantify the extent of the difference – at which point, we would be engaging in a branch of stylistics known as *stylostatistics*, or *stylometrics*.

The larger the sample of data analysed, the more confident our conclusions will be. Stylostatistical studies thus tend to use a small number of carefully chosen textual features and to search for these in as large a body of text as is practicable. Where possible, comparisons are made with statistical data available for the whole language (such as large-scale counts of word frequency). In this way the language acts as a *norm* against which the idiosyncratic features are made to stand out.

Stylostatistics would not normally analyse those features over which individuals have little or no control because they are part of the obligatory structure of a language – such as the way we are obliged in English to put the article before the noun. Where there is no choice, there is no basis for making a stylistic contrast. Style is thus seen as our regular selections from the optional features of language structure. That is what makes individuals distinctive and gives them their personal linguistic identity.

Institutions, as well as people, need to be considered in relation to the definition of style as 'individual identity'. There are certain distinctive linguistic characteristics of newspaper language, for example, which will be found in all instances of the genre; but each paper has its own linguistic identity too, which makes it different from the others. The same principle applies to the study of banks, commercial products, broadcasting channels, and any organization which requires an identity and public image. House styles, letter-heads, newspaper titles, advertising slogans, and many kinds of trade-mark illustrate some of the ways in which institutions rely on stylistic features as a means of promoting corporate identity.

In principle, a detailed stylistic study could be made of a press report, a television commercial, or any other 'everyday' use of language. In practice, most stylistic analyses have attempted to deal with the more complex and 'valued' forms of language found in works of literature (*literary stylistics*). Moreover, it is possible to see in several of these studies a further narrowing of scope, with analysts concentrating on the more striking areas of literary language. Poetic language has attracted most attention, for that reason.

This concentration on the more distinctive forms of literary expression reflects the fact that linguistic analytic techniques are more geared to the analysis of the detailed features of sentence structure than of the broader structures found in whole texts or discourses (§41). The more compact and constrained language of poetry is far more likely to disclose the secrets of its construction to the stylistician than is the language of plays and novels, where the structuring process is less evident, and where dialogue and narrative is often indistinguishable from the norms of everyday speech. A great deal of work, accordingly, has been in the area of poetic language.

But poets are not the only ones who push language beyond its normal limits. All who engage in literary or quasi-literary activity, from novelists and dramatists to journalists and commentators, face similar problems. Nor is the wrestle with words restricted to literature. Humorists, both amateur and professional, are another group who constantly tease new effects out of old words, in their search for good punch-lines. And a further example is provided by the title of a book by the German theologian Paul van Buren, about how people use the word *God* as part of religious discourse: *The Edges of Language*. In his view, theistic language is 'a case of walking language's borders' – an attempt to express insight at the very edge of the 'platform of language', where, if we try to go further, 'we fall off into a misuse of words, into nonsensical jabbering, into the void where the rules give out'. Theologians, like poets, it seems, are continually striving to say what cannot be said.

Some stylistic applications

The focus on a single person's usage has led to a number of important applications of stylistic and stylostatistical studies. One of the most important has been in relation to texts where the authorship is either disputed or unknown – an anonymous essay, for example, or a play written by several authors in collaboration. The procedure is to compare the frequency and distribution of a small number of linguistic features in the problem text with the corresponding features in texts where the authorship is known. Given a judicious selection of features for comparison, it is often possible to make an identification. The authorship of the so-called *Junius letters* – a series of anonymous 18th-century political diatribes written under the pseudonym of *Junius* – was established using this sort of technique. They were shown to be the work of Sir Philip Francis.

The same techniques can be applied to any spoken or written sample. In everyday life, of course, there is usually no reason to carry out a stylistic analysis of someone's usage. But when someone is alleged to have broken the law, stylisticians might well be involved, their subject then forming a part of a *forensic linguistic* enquiry. Typical situations involve the prosecution arguing that incriminating utterances heard on a tape recording have the same stylistic features as those used by the defendant – or, conversely, the defence arguing that the differences are too great to support this contention. A common defence strategy is to maintain that the official statement to the police, 'written down and used in evidence', is a misrepresentation, containing language that would not be part of the defendant's normal usage. If the samples are large enough, the stylostatistical analysis can provide helpful evidence.

Several medical or paramedical professionals spend a great deal of their professional lives attempting to understand idiosyncratic linguistic behaviour. For example, psychiatrists, especially those practising psychotherapy, study their patients' favourite words and sense associations, their errors, and the words they avoid, in order to draw up a linguistic picture of the disorder and use it as a basis for treatment. Psychotherapy, indeed, has been called the 'talking cure'. And a similar characterization could also be applied to the work of speech and language pathologists, who routinely compile *profiles* of the aberrant linguistic behaviour of their patients, during the course of therapy.

The role of rhetoric

Although stylistics, as a branch of linguistics, is a 20th-century development, the task of identifying a person's style is not a new academic exercise. Traditionally it was carried out as part of the field of *rhetoric*, the study of persuasive speech or writing, especially as practised in public oratory. Several hundred *figures* were introduced by classical rhetoricians, classifying the way words could be arranged in order to achieve special stylistic effects. Many were restricted to the patterns found in Latin or Greek, but some achieved a broader currency, especially after the Renaissance, in studies of poetry.

In the Middle Ages, the study of rhetoric became part of the scholastic trivium, along with grammar and logic. Post-Renaissance theorists reduced the five parts to two, *style* and *delivery*, and the subject, as a result, became particularly associated with techniques of verbal expression especially in relation to reading aloud (the concern of *elocution*). Because of this influential tradition, many people think of rhetoric as essentially a matter of 'verbal ornament'.

The modern academic view of the subject, however, involves far more than the special effects of language production. It deals with the whole study of creative discourse, in both speech and writing, including the use of language in the mass media, and the way in which audiences react to and interpret communications directed at them. In effect, it is the analysis of the theory and practice of techniques of argumentation, involving listeners, as well as speakers, readers as well as writers. In its broadest sense, therefore, modern rhetoric studies the basis of all forms of effective communication.

50
How we know where someone is: the contextual issue

The question *Where are you from?*, which signals geographical identity (§45), can be balanced by another locational question, *Where are you now?* Many features of language correlate directly with the circumstances in which a communicative event takes place. Classifications vary, but most approaches recognize the central role played by the following three factors:

- *Setting*: The time and place in which a communicative act occurs, such as in church, during a meeting, at a distance, or upon leave-taking.
- *Participants*: The number of people who take part in an interaction, and the relationships between them, such as the addressee(s) and bystander(s).
- *Activity*: The type of activity in which a participant is engaged, such as cross-examining, debating, or having a conversation.

The interaction between these factors produces a set of constraints on the way we use language.

- *Channel*: They influence the medium chosen for the communication (e.g. speaking, writing, signing, whistling, singing, drumming) and the way it is used.
- *Code*: They influence the formal systems of communication shared

by the participant, such as spoken English, written Russian, American Sign Language, or some combination of these.

- *Message form*: They influence the structural patterns that identify the communication, both small-scale (the choice of specific sounds, words, or grammatical constructions) and large-scale (the choice of specific genres).
- *Subject matter*: They influence the content of the communication, both what is said explicitly and what is implied.

Each of these dimensions is involved in the identification of a communicative event. For example, a sermon (activity) is normally given in a church (setting), by a preacher addressing a congregation (participants), primarily using speech (medium), in a monologue in a single language (code), involving religious forms and genres (message form), and about a spiritual topic (subject matter). This kind of characterization needs immediate refinement, of course. Some sermons permit dialogue as well as monologue; some use chant and song alongside speech; some introduce different languages. But the core identity of sermons – and indeed of all uses of language – can be characterized with reference to the above dimensions.

How setting influences language

The particular time and place in which people interact will exercise its influence on the kind of communication that may occur – or whether communication is permitted at all. In institutionalized settings, such as a church or a court of law, the effect on language use is clear enough. But in many everyday situations, and especially in cultures we find alien, the relationship between setting and language can be very difficult to discover.

At dinner parties, funerals, interviews, council meetings, weddings, and on other occasions, linguistic norms of behaviour need to be intuitively recognized if we are to act appropriately, but they are not always easy to define. For example, how would we begin to define the optimum length of an after-dinner speech, or the proportion of humour its subject matter should contain?

In different times and places we may be obliged, permitted, encouraged, or even forbidden to communicate; and the quality or quantity of the language we use will be subject to social evaluation and sanction. The extent to which we recognize, submit to, or defy these sanctions is an important factor in any study of contextual identity. On the whole, we tend not to notice these constraints when the language is being used appropriately. But we readily react when we notice an inappropriate language use – as letters to broadcasting companies daily testify. Indeed, in a court of law, an inappropriate use of language – such as a failure to use required forms of address – may result in contempt of court and legal sanctions.

How participants influence language

The simple opposition of message *sender* and message *receiver* needs considerable refinement if we are to classify communicative events satisfactorily. Normally a single person acts as sender, or addressor; but we have to allow for unison speech, as in the case of liturgical responses in church or other rituals, group teaching (where the whole class may respond together), popular acclamations (such as during a political address, or in a sports arena), and speeches by the players in a theatrical presentation. The linguistic characteristics of such speech, especially the prosody (§12), will obviously be very different from those found when a person speaks alone.

Similarly, a single person is the usual receiver, or addressee, of a message; but here too we must allow for variations. We may address someone directly, or through an intermediary, such as a secretary, interpreter, or spokesman. A third party may overhear what we are saying, or see what we have written, and we may consider this desirable or undesirable. And speech addressed to a group of people is common enough in everyday conversation, as well as in more formal contexts, such as sermons, toasts, and lectures, and the whole range of circumstances that define the world of spoken and written mass communication.

All of these contexts can influence the language used by the speaker.

For example, if we know we are being overheard by our seniors we may well alter the way we speak, even to the extent of adopting a completely different stylistic level. We may need to defer to the broader audience by altering pronoun forms and using various politeness strategies, as well as by modifying our non-linguistic behaviour (such as our body movements and eye contact, §2). In some circumstances, the knowledge that we are being (or even, are likely to be) overheard may lead to non-fluency or a breakdown in communication, as in the well-known effects that take place when people are asked to speak into a microphone.

Varieties of language can alter completely if there is a perceived change in audience needs. In recent years, for example, there has been a radical shift in the way theologians have begun to talk about God, in the light of their perception that people have become dissatisfied with traditional images and are searching for new ones (p. 319). Such images covered a wide area of language, including terms that were highly abstract and mystical (*supreme being*, *infinite one*, *the unknowable*, *essence*), metaphorical and personal (*father*, *lord*, *judge*, *saviour*), psychological and ethical (*forgiveness*, *love*, *compassion*).

The dissatisfaction is well illustrated by the success of Bishop John Robinson's *Honest to God* (1963), which sold over a million copies. That book questioned the tradition of talking about God in crude spatial metaphors, as if he were *up there*, or *out there*. It argued that, to modern audiences, such language was outmoded and acted as a barrier to understanding, whereas images such as *ground of our being* could more easily be related to current ways of thinking. Several experiments in religious communication followed, in the spirit of this approach, and a new academic discipline was even proposed to study this area – *theography*, a term coined on analogy with *geography*, which aims to 'draw the map' of language that people use to talk about God.

How we accommodate

When two people with different social backgrounds meet, there is a tendency for their speech to alter, so that they become more alike (if the speakers are in rapport) or less alike (if they are not). The process is known as *accommodation* (p. 294) – *convergent* in the first case, *divergent* in the second. Modifications have been observed in several areas of language, including grammar, vocabulary, pronunciation, speech rate, the use of pause, and utterance length.

Everyday examples of convergence are the slower and simpler speech used in talking to foreigners or young children; the way technical information is presented in a less complex manner to those who lack the appropriate background; the rapid development of catch-phrases within a social group; and the way many people cannot stop themselves unconsciously picking up the accent of the person they are talking to. The process has even been observed in a study of babies 'talking' to adults: at twelve months, they were babbling at a lower pitch in the presence of their fathers, and at a higher pitch with their mothers.

These shifts take place in order to reduce the differences between participants, thus facilitating interaction, and obtaining the listener's social approval. It should be noted that linguistic accommodation also has its risks, such as the loss of personal (and sometimes group) identity, or the perceived loss of integrity, such that the listener may react against the speaker's new style. Much depends on how speakers view themselves and the group to which they belong (the *in group*) in comparison with the group to which the listeners belong (the *out group*). But on the whole, the benefits of convergence seem to outweigh these risks, with several social psychological studies showing that people react more favourably to those who move linguistically closer to them.

The opposite effect, speech divergence, takes place when people wish to emphasize their personal, social, religious, or other identity. There may be quite elementary reasons for the divergence, such as a dislike of the listener's appearance or behaviour; or there may be more deep-rooted reasons, such as the deliberate use of a minority language or ethnically distinctive accent or dialect. Threatening contexts readily result in divergence, as has been demonstrated experimentally.

In one study, a group of people in Wales were learning Welsh in a language laboratory. During one of the sessions, they were asked to answer some questions about language learning. The questions were presented to them in their individual booths by an English speaker with an RP accent (p. 64), who at one point arrogantly challenged their reasons for learning what he called 'a dying language with a dismal future'. The accents used in their replies were then compared with those used in responding to a previous question that was emotionally neutral. The test sentence replies showed immediate divergence: speakers used a broader Welsh accent, and some introduced Welsh words into their speech.

How activity influences language

The kind of activity in which we engage will also directly influence the way we communicate. At one level, our activities reflect the social status we have and the roles we perform (§48). But status and role are very general notions, within which it is possible to recognize a much more specific notion of *activity type*. For example, priests have a well-defined status and role within a community; but while exercising their role as priests, they engage in a wide range of activities, such as leading a service, giving a sermon, exorcizing spirits, hearing confession, baptizing, and visiting the sick. Many other occupations involve a similar range of variation; and in all cases there are linguistic consequences of the shift from one activity to another. Linguistically distinct activities are often referred to as *genres* or *registers*.

Activity influence is not restricted to occupational environments. We also engage in many kinds of activity in everyday speech and writing, such as gossiping, discussing, quarrelling, petitioning, visiting, telephoning, and writing out lists. Here too there are linguistic norms and conventions, although they are usually more flexible, and the genres are not always as easy to define as those associated with more formal activities, such as those involved in informational presentations or ceremonial occasions.

Under the heading of *information activities* we would include works of reference (dictionaries, catalogues, almanacs, government leaflets, etc.), instructional material (phrase books, recipe books, do-it-yourself manuals, etc.), newspapers, documents, reports, teletext, and all kinds of academic publication. Some of these materials are so wide-ranging and diverse that it is impossible to make simple generalizations about their linguistic distinctiveness. Newspapers, for example, constitute a clearly identifiable linguistic variety but one that is made up of a large number of *sub-varieties* such as news reports, letters, editorials, and crosswords. But at the opposite extreme, there are many informational linguistic activities that are limited in scope and fairly homogeneous in content and structure – such as cooking recipes and knitting patterns.

Some of the most ornate forms of visual language will be found in materials intended for use on religious and ceremonial occasions, such as in books of religious significance, memorial plaques, certificates (examination, birth, marriage, etc.), and inscriptions. Formal and often archaic language is usual, reflecting the special significance society attributes to these activities.

Probably the most widely encountered variety of visual language is that used for activities which involve the identification of persons, places, and objects. This includes street names, public signs, name tags, compliments slips, publication titles, identity cards, product labels, house numbers, registration plates, letter headings, tickets, shop facias, and much more. Typographical clarity and distinctiveness are the main characteristics, along with considerable grammatical abbreviation and the use of specialized vocabulary.

Finally, there are many linguistic activities where the identity of the visual variety is partly dependent on the active participation of the user. Space may be left for the users to fill in, or opportunity is given for them to reply in their own terms. Included in the first category are questionnaires, official forms, diaries, and various kinds of stationery; in the second are postcards, circulars, letters, and graffiti.

51
How dialects differ from languages

For most languages, the distinction between language and dialect (§45) is fairly clear-cut. In the case of English, for example, even though regional vocabulary and local differences of pronunciation can make communication difficult at times, no one disputes the existence of an underlying linguistic unity that all speakers identify as English, and which is confirmed by the use of a standard written language and a common literary heritage.

The differences between Cockney, Scouse, and Geordie, for example, may be considerable, but, when speakers of these dialects speak slowly, people from other English dialect backgrounds can understand most of what is said; and when such dialects are written down, the similarities with standard English stand out even more clearly. Correspondingly, the differences between dialects of English and dialects belonging to other languages are also easy to perceive. No matter how slowly a speaker of Spanish speaks, and no matter how it is written down, English speakers will not understand it – unless they have taken the trouble to learn Spanish, of course. But they can understand a great deal of Cockney, Scouse, and Geordie without having to learn it.

It is this sense of intelligibility and unintelligibility which allows us to tell the difference between utterances which belong to a dialect of our own language and those which belong to a different language. It is on the grounds of mutual unintelligibility that we distinguish between English, Spanish, German, Swahili, Chinese, and the other 6,000 or so languages of the world (p. 332). It seems a straightforward distinction. However, the criterion of intelligibility does not always work.

How identity outranks intelligibility

The criterion of intelligibility spectacularly fails to work when it comes up against the demands of national identity. A common situation is one where two spoken varieties are mutually intelligible, to a greater or lesser extent, but for political and historical reasons they are referred to as different languages. For example, using just the intelligibility criterion, there are really only two Scandinavian languages: Continental Scandinavian, which includes Swedish, Danish, and the two standard varieties of Norwegian; and Insular Scandinavian, which includes Icelandic and Faeroese. Although there are important linguistic differences between their languages, Swedes, Danes, and Norwegians can on the whole understand each other's speech. But we cannot, on that basis, consider them all to be speakers of the same language.

As soon as non-linguistic criteria are taken into account, we have to recognize three languages under the Continental heading. To be Norwegian is to speak Norwegian; to be Danish is to speak Danish; and to be Swedish is to speak Swedish. In such cases, issues of political identity, with all its historical and cultural associations, take priority over issues of intelligibility. It would be absurd to suggest to Swedes that their language is 'really' Norwegian; or vice versa.

There are many other such cases where political, ethnic, religious, literary, or other identities force a division between two modes of communication where linguistically there is relatively little difference, such as Hindi and Urdu, Bengali and Assamese, Twi and Fante, Xhosa and Zulu. In all such cases, the successful 'upgrading' of a dialect into a language depends on considerations of military, political, religious, economic, or cultural power. A powerless group cannot easily persuade the rest of the world that they want their speech, previously considered a dialect, to be given status as a language. As has often been said, 'A language is a dialect with an army and a navy'.

It need not take long for language identities to manifest themselves with confidence. Everything depends on the sociopolitical situation. For example, before the 1990s people from Croatia, Serbia, and Bosnia in former Yugoslavia were often described as speaking dialects of Serbo-Croatian. But since the 1990s civil war, such a description has become unpalatable to all sides. Today, Croats think of themselves as speaking Croatian, Serbs as speaking Serbian, and Bosniaks as speaking Bosnian. These are not new labels, but they have achieved a new status, as their communities use their new-found political identity to back up their linguistic claims.

The opposite situation is also interesting. Here we find cases where spoken varieties are mutually unintelligible, but for political, historical, or cultural reasons they are nonetheless called varieties of the same language. The three main 'dialects' of Lapp fall into this category, for example. And Chinese is a particularly interesting case, for here two kinds of linguistic criteria are in conflict with each other. From the viewpoint of the spoken language, the hundreds of dialects in China can be grouped into eight main types, which are mutually unintelligible to various degrees. But speakers of all these dialects share the same written language tradition, and those who have learned the system of Chinese characters are able to communicate with each other. Despite the spoken linguistic differences, therefore, Chinese is considered by its speakers to be a single language.

In the above cases, the languages in question have been well studied, and many speakers are involved. When languages have been little studied, or have very few speakers, it is much more difficult for linguists to interpret all the factors correctly. For example, when two languages are in close proximity, they often borrow words from each other – sometimes even sounds and grammar. On first acquaintance, therefore, the languages may seem more alike than they really are, and analysts may believe them to be dialects of the same language. This has proved to be a real problem in such parts of the world as South America, Africa, and South-east Asia, where whole groups of languages may be affected in this way. Similarly, decisions about how to analyse dialect chains (p. 291) will affect our decision as to whether two modes of communication belong to the same language or to different languages.

Language counting

The problem of distinguishing dialects and languages is one of the main reasons why it is so difficult to answer the apparently simple question, 'How many languages are there in the world?' There is no agreed total for the number of languages spoken today. Most reference books give a figure of around 6,000, but estimates have varied from 4,000 to 10,000. The former figure would be approached if we conflated mutually intelligible modes of communication – such as by calling Swedish, Norwegian, and Danish a single *Scandinavian*. The latter would arise if we 'upgraded' many dialects to have the status of separate languages – for example, considering Scots English and Ebonics (African-American Vernacular English), or Northern Welsh and Southern Welsh, to be different languages.

The language total is also affected by other factors. A few new languages do continue to be discovered, even these days, as unexplored regions of the world begin to be opened up. The discovery does not usually take place straight away. Often there are similarities with an already known language which make the investigators assume that what they have found is just a dialect variant of that language. Only after a period of contact does it transpire that the speech is so different that it has to be considered a different language. It takes a language survey to establish the facts, and there are still many countries where such surveys are incomplete or have not even begun. The people may be known, but the identity of their language may not be. Because many such peoples are bilingual or multilingual, and converse with outsiders in lingua francas, it may take a while before linguists come to realize that there is an ethnic language there at all.

The language total is also affected by the way new languages evolve and old languages die. The death of languages is such an important issue that it needs its own section (§52). But new languages do come into being, as they spread from an original heartland. Their speakers lose contact with each other, and gradually their speech evolves into a different language. This is the story of the Romance family of languages, for instance – French, Spanish, Portuguese, Catalan, Italian, Romanian, and so on. A little over a thousand years ago, these were all dialects of Vulgar Latin. Today they are separate languages.

All languages that develop a significant regional spread divide in this way – as has been repeatedly seen in the pidgin and creole languages of the world (§53). The process is less marked these days because of the way people can keep in touch through the mass media. But it still takes place, and no language is exempt. The languages which have developed the widest global spread show the effects most markedly. English, in particular, is rapidly evolving into its own family of languages. The kind of English spoken on the streets in Singapore and the Philippines, for example, is a mixture of English and Chinese (in the first case) and English and Tagalog (in the second). The resulting *Singlish* and *Taglish* are not readily intelligible to monolingual English or Chinese or Tagalog speakers. These are languages in their infancy.

The problem of names

In working on lesser-known language areas, a real problem is deciding what credence to give to a language name. This issue does not arise when discussing European languages, which are usually known by a single name that translates neatly into other languages – German (*Deutsch*), for example, translates neatly into English (*German*), Italian (*Tedesco*), French (*Allemand*), and so on. But in many parts of the world the situation is not so straightforward.

At one extreme, many communities have no specific name for their language. The name they use is the same as a common word or phrase in the language, such as the word for 'our language' or 'our people'. This is often so in Africa (where the name *Bantu*, which is given to a whole family of languages, means simply 'people'), and also in Central and South America. In the latter areas, we find such examples as *Carib* = 'people', *Tapuya* = 'enemy', and *Macu* = 'forest tribes'. Some tribes were called *chichimecatl* (= 'lineage of dogs'), *chontalli* (= 'foreigners'), or *popoloca* (= 'barbarians'), and these labels led to the modern language names *Chichimeca*, *Chontal*, and *Popoloca*. In several Australian Aboriginal languages, the name for the language is the word for 'this': for example, the nine languages within the Yuulngu family are known as *Dhuwala*, *Dhuwal*, *Dhiyakuy*, *Dhangu*, *Dhay'yi*, *Djangu*, *Djinang*, *Djining*, and *Nhangu*. Asking native speakers what language they speak is of little practical help, in such circumstances, if they only answer 'this'!

At the other extreme, it is quite common to find a community whose language has many names. A Native South American tribe, for instance, usually has several names. It will have a name for itself, along the above lines; but adjacent tribes may have given the people a different name – and not always a polite one! The Spanish or Portuguese explorers may have given them a third name – perhaps a characteristic of their appearance (e.g. *Coroado* means 'crowned' in Portuguese). More recently, anthropologists and other investigators may have used another name, often based on the geographical location of the tribe (e.g. *up-river* vs. *down-river*). And lastly, the same language may be spelled differently in Spanish, Portuguese, English, or in its own writing system (if one has been devised). For example, *Machacali*, spoken in Minas Gerais, Brazil, is sometimes spelled *Maxakali*, sometimes *Maxakari*.

There are further complications. Sometimes, the same name is applied to two different languages, as when *mexicano* is used in Mexico to refer to Spanish (otherwise known as *español* or *castellano*) and to the main indigenous language (*nahuatl*). Sometimes, speakers from different backgrounds may disagree about whether their ways of speaking should be related at all. Speakers of Luri, spoken in south-west Iran, say that their speech is a dialect of Persian; speakers of Persian disagree. Asking the native speakers is evidently no solution, for their perceptions will be governed by non-linguistic considerations, especially of a religious, nationalistic, or socioeconomic kind.

When all these factors are taken into account, it is plain that there will be no single answer to the question 'How many languages?' In some parts of the world, there has been a tendency to over-estimate, by taking names too literally and not grouping dialects together sufficiently – the Malayo-Polynesian languages are often cited in this connection. In other places, the totals are likely to have been underestimated – Indonesian languages, for example. Most recent studies have concluded that the total, at the beginning of the new millennium, is somewhere between 6,000 and 7,000. But at the rate at which languages are currently disappearing, this total will halve in the next 100 years.

How dialects differ from languages

52
How languages die

A language dies only when the last person who speaks it dies. Or perhaps it dies when the second-last person who speaks it dies, for then there is no one left to talk to.

There is nothing unusual about a single language dying. Communities have come and gone throughout history, and with them their language. Hittite, for example, died out when its civilization disappeared in Old Testament times. But what is happening today is extraordinary, judged by the standards of the past. It is language extinction on a massive scale. Of the 6,000 or so languages in the world about half are going to die out in the course of the present century: 3,000 languages, in 1,200 months. That means, on average, there is a language dying out somewhere in the world every two weeks or so.

How do we know? In the course of the past two or three decades, linguists all over the world have been gathering comparative data. If they find a language with just a few speakers left, and nobody is bothering to pass the language on to the children, obviously that language is bound to die out soon. And we have to draw the same conclusion if a language has less than 100 speakers. It is not likely to last very long. A 1999 survey showed that 96% of the world's languages are spoken by just 4% of the people. No wonder so many are in danger.

Data compiled by the Summer Institute of Linguistics in 1999 recognized 6,784 languages, with data available for 6,060. There were 51 languages with just one speaker left – 28 of them in Australia alone. There were nearly 500 languages in the world with less than 100 speakers; 1,500 with less than 1,000; and a staggering 5,000 languages with less than 100,000.

Why so many?

Why are so many languages dying? The reasons range from natural disasters, through different forms of cultural assimilation, to genocide. Small communities in isolated areas can easily be decimated or wiped out by earthquakes, hurricanes, floods, and other cataclysms. A habitat may become unsurvivable through unfavourable climatic and economic conditions – famine and drought especially. Communities can die through imported disease – from smallpox to the common cold, and especially, these days, AIDS. Cultural assimilation is an even bigger threat. Much of the present crisis stems from the major cultural movements which began 500 years ago, as colonialism spread a small number of dominant languages, such as English, Spanish, Portuguese, and French, around the world.

When one culture assimilates to another, the sequence of events affecting the endangered language seem to be the same everywhere. There are three broad stages. The first is immense pressure on the people to speak the dominant language – pressure that can come from political, social, or economic sources. It might be 'top down', in the form of incentives, recommendations, or laws introduced by a government or national body; or it might be 'bottom up', in the form of fashionable trends or peer group pressures from within the society of which they form a part; or again, it might have no clear direction, emerging as the result of an interaction between sociopolitical and socioeconomic factors that are only partly recognized and understood. 'To achieve a better quality of life' is a commonly stated reason why someone decides to learn the dominant language.

But wherever the pressure has come from, the result – stage two – is a period of emerging bilingualism, as people become increasingly efficient in their new language while still retaining competence in their old. Then, often quite quickly, this bilingualism starts to decline, with the old language giving way to the new. This leads to the third stage, in which the younger generation becomes increasingly proficient in the new language, identifying more with it, and finding their first language less relevant to their new needs. This is often accompanied by a feeling of shame about using the old language, on the part of the parents as well as their children. Parents use the old language less and less to their children, or in front of their children; and when more children come to be born within the new society, adults find fewer opportunities to use that language to them. Those families which do continue to use the language find there are fewer other families to talk to, and their own usage becomes inward-looking and idiosyncratic, resulting in *family dialects*. Outside the home, the children stop talking to each other in the language. Within a generation – sometimes even within a decade – a healthy bilingualism within a family can slip into a self-conscious semilingualism, and thence into a monolingualism which places that language one step nearer to extinction.

The need for revitalization

Can anything be done? Plainly it is too late to do anything to help many languages, where the speakers are too few or too old, and where the community is too busy just trying to survive to care about their language. But many languages are not in such a serious position. Often, where languages are seriously endangered, there are things that can be done to give new life to them. The term is *revitalization*.

Once a community realizes that its language is in danger, it can get its act together, and introduce measures which can genuinely revitalize. Everything has to be right, of course, for there to be a likelihood of success. The community itself must want to save its language. The culture of which it is a part must need to have a respect for minority languages. There needs to be funding, to support courses, materials, and teachers. And there need to be linguists, to get on with the basic task of *documenting* languages.

That is the bottom line: getting the language documented – recorded (using both sound and film), analysed, written down. The obvious reason for this is educational – the need for literacy. People must be able to read and write, if they or their language is to have a future in an increasingly computer-literate civilization.

But there is a second reason, and this is all to do with why we should care about dying languages at all. We should care for the very same reason that we care when a species of animal or plant dies. It reduces the diversity of our planet. We are talking about the intellectual and cultural diversity of the planet now, of course, not its biological diversity. But the issues are the same. Enshrined in a language is the whole of a community's history, and a large part of its cultural identity. The world is a mosaic of visions. To lose even one piece of this mosaic is a loss for everyone.

We can learn so much from the visions of others. Sometimes the learning is eminently practical, such as when we discover new medical treatments from the folk medicine practices of an indigenous people. Sometimes it is intellectual – an increase in our awareness of the history of our world, as when the links between languages tell us something about the movements of early civilizations. And of course, very often we learn something new about language itself – the behaviour that makes us truly human. That is why it is so important to document these languages as quickly as possible. With every language that dies, another precious source of data about the nature of the human language faculty is lost – and there are only about 6,000 sources in all.

How to save a language

Can we save a few thousand languages, just like that? Of course, if the will and funding were available. So how much would it cost? It is not cheap, when we think of what has to be done – getting linguists into the field, training local analysts, supporting the community with language resources and teachers, compiling grammars and dictionaries, writing materials for use in schools – and all over a period of several years, because it takes a lot of time to revitalize an endangered language. Conditions vary so much that it is difficult to generalize, but a figure of 100,000 dollars a year per language cannot be far from the truth. If we devoted that amount of effort over three years for each of 3,000 languages, we would be talking about some 900 million dollars.

Shall we be neat, and say a billion dollars? It sounds like a lot. But we must put it in perspective. It is equivalent to just over one day's OPEC oil revenues, in an average year. Or a fraction of the profits of the major computer organizations. It would be fine if the companies which have most fostered the linguicidal consequences of globalization in the last century should be the ones to save the world's languages and cultures from extinction in this one. It could be done.

There are very few success stories so far, because the money and political will have not been there, and in many cases it is too soon to say whether long-term survival is certain. But there are some famous cases of what can be done when both will and means are present. Probably the best known is modern Hebrew, resuscitated to serve as the official language of modern Israel. Then we have the case of Welsh, alone among the Celtic languages in not only stopping its steady decline towards extinction but (in the 2001 census) showing signs of real growth. The status of Welsh is protected by two Language Acts now, and its presence is increasingly in evidence wherever you travel in Wales.

On the other side of the world, Maori in New Zealand has been maintained by a system of so-called *language nests*, first introduced in 1982. These are organizations which provide children under five with a domestic setting in which they are intensively exposed to the language. The staff are all Maori speakers from the local community. The hope is that the children will keep their Maori skills alive after leaving the nests, and that as they grow older they will in turn become role models to new generations of young children.

There are cases like this all over the world. A similar language immersion programme has been used in Hawaii, with promising results for Hawaiian. The same applies to Tahitian (in Tahiti) and Yukagir (in Siberia). In North America, Navajo, Seneca, and Mohawk are among several indigenous languages which have begun to benefit from a 'bottom-up' reawakening of interest by local communities, along with 'top-down' political support, in the form of measures guaranteeing language rights. And when the reviving language is associated with a degree of political autonomy, the growth can be especially striking, as shown by Faeroese, spoken in the Faeroe Islands, after the islanders received a measure of autonomy from Denmark.

A language can even be brought back from the very brink of extinction. An example is the Ainu language of Japan, which after many years of neglect and repression had reached a stage where there were only eight fluent speakers left, all elderly. However, new government policies brought fresh attitudes and a positive interest in survival. Several 'semi-speakers' – people who had become unwilling to speak Ainu because of the negative attitudes by Japanese speakers – were prompted to become active speakers again. There is fresh interest now in working with children, and the language is more publicly available than it has been for years.

Several seriously endangered Aboriginal languages of Australia have been maintained and revived, thanks to community efforts, work by Australian linguists, and the help of local linguistic and cultural organizations. And if good descriptions and materials are available, even extinct languages can be resurrected. Kaurna, from South Australia, is an example. This language had been extinct for about a century, but had been quite well documented. So, when a strong movement grew for its revival, it was possible to reconstruct it. The revised language is not the same as the original, of course. It lacks the range that the original had, and much of the old vocabulary. But it can nonetheless act as a badge of present-day identity for its people. And as long as people continue to value it as a true marker of their identity, and are prepared to keep using it, it will develop new functions and new vocabulary, as any other living language would do.

It is too soon to predict the future of these revived languages, but in some parts of the world they are attracting precisely the range of positive attitudes and grass-roots support which are the preconditions for language survival. The interest can be seen in Britain, in the form of enthusiastic revival movements supporting Cornish and Manx, whose last mother-tongue speakers died out long ago. In such unexpected but heart-warming ways might we see the grand total of languages in the world minimally increased.

The alternative: eternal loss

Saving languages is expensive, time-consuming, and energetic work; but it is immensely worth while. It is difficult to convey the sense of joy and pride that people feel when they realize that their language will live on. And conversely, it is difficult to express the sense of loss, when you have not experienced it. Australian author David Malouf puts it this way, in his short story 'The only speaker of his tongue' (1985): 'When I think of my tongue being no longer alive in the mouths of men, a chill goes over me that is deeper than my own death, since it is the gathered death of all my kind'.

Language death is like no other form of disappearance. When people die, they leave signs of their presence in the world, in the form of their dwelling places, burial mounds, and artefacts – in a word, their archaeology. But spoken language leaves no archaeology. When a language dies, which has never been recorded, it is as if it has never been.

53

How languages
are born

It usually does not make sense to talk about languages being 'born'. When was English born? We cannot decide on a moment in time when the language we now know as English came into being. A continuity of change links Old English to Middle English, and Middle English to Modern English in such a way that it would be foolhardy to suggest a point at which the modern language began.

The same point would apply if we tried to identify a starting-point earlier in linguistic history. The language spoken by the Anglo-Saxons when they first arrived on British shores was one already being spoken on the Continent. And that language in turn evolved from still earlier Germanic languages now lost to us. When we search for language origins we usually find ourselves gazing despairingly at pre-history.

But not always. In the case of *contact languages* we can see a language coming into existence in a relatively short period of time. These languages are known as *pidgins*.

How pidgin languages evolve

A pidgin is a system of communication which has grown up among people who do not share a common language, but who want to talk to each other, for trading or other reasons. Pidgins have been variously called 'makeshift', 'marginal', or 'mixed' languages. They have a limited vocabulary, a reduced grammatical structure, and a much narrower range of functions, compared to the languages which gave rise to them. They are the native language of no one, but they are nonetheless a main means of communication for millions of people, and a major focus of interest to those who study the way languages change.

It is essential to avoid the stereotype of a pidgin language, as perpetrated over the years in generations of children's comics and films. The 'Me Tarzan, you Jane' image is far from the reality. A pidgin is not a language which has broken down; nor is it the result of baby talk, laziness, corruption, primitive thought processes, or mental deficiency. On the contrary: pidgins are demonstrably creative adaptations of natural languages, with a structure and rules of their own. Along with creoles (see below), they are evidence of a fundamental process of linguistic change, as languages come into contact with each other, producing new varieties whose structures and uses contract and expand. They provide the clearest evidence of language being created and shaped by society for its own ends, as people adapt to new social circumstances. This emphasis on processes of change is reflected in the terms *pidginization* and *creolization*.

Most pidgins are based on European languages – English, French, Spanish, Dutch, and Portuguese – reflecting the history of colonialism. However, this observation may be the result only of our ignorance of the languages used in parts of Africa, South America, or South-east Asia, where situations of language contact are frequent. One of the best-known non-European pidgins is Chinook Jargon, once used for trading by Native Americans in north-west USA. Another is Sango, a pidginized variety of Ngbandi, spoken widely in west-central Africa.

Because of their limited function, pidgin languages usually do not last for very long – sometimes for only a few years, and rarely for more than a century. They die when the original reason for communication diminishes or disappears, as communities move apart, or one community learns the language of the other. (Alternatively, the pidgin may develop into a creole – see below.) The pidgin French which was used in Vietnam all but disappeared when the French left; similarly, the pidgin English which appeared during the American Vietnam campaign virtually disappeared as soon as the war was over. But there are exceptions. The pidgin known as Mediterranean Lingua Franca, or Sabir, began in the Middle Ages and lasted until the 20th century.

Some pidgins have become so useful as a means of communication between languages that they have developed a more formal role, as regular *auxiliary languages*. They may even be given official status by a community, as lingua francas. These cases are known as *expanded pidgins*, because of the way in which they have added extra forms to cope with the needs of their users, and have come to be used in a much wider range of situations than previously. In time, these languages may come to be used on the radio, in the press, and may even develop a literature of their own. Some of the most widely used expanded pidgins are Krio (in Sierra Leone), Nigerian Pidgin English, and Bislama (in Vanuatu). In Papua New Guinea, the local pidgin (Tok Pisin) is the most widely used language in the country.

How creole languages evolve

A *creole* is a pidgin language which has become the mother tongue of a community – a definition which emphasizes that pidgins and creoles are two stages in a single process of linguistic development. First, within a community, increasing numbers of people begin to use pidgin as their principal means of communication. As a consequence, their children hear it more than any other language, and gradually it takes on the status of a mother tongue for them. Within a generation or two, native language use becomes consolidated and widespread. The result is a creole, or *creolized* language.

The switch from pidgin to creole involves a major expansion in the structural linguistic resources available – especially in vocabulary, grammar, and style, which now have to cope with the everyday demands made upon a mother tongue by its speakers. There is also a highly significant shift in the overall patterns of language use found in the community. Pidgins are by their nature auxiliary languages, learned alongside vernacular languages which are much more developed in structure and use.

Creoles, by contrast, are vernaculars in their own right. When a creole language develops, it is usually at the expense of other languages spoken in the area. But then it too can come under attack.

The main source of conflict is likely to be with the standard form of the language from which it derives (p. 290), and with which it usually coexists. The standard language has the status which comes with social prestige, education, and wealth; the creole has no such status, its roots lying in a history of subservience and slavery. Inevitably, creole speakers find themselves under great pressure to change their speech in the direction of the standard – a process known as *decreolization*.

One consequence of this is the emergence of a continuum of several varieties of creole speech, at varying degrees of linguistic 'distance' from the standard – what has been called the *post-creole continuum*. Another consequence is an aggressive reaction against the standard language on the part of creole speakers, who assert the superior status of their creole, and the need to recognize the ethnic identity of their community. Such a reaction can lead to a marked change in speech habits, as the speakers focus on what they see to be the 'pure' form of creole – a process known as *hypercreolization*. This whole movement, from creolization to decreolization to hypercreolization, can be seen at work in the recent history of African-American English in the USA.

The term *creole* comes from Portuguese *crioulo*, and originally meant a person of European descent who had been born and brought up in a colonial territory. Later, it came to be applied to other people who were native to these areas, and then to the kind of language they spoke. Creoles are now usually classified as English-based, French-based, and so on – though the genetic relationship of a creole to its dominant linguistic ancestor is rarely straightforward, as the creole may display the influences of several contact languages in its sounds, vocabulary, and structure.

Today, the study of creole languages, and of the pidgins which gave rise to them, attracts considerable interest among linguists and social historians. To the former, the cycle of linguistic reduction and expansion which they demonstrate, within such a short time-scale, provides fascinating evidence of the nature of language change. To the latter, their development is seen to reflect the process of exploration, trade, and conquest which has played such a major part in European history over the past 400 years.

Where do pidgins and creoles come from?

The world's pidgins and creoles display many obvious differences in sounds, grammar, and vocabulary, but they have a remarkable amount in common. Two opposed theories have attempted to explain these differences and similarities.

A long-standing view is that every creole is a unique, independent development, the product of a fortuitous contact between two languages. On the surface, this *polygenetic* view is quite plausible. It seems unlikely that the pidgins which developed in South-east Asia should have anything in common with those which developed in the Caribbean. And it is a general experience that these varieties come into use in an apparently spontaneous way – as any tourist knows who has faced a souvenir seller. Would not the restricted features of the contact situations (such as the basic sentence patterns and vocabulary needed in order to trade) be enough to explain the linguistic similarities around the world?

The view is tempting, but there are several grounds for criticism. In particular, it does not explain the *extent* of the similarities between these varieties. Common features such as the reduction of noun and pronoun inflections, the use of particles to replace tenses, and the use of repeated forms to intensify adjectives and adverbs are too great to be the result of coincidence. Why, then, should the pidginized forms of French, Dutch, German, Italian, and other languages all display the same kind of modifications? Why, for example, should the English-based creoles of the Caribbean have so much in common with the Spanish-based creoles of the Philippines? How could uniformity come from such diversity?

Such questions have led to the opposite view, which argues that the similarities between the world's pidgins and creoles can be explained only by postulating that they had a common origin (i.e. are *monogenetic*), notwithstanding the distance which exists between them. Moreover, a clear candidate for a 'proto'-language has been found – a 15th-century Portuguese pidgin, which may in turn have descended from a Mediterranean lingua franca known as Sabir. The Portuguese are thought to have used this pidgin during their explorations in Africa, Asia, and the Americas. Later, it is argued, as other nations came to these areas, the simple grammar of this pidgin came to be retained, but the original Portuguese vocabulary was replaced by words taken from their own languages. This view is known as the *relexification* hypothesis.

There is a great deal of evidence to support the theory, deriving from historical accounts of the Portuguese explorations, and from modern analyses of the languages. For instance, every English-based pidgin and creole has a few Portuguese words, such as *savi* 'know', *pikin* 'child', and *palava* 'trouble'. In Saramaccan, an English-based creole of Suriname, 38% of the core vocabulary is from Portuguese. Early accounts of Chinese pidgin refer to a mixed dialect of English and Portuguese. And on general grounds, relexification of a single 'proto'-pidgin seems a more plausible hypothesis than one which insists on a radical parallel restructuring of several languages.

The shift in approach, implicit in the relexification theory, is fundamental: it is not the case that English, and the other languages, were 'creolized', but that an original (Portuguese) creole was 'Anglicized'. However, not all the facts can be explained in this way. Pitcairnese creole has no Portuguese influence, and yet has much in common with other varieties. What accounts for those similarities? Then there are several pidgins and creoles which have developed with little or no historical contact with European languages – Sango and Chinook, for instance. And there seem to be many structural differences between European and non-European pidgins and creoles, which the common-origin hypothesis finds difficult to explain.

The evidence is mixed. Disentangling the structural similarities and differences between these varieties is a difficult task, and the evidence could be taken to support either a monogenetic or a polygenetic theory. Far more descriptive studies are needed before we rule out one view or the other. Meanwhile, other theories have been proposed, in an attempt to explain these similarities and differences. Other forms of simplified speech have been noted, such as that used by children, or in telegrams and headlines, or in talking to foreigners. It is possible that the processes underlying pidgins and creoles – such as fixed word order, or the avoidance of inflections – reflect some basic preferences in human language.

54
How language began

For centuries, people have speculated over the origins of human language. What is the world's oldest spoken language? Have all languages developed from a single source? What was the language spoken in the Garden of Eden? How did words come to be, in the very beginning? These questions are fascinating, and have provoked experiments and discussion whose history dates back 3,000 years. The irony is that the quest is a fruitless one. Each generation asks the same questions, and reaches the same impasse – the absence of any evidence relating to the matter, given the vast, distant time-scale involved. We have no direct knowledge of the origins and early development of language, nor is it easy to imagine how such knowledge might ever be obtained. We can only speculate, arrive at our own conclusions, and remain dissatisfied.

The Danish linguist Otto Jespersen (1860–1943) grouped commonly held theories about the origins of language into four types, and added a fifth of his own. They are often referred to by nicknames.

- *The 'bow-wow' theory*: Speech arose through people imitating the sounds of the environment, especially animal calls. The main evidence would be the use of onomatopoeic words, such as *splash* and *quack*, but as few of these exist in a language, and as languages vary so much in the way they represent natural sounds, the theory has little support.

- The *'pooh-pooh' theory*: Speech arose through people making instinctive sounds, caused by pain, anger, or other emotions. The main evidence would be the universal use of sounds as interjections, such as *ooh* or *tut-tut*, but no language contains many of these, and in any case the clicks, intakes of breath, and other noises which are used in this way bear little relationship to the vowels and consonants found in phonology. The spelling is never a satisfactory guide.

- The *'ding-dong' theory*: Speech arose because people reacted to the stimuli in the world around them, and spontaneously produced sounds (*oral gestures*) which in some way reflected or were in harmony with the environment. The main evidence would be the universal use of sounds for words of a certain meaning, but apart from a few cases of apparent sound symbolism (such as *teeny-weeny*), the theory has nothing to commend it. Several fanciful examples have nonetheless been cited – *mama* is supposed to reflect the movement of the lips as the mouth approaches the breast, and *bye-bye* or *ta-ta* show the lips and tongue respectively 'waving' good-bye.

- The *'yo-he-ho' theory*: Speech arose because, as people worked together, their physical efforts produced communal, rhythmical grunts, which in due course developed into chants, and thus language. The main evidence would be the universal use of prosodic features (§12), especially of rhythm; but the gap between this kind of expression and what we find in language as a whole is so immense that an explanation for the latter would still have to be found.

- The *'la-la' theory*: Jespersen himself felt that, if any single factor was going to initiate human language, it would arise from the romantic side of life – sounds associated with love, play, poetic feeling, perhaps even song. But again, the gap between the emotional and the rational aspects of speech expression would still have to be accounted for.

Early 'experiments'

The lengths to which some people have gone in order to throw light on the question are truly remarkable – if the accounts are to be believed. One of the best-known reports concerns the Egyptian king Psamtik I, who reigned in the 7th century BC. According to the Greek historian Herodotus, Psamtik wished to find out which of all the peoples of the world was the most ancient. His way of determining this was to discover the oldest language which, he thought, would be evidence of the oldest race.

> He gave two new-born babies of ordinary men to a shepherd, to nurture among his flocks after this manner. He charged him that none should utter any speech before them, but they should live by themselves in a solitary habitation; and at the due hours the shepherd should bring goats to them, and give them their fill of milk, and perform the other things needful. Thus Psammetichus [Psamtik] did and commanded because he desired, when the babes should be past meaningless whimperings, to hear what tongue they would utter first.

> And these things came to pass; for after the shepherd had wrought thus for a space of two years, when he opened the door and entered in, both the babes fell down before him, and cried *becos*, and stretched out their hands. Now when the shepherd heard it for the first time, he held his peace; but when this word was often-times spoken as he came to care for them, then he told his lord, and brought the children into his presence when he commanded. And when Psammetichus had also heard it, he enquired which nation called anything *becos*; and enquiring, he found that the Phrygians call bread by this name. Thus the Egyptians, guided by this sign, confessed that the Phrygians were elder than they. That so it came to pass I heard of the priests of Hephaestus in Memphis.

Phrygian is now extinct, but at the time it was spoken in an area corresponding to the north-western part of modern Turkey.

Psamtik's conclusion was wrong, for we know from philological studies that Phrygian is but one of several languages which had developed in that period of history. So why did the children say *becos*? Doubtless they had begun to babble naturally and repetitively to each other, in a similar way to twins, and this was one of the 'snatches' that the shepherd recognized. Some commentators have even suggested that they were imitating the sound of the goats!

Whether the Psamtik experiment ever took place is open to question. Possibly the origins of the story lie in a fiction invented by someone to discredit the Egyptians. But whatever the reality, the initiative credited to Psamtik has apparently had its parallels in several later times and places. At least two similar experiments have been reported – though again, there are doubts as to their authenticity.

Scientific approaches

By contrast with the informal discussion and speculation of preceding centuries, serious attempts have been made in recent years to see if modern science can throw any light on the question of the origins of language. The study is sometimes called *glossogenetics* – the study of the formation and development of human language, in both the child and the race. Might it be possible to deduce, from the fossil record of early hominids, the point at which speech began? The matter has been well investigated, but the results are not conclusive.

It is possible to make plaster casts of the bony cavities within the skulls which have been found. It can be shown, for example, that both Neanderthals and Cro-Magnons (pre-30,000 BC) had similar brain sizes to that of modern humans. But this information is of limited value. The relative size and shape of the brain can be established, but none of the more relevant detail. In any case, there is no direct correlation between the size of a brain and the use of language: language is found in people with small brains, such as nanocephalic dwarfs, or children who have had large areas of brain removed – and some gorillas have a brain size close to these. It is plausible that an increase in the number of brain cells increases intellectual or linguistic capacity, but no correlation has been established.

Another way of looking at the problem is to ask whether primitive people had the physiological capacity to speak, and this has led to a great deal of interesting research. The problem is that only the shape of the jaws and the oral cavity are preserved in fossils; there is no direct information about the size and shape of the soft tissues of tongue, pharynx, or larynx, nor about the ability to move these organs (§4). Most of the reasoning has therefore had to be based on reconstruction using plaster casts, and comparison with the physiology and vocalization of present-day primates and human infants.

It is possible to say with some conviction, using this kind of argument, that the older hominids did not possess speech; but the position of the more recent remains is unclear. It is unlikely that Australopithecus (who appeared around 4–5 million BC) could speak, but the evidence is ambiguous for Neanderthals (70–35,000 BC). Linguists and anatomists have compared the reconstructed vocal tract of a Neanderthal skull with those of a newborn and an adult modern human. The newborn and Neanderthal vocal tracts are remarkably similar. Neanderthals would have been able to utter only a few front consonant-like sounds and centralized vowel-like sounds, and may have been unable to make a contrast between nasal and oral sounds. This is well below what is found in the phonologies of the world's languages today (§11). It would have been possible to construct a linguistic code out of these limited sounds, but it would have required a level of intellectual ability apparently lacking at that evolutionary stage. On the other hand, these phonetic abilities are far ahead of modern primates. It has thus been concluded that Neanderthals represent an intermediate stage in the gradual evolution of speech. Cro-Magnons (35,000 BC), by contrast, had a skeletal structure much more like that of modern humans.

It would seem that the human vocal tract evolved from a non-human primate form to enable fast and efficient communication to take place. Speech is not merely the incidental result of a system designed for breathing and eating. The changes that took place in the larynx, pharynx, and mouth came about at the cost of less efficient breathing, chewing, and swallowing. Modern humans can choke from food lodged in the larynx;

monkeys cannot (p. 25). The survival value of speech must be considerable to compensate for such deficiencies. The human being, in short, seems to have evolved as a speaking animal – *homo loquens*.

Some hominids had a human-like vocal tract as far back as 200,000 BC, but they probably did not have a sufficiently developed nervous system to control it. There is general agreement on a time-scale from 100,000 to 20,000 BC for the development of speech. If the Neanderthal evidence is accepted, this scale narrows to 50–30,000 BC, in the latter part of the Upper Palaeolithic period.

This is the conclusion regarding speech. But the lack of physical similarities with modern humans does not prove that there was no language in an abstract sense, or other modes of communication (§2). At the time indicated above, cultural development was relatively advanced, and there must have been some efficient way of transmitting information about skills from one generation to the next. Any degree of social interdependence – as found in tribal grouping, religious activity, or group hunting techniques – would seem to require a communication system. Cave drawings of the period also suggest the existence of an intellectual capability such as would be required for language.

An elaborate gesture system is one possibility. The early development of language may well have been assisted by some kind of signing, which would have been the simplest way of communicating basic meanings – such as how to use tools. Hands were no longer necessary for locomotion, so they could be used for other activities. Perhaps primitive people who were skilful in using signs stood a better chance of survival. Natural selection could then have led to the development of the intellectual faculties prerequisite for speech.

Learning to use tools, and to pass the skills on, would be most efficiently done through language. It has even been suggested that learning to use tools and learning language are interrelated skills. They are localized in the same general area of the brain; and both tool using and gesture require sophisticated use of the hands. However, some non-human primates can use tools, and it is unlikely that the hands could have been used for two such different purposes for long. Nonetheless, in an indirect way, tools could have promoted the development of speech. Sounds made at the same time as the gestures might have come to be associated with various activities. The idea has been proposed that, as tools came to be used for more advanced purposes, food would be stored, so that there would be intervals between meals, and thus more time available for the mouth to be put to other uses – such as the development of spoken language.

We can only speculate about the link between oral and gestural language. Similarly, the gap between human language and the communication systems of the nearest primates remains vast, and there is no sign of a language-like increase in communicative skills as one moves from lower to higher mammals. Human language seems to have emerged within a relatively short space of time, perhaps as recently as 30,000 years ago. But that still leaves a gap of over 20,000 years before the first unequivocal evidence of written language (§17).

55

How language changes

However language began, one thing is certain – it immediately began to change, and has been changing ever since. Languages are always in a state of flux. Change affects the way people speak as inevitably as it does any other area of human life. Language purists do not welcome it, but they can do very little about it. Language would stand still only if society did. A world of unchanging linguistic excellence, based on the brilliance of earlier literary forms, exists only in fantasy. The only languages that do not change are dead ones.

During the greater part of the 19th century, linguists began to use a comparative method to establish the facts of language change. What features of language have changed in the past? When did they change? How did they change? During the 20th century, especially as a consequence of recent trends in sociolinguistics (p. 299), the emphasis shifted towards a search for explanations. *Why* do languages change?

How we know what old languages sounded like

How do we know, in the days before recorded sound, how languages were pronounced? The question applies as much to earlier states of a modern language (such as the language of Shakespeare) as to languages that are no longer spoken (such as Hittite). There are several kinds of evidence.

When European languages first came to be written down, those who devised the alphabets borrowed symbols from alphabets already in use elsewhere – usually Latin. They would then modify or add to these symbols whenever they came across sounds which the older alphabet could not cope with. It is thus possible to use these changes as evidence of differences in the way the two languages were spoken. For example, when the Latin alphabet was used for Anglo-Saxon, the symbol æ was added – presumably because the missionaries felt that Latin *a* and *e* were inadequate to represent the sound they heard.

Writers sometimes give an account of contemporary pronunciation features. In 16th- and 17th-century England, for example, detailed accounts were provided by *orthoepists*, specialists in the study of pronunciation. They included Bishop John Wilkins (1614–72) and the mathematician John Wallis (1616–1703). In the *Orthographie* of John Hart (d. 1574), for instance, which was published in 1569, we find detailed descriptions of the organs of speech and of the sounds of 16th-century English.

The way in which early poets pun, made words rhyme, or gave their lines a particular metrical pattern, provides a great deal of evidence about where the stress fell in a word, and the way vowels were pronounced. The name *Rosaline*, for example, can be pronounced with an ending which rhymes with *pin* or with *pine*. In Shakespeare's *Romeo and Juliet*, we hear him rhyming it with *mine*. Or again, we can infer from the way Chaucer rhymes *was* with the French *par cas* that its pronunciation must have been something like 'wass'. Such comparisons do not tell us exactly how the words were pronounced, nor whether these were normal pronunciations of the time; but they do provide the historical linguist with valuable clues.

Another procedure is *comparative reconstruction*. We work backwards from languages whose pronunciations are known, comparing the way languages have changed in order to reconstruct earlier forms. Most of our information about the oldest states of languages derives from this method. But the further back in history we travel, the less certain our phonetic deductions are likely to be. It may be clear that an early language contrasted two sounds, but quite unclear as to how this contrast was actually realized in speech.

How does language change?

During the later part of the 19th century, it was believed that a sound change affected the whole of a language simultaneously: one sound system would smoothly develop into the next, and all words which contained a particular sound would be affected in the same way.

We now know that linguistic change does not operate in such an 'across-the-board' manner. Some speakers introduce the change into their speech before others; some use it more frequently and consistently than others; and some words are affected before others. A more accurate view is to think of a change gradually spreading through the words of a language – a view that is known as *lexical diffusion*. At first just a few people use the change sporadically in a few words (commonly occurring words are influenced very quickly); then a large number of words are affected, with the sound gradually being used more consistently; then the majority of the words take up the change.

The evidence for this kind of process has largely come from sociolinguistic studies of contemporary linguistic variation. Pioneered by William Labov (1927–), these studies proceed on the assumption that the variation in language use which is found in any community is evidence of change in progress in a language. Detailed observations are made of the way in which different kinds of people speak in different social settings. The parameters along which these differences can be plotted are known as *linguistic variables* (p. 300). By examining the frequency with which different people used a variable, Labov was able to draw conclusions about the motivation, direction, and rate of linguistic change.

These are small-scale studies, but they have large-scale implications. It is likely that the same gradual process of change affects whole languages as well as dialects. The metaphor of a *wave* has proved particularly attractive since the late 19th century: a change spreads through a language in much the same way as a stone sends ripples across a pool. But even this implies too regular a movement to account for the reality of sociolinguistic variation.

Why does language change?

It is easy to recognize a change in language – but only *after* it has taken place. It is not difficult to reflect on how people spoke several years ago, to point to a new word which has recently entered the language, or to express an opinion about the emergence of a cliché. What is almost impossible is to *predict* a language change. Which sounds, words, or grammatical constructions will change in the next ten, twenty . . . years?

It is just as difficult to be precise about the origins of a change in language. Who first used the new form? Where was it used? And when, exactly? Historical dictionaries always give an approximate date of entry for a new word or meaning – but these dates invariably reflect the earliest known use of that word in the *written* language. The first use of the word in speech is always an unknown number of years previously.

To obtain answers to these questions, we need to know more about why language changes. If we understood the causes of change, we could begin to make predictions about when a change was likely to take place, and observe it while it was happening. There has long been imaginative speculation on the matter, with suggested causes coming from fields as far apart as theology (that change is a consequence of human arrogance, as manifested in the Tower of Babel) and climatology (that change is the consequence of human physical location – the mountain-dweller having a physiologically different capacity for speech compared with the valley-dweller). Some scholars have adopted a highly pessimistic view, feeling that the causes can never be found.

These days, the speculation and pessimism are being replaced by an increasing amount of scientific research, which has shown that there is no single reason for language change. Several factors turn out to be implicated, some to do with the nature of society, and some to do with the nature of language structure.

Social factors

Geographical distance

When people move away from each other, their language will diverge. The two groups will have different experiences, and at the very least their vocabulary will change. Similarly, when people come into contact with each other, their language will converge. The sounds, grammar, and vocabulary of one group are likely to exercise some influence on the other. These days, the increased mobility of people, within and between countries, makes this a major factor.

Cultural developments

New objects and ideas are continually being created, and language changes to take account of them. At the same time, old objects and ideas fall out of daily use, and the language becomes obsolete.

Imperfect learning

Some change is the result of one population imperfectly learning the language of another. This is a common occurrence, as illustrated by many immigrant groups, or the levels of bilingualism found in contact areas. The minority language forms a *substratum* which in the long term influences majority usage. For example, several varieties of American English display the influence of the West African linguistic background of its black population.

Social prestige

People come to talk like those they identify with or admire – a process which may be conscious or subconscious (p. 325). Conscious change can be observed in those cases where people go out of their way to use or avoid a certain feature in their spoken or written language – such as *whom* or intrusive /r/ (p. 452). Subconscious change, where people are not aware of the direction in which their speech is moving, is less noticeable, but far more common. The movement may be towards a favoured accent or dialect (one which has *positive prestige*), or away from one which is held in low esteem (*negative prestige*). The speakers are usually aware of the existence of linguistic differences (saying such things as *I don't like the way those people talk*), but unaware of any trend in their own speech related to their attitude.

Research in sociolinguistics has shown the way in which patterns of change relate to social prestige. For example, the work of Labov and others has shown that conscious change in American and British English is usually in the direction of those linguistic forms which are widely and openly recognized as prestigious (they have *overt prestige*, as in the case of standard English). This kind of change is often initiated by people from the lower middle-class or upper working-class – especially women, who seem to be more aware of these factors than men. By contrast, subconscious change is usually in the opposite direction, away from overt prestige. It is often initiated by working-class men, and associated with such attributes as toughness and virility, which carry *covert prestige*.

Linguistic factors

Social factors can motivate people to change their language, but is there anything in language itself which, so to speak, 'welcomes' a change? Several trends have been noted.

Ease of articulation

In the 19th century, it was widely felt that sounds changed because speakers would want to speak using as little effort as possible. On this basis, sounds and sound systems should become simpler over long periods of time. Some types of sound change do provide evidence for this view – such as the trend in many languages to weaken or drop final consonants, or to allow adjacent sounds to influence each other. But there are also many cases where articulatory complexity is unaffected by a sound change – and even cases where it seems to have increased. Only a small part of language change can be explained by the principle of *least articulatory effort*.

Analogy

Irregular features in the grammar of a language are often influenced by its regular patterns: the exceptions are made to conform to the rule. A well-studied case is the verb system in the history of English. Several of the irregular verbs of Anglo-Saxon have fallen under the influence of the regular verbs in the past 1,000 years. For example, *helpan* ('help') had *healp* as a past tense and *holpen* as a past participle; but by the 14th century, the verb had become regular, using the normal *-ed* ending – *helped*. During the early Middle English period, over forty other verbs (including *walk*, *climb*, *burn*, and *step*) were influenced in the same way. Social factors, such as the development of the standard language, and the growth of printing, slowed the change down, so that present-day English still has many irregular verbs. But the force of analogy can still be heard, when people use non-standard forms (such as *knowed*), or when children, learning the language, experiment with such forms as *goned*.

Randomness

Might language change have no systematic explanation? It has been proposed that change might be essentially unpredictable – the result of arbitrary changes in fashion or chance errors in articulation. Certainly, many changes in vocabulary are isolated and arbitrary; but there is no strong case for randomness in phonology or grammar. On the contrary, similar processes of change have been found in unrelated languages all over the world.

56
How language families work

The first scientific attempts to discover the history of the world's languages were made at the end of the 18th century. Scholars began to compare groups of languages in a systematic and detailed way, to see whether there were correspondences between them. If these could be demonstrated, it could be assumed that the languages were related – in other words, that they developed from a common source, even though this might no longer exist.

Evidence of a common origin for groups of languages was readily available in Europe, in that French, Spanish, Italian, and other Romance languages were clearly descended from Latin – which in this case is known to have existed. The same reasoning was applied to larger groups of languages, and by the beginning of the 19th century there was convincing evidence to support the hypothesis that there was once a language from which many of the languages of Eurasia have derived. In 1786, Willliam Jones (1746–94), a British orientalist and jurist, gave a presidential address to the Bengal Asiatic Society. It contained the following observation, generally quoted as the first clear statement asserting the existence of this earlier language, now generally referred to as Proto-Indo-European:

> The Sanskrit language, whatever be its antiquity, is of a wonderful structure; more perfect than the Greek, more copious than the Latin, and more exquisitely refined than either, yet bearing to both of them a stronger

affinity, both in the roots of verbs, and in the forms of grammar, than could possibly have been produced by accident; so strong, indeed, that no philologer could examine them all three, without believing them to have sprung from some common source, which, perhaps, no longer exists.

The resemblances between European languages and Sanskrit, the oldest-attested language of the Indian subcontinent, had been noted as early as the 16th century, but the explanation advocated was that Sanskrit was the parent of the European languages. During the 19th century, the procedures of *comparative philology* validated the common-source hypothesis beyond question. Minutely detailed investigations of all the major European languages, and several of their dialects, were carried out by such scholars as Franz Bopp, Jakob Grimm, and August Schleicher, and their work established Germany as the centre of comparative philology.

How the comparative method works

In historical linguistics, the *comparative method* is a way of systematically comparing a series of languages in order to prove a historical relationship between them. Scholars begin by identifying a set of formal similarities and differences between the languages, and try to work out (or *reconstruct*) an earlier stage of development from which all the forms could have derived. The process is known as *internal reconstruction*. When languages have been shown to have a common ancestor, they are said to be *cognate*.

The clearest cases are those where the parent language is known to exist. For example, on the basis of the various words for *father* in the Romance languages, such as *père* and *padre*, it is possible to work out how they all derived from the Latin word *pater*. If Latin no longer existed, it would be possible to reconstruct a great deal of its form, by comparing large numbers of words in this way. Exactly the same reasoning is used for cases where the parent language does not exist, as when the forms in Latin, Greek, Sanskrit, Welsh, etc. are compared to reconstruct the Indo-European form *pəter*.

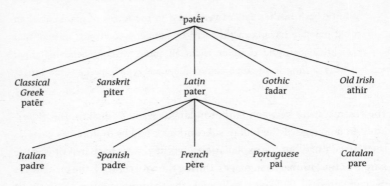

Fig. 18. Some words for *father* in Indo-European

The asterisk in front of a form, in historical linguistics, shows that the form in question is a reconstruction which has not been attested in written records. Exactly how such reconstructed forms were pronounced is a matter of (at times fierce) debate: some scholars are happy to assign phonetic values to the forms, and pronounce them as if they were part of a real language; others argue that the forms are little more than abstract formulae, summarizing the sets of correspondences which have been noted.

How to show historical relationships

The main metaphor that is used to explain the historical relationships is that of the *language family*, or *family tree*. Within the Romance family, Latin is the *parent* language, and French, Spanish, etc. are *daughter* languages; French would then be called a *sister* language to Spanish and the others. The same approach is used with larger groups. Within the Indo-European family, Proto-Indo-European is the parent language, and Latin, Greek, Sanskrit, and others are the daughter languages. In a large family, it will be necessary to distinguish various *branches*, each of which may contain several languages, or *sub-families* of languages.

This way of talking must not be taken too literally. A parent language does not always live on after a daughter language is 'born', nor do

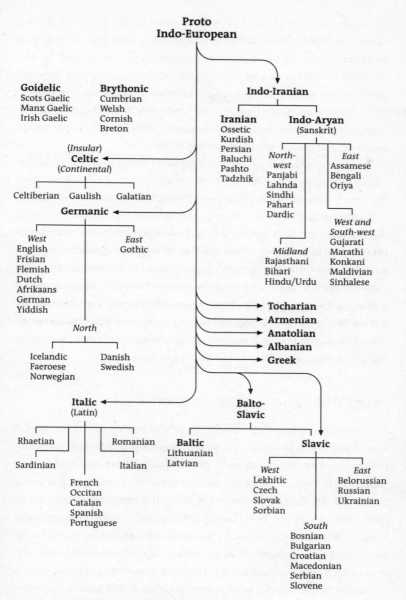

How language families work

Fig. 19. The Indo-European family of languages

languages suddenly appear in the way implied by the metaphor of birth. Nor is it true that, once branches of a family begin to emerge, they develop quite independently, and are never afterwards in contact with each other. Languages converge as well as diverge. Furthermore, stages of linguistic development are not as clear-cut as the labels on a family tree suggest, with change operating smoothly and uniformly throughout. Linguistic change, we now know, is much more uneven, with different social groups responding to change in different ways (p. 360).

Since the 19th century, other classificatory terms have come into use. *Family* is still used as a general term for any group of languages where there is a likelihood of a historical relationship. But in some classifications, a distinction is drawn in terms of how definite the relationship is. If there is clear linguistic evidence of a close relationship, the term *family* continues to be used; but where the relationship is less definite, or more remote, the grouping is referred to as a *phylum*. Sometimes the term *macro-phylum* is used for yet more general and less definite groupings. It is evident, for example, that all the Aboriginal languages of Australia are related, but as there is no clear-cut historical evidence which bears on the matter, and little typological work, scholars often refer to the Australian *(macro)phylum* rather than to the Australian *family*.

Types of linguistic classification

There are two main ways of classifying languages: the *genetic* (or *genealogical*) and the *typological*. The genetic approach is a historical classification, based on the assumption that languages have diverged from a common ancestor. It uses early written remains as evidence, and when this is lacking, deductions are made using the comparative method to enable the form of the parent language to be reconstructed. The approach has been widely used, since its introduction at the end of the 18th century, and provides the framework within which all world-wide linguistic surveys to date have been carried out. However, the success of the approach in Eurasia, where copious written remains exist, is not matched in most other parts of the world, where written remains may be absent.

How Language Works

The typological classification is based on a comparison of the formal similarities which exist between languages. It is an attempt to group languages into structural types, on the basis of phonology, grammar, or vocabulary, rather than in terms of any real or assumed historical relationship. For example, it is possible to group languages in terms of how they use sounds – how many and what kinds of vowels they have, whether they use clicks, whether they use tones, and so on. Languages can also be classified in terms of whether their word order is fixed or free, and which order is favoured.

The earliest typologies were in the field of morphology (§37). These, propounded by August von Schlegel (1767–1845) and others in the early 19th century, recognized three main linguistic types (the first three below), on the basis of the way a language constructs its words, and a fourth type is often added:

- In *isolating* languages (also called *analytic* or *root* languages), all the words are invariable: there are no endings, and grammatical relationships are shown through the use of word order. Chinese, Vietnamese, and Samoan are clear cases.
- In *inflecting* languages (also called *synthetic* or *fusional* languages), grammatical relationships are expressed by changing the internal structure of the words – typically by the use of inflectional endings which express several grammatical meanings at once. Latin, Greek, and Arabic are clear cases.
- In *agglutinative* languages (also called *agglutinating* languages), words are built up out of a long sequence of units, with each unit expressing a particular grammatical meaning, in a clear one-to-one way. Turkish, Finnish, Japanese, and Swahili form words in this way.
- In *polysynthetic* languages (also called *incorporating* languages), words are often very long and complex, containing a mixture of agglutinating and inflectional features, as in Eskimo, Mohawk, and Australian languages.

Both typological and genetic classifications have their limitations. In particular, they ignore the relevance of cultural links between languages

– the fact that languages influence each other by contact, such as by borrowing words from each other. Sometimes languages that have no historical relationship can converge so that they seem to be members of the same family. Conversely, related languages can be influenced by other languages so much that the differences become more striking than the similarities. The role of cultural contact is a real problem in studying many language families, because it can be totally unclear whether two languages are similar because they share a common origin, or because they have borrowed from each other.

It is also important to stress that languages often display mixtures of features, and do not neatly fall into one or the other category. English is a case in point. We know that it is a Germanic language, according to the genetic method of classification. But from other points of view, the picture alters. Culturally, it displays many similarities with Romance or its Classical antecedents, in view of the large number of loan words it has taken in from French and Latin, and the way these languages have even exercised some influence on grammar (such as the adjective coming after the noun in *chicken supreme*) and phonology (such as the use of final 'zh' sound in some pronunciations of words like *garage*).

From a typological viewpoint, English is in fact more similar to an isolating language like Chinese than Latin: there are few inflectional endings, and word order changes are the basis of the grammar. It displays isolating characteristics in such sentence relationships as *The dog will chase the cat* vs. *The cat will chase the dog*. It displays inflecting characteristics in such sentences as *The largest dogs have been chasing the smallest cats*. And it displays agglutinating characteristics in such possible word coinages as *anti-de-nation-al-iz-ation*. Admixtures of this kind are found in many languages of the world.

57

How the Indo-European family is organized

Indo-European is the name scholars have given to the family of languages that first spread throughout Europe and many parts of southern Asia, and which are now found, as a result of colonialism, in every part of the world. The parent language, generally known as *Proto-Indo-European*, is thought to have been spoken before 3000 BC, when the Greek, Anatolian, and Indo-Iranian languages are first attested.

Archaeological evidence shows the existence of a semi-nomadic population living in the steppe region of southern Russia around 4000 BC, who began to spread into the Danube area of Europe and beyond from around 3500 BC. The people are known as the Kurgans, because of their burial practices (*kurgan* being the Russian for 'burial mound'). Kurgan culture seems to have arrived in the Adriatic region before 2000 BC, and this coincides well with the kinds of time-scale needed to produce large amounts of linguistic change. The ancestors of the Kurgans are not known, though there are several similarities between Proto-Indo-European and the Uralic family of languages (p. 384), spoken further east, and these may well have had a common parent, several thousand years before.

By comparing the similar vocabulary of the extant Indo-European languages, it is possible to draw some conclusions about the geographical origins and life-style of the people. For instance, many family words (such as 'mother', 'husband', 'brother') can be reconstructed for Proto-Indo-European. These include several words for 'in-laws', which seem to have been used solely with reference to the bride. Evidence of this kind suggests that it was the wife who was given a position within the husband's family, rather than the other way round, and that the society must therefore have been patriarchal in character.

The reconstructed language has words for horses, dogs, sheep, pigs, and other animals; there is a word for some kind of vehicle, and this vehicle definitely had wheels; there are many words for parts of the body; there are several words relating to farming, and a few words relating to tools and weapons; numerals went to at least 100.

Words relating to fauna and flora are of particular interest, for they can provide clues as to the place of origin of the people. There are no words for 'palm tree' or 'vine', for example, which suggests, independently of any archaeological evidence, that the migrations did not begin in the Mediterranean area. But other clues often seem contradictory. The word for 'beech tree' is widely attested, and, as this tree does not grow in Asia, it has been suggested that the Indo-Europeans must have originated in north-central Europe. On the other hand, there is little evidence of a common word for 'oak', which is also a European tree, and if this word was not known to the Indo-Europeans, then perhaps their migration must have begun in Asia after all. Indo-European philology raises many fascinating questions of this kind.

There are ten branches in the Indo-European family tree.

Albanian

This language forms a single branch of the Indo-European family, spoken by nearly 6 million people in Albania, and nearby parts of the Balkans, Greece, Turkey, and in Italy. Albanian has two main dialects, known as Gheg (in the north) and Tosk (in the south), but these contain many further dialect divisions, not all of which are mutually intelligible. The history of the language is obscure, and it is not possible to demonstrate a clear relationship with any other Indo-European group. This is partly because of the many loan words which have shaped the modern language, and partly because so few written remains of earlier times exist, dating only from the 15th century, largely on religious themes. An official alphabet was not introduced until 1909, using roman characters. Since the Second World War, the official language has been based on the Tosk dialect.

Anatolian

This group of languages, now extinct, was spoken from around 2000 BC in parts of present-day Turkey and Syria. The main Anatolian language is Hittite, shown to be Indo-European only as recently as 1915. Its written remains, consisting of tablets inscribed with cuneiform writing, date from the 17th century BC. The earliest forms of Hittite (Old Hittite) are the oldest Indo-European texts so far discovered. More of the texts have religious themes, but they also contain a great deal of historical and social information. Other languages of the group are Palaic, Lydian, Lycian, and Luwian, represented in cuneiform and hieroglyphic systems (§17). Also grouped under this heading are certain languages which do not belong to the Indo-European family (Hurrian, Urartian) or where the relationship is not certain (Phrygian).

Armenian

This branch of Indo-European consists of a single language, spoken in many dialects by between 5 and 6 million people in Armenia and Turkey, and (through emigration) in parts of the Middle East, Europe, and the United States. The spoken language may have been established soon after 1000 BC, but there was no written form until after the introduction of Christianity. Classical Armenian, or Grabar, is the language of the older literature, and the liturgical language of the Armenian church today. The oldest writings date from the 5th century, and the 38-letter alphabet, invented by St Mesrop, is still widely used. Modern literary Armenian exists in two standard varieties: East Armenian is the official language of Armenia; West Armenian is the dominant variety elsewhere. Because of the large numbers of loan words which have come into the language, its basic Indo-European character is often obscured.

Balto-Slavic

Baltic languages and Slavonic languages are often placed together as a single branch of Indo-European, because of their similarities, though there is some dispute over whether these constitute evidence of common origin rather than of more recent mutual influence, and in the Baltic countries one can encounter considerable political opposition to the grouping. Taken together, these languages are spoken by about 300 million people, more than half of whom speak Russian.

The main Baltic languages are Latvian (also known as Lettish) and Lithuanian, with written texts dating from the 14th century. There are around 4 million speakers in the Baltic area, with a further million abroad, mainly in the United States. Both languages have standard forms, and many dialects. Several other languages of this group are now extinct, though there are a few written remains of Old Prussian.

The Slavonic (or Slavic) languages are more numerous, and are usually divided into three groups: South Slavonic, found in Bulgaria, the countries of former Yugoslavia, and parts of Greece, includes Bulgarian, Macedonian, Serbian, Croatian, and Slovene; West Slavonic, found in the Czech Republic, Poland, and eastern areas of Germany, includes Czech, Slovak, Sorbian, and Polish; East Slavonic, found in the countries which replaced the USSR, includes Russian, Belorussian, and Ukrainian. The name Lekhitic is sometimes given to a group of West Slavonic languages originally spoken along the Baltic between the Vistula and the Oder, including Polish, Kashubian, Polabian (died out in the 18th century), and Slovincian.

Each of the main Slavonic languages has an official status as a standard; but there are numerous dialect differences within these groupings. Old Church Slavonic is evidenced in texts dating from the 9th century, and its later form (Church Slavonic) is still used as a liturgical language in the Eastern Orthodox Church. The distinctive Cyrillic alphabet, attributed to Saints Cyril and Methodius in the late 9th century, is still used for writing Bulgarian, Serbian, Macedonian, and all the East Slavonic languages. In modified forms, it is also used for about 100 non-Slavonic minority languages of Russia.

Celtic

The Celts were the first Indo-European people to spread across Europe. Known to the Greeks as Keltoi, they emerged in south-central Europe around the 5th century BC, speaking a language which has been reconstructed under the name of Common (or Proto-) Celtic. In a series of waves they spread throughout most of Europe, reaching as far as the Black Sea and Asia Minor, south-west Spain, central Italy, and the whole of Britain.

The main migration was by the Galli, or Gauls, into France, northern Italy, and the north of Europe. Evidence of the Gaulish language is found throughout this area in place names and inscriptions. In other places, the language goes under different names. The Celts who went into the Balkans and Asia Minor were called Galatae by the Greeks, and Galatian remained in use until around the 5th century AD. The Celts who went into Spain were known as Celtiberi, and Celtiberian is found in inscriptions (only partly decipherable), especially in the north and east. Some 2nd-century BC inscriptions in Switzerland are often referred to as Lepontic.

The range of Celtic dialects spoken on the Continent of Europe has been labelled Continental Celtic. Insular Celtic refers to the dialects which came to be spoken in the British Isles and Brittany, and almost all our information about the Celtic languages comes from this area. There seem to have been two waves of invasion: the first, into Ireland in the 4th century BC, led to a type of Celtic known as Goidelic (or Gaelic) which later reached Scotland and the Isle of Man; the second, into southern England and Wales, and later over to Brittany, produced a type of Celtic known as Brythonic (or, simply British). Linguistically, the first language group is known as *Q-Celtic*, because it retained the /kw-/ sound of Proto-Indo-European, writing it as *q*, later *c*; the second group is referred to as *P-Celtic*, because /kw-/ developed into /p-/. The contrast can be seen in such pairs of words as modern Irish Gaelic *ceathair*, Welsh *pedwar* 'four'.

In Europe, the most noticeable modern characteristic of this language family is its dramatic decline, under the influence of its powerful linguistic neighbours, English and French. But equally dramatic is the 20th-century revival of interest in Celtic languages, as symbols of nationalistic unity, and as keys to earlier periods of cultural and literary brilliance. Today, over 1.2 million people speak a Celtic language.

Germanic

The various branches of the Germanic family of languages derive from the migrations of the Germanic tribes who lived in northern Europe during the 1st millennium BC. Some Germanic words are recorded by Latin authors, and Scandinavian inscriptions in the runic alphabet are recorded from the 3rd century AD. The earliest main text is the Gothic bible of Bishop Ulfilas (or Wulfila), translated around AD 350, using an alphabet of his own devising. Anglo-Saxon and Old High German are recorded from the 8th century, and the oldest forms of Scandinavian languages from the 12th century.

Germanic languages are used as a first language by over 550 million people, largely because of the world-wide role of English. They are usually classified into three groups. East Germanic languages are all extinct, and only Gothic is preserved in manuscript to any extent – most recently, in a few words recorded in the Crimea in the 16th century. North Germanic includes the Scandinavian languages of Swedish and Danish (East Scandinavian), Norwegian, Icelandic, and Faeroese (West Scandinavian), and the older states of these languages, most notably the literary variety of Old Icelandic known as Old Norse – the language of the Icelandic sagas. West Germanic comprises English and Frisian (often grouped as Anglo-Frisian), and German, Yiddish, Netherlandic or Dutch (including local Flemish dialects in Belgium), and Afrikaans (sometimes grouped together as Netherlandic-German). Dialect similarities often blur the distinctions suggested by these labels.

Greek

This branch of Indo-European consists of a single language, represented in many dialects, and attested from around the 14th century BC. The earliest evidence of the language is found in the inscriptions discovered at Knossos and other centres in Crete, written mainly on clay tablets in a syllabic script known as Linear B, and discovered to be Greek only as recently as 1952. This period of the language is referred to as Mycenaean Greek, to be distinguished from the later, classical Greek, dating from the 8th century BC, when texts came to be written in the Greek alphabet – notably the epic poems *Iliad* and *Odyssey*.

The great period of classical drama, history, philosophy, and poetry ended in the 4th century BC. A later variety of Greek, known as *koine* (or 'common') Greek, was spoken throughout the eastern Mediterranean from around the 4th century BC for nearly a thousand years. In its written form, it was the language of the New Testament. The modern varieties of Greek, now spoken by over 11 million people in Greece, Cyprus, Turkey, the United States, and other localities, derive from this koine.

Indo-Iranian

This branch of Indo-European comprises two large groups, known as Indo-Aryan (or Indic) and Iranian. There are over 200 Indo-Aryan languages, spoken by over 825 million people in the northern and central parts of the Indian subcontinent. They may be divided into several groups, on a broadly geographical basis: the Midland group mainly includes Hindu/Urdu, the Bihari languages, and the Rajasthani languages; the Eastern group includes Assamese, Bengali, and Oriya; the West and South-west groups include Gujarati, Konkani, Maldivian, Marathi, and Sinhalese; and the North-west group includes Panjabi, Sindhi, Lahnda, the Dardic languages, and the Pahari languages. The Romani languages of the gypsies is also a member of Indo-Iranian. The early forms of Indo-Aryan, dating from around 1000 BC, are collectively referred to as Sanskrit – the language in which the Vedas, the oldest sacred texts, are written. Later forms, the Prakrits, lasted 1,000 years, and were the medium of Buddhist and Jain literature.

During the same period, the Iranian languages were being spoken in an area centred on modern Afghanistan and Iran – especially Old Persian and Avestan (the sacred languages of the Zoroastrians), both of which have texts dating from the 6th century BC. The group has over seventy languages spoken by over 75 million people, but many of these languages, and innumerable dialects, have not received a definite classification. Major languages include the closely related Persian (or Farsi) and Tadzhik, as well as Pashto, Ossetic, Kurdish, and Baluchi.

Italic

The main language of this family is Latin, the language of Rome and of its surrounding provinces, preserved in inscriptions from the 6th century BC, and most systematically in literature from the 3rd century BC. Other languages of the period include Faliscan, Oscan, Umbrian, and Venetic, spoken in and to the north-east of modern Italy. From the spoken, or *vulgar* form of Latin, used throughout the Roman empire, developed the Romance languages – French, Spanish, Portuguese, Italian, and Romanian, along with Sardinian, Occitan (in southern France), Rhaetian (various dialects in northern Italy and Switzerland), Galician (in north-west Spain), and Catalan (predominantly in north-east Spain). A Romance language known as Dalmatian, spoken along the Croatian coast, became extinct when its last known speaker died in 1898. But the main Romance languages have spread, as a result of colonialism, throughout the world, so that today around 650 million people speak a Romance language, or one of the creoles (§53) based on French, Spanish, or Portuguese.

Tocharian

This language, now extinct, was spoken in the northern part of Chinese Turkistan during the 1st millennium AD. The first evidence of Tocharian was discovered only in the 1890s, in the form of various commercial and Buddhist religious documents, dating from around the 7th century, and on the basis of these discoveries two dialects were established – an eastern variety, from the Turfan region, which was labelled Tocharian A, and a western variety, from the Kucha region, which was labelled Tocharian B. The functions of these dialects, and the identity of their speakers, have been sources of controversy in comparative philology, as has the very name of the language (based on that of the Tochari people, who lived further east, and who were probably speakers of an Iranian language). But the status of Tocharian as an independent Indo-European language is not in doubt.

58
How other Eurasian families are organized – part one

Several other language families are to be found in or around the territory where Indo-European languages are most prominent.

Altaic

The Altaic family of languages covers a vast area, from the Balkan peninsula to the north-east of Asia – an area which includes the Altai mountain region of central Asia, from which the family receives its name. It comprises about sixty languages, classified into three groups: Turkic, Mongolian, and Tungusic. The common ancestry of these groups is maintained by many scholars; but this hypothesis is contested by those who feel that the linguistic similarities could be explained in other ways – such as the mutual influences displayed when languages are in contact with each other.

Over half of the Altaic languages belong to the Turkic group, whose best-known member is Turkish, spoken by around 50 million people in Turkey and surrounding territories. Other main languages of the south-west are Azerbaijani (14 million) and Turkmen (around 3 million), both spoken mainly in Russia, Iran, and Afghanistan. In the south-east, there is Uzbek (over 15 million), spoken mainly in Uzbekistan, and Uighur (around 7 million), mainly found in China (Xinjiang) and nearby Russia. In the north-west, the main languages are Tatar (over 5 million), Kazakh (over

7 million), Kirghiz (over 2 million), and Bashkir (around 1 million), found largely in Kazakhstan, Kirghizstan, and Russia, with some speakers in China and nearby territories. In the north-east, languages are spoken by smaller numbers. There are over 300,000 speakers of the geographically isolated language Yakut, and 190,000 speakers of Tuva (or Tuvinian), but other languages number only tens of thousands (including one named Altai – formerly, Oirot – which should not be confused with Altaic, the name of the family as a whole). Chuvash, spoken by over 1.5 million in the middle Volga region, is usually listed along with other Turkic languages, but many consider it to be a separate branch within the Altaic family.

The main Mongolian language is known as Mongol (or Khalka), spoken in two main varieties by over 4 million people in the Mongolian People's Republic and nearby China. Related languages in the same region are Buryat (around 300,000), Dongziang or Santa (around 280,000), Dagur, and Tu or Monguor (both fewer than 100,000). Further west, the group is represented by Oirat, Kalmyk (both over 270,000), and Mogol (around 50,000). There are many uncertainties of classification in this area, due principally to problems of applying the distinction between language and dialect.

The Tungusic (or Manchu-Tungus) group is spoken in a large number of dialects over a wide area. Evenki (formerly Tungus) may have as many as 20,000 speakers; but the other languages have fewer than 10,000 – Lamut (or Even), Nanai, and Manchu. The Manchu people of north-east China number over 4 million, but less than 1,000 now speak the once important Manchu language – a lingua franca between China and the outside world for over 200 years.

There is little evidence of the early development of the Altaic family. Written remains of Turkic are found in a runic script dating from the 8th century AD; but Mongolian script dates only from the 13th century; and the earliest Manchu records are even more recent – mid-17th century. Several writing systems seem to have been used throughout the early period.

In the 20th century, the most notable developments came from the major political changes which affected the area following the First World War. There was a considerable effort to modernize the languages, especially by promoting fresh vocabulary. Several new literary languages emerged, based on local languages (as in the case of Uzbek), and some of the older written languages were reformed (seen most dramatically in the case of Turkish, which in 1929 replaced Arabic by Latin script).

Caucasian

The area between the Black Sea and the Caspian Sea, surrounding the Caucasus Mountains, is relatively small and compact – not quite twice the size of the United Kingdom – but it contains one of the highest concentrations of languages in the world. Leaving aside the Indo-European, Semitic, and Altaic languages which have infiltrated the area in the past 3,000 years, there are nearly forty languages which are recognized as belonging to a single Caucasian family. They are classified into four regionally based types: the North-west Caucasian, or Abkhazo-Adyghian group; the North-central Caucasian group; the North-east Caucasian group; and the Southern Caucasian (or Kartvelian) group.

The family as a whole is represented by nearly 8 million speakers, almost all to be found in the Caucasus region. Over 4 million of these live in Georgia, speaking a Kartvelian language – mainly one of the dialects of Georgian, which is the state language, used throughout the area. Other languages of the south are Zan (including Mingrelian and Laz) and Svan. Only Georgian has a written form, which dates from the 5th century AD.

In the north-west, the main languages are Kabardian (or Circassian), with over 350,000 speakers, Adyghe (over 250,000), and Abkhaz (around 90,000). There are around 45,000 speakers of Abaza. In the 1980s, only one person was known to speak Ubykh – a language whose large number of consonants (eighty) illustrates the special place of this family in phonological studies (§11).

Most of the languages of the north-east belong to the Dagestanian group. The main languages are Avar (over 450,000), Lezghian or Kuri (around 350,000), Dargwa or Khjurkili (over 250,000), Lak (over 90,000), and Tabassaran (over 70,000). Several other languages are spoken by 10,000 or fewer. Also in the north-east, the Nakh group of languages comprises Chechen (over 900,000), Ingush (over 190,000), and Bats (around 3,000), found in a single village in Georgia. The linguistic profile of this area is complicated by the difficulty of drawing a clear line between language and dialect (§51), and this has led to several different estimates of the number of languages in the Caucasian family.

Several of the northern languages have a written form, based on the Cyrillic alphabet (p. 374), and are used as state languages. There is much evidence of the influence of previous periods of contact with adjacent families (such as Arabic and Persian). Today, the most noticeable influence on the family, especially in the area of vocabulary, is Russian.

Dravidian

The Dravidian family is a group of over twenty-five languages, most of which are found close together in the southern and eastern areas of India – though one language (Brahui) is curiously isolated, being spoken 1,000 miles away from the main family, in the north of Pakistan. Through emigration, speakers of the main Dravidian languages are today found throughout South-east Asia, in eastern and southern regions of Africa, and in cities in many parts of the world.

Tamil has the oldest written records of this family, dating from the 3rd century BC, and scholars believe it to be close to the ancestor language, known as Proto-Dravidian. But, despite the historical records and associated reconstruction, there is little agreement about the origins of the language, or its speakers. One tradition speaks of migration from lands to the south, now submerged; other views suggest a movement from Asia, via the north-west, perhaps around 4000 BC. A relationship has been proposed with both the Uralic and the Altaic language families, but the hypothesis is controversial. There is, however, strong support for the view that Dravidian languages were once spoken in the north of India, and were gradually displaced by the arrival of the Indo-European invaders (p. 371).

The four main languages of the family are Telugu, Tamil (both with over 50 million speakers), Kannada (also known as Kanarese), and Malayalam (both with over 26 million speakers). Each language can be identified with a state in southern India – Andhra Pradesh, Tamil Nadu, Mysore, and Kerala, respectively. Of the four, Tamil has the greatest geographical spread, including several million speakers in Sri Lanka, Malaysia, Indonesia, Vietnam, parts of East and South Africa, and many islands in the Indian and South Pacific Oceans. The other languages are not so widely used outside India, though both Telugu and Malayalam have some currency. Written records date from the 5th century AD for Kannada, the 7th century for Telugu, and the 9th century for Malayalam.

Other languages with over a million speakers include Gondi (nearly 2 million), Brahui (1.7 million), Kurukhi (or Oraoni), and Tulu. Kui has around half a million. Malto, isolated from the other languages in the north-east, is spoken by around 90,000 people. The remaining languages of the family have many fewer speakers, sometimes numbering only a few thousand – but it is not always obvious how to draw the line between language and dialect. New languages continue to be reported – Naiki, Pengo, and Manda have been identified only since the early 1960s – and there are some forty-five other languages which are often listed along with the Dravidian family, though lacking clear genetic affiliation.

Uralic

The Uralic family consists of over thirty languages which have descended from an ancestor, called Proto-Uralic, spoken in the region of the north Ural Mountains in Russia over 7,000 years ago. Uralic languages are attested in written form from the 13th century. The most noticeable trend in the 20th century has been the decline of many of the languages, under the influence of dominant neighbours, especially Russian.

Two main branches of the family are represented today: Finno-Ugric and Samoyedic. The Finno-Ugric group of languages is found in one part of central Europe, and in those northern territories where Europe and Asia meet. In the north, the Finnic branch of the family is located in the region between northern Norway and the White Sea, the whole of Finland, and parts of adjacent Soviet territory. The main language of the group is Finnish, with over 5.5 million speakers in Finland, Sweden, Russia, and (through emigration) the USA. Estonian has over 1 million, mainly in Estonia. There are only around 25,000 speakers of the Sami group of languages (formerly known as Lappish), but they are spread throughout the whole of the north.

Curiously isolated from the rest of the family is the main language of the Ugric branch – Hungarian (or Magyar). This is spoken by nearly 11 million people as a national language in Hungary, and by a further 3 million in surrounding areas, and through emigration in many parts of the world. Two other Ugric languages are found to the east of the Urals, around the River Ob, and are known as Ob-Ugric. They are Khanty (or Ostyak), with over 13,000 speakers, and Mansi (or Vogul), with around 3,000.

The remaining Finno-Ugric languages are spoken within Russia. One group is found in the Kola Peninsula in the north, and southwards towards the Gulf of Riga. Some of these languages (Ingrian, Livonian, and Votic) have very few speakers, and may not survive for long. Karelian, the most widespread, has over 100,000 speakers. Vepsian has only some 2,000. A second group is found further into the Soviet Union, scattered around the central Volga. The most widely used languages are Mordvin (or Erza), with over 800,000 speakers; Mari (or Cheremis), with over 600,000; Udmurt (or Votyak), with over 500,000; and Komi (or Zyryan), with around 250,000.

The other branch of the Uralic family is spoken by the Samoyeds – fewer than 30,000 people scattered throughout a vast area in Siberia and Arctic Russia, whose economy is largely based on reindeer hunting and breeding. The most widely spoken language is Nenets (or Yurak), with around 27,000 speakers. Selkup (or Ostyak Samoyed) has around 1,700. The other languages still spoken are Nganasan (Tavgi, or Aram), with around 1,000 speakers, and Enets (or Yenisey), which had less than 100 speakers in 1989. The last of a group of languages once spoken in the Sayan Mountain area now seems to have died out.

Palaeosiberian

The once-extensive Palaeosiberian culture is now represented by only a few thousand people scattered throughout north-eastern Siberia. The languages they speak have been classified into four groups, and since the 19th century these have been studied together under the Palaeosiberian heading; but the groups are not genetically related to each other, and therefore they do not constitute a family in the linguistic sense. Nor are the links with other families any clearer, though several attempts have been made to trace connections with other families found in the region.

The Luorawetlan group is the best represented, in the far north-east, consisting of Chukchi (about 11,000), Koryak (or Nymylan, 5,000), and Kamchadal (or Itelmen), Aliutor and Kerek, with only a few hundred speakers between them. To the west, the Yukaghir group is now represented by just a single language (Yukaghir, or Odul), spoken by around 150 people. Further west again, along the Yenisey River, about 900 people speak the only surviving member of the Yeniseian group – Ket (or Yenisey-Ostyak). And to the south, about 400 speak Gilyak (or Nivkhi), which has no known relatives. Since the early 20th century, each of these languages has been given a written form, based on the Cyrillic alphabet.

59
How other Eurasian families are organized – part two

South-east Asia and the western Pacific rim contain three major language families, as well as a number of language groups of uncertain relationship, and several languages of no known relationship to any other (*isolated languages* or *isolates*).

Austro-Asiatic

Most of the languages of this family are spoken in South-east Asia, in the countries between China and Indonesia; but a few are found further west, in the Nicobar Islands and in parts of India. The membership of the family, and its main subdivisions, are not entirely clear. Few of the languages have a written history. Links between this and other families (in particular, the Austronesian family) have been proposed, but are uncertain.

Three main branches of the family are generally recognized. The largest branch is the Mon-Khmer group of languages, spoken throughout the south-eastern mainland, mainly in North and South Vietnam, Laos, Cambodia, and parts of Myanmar (Burma) and Malaysia. It has three main languages. Mon (or Talaing) is spoken in Myanmar and Thailand by nearly half a million; Khmer (or Cambodian), the official language of Cambodia, is spoken by over 7 million people. Inscriptions in both languages date from the 6th–7th centuries AD.

The main language of the group, Vietnamese, poses something of a problem. This language is spoken by around 55 million people in North and South Vietnam, Laos, and Cambodia, and in recent years small groups of emigrants have taken it to many parts of the world. Its status in the Mon-Khmer group has, however, been disputed: some scholars see it as a marginal member, while some relate it to the Tai family (p. 390). Its early history is obscured by the use of Chinese throughout South-east Asia – the result of over 1,000 years of rule by China, which lasted until the 10th century AD. The modern Latin-based alphabet, known as Quoc-ngu ('national language'), was introduced only in the 17th century.

The other two language groups are clearly separated geographically from the Mon-Khmer. The Munda group of languages is spoken in several parts of India, mainly in the north-east, but also in a few central areas. Mundari (around 800,000) and Santali (around 4 million) are the most widely used languages. Lastly, a tiny group of languages is spoken by around 20,000 people on the Nicobar Islands in the Bay of Bengal. These have been considered a separate, Nicobarese branch of the Austro-Asiatic family, but there is some evidence to suggest that they are a branch of Mon-Khmer.

There are over 170 Austro-Asiatic languages, spoken by over 75 million people. A few other languages spoken in Malaysia and India have at times been proposed as members of the family. Nothing is known about the early movements of the peoples involved. It is possible that the various groups of languages which make up the Mon-Khmer branch began to split up in the 2nd millennium BC, but where the Austro-Asiatic peoples came from, and when they migrated, remains pure guesswork.

Sino-Tibetan

The membership and classification of the Sino-Tibetan family of languages is highly controversial. The *Sinitic* part of the name refers to the various Chinese languages (often, misleadingly, referred to as 'dialects'); the *Tibetan* part refers to several languages found mainly in Tibet, Myanmar (Burma), and nearby territories. But as there are notable similarities with many other languages of the region, some scholars – notably in China –

adopt a much broader view of the family, so as to include the Tai and Miao-Yao groups.

The Sinitic languages are spoken by over 1,000 million people. The vast majority of these are in China (over 980 million) and Taiwan (19 million), but substantial numbers are to be found throughout the whole of South-east Asia, especially in Hong Kong, Indonesia, Malaysia, Thailand, and Singapore. Important Chinese-speaking communities are also found in many other parts of the world, especially in the USA.

Because there has long been a single method for writing Chinese, and a common literary and cultural history, a tradition has grown up of referring to the eight main varieties of speech in China as 'dialects'. But in fact they are as different from each other (mainly in pronunciation and vocabulary) as French or Spanish is from Italian, the dialects of the south-east being linguistically the furthest apart. The mutual unintelligibility of the varieties is the main ground for referring to them as separate languages.

- *Cantonese* (Yúe) Spoken in the south, mainly Guangdong, southern Guangxi, Macau, Hong Kong. (46 million)
- *Gan* Spoken in Shanxi and south-west Hebei. (21 million)
- *Hakka* Widespread, especially between Fujian and Guangxi. (26 million)
- *Mandarin* A wide range of dialects in the northern, central, and western regions. North Mandarin, as found in Beijing, is the basis of the modern standard language. (720 million)
- *Northern Min* Spoken in North-west Fujian. (10 million)
- *Southern Min* Spoken in the south-east, mainly in parts of Zhejiang, Fujian, Hainan Island, and Taiwan. (26 million)
- *Wu* Spoken in parts of Anhui, Zhejiang, and Jiangsu. (77 million)
- *Xiang (Hunan)* Spoken in the south-central region, in Hunan. (36 million)

There are some 275 languages in the Tibeto-Burman family, and these have been classified in several different ways. It is possible to identify 'clusters' of languages which have certain features in common, such as the forty-five or so Lolo languages, spoken by around 3 million people in parts of Myanmar, Thailand, Vietnam, Laos, and China. The fifty or so Naga, Kuki, and Chin languages, spoken in Myanmar and India, comprise another group. But groupings of this kind display many differences as well as similarities, and it has not yet proved possible to find a neat way of classifying these, and the other groups thought to belong to the same family, into two or three types. It is by no means clear, for example, whether the small group of Karen languages, spoken by around 4 million people in Myanmar and Thailand, should be included or excluded from the Sino-Tibetan family.

After Chinese, Burmese and Tibetan are the two main languages of this family. Burmese is spoken by around 22 million people in Myanmar as a mother tongue, and several million more use it as a second language throughout the region. It has written records dating from the 11th century. Speaker estimates for Tibetan are very uncertain, largely because of the influence of Chinese in recent years; but a figure of 4 million seems likely, chiefly in China and Nepal. There are several major dialects, which are sometimes viewed as separate languages. Written records date from the 8th century AD, treating largely of Buddhist religious subjects. The alphabet of this period, which reflects the pronunciation of the time, is still in use today, with the result that there is considerable divergence between spelling and modern Tibetan speech.

Tai

The Tai family of languages are all found in South-east Asia, in an area centred on Thailand, and extending north-eastwards into Laos, North Vietnam, and China, and north-westwards into Myanmar and India. The spelling *Tai* is used to avoid confusion with the main language of the family, Thai (or Siamese), which is the official language of Thailand.

The sixty or so Tai languages are usually divided into three groups: South-western, Central, and Northern. Most speakers belong to the South-western group, which includes Thai, spoken by over 20 million people in a wide range of dialects, and Lao (or Laotian), widely spoken in Thailand,

and the official language of Laos (3 million). Isan (Thailand) has some 15 million; the two varieties of Zhuang (China) have over 12 million; Lanna or Yuan (Thailand) has over 6 million; and Shan, Tho, Buyi, Dong, and Nung each have over a million. But in this part of the world, such estimates are very approximate.

The relationship between the Tai family and other languages is unclear. Written remains of the south-western group date from around the 13th century. Links have been proposed both with the Sino-Tibetan and the Austronesian families. In particular, several languages of south-west China, belonging to the Kadai and Kam-Sui groups, display interesting similarities to Tai.

Miao-Yao

This is a small group of about fifteen languages, also called Hmong-Mien, spoken in southern China and adjacent parts of South-east Asia – especially northern Laos, Thailand, and Vietnam. The two chief languages, which give the group its name, are Miao (also called Hmong), spoken in several varieties by 4.5 million people, and Yao (also called Mien), spoken by nearly a million. The sub-classification of the group into languages and dialects is controversial, as indeed is its status as a separate language family. Links with Tai, Mon-Khmer, and Sino-Tibetan have been suggested, and it is within the latter family that Miao-Yao languages are most often placed.

Korean

There are evident similarities between the Korean language and the Altaic family, but it is not clear whether these can best be explained by a hypothesis of common descent or one of influence through contact. Thus in some classifications the language is placed with the Altaic family, and in others it is left isolated. A relationship with Japanese has also been suggested.

Korean is spoken by over 60 million people in North and South Korea (where it is an official language), China, Japan, and Russia. The language has been much influenced by Chinese: more than half its vocabulary is of Chinese origin, and the earliest records of the language, dating from before the 12th century, are written in Chinese characters.

Japanese

The genetic relationship between Japanese and other languages has not been clearly established. It is most often considered to be a member of the Altaic family, but resemblances with other language families of the region have also been noted. There are several varieties, those in the south (and especially in the Ryukyu Islands) displaying major differences from the standard language based on the Tokyo dialect.

Japanese is spoken by around 121 million people on the islands of Japan, and by a further 5 million in other parts of the world, especially in Brazil and the United States. Apart from a few isolated forms, the first written records of Japanese date from the early 8th century, using Chinese characters, or *kanji*.

How the Indo-Pacific island families are organized

Three other families, Austronesian, Indo-Pacific, and Australian, cover most of the islands, large and small, of the Indian and Pacific Oceans.

Austronesian

The Austronesian language family covers a vast geographical area, from Madagascar to Easter Island, and from Taiwan and Hawaii to New Zealand, a territorial range which is reflected in an alternative name sometimes given to the family: Malayo-Polynesian. It is one of the largest families, in terms of both number of speakers (around 270 million) and number of languages (over 1,200).

In this part of the world, it is particularly difficult to establish language identities. Apart from the usual problems of distinguishing dialects from languages (§51), several different names may be used with reference to the speakers in an area, and it is never obvious whether these names refer to different languages, or are simply alternative names for the same languages. For example, over seventy names have been recorded for the various dialects of the Dayak language of north-western Borneo and south Sarawak, but it is possible that research will show several of these to be so different that they could legitimately be counted as distinct languages. The linguistic picture is also complicated by the existence of many pidgins and creoles (§53) which have grown up as the result of trade contacts in the area. Moreover, several languages have come to be extensively used as lingua francas – notably Bahasa Indonesia, Bazaar Malay, Chinese, English, and French.

The classification of the languages of the Austronesian family is controversial. One influential approach distinguishes a Formosan group of about twenty languages, spoken in Taiwan by some 300,000 people, from the rest, which are collectively called Malayo-Polynesian (in a slightly narrower sense than that used above). The latter group is then divided into three branches. The Western branch contains over 500 languages, spoken in Madagascar, Malaysia, the Indonesian Islands, the Philippines, parts of Vietnam and Cambodia, and the western end of New Guinea. Two languages of Micronesia (Chamorro and Palauan) are also included. The Central branch of 150 languages is spoken by about 4.5 million people in the central islands of Indonesia, such as Timor, Flores, and Maluku (the Moluccas). The Eastern branch of over 500 languages is spoken over most of New Guinea, and throughout the 10,000 or more islands of Melanesia, Micronesia, and Polynesia. Most of them form a family usually referred to as Oceanic. Despite its geographical and linguistic diversity, only a small minority of speakers (about 2.5 million) belongs to the eastern branch.

Because of the many structural differences between the languages, it is estimated that the Austronesian family has a history of development of over 4,000 years, with archaeological and linguistic evidence suggesting a probable geographical origin in the New Guinea area. But despite extensive research into Austronesian languages in recent years, the early history of this family remains obscure and controversial, and several competing linguistic sub-classifications have been proposed.

Indo-Pacific

There are over 650 languages spoken in New Guinea, which do not belong to the Austronesian family, and about a further 100 spoken in the islands to the immediate east and west. Two small language groups lie much further away from those spoken in the New Guinea region, and some scholars believe that there is enough evidence to justify their placement within this group: Andamanese, from the Andaman Islands in the Bay of Bengal; and Tasmanian, now extinct, from the island of Tasmania, to the south of Australia. About 3.5 million speakers are involved.

Over half of the Indo-Pacific languages have been shown to be related, especially many of those in central New Guinea. But the linguistic picture is by no means certain: in the more inaccessible parts of New Guinea, there are still tribes who have not been contacted, and whose languages are not known; and data are sparse on many others, which may have only tens or hundreds of speakers. Many different classifications have been proposed, some of which recognize over 100 sub-families. Other names for the family, such as Papuan, are also in use. There is no clear genetic basis for the Indo-Pacific grouping: it is a convenience, bringing together the languages of the New Guinea region which are not Austronesian.

There is nowhere to compare with the multilingual diversity of New Guinea – so many languages crammed into a land area of only 300,000 square miles, and containing a total population of only around 6 million. A sense of this complexity can be obtained by 'translating' these figures into British terms: Britain, one third of the size, would find itself containing nearly 200 languages, separated from each other by distances of only twenty miles.

Australia

No clear relationship has yet been found between Australian Aboriginal languages and the rest of the world's languages. With no written records, historical discussion is largely speculation. In the 18th century, there may have been over 500 Aboriginal languages in Australia, spoken by over 300,000 people. Today, about 250 languages are documented from many parts of Australia (but excluding Tasmania). Only five languages have more than 1,000 speakers; most have very few; and at least half are nearly extinct.

A frequently cited estimate is that fewer than 30,000 people speak the languages today, with different levels of ability. But, for many reasons, population estimates are difficult. Aboriginal people often live in isolated areas; most are bilingual to differing degrees; and it is not always easy to obtain accurate information from the speakers themselves, many of whom overestimate or underestimate their ability to use the language, for social or political reasons. By the same token, scepticism is sometimes expressed about the results of national surveys, which might be used as evidence for or against the provision of educational or social facilities for Aboriginal groups.

Aboriginal languages have been grouped into twenty-eight families, all of which are thought to be related. All but one of these are found in the northern parts of Western Australia, Northern Territory, and Queensland, in an area comprising no more than one-eighth of the continent. Arnhem Land in particular shows a high concentration of these languages. By contrast, a single family, Pama-Nyungan, covers the remainder of the continent; about 175 languages once belonged to this family, but fewer than fifty are spoken today, most of these surviving in the north-west.

The languages with the largest number of speakers are Tiwi, Walmatjari, Warlpiri, Aranda, Mabuyag, and Western Desert – all but the first belonging to the Pama-Nyungan family. Several of the languages have come to be used as lingua francas. Gunwinygu is used in this way in much of north-east Arnhem Land, and Pitjantjatjara in much of northern Western Australia, partly as a church language. Warlpiri is one of the most vigorous of these languages, spoken in many central and southern parts of Northern Territory. Several pidgins and creoles (§53), related to English, have also developed in northern areas.

The future of Aboriginal languages is uncertain, but several of the languages now have a written form, and bilingual school programmes have been devised. Organizations such as the Australian Institute of Aboriginal Studies promote the study of these languages, their history, and their contemporary social and political status. It therefore seems likely that a small number of these languages will remain vigorous for some time to come.

61

How African families
are organized

Africa contains more languages than any other continent – some 2,000, spoken by over 480 million people. The language total is uncertain, because many areas are inaccessible, and many dialect groups have not been well investigated, but it is probably an underestimate. Very few of these languages are spoken by large numbers: less than 5% have more than a million speakers.

As a consequence, Africa is a continent of lingua francas. Arabic is used throughout the north and north-east; Swahili is used throughout most of East Africa; English and French are widespread, often as official languages, in former colonial territories; and, especially in West and Central Africa, several languages have come to be used as ways of fostering communication between different tribes (such as Hausa, Bambara-Malinka, Wolof, Kongo, Lingala, and various pidgins and creoles, such as Pidgin English, Krio, and Sango).

The most widely used classification of African languages, made by Joseph Greenberg in the 1960s, recognizes four main families, though there is considerable difference of opinion about the boundaries between them, and about several of the language groups which they subsume. There is little historical evidence available to aid classification. Written records of most African languages have existed only since missionary activities began on the continent, less than 150 years ago. As a consequence, the field of African languages has proved to be one of the most controversial areas within the domain of comparative linguistics.

Niger-Congo

This is the largest African family, with around 1,350 languages, and several thousand dialects, whose status is often difficult to determine. The family spreads across the whole of sub-Saharan Africa, west of the River Nile, and extends along the eastern half of the continent as far north as the Horn of Africa. It is divided into several groups of languages which are estimated to have diverged well over 5,000 years ago, though the order and rate of divergence is controversial. There are also several isolated languages. Accurate statistics are impossible in some areas, especially those affected by civil war (in the 1990s, notably Rwanda).

The largest group is the Benue-Congo – around 800 languages spoken by about 150 million people throughout central and southern Africa, over half of them (spoken by two-thirds of these people) belonging to the Bantu sub-group. The main Bantu languages are Yoruba (20 million), Igbo (12 million), Lingala and Luba (both 8 million), Shona and Rwanda (both 7 million), Xhosa and Zulu (sometimes considered dialects of the same language, but considered by their speakers to be different languages – both over 6 million), and Kongo and Makua (both 5 million). Swahili also has 5 million native speakers, but is additionally used by around 30 million speakers as a lingua franca in parts of East Africa. Some classifications include Yoruba and Igbo as members of the Kwa family. The largest non-Bantu languages are found in Nigeria: Efik (4 million, chiefly as a second language), and Tiv (2 million).

The Kwa group of over seventy-five languages is spoken by about 14 million in the southern part of the bulge of West Africa. Major languages are Akan (7 million), and Ewe (2 million). Ijo is now thought to be part of a separate branch (Ijoid), spoken by about 1.5 million. English or French are official languages in the area.

The Adamawa-Ubangi group of around 180 languages is spoken by about 6 million people in the remote, northern part of central Africa, between Nigeria and Sudan. Its main members are Sango, a creolized language used throughout the Central African Republic and nearby areas (about 5 million, including second-language speakers) and Gbaya (850,000). Several pidgins and creoles are spoken in the area.

The Gur group consists of over eighty languages spoken by about 11 million people in a broad area around the Upper Volta River, between Mali and Nigeria. Its main member is Mooré (or Mossi), spoken by around 4 million.

The Atlantic (or West Atlantic) group, as its name suggests, consists of over sixty languages spoken in the extreme western part of the African bulge. Fula (or Fulfulde) is the most widespread language, spoken in most West African states by around 13 million in several varieties, some mutually unintelligible. Other languages include Wolof and Fuuta Jalon, both spoken by over 2 million.

The Mande group of over forty-five languages is also spoken by over 12 million in the western part of the bulge. Its main members are Bambara (2 million), Malinka (3 million), Dyula, and Mende (each over 1 million).

About thirty Kordofanian languages are spoken in the Nuba Mountains area of central Sudan by less than half a million people.

Nilo-Saharan

The major group of languages in this family is spoken in two areas around the upper parts of the Chari and Nile rivers, and is generally referred to by the name Chari-Nile. It contains around 180 languages, whose subclassification has given rise to much controversy. In particular, scholars have argued for over 100 years about the best way of classifying the languages spoken along the Nile, in Sudan, Uganda, and nearby territories (the so-called Nilotic group).

An Eastern Sudanic group includes such languages as Luo (3.2 million), Dinka (spoken in several varieties by over 2 million), Kalenjin and Teso (both 1.4 million), Acholi, Alur, Bari, Lango, Maasai, and Nuer (all with over half a million speakers). A Central Sudanic group includes Lugbara (nearly 1 million), Lendu, Mangbetu, and Ngambai (all over half a million).

Nile Nubian, or Dongolawi, is spoken in Sudan and Egypt by around a million speakers. It is the only language of this group to have a long written history, with manuscripts in a modified Coptic alphabet dating from the 8th century AD (Old Nubian).

Argument also surrounds the relationship between the Chari-Nile languages and the twenty-five or so other languages which have been grouped into the Nilo-Saharan family. Particularly unclear is the status of the Songhai group, spoken by over 2 million people in a wide area between Mali and Nigeria. Fur is another isolated language, spoken by around 500,000 in the Sudan and Chad. The remaining languages have been classified into small groups: Saharan, Maban, and Komuz. The Saharan language, Kanuri, is the largest, with around 4 million speakers.

Khoisan

This is the smallest language family in Africa, consisting of fewer than forty languages, spoken by about 300,000 people; but they are a well-known group because of their use of click consonants (p. 22). They are spoken in the southern part of Africa, in an area around the Kalahari Desert extending from Angola to South Africa, though two click languages are spoken as far north as Tanzania (Sandawe and Hatsa). *Khoisan* derives from the name of the largest Hottentot group (the Khoi-Khoin) and that of the Bushmen in the Nama region of Namibia (San). Only about a third of these languages have over 1,000 speakers. Nama (spoken chiefly in Namibia) may have as many as 150,000; Sandawe (spoken in Tanzania) has about 70,000. The numbers are diminishing, and several languages have recently become extinct. About half of the languages have been given a written form by missionaries and others.

Afro-Asiatic

This family, formerly known as Hamito-Semitic, is the major family to be found in North Africa, the eastern horn of Africa, and South-west Asia. It contains over 300 languages, spoken by nearly 250 million people.

There are five (in some classifications, six) major divisions which are thought to have derived from a parent language that existed around the 7th millennium BC.

The Semitic languages have the longest history and the largest number of speakers. They are found throughout South-west Asia, including the whole of the Saudi Arabian peninsula, and across the whole of North Africa, from the Atlantic to the Red Sea. The oldest languages of the group, now extinct, date from the 3rd millennium BC; they include Akkadian, Amorite, Moabite, and Phoenician, all once spoken in and around the Middle East. There was a vast literature in Akkadian, written in cuneiform script (p. 111). Hebrew dates from the 2nd millennium BC; its classical form was preserved as the written language of Judaism; its modern spoken and written form is used by over 3 million people in Israel and a further million throughout the world. Old Aramaic, the language of Jesus and the Apostles, also dates from this period. Syriac, a variety of Late Aramaic, was the literary and religious language of Christians throughout the Middle East for several centuries. Aramaic dialects are still spoken by some 200,000 people in tiny groups in the region.

The major language of the group is Arabic, spoken in eight major varieties by over 180 million people as a mother tongue, and used by several million more as a second language. It exists in both classical and colloquial forms. Classical (or literary) Arabic is the sacred language of Islam, and is used as a lingua franca of educated people throughout the Arabic-speaking world. Colloquial Arabic exists in many modern varieties, not all of which are mutually intelligible – they include Algerian, Moroccan, Egyptian, Syrian, Iraqian, and several dialects of Arabia and the Sahara. Maltese, spoken by over 300,000 people on the island of Malta, is also a development from Arabic.

In the south of the region, in Ethiopia, there are several Semitic languages, notably Tigrinya (4 million), Amharic (the official language of Ethiopia, used by around 14 million), and varieties of Gurage (around 1 million).

The remaining branches are less widespread. Egyptian is now extinct: its history dates from before the 3rd millennium BC, preserved in many hieroglyphic inscriptions and papyrus manuscripts (p. 109). Around the 2nd century AD, it developed into a language known as Coptic. Coptic may still have been used as late as the early 19th century, and is still used as a religious language by Monophysite Christians in Egypt.

There are over thirty Berber languages spoken throughout North Africa by around 10 million people, mainly in Algeria and Morocco. They include Riff, Kabyle, Shluh, and Tamashek, the widely scattered language of the Tuareg nomads. There are about fifty Cushitic languages, spoken by around 24 million people. The largest is Oromo (or Galla), several varieties of which are spoken in Ethiopia and Kenya by over 10 million people; and Somali, spoken in Ethiopia, Somalia, and Kenya by over 5 million. There are over 160 Chadic languages, whose status within the Afro-Asiatic family is less clear. These languages are spoken by over 28 million people in an area extending from northern Ghana to the Central African Republic. Hausa is undoubtedly the most important language of this group, spoken by around 25 million people as a mother tongue, and by several million more as a second language throughout the region. It is the only Chadic language to have a written form – a roman alphabet now being used in place of the Arabic script introduced in the 16th century.

Lastly, there are over twenty Omotic languages, spoken by nearly 3 million people in western Ethiopia and northern Kenya. About two-thirds of these are speakers of Wolaytta. Omotic is sometimes classified as a separate branch of Afro-Asiatic, and sometimes as a western branch of Cushitic.

62

How American families are organized

North America

There were originally around 300 languages spoken by the indigenous Native American (or Amerindian) tribes, but this number had more than halved by the 1970s. Many of the languages are now spoken by only a few old people. Only about fifty of the languages have more than 1,000 speakers; only a handful have more than 10,000. In the mid-1980s, the total number of speakers was estimated at around 500,000.

The Amerindian languages have been classified into over fifty families, showing many kinds and degrees of interrelationship. However, this allows a great deal of scope for further classification, and Amerindian linguistics has thus proved to be a controversial field, generating many proposals about the links between and within families. It is not known whether the languages have a common origin. The peoples are thought to have migrated from Asia across the Bering Strait, perhaps in a series of waves, but the only North American languages which show any clear links with Asian languages are those belonging to the Eskimo-Aleut family.

Eskimo-Aleut is the name given to a small group of languages spoken in the far north, in Alaska, Canada, and Greenland, and stretching along the Aleutian Islands into Siberia. Eskimo is the main language, spoken in many varieties by around 60,000. Its two main branches – Yupik in Alaska and Siberia, Inupiaq (Inuit, or Inuktitut) elsewhere – are sometimes classified as separate languages. Greenlandic Eskimo has official status in Greenland, alongside Danish. A standard written form dates from the mid-19th century. There are also a few hundred remaining speakers of Aleut.

Further south, the Na-Dené group consists of about fifty languages, spoken in two main areas: Alaska and north-west Canada, and south-west-central USA. Most of the languages belong to the Athabaskan family, whose best-known member is Navajo, with around 130,000 speakers – one of the few Amerindian languages which has actually increased in size in recent years. The various dialects of Apache are closely related to Navajo.

The Algonquian (or Algonkian) family is geographically the most widespread, with over thirty languages covering a broad area across central and eastern Canada, and down through central and southern USA. Many well-known tribes are represented – the Arapaho, Blackfoot, Cheyenne, Cree, Fox, Micmac, Mohican, Ojibwa, Potawatomi, and Shawnee – though only Cree and Ojibwa have substantial numbers of speakers (each around 35,000).

The remaining languages defy easy classification. Some scholars have proposed genetic links between the twenty or so Siouan languages (which include Crow and Dakota, or Sioux), the fifteen or so Iroquoian languages (which include Mohawk and Cherokee), and other small groups, but the relationships are controversial. There are many isolates (p. 407).

The main linguistic bridge between North and South America is formed by the (Macro-) Penutian group, which in its broadest interpretation consists of over sixty languages (many of these grouped into smaller families), spoken from south-west Canada down through the western states of the USA, throughout Mexico and Central America, and into south-west South America. In a narrower interpretation, only the twenty-five or so North American languages, none of which has many speakers, are subsumed under this heading.

The broader interpretation includes the languages of the Mayan family – about thirty languages, some in several mutually unintelligible varieties, spoken by over 3 million people in Mexico and Central America. They include Yucatec and the many varieties of Quiché, both with over half a million speakers, and Mam, Kekchi, and Cakchiquel, each with over a quarter of a million. In South America, the main candidate for membership of Penutian is Mapudungan (or Araucano), spoken mainly in Chile by around 400,000. Chipayan and Uru (spoken by a few hundred people in Bolivia) have also been proposed as belonging to Penutian.

The Hokan group of around twenty languages is spoken by small numbers in parts of western and south-west USA, and eastern Mexico. Similarly, most of the fifty or so languages which belong to the Uto-Aztecan group have few speakers today. The group, which is distantly related to the Tanoan languages (a proposed Aztec-Tanoan family), includes the languages of such well-known tribes as the Comanche, Paiute, Shoshone – and also the Hopi. Three Uto-Aztecan languages are still widely spoken (in several varieties) in Mexico: Nahuatl (around a million speakers), Tarahumar (over 50,000), and Pima-Papago (around 15,000).

Central America

The indigenous languages of Central America are generally known as Meso-American (or Middle American) Indian languages. In an area extending from Mexico to Nicaragua, there are some 250 languages which some approaches have classified into about ten families, spoken by around 7 million people. Several of the languages belong to one of the North American families (Penutian, Hokan, Aztec-Tanoan); some belong to South American families (grouped under Macro-Chibchan). The only group which is restricted to this region is Oto-Manguean. Almost all Oto-Manguean languages are spoken within a small area centred on the state of Oaxaca, Mexico. The main languages (all spoken in several varieties, some mutually unintelligible), are Zapotec (about half a million speakers), Otomí, and Mixtec (each about a quarter of a million).

South America

Indigenous languages are used throughout the whole of the continent of South America, including the southern part of Central America and the

Antilles group of islands. They are spoken by over 11 million people. In former times, as many as 2,000 languages may have been spoken in the area, but only 400–500 of these have been attested. Despite the considerable efforts of ethnographers and missionaries, especially in the 20th century, few languages have been completely described. Many tribes consist of small numbers living in extremely remote jungle areas. Even in the more accessible cases, there is considerable uncertainty over the identity of the languages, and what kind of language/dialect boundaries operate (p. 329). Many are under threat of extinction as western civilization (in the linguistic shape of Spanish and Portuguese) opens up the area. It seems likely that over 1,000 tribes have become extinct before their languages could be recorded.

In spite of this decline, South America remains one of the most linguistically diversified areas of the world. Some accounts suggest that there are more than 100 language families on the continent. However, because of the difficulties in obtaining accurate information, classifications of the languages have tended to be very general, and there are many differences among the sub-groupings which have been proposed. At the most general level, three major groups have been suggested.

The Chibchan group is one of the most widespread, being found in Central America, Columbia, Venezuela, and south into Bolivia and Brazil. There are over twenty languages in the group, but only a few, such as Guaymi (45,000), Kuna or Cuna (35,000), and Waika (16,000), have reasonably large numbers of speakers, and several are on the verge of extinction. Several other languages have been proposed as part of a Macro-Chibchan group.

The Gê-Pano-Carib group of nearly 200 languages is spoken east of the Andes along most of the length of the continent and along the Brazilian Amazon basin. It has a very small number of speakers (perhaps a million) for such a vast area. The Macro-Gê family has over thirty languages, spoken mainly in eastern Brazil. Panoan is a family of about thirty languages spoken from Peru and Bolivia eastward to Brazil, and southward to Paraguay and Argentina. The Carib family, also within this group, is one of the largest in South America, containing over thirty languages spoken by tiny numbers throughout the whole northern region. Several other small language families have been associated with this group.

The Andean-Equatorial group consists of about 250 languages, and contains many subdivisions. Within the Equatorial division, for example, there is the Arawakan group of nearly seventy languages, which once extended into North America, and is still widespread, being spoken by about 350,000 from Central America to southern Brazil, and from the Andes to the east coast. Goajiro (over 120,000), Black Carib (100,000), and Campa (50,000) make up 80% of the speakers of this group.

Within the Andean division, the Quechumaran group is pre-eminent in the Andes highlands between Colombia and Argentina. Aymará was once a major language throughout the central Andes, but is now restricted to around 600,000 speakers in Bolivia and Peru. Quechua, the official language of the Incas, is now spoken in over thirty varieties by nearly 7 million from Colombia to Chile. It is widely used as a lingua franca, and its literary history dates from the 17th century.

In the south, in Paraguay, the indigenous language of Guaraní (a member of the Tupian family of about sixty languages) is spoken by over 3 million people (mainly non-Indians), and is the majority language of that country – the only indigenous language to achieve such a status. By contrast, over a dozen Tupian languages became extinct in the first half of the 20th century.

The Native South Americans migrated from the north, but hardly any of the languages of the area are plausibly related to the language families of North and Central America. The only links which have attracted support are under the heading of Penutian, where some scholars have placed Araucanian, Chipayan, and Uru. Others, however, see these languages as part of the Andean-Equatorial group.

Isolates

There are over thirty languages whose relationship to the main language groups in North America has not so far been determined. About twenty of these isolates (p. 387) are the Salish languages, spoken along the

Canadian/USA Pacific coastline, and some way inland. They include Bella Coola, Okanogan, Shuswap, and Squamish. These days, the numbers of speakers are very small – mostly fewer than 1,000 and in several cases fewer than ten. Pentlach, spoken on Vancouver Island, was already extinct in the 1970s. The five languages of the Wakashan family, spoken on the British Columbia coast (notably, Nootka and Kwakiutl) constitute another isolated group.

63
How multilingualism works

The language families of the world have an intrinsic fascination, because of their range and diversity, but they draw attention to a principle of fundamental significance: multilingualism is the normal human condition. It is a principle which often takes people by surprise. If you have lived your whole life in a monolingual environment, you could easily come to believe that this is the regular way of life around the world, and that people who speak more than one language are the exceptions. Exactly the reverse is the case.

Speaking two or more languages is the natural way of life for three-quarters of the human race. There are no official statistics, but with over 6,000 languages co-existing in fewer than 200 countries (§51) it is obvious that an enormous amount of language contact must be taking place; and the inevitable result of languages in contact is multilingualism, which is most commonly found in an individual speaker as bilingualism.

There is no such thing as a totally monolingual country. Even in countries that have a single language used by the majority of the population, such as Britain, the USA, France, and Japan, there exist sizeable groups that use other languages. In the USA, around 10% of the population regularly speak a language other than English. In Britain, over 350 minority languages are in routine use. In Japan, one of the most monolingual of countries, there are substantial groups of Chinese and Korean speakers. In Ghana, Nigeria, and many other African countries that have a single official language, as many as 90% of the population may be regularly using more than one language.

It is impossible to generalize about the way multilingualism manifests itself around the world; there are vast differences in social and cultural situations. Often the majority of a population is bilingual, such as in Paraguay, where Spanish is used as the official language, and Guaraní as the national language. Often only a small minority may be affected, as with Gaelic speakers in Scotland. The majority of the bilingual speakers may be concentrated in the cities, or they may be found throughout the country, with focal points in those rural areas where languages are in contact. The bilingualism may be due to a long-standing coexistence of different groups (as in Belgium) or to a more recent and shifting coexistence, as with many migrants within the European Union.

An important characteristic of these situations is their fluidity. It is rare to find a setting where the languages are stable and balanced, and where social controversy over government policy is not a major issue. Usually the language balance is changing, either spontaneously or because of government pressure. In some areas, the level of bilingualism is increasing; in others it is decreasing, with second- and third-generation immigrants becoming increasingly monolingual.

A distinction is commonly drawn between cases where one language is holding its own despite the influence of powerful neighbours (*language maintenance*) and cases where a language has yielded to this influence, and speakers have assimilated to the dominant culture (*language shift*). Other possibilities include extensive vocabulary borrowing by one of the languages, or the emergence of a new 'hybrid' as a result of the contact, as with pidgins and creoles (§53). And the contact can lead to a language being completely eliminated, an outcome which is being encountered with regrettable frequency in the 21st century (§52).

What causes multilingualism?

A multilingual situation can develop for reasons which may be difficult to disentangle because of their obscure historical origins. Often the situation is of the people's own choosing; but it may also be forced upon them by other circumstances.

- *Politics*: Annexation, resettlement, and other political or military acts can have immediate linguistic effects. People may become refugees, and have to learn the language of their new homes. After a successful military invasion, the indigenous population may have to learn the invader's language in order to prosper.
- *Religion*: People may wish to live in a country because of its religious significance, or to leave a country because of its religious oppression. In either case, a new language may have to be learned.
- *Culture*: A desire to identify with a particular ethnic culture or social group usually means learning the language of that group. Nationalistic factors are particularly important (§47).
- *Education*: Learning another language may be the only means of obtaining access to knowledge. This factor led to the universal use of Latin in the Middle Ages, and today is one of the motivating factors behind the international use of English (§65).
- *Economy*: Very large numbers of people have migrated to find work and to improve their standard of living. This factor alone accounts for most of the linguistic diversity of the USA, and an increasing proportion of the bilingualism in present-day Europe.
- *Natural disaster*: Floods, volcanic eruptions, famine, and other such events can be the cause of major movements of population. New language contact situations then emerge as people are resettled.

Being bilingual

Research into bilingualism usually distinguishes between large-scale analyses of multilingual societies (*societal* bilingualism) and small-scale analyses of the settings in which bilingual speakers interact (*individual* bilingualism). But in both cases, a basic question arises: what does it mean to be bilingual? The obvious answer is: someone who speaks two languages. But this answer will not do.

It does not allow for those who make irregular use of one or other language, or those who have not used the language at all for many years (so-called *dormant* bilinguals). Nor does it allow for the many people who have developed a considerable skill in comprehending a foreign language, but who do not speak it; or those who have learned to read in another language, but who cannot speak or write it. It leaves unclear the relationship between different languages and different dialects, styles, or levels of the same language (as in the case of diglossia, p. 312). And above all, this definition says nothing about the level of proficiency that has to be attained before speakers can legitimately claim to be bilingual.

The notion of proficiency raises some very complex issues. Again, the 'obvious' answer is to say that people are bilingual when they achieve native-like fluency in each language. But this criterion is far too strong. People who have 'perfect' fluency in two languages do exist, but they are the exception, not the rule. The vast majority of bilinguals do not have an equal command of their two languages: one language is more fluent than the other, interferes with the other, imposes its accent on the other, or simply is the preferred language in certain situations. I know a child of French/English parents who went to school and university in France. She became a geography teacher, married a British doctor, and came to live in England, where she had her first child. In general conversation, she could cope with ease in either language; but she found herself unable to teach geography in English, and she was extremely reluctant to discuss baby care in French. In each case she knew the slang, jargon, and phrasing which is naturally assimilated when learning a new skill – but this was available in only one of her languages. Her linguistic competence certainly did not resemble that of monolingual teacher-mothers.

This situation seems to be typical. Studies of bilingual interaction have brought to light several differences in linguistic proficiency, both within and between individuals. Many bilinguals fail to achieve a native-like fluency in either language. Some achieve it in one (their *preferred* or *dominant* language), but not the other. For such reasons, scholars now tend to think of bilingual ability as a continuum: bilingual people will find themselves at different points on this continuum, with a minority approaching the theoretical ideal of perfect, balanced control of both languages, but most being some way from it, and some having very limited ability indeed. However, the notion is a difficult one to make precise, because so many different abilities are involved – in speaking, listening, reading, and writing, as well as in phonology, grammar, vocabulary, and pragmatics.

Why be bilingual?

Here too there is an 'obvious' answer: to communicate with people of different language backgrounds. And once again, the obvious answer will not account for the remarkable range of linguistic behaviour that can be observed in adult bilinguals. The 'easy' cases are those where a bilingual meets different monolingual people within a multilingual society, and changes from one language to the other in order to communicate with them. Somewhat more complex are cases where a bilingual chooses to use one language knowing that the listener would prefer the other (for example, electing to be tried in the language of a minority group, in order to embarrass the authorities). Here, language choice is a symbol of national identity.

But such bilingual/monolingual interactions and confrontations account for only a minority of cases. More often, in a multilingual society, bilinguals interact with other bilinguals, and opt to use their different languages in a complex network of interaction that proves extremely difficult to describe and explain. The choice of language will vary depending on the type of person addressed – members of the family, school-mates, colleagues, superiors, friends, shopkeepers, officials, transport personnel, neighbours, and others. It will also vary depending on the location or social setting. The members of a family may vary their language use depending on whether they are at home, in the street, or in church. At the office, someone may talk to a colleague in language X, but over lunch talk to the same person using language Y.

Even more complex, and not well understood, are the many cases when a bilingual talks to another bilingual with the same language background, and yet changes from one language to another in the course of the conversation. The phenomenon is known variously as *language mixing*, *language switching*, or *code switching*.

Language switching

Switching between languages is extremely common and takes many forms. A long narrative may switch from one language to the other. Sentences may alternate. A sentence may begin in one language, and finish in another. Phrases from both languages may succeed each other in apparently random order (though in fact grammatical constraints are frequently involved). Such behaviour can be explained only by postulating a range of linguistic or social factors such as the following.

- Speakers cannot express themselves adequately in one language, so switch to the other to make good the deficiency. This may trigger a speaker to continue in the other language for a while. This tends to happen a great deal when the speaker is upset, tired, or otherwise distracted.
- Switching to a minority language is very common as a means of expressing solidarity with a social group. The language change signals to the listener that the speaker is from a certain background; if the listener responds with a similar switch, a degree of rapport is established. The same switch may of course also be used to exclude other people, who do not know the language, from the group.
- The switch between languages can signal the speaker's attitude towards the listener – friendly, irritated, distant, ironic, jocular, and so on. Monolinguals can communicate these effects to some extent by varying the level of formality of their speech; bilinguals can do it by language switching. If two bilinguals normally talk to each other in language X, the choice of Y is bound to create a special effect. A common example is for a mother to tell her child to do something in one language, and then, if the child fails to obey, to switch to another language, thereby showing her stronger emphasis or displeasure.

These are but some of the sociolinguistic functions that language switching can perform. The phenomenon is evidently a complex and subtle one, with speakers usually being totally unaware of the extent to which they have been switching in a conversation. If interrupted, they may even be unable to say which language they were using in their last sentence. Monolinguals often dismiss or satirize language switching, using such pejorative labels as *Franglais*, *Spanglish*, or *Tex-Mex* (= Texan Mexican). Perhaps because of this kind of criticism, many bilingual people come to be very self-conscious about their switching, and try to avoid it in talking to strangers or on formal occasions. But in informal speech, it is a natural and powerful communicative feature of bilingual interaction, which presents linguists with one of their most intriguing analytical challenges.

64

How we cope with many languages: translate them

Although multilingualism is the normal human condition, individuals typically do not achieve great proficiency in more than two or three languages. We remain rightly in awe of linguistic legends, such as Cardinal Giuseppe Mezzofanti (1774–1849), librarian at the Vatican, who is reputed to have been able to speak 50 languages (most with great fluency), to understand a further 20, and to translate 114. However, that is still less than 2% of the world's languages. So even he would have found himself, from time to time, having to cope with the problem of language when it becomes a barrier to communication.

The discovery of the language barrier is quickly made by all who travel, study, govern, or sell. Whether the activity is tourism, research, government, policing, business, or data dissemination, the lack of a common language can severely impede progress and can halt it altogether. Communication problems of this kind must happen thousands of times each day, but very few become public knowledge. Publicity comes only when a failure to communicate has major consequences, such as strikes, lost orders, legal problems, or fatal accidents – even, at times, war.

There are four ways of getting around the foreign-language barrier.

- Increase the number and availability of translating and interpreting services.
- Invent an auxiliary language that everyone will understand (§65).

- Introduce an existing language as a world language that everyone will understand (§66).
- Provide increased motivation and opportunity to learn foreign languages (§67).

Translating

When people are faced with a foreign-language barrier, the oldest and usual way round it is to find someone to interpret or translate for them. The term *translation* is the neutral term used for all tasks where the meaning of expressions in one language (the *source* language) is turned into the meaning of another (the *target* language), whether the medium is spoken, written, or signed. In specific professional contexts, however, a distinction is drawn between people who work with the spoken or signed language (*interpreters*), and those who work with the written language (*translators*). The two roles are seen as quite distinct, and it is unusual to find one person who is equally happy with both occupations.

It is sometimes said that there is no task more complex than translation – a claim that can be readily believed when all the variables involved are taken into account. Translators not only need to know their source language well; they must also have a thorough understanding of the field of knowledge covered by the source text, and of any cultural or emotional connotations that need to be specified in the target language if the intended effect is to be conveyed. The same special awareness needs to be present for the target language, so that points of special phrasing, contemporary fashions or taboos in expression, local expectations, and so on, can all be taken into account. On the whole, translators work into their mother tongue (or language of habitual use), to ensure a result that sounds as natural as possible – though some argue that, for certain types of text (e.g. scientific material) where translation accuracy is more crucial than naturalness, it makes sense for translators to be more fluent in the source language.

The aim of translation is to provide semantic equivalence between source and target language. This is what makes translation different from other kinds of linguistic activity, such as adapting, précis writing, and abstracting. However, there are many problems hidden within this apparently simple statement, all to do with what standards of equivalence should be expected and accepted. Exact equivalence is of course impossible: no translator could provide a translation that was a perfect parallel to the source text, in such respects as rhythm, puns, and cultural allusions. Such a parallel is not even possible when paraphrasing within a single language: there is always some loss of information.

On the other hand, there are many kinds of inexact equivalence, any of which can be successful at a certain level of practical functioning. It therefore follows that there is no such thing as a 'best' translation. The success of a translation depends on the purpose for which it was made, which in turn reflects the needs of the people for whom it was made. An inelegant, rough-and-ready translation of a letter can suffice to inform a firm of the nature of an enquiry. A translation of a scientific article requires careful attention to meaning, but little attention to aesthetic form. The provision of a dubbed film script will warrant scrupulous care over the synchronization of lip movements, often at the expense of content. Literary work requires a sensitive consideration of form as well as content, and may prompt several translations, each of which emphasizes a different aspect of the original. It is easy to see that what might be 'best' for one set of circumstances may be entirely unsuitable for another.

Translators aim to produce a text that is as faithful to the original as circumstances require or permit, and yet that reads as if it were written originally in the target language. They aim to be 'invisible people' – transferring content without drawing attention to the considerable artistic and technical skills involved in the process. The complexity of the task is apparent, but its importance is often underestimated, and its practitioners' social status and legal rights undervalued. Some countries view translation as a menial, clerical task, and pay their translators accordingly. Others (such as the Japanese) regard it as a major intellectual discipline in its own right. The question of status is currently much debated.

Interpreting

Interpreting is today widely known from its use in international political life. When senior ministers from different language backgrounds meet, the television record invariably shows a pair of interpreters hovering in the background. At major conferences, the presence of headphones is a clear indication that a serious linguistic exercise is taking place. In everyday circumstances, too, interpreters are frequently needed, especially in cosmopolitan societies formed by new generations of immigrants. Often, the business of law courts, hospitals, local health clinics, classrooms, or industrial tribunals cannot be carried on without the presence of an interpreter.

There are two main kinds of interpreting. One procedure, known as *consecutive* interpreting, is doubtless as old as language itself. Here, the interpreter translates after the speaker has finished speaking, either in short bursts between sentences, or at the very end of a discourse. This approach is widely practised in informal situations, as well as in committees and small conferences. In larger and more formal settings, however, it has been generally replaced by *simultaneous* interpreting – a development that arose from the availability of modern audiological equipment and the advent of increased international interaction following the Second World War.

Of the two procedures, it is the second that has attracted most interest, because of the special complexity of the task and the remarkable skills required. In no other context of human communication is anyone routinely required to listen and speak at the same time, preserving an exact semantic correspondence between the two modes. Moreover, there is invariably a delay of a few words between the stimulus and the response, because of the time it takes to assimilate what is being said in the source language and to translate it into an acceptable form in the target language. This *ear–voice span* is usually about two or three seconds, but it may be as much as ten seconds or so, if the text is complex. The brain has to remember what has just been said, attend to what is currently being said, and anticipate the construction of what is about to be said.

How it is all done is a bit of a mystery. That it is done at all is a source of some wonder, given the often lengthy periods of interpreting required, the confined environment of an interpreting booth, the presence of background noise, and the awareness that major decisions may depend upon the accuracy of the work. Research projects have now begun to look at these factors – to determine, for example, how far successful interpreting is affected by poor listening conditions, or the speed at which the source language is spoken. It seems that an input speed of between 100 and 120 words per minute is a comfortable rate for interpreting, with an upper limit of around 200 w.p.m. But even small increases in speed can dramatically affect the accuracy of output.

The problem in Europe

Nowhere does the foreign language barrier exist so markedly as in the offices of the European Commission, whose Directorate-General for Translation is the largest translation service in the world, translating written text into and out of all the EU's official languages, exclusively for the European Commission. (Interpretation of speech is handled by the *Directorate-General for Interpretation*.) Located in Brussels and Luxembourg, at the beginning of 2004 it had a permanent staff of some 1,300 linguists and 500 support staff.

However, in 2004 the number of countries in the EU increased from eleven to twenty-five, and the number of official languages, in which legislation has to be published, rose by 82%, from eleven to twenty: Czech, Danish, Dutch, English, Estonian, Greek, Finnish, French, German, Hungarian, Italian, Latvian, Lithuanian, Maltese, Polish, Portuguese, Slovak, Slovene, Spanish, Swedish. The number of pages to be translated immediately expanded – from 1.5 million in 2003 to 2.4 million in 2005. The additional permanent staff required was sixty translators per language, along with support staff.

The scale of the problem is evident, and is especially marked in interpreting. Even in the days of eleven EU languages it was impossible to find expert interpreters for all language pairs, or to provide maximum coverage on all occasions. Pragmatic solutions therefore had to be found. One is the use of a relay system: if there is no Finnish/Portuguese interpreter, for example, English might be used as an intermediary language. Also, every effort is made to find interpreters who each know three or four languages. But there is always a shortage of trained interpreters, especially for the languages with small populations, such as Maltese.

Machine translation

Is automation the solution? The idea of using machines to provide translations between natural languages has been recognized since the 1930s, but an appropriate climate for development did not arise until the years following the Second World War. At that time, the rise of information theory, the success of advanced code-breaking techniques, and the invention of the electronic computer all indicated that machine translation (MT) could be a reality. However, initial results were not encouraging. The systems proved to be very limited in the kind of data they could handle. Translations were crude, full of errors, and required so much human post-editing that they proved to be more expensive than having a human translator carry out the whole task in the first place.

A new climate has emerged in recent years, following the major intellectual and technological developments in linguistics, computing, and artificial intelligence. The main developments have been to provide systems of analysis that allow for grammatical and semantic complexity. The first steps were in devising automatic procedures for parsing the syntactic structure of a sentence, and for carrying out an analysis of word structure. Later developments began to introduce semantic information and to use artificial intelligence techniques to simulate human thought processes (*knowledge-based MT*). If the computer is given enough data on the meaning of words and about the context of a sentence, it is argued, it should be able to work out for itself what analysis to make in cases where individual words or sentences are ambiguous.

The principle is undeniable, but it has proved extremely difficult so far to write programs that can handle more than fragments of discourse.

It is therefore unlikely that machines will replace human translators in the forseeable future; but they can already help to take a great deal of the drudgery out of routine translation work, and enable far more material to be processed than would otherwise be the case. In the rapidly developing world of *machine-aided translation*, computationally organized databanks and all kinds of peripheral equipment help translators in their daily work. But the distance we have to travel, before MT becomes a satisfactory reality, can be seen every day on the Internet, where automatic translation services desperately seek to transcend the limitations of unidiomatic gist. The goal of idiomatic accuracy is still a generation away.

65

How we cope with many languages: supplement them

An alternative solution to the problem presented by the language barrier (§64) is not to engage teams of translators and interpreters but to have everyone – or, at least, all who travel, study, govern, or sell – learn a common language, or *lingua franca*, in addition to their mother tongue. Three approaches have been used.

Devising an artificial language

The first approach is to devise an *artificial* or *auxiliary language* (AL) – one specially invented to facilitate international communication. Several hundred ALs have been recorded, and new ones continue to be devised. The desire for a universal language can be traced back to Classical times, but the idea began to flourish only in the 17th century, when world exploration brought to light many new languages, and Latin began to fall from favour as a universal medium.

The hope was that things could be represented by *real characters* – special symbols or numbers – which would be understood regardless of language, instead of the usual letters or sounds. However, all such systems, though simple, logical, and plausible at the outset, become extremely arbitrary and complicated as they are developed. The learner ends up being presented with a virtually impossible memory load, with thousands of symbols, and a rigid classification within which it proves difficult to incorporate new knowledge.

Such schemes fell out of favour at the end of the 17th century, though they had a revival a century later, with the rise of a movement which aimed to discover universal principles of thought behind the variety of grammatical forms in language. There was much more at stake here than international communication: it was felt that a good philosophy of signs, or *ideology*, would help to eliminate vagueness and ambiguity from language, provide a better vehicle for thought, and be a more efficient means of spreading knowledge. But the resurgence of interest was short-lived.

In the last quarter of the 19th century, there was another flurry of enthusiasm, with several AL proposals competing with each other for public support. These were based on a different principle: their elements were drawn not from abstract notions but from natural languages. The first large-scale movement was Volapük, followed closely by Esperanto, Idiom Neutral, Ido, and several dozen other systems. Most of the proposals had very short lives, but some, such as Esperanto, have achieved an impressive international use.

An enormous amount of time, energy, money, and ingenuity has been expended on the invention and dissemination of AL proposals. In the early years they were usually seen by their supporters as a key to a world of mutual understanding, clearer thinking, and peaceful coexistence. The use of a common language does not guarantee peace, however, as is plain from the civil wars that have taken place throughout history. In recent years, therefore, there has been a tendency to adopt less ambitious goals, and there have been several local successes, with different countries and organizations (especially on the Continent of Europe) being persuaded to introduce an AL dimension into aspects of their daily life – in hotels, telephone boxes, telegrams, advertisements, and timetables. Even with the most successful of these movements, however, very limited progress has been made towards the goal of an internationally recognized and universally used auxiliary language.

Esperanto has come nearest to this goal, the invention of a Polish oculist, Ludwig Lazarus Zamenhof (1859–1917). He first published the scheme in Russian in 1887 using the pseudonym *Doktoro Esperanto* ('Doctor Hopeful'). The first Esperanto journal was published in 1889, and the First Universal Congress of Esperanto was held in 1905, bringing together nearly 700 delegates from twenty countries. That year also saw the publication of the *Fundamento de Esperanto*, an authoritative statement of the language's structure and vocabulary, which was to be the 'obligatory basis for Esperantists of all time'.

Today Esperanto is frequently encountered at international conferences. Several journals and newspapers are published in the language, and there is a large translated literature, including the Bible and the Qur'an. There is extensive original work in the language, and several countries transmit radio broadcasts in Esperanto. Estimates vary greatly about the number of fluent speakers, but tend to fall between 1 and 2 million, almost all being second-language speakers at various levels of proficiency. It has still to achieve official status as an international language.

The international acceptance of any AL is a long uphill battle for its supporters, who have to overcome problems of a social, linguistic, and political kind.

Motivation

How is the inventor of an AL to persuade people to learn it, when no one else knows it? To avoid this problem, there has to be a massive period of simultaneous learning, which is extremely difficult to organize.

Identity

One of the chief functions of natural language is to express identity, and to foster internal variation in the form of dialects (§45), but ALs do not welcome variety differences. They are therefore in conflict with the aspirations of movements where there is a desire to retain and express national, regional, or social identities.

Linguistic bias

It is not easy to develop a simple and common language. Most ALs are based on western Indo-European languages, and this acts as a barrier to speakers from other language families. There is still a marked European linguistic parochialism among ALs, which tend to underestimate the diversity of the world's languages.

Semantic differences

Insufficient attention is paid to the semantic differences that exist between languages. Speakers of different languages may translate their mother-tongue words into an AL, but this does not necessarily mean that they understand each other any better.

Antagonism

Many people who are sympathetic to the general idea of a universal language are put off by the great fervour with which proponents of ALs present their causes. Several AL organizations arrange public occasions with songs and hymns, each displaying a faith in the efficacy of its own AL which can reach evangelical proportions.

Modify a natural language

The language barrier has also been attacked by several proposals to simplify the structure of a natural language, usually by reducing the complexity of its grammar or the size of its vocabulary. All the main western European languages have been modified in this way, the most famous approach being that of Charles Kay Ogden (1889–1957), known as *Basic English* (1930).

BASIC is an acronym for 'British American Scientific International Commercial'. It consists of 850 words selected to cover everyday needs: 400 general nouns, 200 picturable objects, 100 general qualities, 50 opposites, and 100 operations (adverbs, particles, etc.). The working principle is that all words not on this list can be replaced by those that are (permitting several inflectional variations). The basic vocabulary is supplemented by several international and scientific words (e.g. *radio, geography, radium,* names of countries and currencies).

The system was strongly supported in the 1940s by such people as

Churchill and Roosevelt, but there were also many criticisms. The simplification of the vocabulary is achieved at the expense of a more complex grammar and a greater reliance on idiomatic construction. The replacement forms are often unwieldy, involving lengthy circumlocutions. And although BASIC proved easy to learn to read, it proved very difficult to write in the language in such a way that meaning was clearly preserved. The system is now largely of historical interest.

Promote a natural language

Many people feel that the only realistic chance of breaking the foreign-language barrier is to use a natural language as a world lingua franca. The history of ideas already provides precedents, with Latin employed as a medium of education in western Europe throughout the Middle Ages, and French from the 17th to the 20th centuries. Today, English has emerged as the leading contender for the position of world lingua franca.

English is an official or semi-official language in over sixty countries, and is either dominant or well established in every continent. It is the main language of books, newspapers, airports and air-traffic control, international business and academic conferences, science, technology, medicine, diplomacy, sports, international competitions, pop music, and advertising. Over two-thirds of the world's scientists write in English. Of all the information in the world's electronic retrieval systems, 80% is currently stored in English.

There are few competitors to English. Several other languages have an important local role as a lingua franca but no comparable international level of use, such as Russian in eastern Europe, Spanish in South and Central America, or French in Africa. More people in the world speak Chinese as a mother tongue than any other language, but Chinese is too unfamiliar in the West to be a serious contender.

According to conservative estimates, mother-tongue speakers of English have now reached around 400 million, but these are far exceeded (in a ratio of three to one) by those who have learned English as a second or foreign language. Estimates of all English speakers in the world in 2005 range from 1,500 to 2,000 million – between a quarter and a third of the world's population. Much depends on the rate at which the language is being learned in India (with some 350 million speakers in 2005) and China (with some 220 million), the latter introducing a great push in its English-teaching as it anticipates the arrival of the Olympics in 2008.

Many factors contribute to the gradual spread of a language – chiefly political and military might, economic power, cultural power, and religious influence. These same factors mean that the development of a world language is not always viewed with enthusiasm by those who would have to learn it. Such a language, it can be argued, would give its originating culture an unprecedented influence in world affairs and scientific research. Furthermore, it is thought, a world language would inevitably erode the status of minority languages and pose a threat to the identity of nations. Many people thus view the current progress of English towards world-language status with concern and often with antagonism. But with millions voting with their mouths, the only realistic option seems to be to find ways of managing the problems caused by this progress, as they arise, rather than trying to reverse it.

Ironically, the main danger to the growth of a world language comes from within. As English becomes used in all corners of the world, by people from all walks of life, so it begins to develop new spoken varieties which are used by local people as symbols of their identity. And in the course of time, some of these new varieties will become mutually unintelligible. One prediction is that eventually there will emerge a new English family of languages, and we will be back where we started. An alternative view suggests that this variety will emerge only at a colloquial, grass-roots level, and that, at the levels of formal speech and writing, standard English – already globally present as a medium of print and satellite broadcasting channels – will retain its unifying role.

Some people think they already see signs of the break-up of the language when they find difficulty in understanding the English used in India, West Africa, or other parts of the world. Variation can also be seen in the written language, mainly in a distinctive regional lexicon. An English edition of an Indian newspaper, for example, might refer routinely to *roti, kapra, and makan* ('bread, clothing, and dwelling'), a *rail roko* ('railway strike'), and to such quantities as a *crore* ('10 million') or *lakh* ('100,000'). In some international varieties of English, the local standard vocabulary (including words for local food, fauna, or flora) may run to thousands of items.

This variation raises a question mark against the notion of 'world' English. With so many varieties, which one should be used as the international medium? Should it be American, British, Indian, Australian . . . ? Teachers in particular are faced with a conflict of aims: should they teach British or American English, both, or neither, focusing on the variety found in their own country? What effect will their decision have on the ability of their students to communicate at an international level? These are major questions at the beginning of the new millennium.

66
How we cope with many languages: learn them

To many people, the most obvious way of reducing some of the power of the language barrier (§64) is to promote the learning and teaching of foreign languages in a variety of child and adult educational settings. This widely practised approach is undoubtedly very successful, as can be judged by the millions who succeed in mastering a foreign language, even to levels that are comparable to those achieved by 'natural' bilinguals (§63).

English-speaking monoglots often express amazement at the linguistic proficiency displayed by foreigners – not least, the standards routinely achieved in English – and conclude that foreigners must have a 'gift' for language learning, which they lack, or that English must be a particularly easy language to learn. There is no basis for these suggestions. A few gifted language learners do exist, but most people arrive at their fluency only as a result of hard work, expended over a considerable period of time.

On the other hand, there is also a great deal of educational failure and lack of achievement in the language-learning field, which also requires explanation. Many people, from a variety of linguistic backgrounds, are actually embarrassed by their linguistic inadequacy when travelling abroad, and wish to overcome it. Many have tried to learn a foreign language, but have made little progress in it. 'I was never very good at languages in school' is a widely heard complaint. It is therefore important to study the factors that govern success or failure in this field.

There are two sides of the coin: *foreign language learning* (FLL) and *foreign language teaching* (FLT). FLL was at one time thought to be exclusively a matter of teaching techniques; it was felt that, if teaching was above a certain minimum level of efficiency, learning would automatically follow. Teaching was the active skill; learning, the passive one. Today, the active role of the learner is an established principle. It is recognized that there are important individual differences among learners, especially in personality and motivation, that can directly influence the teaching outcome. Research is therefore now directed not only at the way teachers teach (§67), but also at the way learners learn.

Several terminological distinctions have to be recognized. A person's *mother tongue* or *first language* (L1) is distinguished from any further languages that may be acquired (L2, L3, etc.). The term *foreign language* is popularly used to refer to any language that is not a native language in a country; and *second language* is also commonly used in this way, especially in the USA (a usage which is increasing world-wide). But many linguists distinguish between *foreign* and *second* language use, recognizing major differences in the learning aims, teaching methods, and achievement levels involved.

A *foreign language* (FL), in this more restricted sense, is a non-native language taught in school that has no status as a routine medium of communication in that country. A *second language* (SL) is a non-native language that is widely used for purposes of communication, usually as a medium of education, government, or business. In this usage, English, for example, has foreign language status in Japan, but second language status in Nigeria. The latter term is also used with reference to immigrants and indigenous groups whose L1 is a minority language: in the USA, for example, English is a second language for millions of immigrants from a wide range of language backgrounds as well as for speakers of Native American languages.

Why learn foreign languages?

The question requires an answer, in a world where we frequently find indifference or hostility expressed towards foreign languages and foreign people, where teaching resources are limited, and where other subjects clamour for extra slots within the school timetable. The criticisms come mainly from within the English-speaking world, where many people think that FLL is unnecessary in a world where an increasing number of people understand English (§65). However:

- FFL is no longer a luxury, in an international world. It is a necessity, if a country is to exercise a role in world affairs. Especially in Europe, it is seen as a criterion of responsible international citizenship. It is a strength to be able to meet people from other countries on equal linguistic terms.

- FLL has an essential role in preparing children to cope with the new perspectives brought about by a rapidly changing society, not only abroad, but within their own community. It can help overcome their insecurity and develop their confidence as they face up to the demands of social and personal relationships not usually encountered in a mother-tongue context.

- FLL promotes understanding, tolerance, and respect for the cultural identity, rights, and values of others, whether abroad, or at home in minority groups. People become less ethnocentric, as they come to see themselves and their society in the eyes of the rest of the world, and encounter other ways of thinking about things. Language learning, as well as travel, broadens the mind.

- Success in the international world of commerce and industry is becoming more and more dependent on FLL. Young people now find they have more career opportunities when they know a foreign language and are increasingly moving to localities where some degree of FL competence is required of them. This mobility no longer affects only executives, but is found with all grades and categories of personnel, such as marketing staff, legal specialists, secretaries, and technicians.

- FLL is becoming increasingly important as unemployment and reduced working hours add to people's leisure time. Tourist travel is a major motivation, but many have come to find FLL a satisfying leisure activity in its own right, enabling them to have direct access to the world of foreign cinema, radio and television, vocal music, literature, and the history of ideas.

How we learn a foreign language

Several theories of the nature of the FLL process have been propounded. A great deal of language learning and teaching in the 1950s and 1960s was influenced by the tenets of behaviourism. In this view, FLL is seen as a process of imitation and reinforcement: learners attempt to copy what they hear, and by regular practice they establish a set of acceptable habits in the new language. Properties of the L1 are thought to exercise an influence on the course of L2 learning: learners *transfer* sounds, structures, and usages from one language to the other.

This account faces several problems. Imitation alone does not provide a means of identifying the task facing learners, who are continually confronted with the need to create and recognize novel utterances that go beyond the limitations of the model sentences they may have practised. Nor does imitation suffice as an explanation of the way learners behave: not many of the errors that are theoretically predicted by the differences between L1 and L2 in fact occur in the language of learners; and conversely, other errors are found that seem unrelated to the L1. The systematic comparison of L1 and L2, in order to predict areas of greatest learning difficulty – a procedure known as *contrastive analysis* – explains only a small part of what goes on in FLL.

The main alternative to the behaviourist approach sees as central the role of cognitive factors in language learning. In this view, learners are credited with using their cognitive abilities in a creative way to work out hypotheses about the structure of the FL. They construct rules, try them out, and alter them if they prove to be inadequate. Language learning, in this account, proceeds in a series of transitional stages, as learners acquire more knowledge of the L2. At each stage, they are in control of a language system that is equivalent to neither the L1 nor the L2 – an *interlanguage*.

Error analysis plays a central role in this approach. Errors are likely to emerge when learners make the wrong deductions about the nature of the L2, such as assuming that a pattern is general, when in fact there are exceptions. The errors provide positive evidence about the nature of the learning process, as the learner gradually works out what the FL system is. For example, learners of French who say *vous disez* instead of *vous dites* 'you say' have assumed, wrongly, that the *-ez* ending found after *vous* in most other French verbs (*marchez*, *donnez*, etc.) also applies to *dire* 'say'. The error in this case indicates that a faulty generalization has been made.

Since the 1970s, cognitive approaches to FLL have been in the ascendant. However, the analysis of errors turns out to be a highly complex matter, involving other factors than the cognitive. Some errors are due to the influence of the mother tongue, as contrastive analysis claims. Some come from external influences, such as inadequate teaching or materials. Moreover, not all errors are equally systematic, disruptive, or unacceptable. Errors of vocabulary, for example, are less general and predictable than errors of grammar, but they are usually more disruptive of communication. Some errors, indeed, become so acceptable that they do not disappear: they become *fossilized* – tolerated by learners because they do not cause major problems of communication. A good example would be the pronunciation errors that are heard in a foreign accent.

Achieving success in language learning

There is as yet no single theory that can account for the diversity of FLL behaviour, and explain why some learners succeed in their task, whereas others fail. Many variables are involved.

- It is unclear how far there may be a genuine *aptitude* for FLL. Given sufficient motivation, intelligence, and opportunity, anyone can learn a language; but the task is likely to be less onerous if certain general personal qualities are present. Among these, it has been suggested, are empathy and adaptability, assertiveness and independence, with good drive and powers of application. People need to be capable of assimilating knowledge in difficult conditions. They should have a good memory, and be good at finding patterns. Of particular importance is an ability to detect phonetic differences (e.g. of stress, melody, vowel quality) – something which can manifest itself in other domains, such as drama or music.

- *Motivation* is a central factor. Students need to see that foreign languages are taken seriously by those whom they respect, especially in the community at large (encouragement from local employers, civic interest in town twinning, etc.). It is critical to take the language out of the classroom, so that students see its use in a native community. Moreover, motivation applies to teacher as well as student: it is difficult to teach enthusiastically if it is known that most of the class are going to drop their language at the earliest opportunity, or that society places little store by it.

- *Attitude* towards the foreign language is important. If a student perceives a country or culture to be unpleasant, for whatever reason (e.g. its politics, religion, eating habits), the negative attitude is likely to influence language learning achievement – and conversely.

- Students can benefit from being taught to 'learn how to learn' foreign languages – useful *strategies*, such as silent rehearsal, techniques of memorization, and alternative ways of expressing what they want to say (paraphrase). They may also benefit from training in the kinds of basic skills involved in FLL, such as those identified above.

- *Exposure* to the foreign language needs to be regular – a problem which particularly affects FLT in schools, where timetable pressure, examinations, and holidays may lead to discontinuities. Whenever possible, the aim should be to teach 'little and often'. Too much exposure at any one time can be as ineffective as too little, readily leading to fatigue and superficial assimilation ('quickly learned is quickly forgotten').

- Exposure to native users of the foreign language is a real benefit, through the use of authentic materials (e.g. audio tape, video tape, newspaper library) and in school, foreign language teaching assistants. A parallel emphasis on output, as well as input, is desirable:

'practice makes perfect'. An important dimension is the use of educational visits abroad – but these need to be properly prepared and followed up in class, and the experience should enable children to be genuinely integrated within the FL environment. Out-of-school activities should be encouraged, such as pen friends, private exchanges, and weekend culture simulation courses.

When should we learn a foreign language?

Traditionally, L2s have been introduced at a relatively late stage of development – usually around the age of 10 or 11. In recent decades, the benefits of an early start have been urged, given the natural way in which young children learn language (§14), the positive results of some immersion programmes, and the likelihood that they can devote more time to the task. Several experimental FL programmes have been tried out in primary school.

The results have been mixed. FLL with young children can work well, but only if learning conditions are optimal. The teaching objectives need to be limited, graded, and clearly defined. Specialist teachers need to be available. Methods need to be devised that are appropriate to the interests and cognitive level of the children. And the transition to secondary school needs to be borne in mind, because a lack of continuity can negate previous work.

However, even if formal FLT is not introduced, it is still possible to develop young children's general language awareness – to sensitize them towards the existence and variety of the languages of others as well as of their own language – and to foster the enjoyment that can come from being in contact with foreign languages. Children can learn FL games, songs, rhymes, sayings, everyday greetings, and many basic notions (e.g. counting, parts of the body, telling the time). In particular, if pupils from other language backgrounds are present, the multilingual setting can be used to generate a mutual linguistic and cultural interest. And the experience can provide a valuable foundation for the systematic study of foreign languages at later ages.

67
How we cope with many languages: teach them

But how? In the long search for the best way of teaching a foreign language, hundreds of different approaches, or methods, have been devised. Each method is based on a particular view of language learning (§66), and usually recommends the use of a specific set of techniques and materials, which may have to be implemented in a fixed sequence. Ambitious claims are often made for a new teaching method, but none has yet been shown to be intrinsically superior.

The contemporary attitude is flexible and utilitarian: it is recognized that there are several ways of reaching the goal of foreign language (FL) competence, and that teachers need to be aware of a range of methods, in order to find the one most appropriate to the learner's needs and circumstances, and to the objectives of the course. It is frequently necessary to introduce an eclectic approach, in which aspects of different methods are selected to meet the demands of particular teaching situations.

Several classifications of teaching methods have been made, in an attempt to impose some degree of order on what is a highly diverse and idiosyncratic field. Certain methods are widely recognized because of their influential role in the history of ideas surrounding this subject.

The grammar translation method

This method derives from the traditional approach to the teaching of Latin and Greek, which was particularly influential in the 19th century. It is based on the meticulous analysis of the written language, in which translation exercises, reading comprehension, and the written imitation of texts play a primary role. Learning mainly involves the mastery of grammatical rules and the memorizing of long lists of literary vocabulary, related to texts which are chosen more for their prestigious content than for their interest or level of linguistic difficulty. There is little emphasis laid on the activities of listening or speaking.

This approach dominated early work in modern language teaching. A minority still find its intellectual discipline appealing; but the vast majority of teachers now recognize that the approach does little to meet the spoken language needs and interests of today's language students.

The direct method

This approach, also known as the *oral* or *natural* method, is based on the active involvement of the learner in speaking and listening to the foreign language in realistic everyday situations. No use is made of the learner's mother tongue; learners are encouraged to think in the foreign language, and not to translate into or out of it. A great deal of emphasis is placed on good pronunciation, often introducing students to phonetic transcription (§9) before they see the standard orthography. Formal grammatical rules and terminology are avoided.

The direct method continues to attract interest and enthusiasm, but it is not an easy approach to use in school. In the artificial environment of the classroom, it is difficult to generate natural learning situations and to provide everyone with sufficient practice. Several variants of the method have thus evolved. In particular, teachers often permit some degree of mother-tongue explanation and grammatical statement to avoid learners developing inaccurate fluency ('school pidgin').

The audio-lingual method

Also known as the *aural–oral* method, this approach derives from the intensive training in spoken languages given to American military personnel during the Second World War, which resulted in a high degree of listening and speaking skill being achieved in a relatively short time-span. The emphasis is on everyday spoken conversation, with particular attention being paid to natural pronunciation. Language is seen as a process of habit formation: structural patterns in dialogues about everyday situations are imitated and drilled (first in choral speech, then individually) until the learner's responses become automatic. There is a special focus on areas of structural contrast between L1 and L2. There is little discussion of grammatical rules. Language work is first heard, then practised orally, before being seen and used in written form.

The approach can instil considerable conversational fluency in a learner, and was widely used, especially in the 1950s and 1960s. Its reliance on drills and habit-formation makes it less popular today, especially with learners who wish for a wider range of linguistic experience, and who feel the need for more creative work in speech production.

Communicative teaching

During the 1970s, there was a widespread reaction against methods which stressed the teaching of grammatical forms and paid little or no attention to the way language is used in everyday situations. A concern developed to make FLT *communicative* by focusing on learners' knowledge of the functions of language, and on their ability to select appropriate kinds of language for use in specific situations. Increased interest was shown in the situations themselves, and in the kind of language the learner would be likely to meet – for example, at a bank, or when eating out. *Situational* syllabuses aimed to recreate these situations, and to teach the various linguistic activities involved, such as requesting, thanking, complaining, and instructing.

Notional (or *functional*) syllabuses provided a major alternative to the emphases of formal language teaching. Here, the content of a course is organized in terms of the meanings (*notions*) learners require in order to communicate in particular functional contexts. Major communicative notions include the linguistic expression of time, duration, frequency, quantity, location, and motion. Major communicative functions include evaluation, persuasion, emotional expression, and the marking of social relations.

Humanistic approaches

In the later decades of the 20th century, a number of new and radically different approaches came to the fore, often grouped together under the heading *humanistic* because of the way they focused on tapping into innate skills and abilities assumed to be present in all learners. For example, *Suggestopedia* is based on the view that the brain has great unused potential which can be exploited through the power of suggestion. In their opening lesson, learners are presented with large amounts of the foreign language. The text is translated, then read aloud in a dramatic way against a background of classical music. The aim is to provide an atmosphere of total relaxation and enjoyment, in which learning is incidental. By using a large amount of linguistic material, the suggestion is conveyed that language learning is easy and natural. In a later session, students use the material in various communicative activities.

Another example is *The Silent Way*. This aims to provide an environment which keeps the amount of teaching to a minimum and encourages learners to develop their own ways of using the language elements introduced. In the first lesson, the teacher introduces a small L2 vocabulary to talk about a set of coloured rods, using a few verbs (equivalent to 'take', 'give', 'pick up', and 'put'), adjectives, pronouns, etc., and gradually extending the length of the sentence (e.g. *Take the green rod and give it to Michael*). The aim is to help the learners to become self-reliant – to select their own sentences and be in control of them, with good intonation and rhythm. The teacher does not repeat the material or provide sentences for students to imitate; and no use is made of the learners' L1. Charts containing vocabulary and colour-coded guides to pronunciation are made available to enable the teacher to guide the student's learning while saying as little as possible. As students say more to each other, so the teacher says less – hence the 'silent' way.

Teaching materials

The days are long gone when FLT materials consisted only of a grammar book and a dictionary. Today, there is a vast variety of printed materials – course books, workbooks, readers, programmed courses, collections of facsimile material, simplified literature, cue cards, charts, newspapers, magazines, posters, picture cards, cut-outs, and much more. These are supplemented by a range of materials using other media, such as CDs, records, audio tapes, slides, transparencies, filmstrips, video tapes, toys, games, and puppets. The advent of computer technology introduces a further potentially inexhaustible domain of ancillary equipment and a wide range of new interaction techniques and settings, such as Internet chatrooms.

Today, learning a foreign language is likely to mean learning a great deal about the foreign civilization and culture at the same time. Books and materials increasingly incorporate information about such matters as the physical geography, economy, history, politics, religion, social institutions, educational system, literature, art, music, science, technology, media, and sport, as well as about daily life-style, popular beliefs, folk customs, and social values. The material is inevitably very selective; but it helps the learner to become more fully aware of differing ways of behaviour, and reduces the risks of culture shock, foreigner stereotyping, and intolerance.

A cultural frame of reference becomes increasingly important the greater the 'distance' between languages. To succeed in an oriental language, for example, a westerner needs the support of several of the above studies. But a cultural perspective is needed even with 'nearby' languages, in order to grasp the social significance of a linguistic feature or to follow the subject matter of daily conversation. For example, in every country, knowing the names of the most famous men and women of a culture, whether they are political figures, folk heroes, or media stars, is a major factor in really understanding the meaning of a newspaper report, a debate on television, or the course of a conversation.

The language laboratory

The best-known technological aid in FLT is undoubtedly the language laboratory – a room, usually divided into booths, where students can listen individually to tape recordings of FL material, and where they may record and play back their own responses, while being monitored by a teacher.

When these laboratories were first introduced, they were heralded as a technique that would vastly improve the rate and quality of FLL. They would take the burden of repetitive drills away from the teacher, provide more opportunities for learners to practise listening and speaking, and enable them to develop at their own rates and monitor their own progress. Many schools were quick to install expensive laboratory equipment. However, within a few years, it became apparent that there would be no breakthrough. The expected improvements did not emerge, and the popularity of the *language lab* showed a marked decline.

There were several reasons for the failure to live up to expectations. The taped materials were often poorly designed, leading to student frustration and boredom. The published programmes failed to reflect the kind of work the student was doing in class. Few modern languages staff had received training in materials design or laboratory use. And it proved difficult to maintain the equipment once it had been installed.

Today, the strengths and limitations of the laboratory are better realized, and the vastly increased potential of modern electronic hardware has led to a certain revival. There is now considerable interest in language-learning laboratories, which contain much more than the traditional systems – in particular, the introduction of interactive computational aids and video materials has proved to be extremely popular. *Computer-assisted language learning* (CALL) is today's trend.

It is now clear that, when used properly, laboratories can add a valuable extra dimension to FLT. For example, the taped material can provide a variety of authentic and well-recorded models for the training of listening comprehension. And laboratories can be used as resource centres, or libraries, giving learners extra opportunities to practise at their chosen level.

At the same time, the limitations of laboratories must be borne in mind. Their value will always depend on the development of appropriate teaching materials which reinforce what has been taught in class and provide opportunities for creative use; and here there is an urgent need for research into the efficacy of the different approaches which have been devised. Laboratory software, it seems, has some way to go before it can compare in sophistication with the hardware. But the arrival of the Internet has given language software developers a new lease of life.

Political considerations

No matter how much we come to understand about excellence in FLL and FLT, the knowledge is useless if a country's political policy gives no opportunity to put it into everyday practice. It is usually more economics than ideology which drives a country's language strategy. Questions of class size, technology availability, length of course, and teacher training all give rise to considerations of cost. But before these can be resolved, a country first has to have a coherent language policy (§68).

68
How we cope with many languages: plan them

Language, sooner or later, proves to be a thorn in the flesh of all who govern, whether at national or local level. Different social groups wish to see their linguistic identities and interests maintained, and may actively campaign for recognition. Governments have to react to these differences, officially or unofficially: they may wish to reconcile them, or try to eliminate them. With the pace of change increasing, and countries becoming more heterogeneous, cosmopolitan, and internationally aware, it is not possible to rely on the slow course of natural linguistic evolution to resolve the many pressures and conflicts that arise. Many governments, accordingly, try to solve their problems by engaging in conscious, principled *language planning*, or *linguistic engineering*.

Language planning involves the creation and implementation of an official policy about how the languages and linguistic varieties of a country are to be used. Decisions of a fundamental nature may need to be made, especially in the developing countries. But planning issues are to be found in all countries, as people debate such topics as the place of minority languages, foreign language teaching and learning (§66), the role of an academy in safeguarding standards, the influence of the media on usage, the value of spelling reform, the avoidance of sexist language, the need for plain English, stylistic standards in publishing, and the maintenance of oracy and literacy levels in school.

Language planning is carried out by a variety of government depart-

How Language Works

ments and agencies, academies, committees, popular societies, and individuals. Activities range from the political and judicial, at one extreme, to the unofficial and illegal, at the other. Popular attitudes towards planning proposals include everything from complete support, through partial approval, general indifference, and mild antagonism, to total antipathy. Historical, political, economic, religious, educational, judicial, and social factors all have to be disentangled.

There are two main types of language-planning activities, based on whether the changes chiefly affect linguistic structure or linguistic use. In *corpus planning*, the changes are introduced into the structure (or *corpus*) of a language/variety – as when changes are proposed in spelling, pronunciation, grammar, or vocabulary. In *status planning*, changes are proposed in the way a language/variety is to be used in society (thus altering its status), as when it is permitted for the first time in law courts or in official publications. The distinction is not clear-cut, because not all kinds of planning activity can be neatly classified in this way, but it is widely encountered in language-planning research.

Planning in practice

In a multilingual environment – which means most environments around the world (§63) – several steps have to be taken in implementing a language policy.

- *Selecting the norm*: If several languages are spoken within a country, it is usually necessary to choose a single language as a norm for official, educational, and other purposes. It may prove possible to use one of the indigenous languages, but intergroup rivalry may make it necessary to introduce a language from elsewhere as a lingua franca (e.g. Hindi in India, English in Ghana), in which case the relative merits of these languages will need to be debated. In addition, it may be necessary to choose a particular variety of a language, or to construct a new variety, taking into account such factors as formality, social class, regional dialect, and previous literary use.

- *Codification*: If an indigenous language is chosen, it will need to be developed to meet the demands placed upon it as a medium of national or international communication. If the language has previously existed only in spoken form, or in an unusual writing system, an alphabet will have to be devised, along with rules of spelling and punctuation. An early aim will be the codification of the pronunciation, grammar, and vocabulary to provide a set of norms for standard use, especially if there is a great deal of local variation.

- *Modernization*: The vocabulary will need to be modernized, to enable foreign material (in such areas as science, medicine, or the consumer society) to be translated in a consistent way. Principles will have to be agreed for the introduction of new terms; for example, should they be loan words, or coinages based on native roots? New styles of discourse may need to be developed, for use on radio or in the press. Decisions will need to be made about new or uncertain usages, especially in technical contexts (e.g. how to abbreviate scientific terms).

- *Implementation*: The chosen standard will need to be officially implemented, by using it for government publications, in the media, and in schools. Inevitably, it will come to be viewed as the 'best' form of language in the speech community, because it will be associated with educational progress and social status. It will also provide the norm for literary style, and may be associated with factors of a nationalistic, cultural, or religious kind. In due course, it is likely to be promulgated as a norm through an official body, such as an academy, or through prescriptive grammars, dictionaries, and manuals of usage.

Educational policy

One of the most important ways in which a country's language policy manifests itself is in the kind of provision it makes for the linguistic education of children. Which languages and language varieties are to be taught in schools, from what age, and for how long? These questions are only partly answerable with reference to the field of foreign-language learning and teaching (§66); far more fundamental are factors arising out of government policy and popular opinion, where a wide range of positions is found. Languages can be actively promoted, passively tolerated, deliberately ignored, positively discouraged, and even banned.

The results of active promotion are most clearly shown by the progress of English towards world-language status (§65). Many countries encourage the teaching of English in school, often at the expense of other languages: a recent case is Spain, where the early 1980s saw the widespread replacement of French by English as the first foreign language. At the other extreme, there are many examples of languages receiving official disapproval, as in the reluctance of several countries to teach German after the Second World War.

The fortunes of minority languages are closely bound up with the political aspirations of their speakers, and the extent to which the government of the day perceives these to be a threat. Again, the whole gamut of official attitudes can be found. There may be a strong local government policy of language maintenance (p. 410), as happens with the teaching of Welsh in Wales. On the other hand, there are many instances of languages being discouraged or banned (e.g. Catalan in Franco's Spain).

Official attitudes today are generally sympathetic, with an increasing number of countries supporting (at least in principle) a bilingual or multilingual educational policy. Progress varies greatly from country to country, however, with some countries (such as Britain) providing immigrants with relatively little by way of mother-tongue education, and others (such as Sweden) providing a great deal. Conflict is never far away, as progress towards linguistic recognition inevitably proves to be too slow for some people, and too rapid for others. Vocal and vigorous objections to educational linguistic policies are thus commonly encountered all over the world.

Bilingual programmes

There has been an extremely rapid growth in bilingual education programmes, with reference to minority languages, in recent years. However, the reasons for introducing such programmes vary greatly. In some countries, the aim is to find a single language capable of unifying the nation (e.g. Bahasa Indonesia). In Russia, the teaching of Russian to speakers of regional languages has promoted ideological assimilation and national solidarity. The teaching of English in many African countries ensures greater access to world opportunities. In the USA, the primary concern is to guarantee the civil rights and equal opportunities of minority groups. In all cases, bilingual education is not simply a matter of language learning: it involves the acquisition of all the knowledge and skills that identify the minority culture.

Bilingual programmes have always attracted controversy. Two main views are argued (with many variant positions).

- A *maintenance* view: Maintaining the mother tongue is said to develop a desirable cultural diversity, foster ethnic identity, permit social adaptability, add to the psychological security of the child, and promote linguistic (and perhaps even cognitive) sensitivity. To achieve this, bilingual instruction needs to be retained throughout the whole of a child's school career.

- A *transitional* view: A permanent dual-language policy may foster social divisions and narrowness of outlook (through ethnocentric churches, media, schools, etc.); the children may become 'trapped' in their mother tongue, and fail to achieve in the majority language, thus reducing their access to prosperity; and where there is inadequate teacher preparation, timetabling, and materials, they may fail to achieve in their mother tongue also. They should therefore be educated in their mother tongue only until they are able to continue in the majority language.

Although many bilingual programmes subscribe in principle to a maintenance view of bilingual education, in practice the majority (in the USA and

Britain, at least) are of the transitional type – though often accompanied by maintenance elements (e.g. in literature, music, dance) in a continuing parallel teaching programme.

These views about the nature of bilingual education continue to be emotionally debated, for they reflect fundamentally different conceptions of the kind of nation people want to see around them. Maintenance views anticipate a society that is characterized by cultural pluralism and linguistic diversity; transitional views look towards a culturally homogeneous society, characterized by minority assimilation and language shift (p. 410). However, the issues are more complex than this simple opposition suggests, for there are many kinds and degrees of support for both positions, and compromise views have also been proposed.

Case studies show that the notion of *language loyalty* is never a simple one. For example, within an immigrant group, some members may wish (with varying degrees of conviction) to have their children retain their linguistic identity; others may wish them to 'shift' to the majority language as quickly as possible in order to participate fully in the new society; and yet others may wish to have them use their new language in public, but to retain their mother tongue for a range of private occasions (e.g. home, church, club). There are many further possible positions, reflecting the different influences of racial, geographical, political, cultural, economic, religious, and other factors.

Language immersion

In Quebec, in the 1960s, a new kind of bilingual education programme was introduced, which has since proved to be popular and successful. The proposal came from the English-speaking minority, who wished to make their children proficient in a second language, French, in order to cope with a society where the role of French was becoming increasingly dominant. The idea was to arrange for the whole of their children's first encounter with schooling to be in the second language (§63) – a programme of *immersion*. The children would speak in their mother tongue to a bilingual teacher, who would reply in the second language. Gradually, the children would come to use the second language themselves. Then, at a later stage, English would be introduced into the classroom.

After several years of experimentation, two patterns have come to be established. *Primary* immersion starts at kindergarten, entirely in French. Gradually an element of English is introduced, until by mid-primary level the children are taught 60% in English and 40% in French. *Secondary* immersion usually starts in the first year of secondary school with a booster year in which all teaching is done in French. This is followed by a *post-immersion* teaching programme which follows the proportions of the primary school.

The approach continues to attract support, and has been used in many other countries. The children acquire a much higher level of competence than they would through traditional teaching methods (though this is still a long way from native-like proficiency, and doubts have been expressed over how effective the children's linguistic skills are outside of school). Their attitudes towards French-Canadian people tend to be more positive (though evidence is mixed on this point). And their mother-tongue abilities do not seem to suffer from the experience, but may even improve in certain respects. However, for this last outcome to be certain, there needs to be a supportive and strong first-language environment in the community. With speakers of minority languages where the home linguistic situation is weak or unstable, an immersion programme would be unlikely to result in maintenance, but would probably hasten the process of assimilation to the majority language.

69

How not to look
after languages

If this had been a 'how it works' book about cars or bicycles, people would expect it to contain information about how to take care of their purchase. There would be at least one section called 'How to look after your car' or 'Troubleshooting'. As we have seen in relation to language planning (§68), language is no different. Multilingualism requires managing. But even within a single language there are issues of management which require regular attention by institutions and individuals alike. And the problem we have to face, at the beginning of the 21st century, is that we are still some way from achieving an appropriate theory and practice of language management.

Mechanics, quacks, and thieves

When it comes to maintenance, there is a big difference between our vehicles and our language. With cars we know there is a cadre of individuals who will sort out our problems: they are called mechanics, and we happily respect their ability to do the work. With language, everyone thinks they can be a mechanic. And some people, without any training at all, even go so far to write repair manuals about language, and expect other people to live by their recommendations. Such usage manuals, written by civil servants, bishops, broadcasters, and other well-intentioned pundits, have been with us for over 200 years.

the people who write the manuals are more akin to doctors ~~nics~~, because they take the view that a great deal of language ~~thy~~, and that a large proportion of the population is linguisti- ~~y ... ...~~thout realizing it. Having persuaded others that they are unwell, they then offer remedies in the form of usage tablets of their own devising. Talk or write like me, they say, and you will be well again. The word *doctor* was wrong: these are the equivalent of the 19th-century quacks.

A few go even further, taking the view that a large proportion of the population is linguistically criminal. Believing in the inviolability of the small set of rules that they have managed themselves to acquire, they condemn others from a different dialect background, or who have not had the same educational opportunities as themselves, for not following those same rules. Enthused by the Stalinesque policing metaphor, they advocate a policy of *zero tolerance*, to eradicate all traces of the aberrant behaviour. This extreme attitude would be condemned by most people if it were encountered in relation to such domains as gender or race, but for some reason it is tolerated in relation to language. Welcomed, even, judging by the phenomenal sales of *Eats, Shoots and Leaves*.

Prescribing remedies

Where did such attitudes come from? How long have people been setting themselves up as linguistic salvationists? The underlying mindset is ancient, embedded in Classical canons of stylistic correctness and propriety. It is usually referred to as *prescriptivism*, the view that one variety of language has an inherently higher value than others, and that this ought to be imposed on the whole community. It was especially developed with reference to Latin, and manifested itself strongly in the language Academies established by the Romance nations.

For English, we can trace prescriptive attitudes back to the 17th century. A proposal for an Academy in England had the support of John Dryden and Daniel Defoe, and it is the latter who was one of the first to introduce the crime analogy. In Defoe's view, the reputation of the members of this Academy 'would be enough to make them the allowed judges of style and language; and no author would have the impudence to coin without their authority ... There should be no more occasion to search for derivations and constructions, and it would be as criminal then to coin words as money.'

The proposal did not achieve support – observers noted that the French Academy had been a total failure in stopping the French language from changing – and it is only in the second half of the 18th century that we find prescriptivism really taking hold in Britain. This was the period of Dr Johnson's dictionary, Bishop Lowth's and Lindley Murray's grammars, and John Walker's pronunciation dictionary. It was a period when the grammars first incorporated such rules as not ending sentences with prepositions, distinguishing between *will* and *shall*, and avoiding double negatives. It was also a period in which correctness in spelling – and later punctuation – finally became a recognized index of an educated background. It was a period which lasted some 250 years, continuing in the British educational system until the 1960s, and introducing a mindset which, as we have seen, still exercises considerable influence today.

The aims of the early grammarians were threefold. They wanted to codify the principles of their languages, to show that there was a system beneath the apparent chaos of usage. They wanted a means of settling disputes over usage. And they wanted to point out what they felt to be common errors, in order to 'improve' the language. The authoritarian nature of the approach is best characterized by its reliance on rules of grammar. Where usage was divided, one version would be *prescribed*, to be learnt and followed accurately; others would be *proscribed*, to be avoided. In this early period, there were no half measures: usage was either right or wrong, and it was the task of the grammarian not simply to record alternatives, but to pronounce judgement upon them.

It is important to appreciate that only a few dozen rules were ever the focus of grammatical prescriptivism – around 1% of the 3,500 or so features of English grammar (p. 230). The vast majority of grammatical rules are shared by speakers and writers of English, regardless of their dialect background. But the disproportionate critical attention devoted to the problem cases made them famous, so that most people have heard, for example, of *split infinitives* and *double negatives*, even if they are not exactly sure what such terms mean.

It seems remarkable, today, that just a handful of people – Johnson, Lowth, Walker, Murray – should have achieved such acceptance as language authorities. But the 18th century – the century of manners, as it is often called – was one in which upper-class people were anxious to avoid accusations of social ineptness at all costs, and with language the most pervasive means of expressing social identity (p. 309), it is not surprising that linguistic behaviour became pre-eminent as the means of conveying class most subtly and flexibly. Nor should it be surprising that, in the later 20th century, when old-style class distinction began to die away, the linguistic reflection of this distinction should also start to fade.

In fact, there was criticism of the prescriptive attitude from the outset. Joseph Priestley, for example, wrote an English grammar in 1761 in which he insists that 'the custom of speaking is the original and only just standard of any language'. Linguistic issues, he argues, cannot be solved by logic and legislation. And this focus on the facts of linguistic usage is one which has grown in importance in our day, becoming a tenet of modern descriptive linguistics.

The opposition between *descriptivists* and *prescriptivists* has often become extreme, with both sides painting unreal pictures of the other. Descriptive grammarians have been presented as people who do not care about standards, because of the way they see all forms of usage as equally valid. Nothing could be further from the truth. I would call myself a descriptive linguist, but I am just as concerned about clarity, ambiguity, and intelligibility as anyone with a prescriptivist temperament. But I am not so stupid as to think that we shall achieve any gain in clarity by avoiding split infinitives or not ending sentences with prepositions. And I am not so insensitive as to blame others who have not had the opportunity I have had to acquire an effective command of standard English.

Potato's as a test case

If the Trussians of this world chose the right examples, there would be no argument. But – to take just one example – to focus attention on the so-called 'green-grocer's apostrophe' (as in *potato's*) and to condemn its writers so unequivocally, is to introduce red-herrings into the argument. All people who complain about punctuation errors do so on the grounds that a mistake in punctuation is a loss of clarity, and indeed there are many cases where bad punctuation is misleading and needs correction. But *potato's* is not one of them. There is not the slightest ambiguity, when we see a sign outside a shop advertising *potato's*. We know it must be a plural, for the obvious reason that we know potatoes do not have the ability to possess things.

People who object do so because they know the 'correct' spelling. They are the lucky ones; they have had the right kind of opportunity and exposure in their education to learn standard English well. But before they lash out at others who have not been so fortunate they should reflect on the fact that the spelling about which they want to express their intolerance was not always incorrect. In the 18th century, the spelling *potato's* would have been perfectly acceptable. We find *volcano's*, for example, in Johnson's dictionary. The reason for the apostrophe is that words like *potato* end in a vowel, and this is an unusual type of English word. Adding an -*s*, as a normal plural, would suggest the wrong pronunciation (*potatos*), and an obvious solution is to add an apostrophe. Alternatively, one can get round the problem by marking the long vowel in some other way, and this was the solution (adding -*es*) eventually adopted in standard English.

The apostrophe solution was possible in the 18th century because this mark of punctuation was still coming into English at the time. The rules governing its chief use as a marker of possession were not established for another century, so that in the 1700s it was quite often used to mark a plural. Indeed, we still have this option today, as when we write *1700's*. So to condemn someone for using such forms as *potato's* is actually to display linguistic ignorance – an ignorance of the logic behind such forms which the modern users are unconsciously manifesting.

None of this is to deny the importance of having people learn the standard spelling and punctuation. Written languages need to follow a standard, if they are to be successful. That is why standard languages evolve in the first place. There was no standard English in the Middle Ages, but as literacy grew it proved essential for it to evolve, to ensure intelligibility. There are many important rules of spelling and punctuation, which to get wrong would result in chaos. The problem with prescriptivists is that they have never understood the difference between rules which are important for clarity and those which are not. A zero tolerance policy ignores the difference.

Standard English was never a totally homogeneous phenomenon. Even today, some 25% of the words in an English dictionary display usage variation – *judgement/judgment, criticise/criticize, paediatrics/pediatrics, color/colour*, and so on. English copes with all this. Languages, like buildings and bridges, have tolerances built into them so that they can survive changing circumstances. The aim of prescriptivists is to remove these tolerances. If they were ever successful, languages, like buildings and bridges, would then indeed break down. This is not how to look after a language. There has to be a better way (§70).

70
How to look after languages: recognizing principles

We should look after languages like we look after our cars, by increasing our understanding of how they work. That is why I have written this book. The more we understand about the history, structure, and use of language, the more we will be in a position to employ language effectively for our own purposes, appreciate the way other people are employing it, and manage the very real problems which come from differences of opinion about the way it should be employed. And this principle applies to languages, in the plural, as much as to our competence in an individual language.

Understanding has both negative and positive sides. There are myths and beliefs about language whose unreality can seriously mislead; and there are properties and possibilities in language which we need to appreciate for what they are. The prescriptive approach to language study (§69) introduced a set of class-conscious beliefs about the nature of language from whose limitations we are only now beginning to escape. There are other beliefs, even more deep-rooted, which – thanks to the growth of linguistics as a science – we are able to explore and evaluate more fully than was ever possible before. And it is on the foundation of these evaluations that a sound philosophy of language management can be based.

Recognizing language change

The phenomenon of language change probably attracts more public notice and criticism than any other linguistic issue. There is a widely held belief that change must mean deterioration and decay. Older people observe the casual speech of the young, and conclude that standards have fallen markedly. They place the blame in various quarters – most often in the schools, where patterns of language education have changed a great deal in recent years, but also in state public broadcasting institutions, where any deviations from traditional norms provide an immediate focus of attack by conservative, linguistically sensitive listeners. The concern can even reach national proportions, as in the widespread reaction in Europe against what is thought of as the 'American' English invasion.

It is understandable that many people dislike change, but the criticism of linguistic change is misconceived. It is widely felt that the contemporary language illustrates the problem at its worst, but this belief is shared by every generation. Moreover, many of the usage issues recur across generations: several of the English controversies which are the focus of current prescriptivist attention can be found in the books and magazines of the 18th and 19th centuries – the debate over *it's me* and *very unique*, for example. In *The Queen's English* (1863), Henry Alford, the Dean of Canterbury, lists a large number of usage issues which worried his contemporaries, and gave them cause to think that the language was rapidly decaying. Most are still with us, with the language not obviously affected. Indeed, the English language has grown immensely in range and expressiveness over the past hundred years.

There are indeed cases where linguistic change can lead to problems of unintelligibility, ambiguity, and social division. If change is too rapid, there can be major communication problems. But as a rule, the parts of language which are changing at any given time are tiny, by comparison with the vast, unchanging areas of language. Indeed, it is because change is so infrequent that it is so distinctive and noticeable. Some degree of caution and concern is therefore always desirable, in the interests of maintaining precise and efficient communication; but there are no grounds for the extreme pessimism and conservatism which is so often encountered – and which in English is often summed up in such slogans as 'Let us preserve the tongue that Shakespeare spoke'.

For the most part, language changes because society changes (§55). To stop or control the one requires that we stop or control the other – a task which can succeed to only a very limited extent. Language change is inevitable and rarely predictable, and those who try to plan a language's future waste their time if they think otherwise. The time would be better spent in devising fresh ways of enabling society to cope with the new linguistic forms that accompany each generation. These days, there is in fact a growing recognition of the need to develop a greater linguistic awareness and tolerance of change, especially in a multi-ethnic society. This requires, among other things, that schools have the knowledge and resources to teach a common standard, while recognizing the existence and value of linguistic diversity. Such policies provide a constructive alternative to the emotional attacks which are so commonly made against the development of new words, meanings, pronunciations, and grammatical constructions. But before these policies can be implemented, it is necessary to develop a proper understanding of the inevitability and consequences of linguistic change.

Some people go a stage further, and see change in language as a progression from a simple to a complex state – a view which was common as a consequence of 19th-century evolutionary thinking. But there is no evidence for this view. Languages do not develop, progress, decay, evolve, or act according to any of the metaphors which imply a specific endpoint and level of excellence. They simply change, as society changes. If a language dies out, it does so because its status alters in society, as other cultures and languages take over its role: it does not die because it has 'got too old', or 'become too complicated', as is sometimes maintained. Nor, when languages change, do they move in a predetermined direction. Some lose inflections; some gain them. Some move to an order where the verb precedes the object; others to an order where the object precedes the verb. Some languages lose vowels and gain consonants; others do the opposite. If metaphors must be used to talk about language change, one of the best is that of the tide, which always and inevitably changes, but never progresses, while it ebbs and flows.

Recognizing language equality

It comes near to stating the obvious that all languages have developed in order to express the needs of their users, and that all languages are, in a real sense, equal. But this tenet of modern linguistics has often been denied, and still needs to be defended. Part of the problem is that the word *equal* needs to be used very carefully. It is difficult to say whether all languages are structurally equal, in the sense that they have the same 'amounts' of grammar, phonology, or semantic structure (§28). But all languages are arguably equal in the sense that there is nothing intrinsically limiting, demeaning, or disabling about any of them. All languages meet the social and psychological needs of their speakers, and can provide us with valuable information about human nature and society. This view is the foundation on which the whole of the present book is based.

There are, however, several widely held misconceptions about languages which stem from a failure to recognize this view. The most important of these is the idea that there are such things as *primitive* languages – languages with a simple grammar, a few sounds, and a vocabulary of only a few hundred words, whose speakers have to compensate for their language's deficiencies through gestures. In the 19th century, such ideas were common, and it was widely thought that it was only a matter of time before explorers would discover a genuinely primitive language.

The fact of the matter is that every culture which has been investigated, no matter how 'primitive' it may be in cultural terms, turns out to have a fully developed language, with a complexity comparable to those of the so-called 'civilized' nations. Anthropologically speaking, the human race can be said to have evolved from primitive to civilized states, but there is no sign of language having gone through the same kind of evolution. There are no 'bronze age' or 'stone age' languages.

At the other end of the scale from so-called 'primitive' languages are opinions about the 'natural superiority' of certain languages. Latin and

Greek were for centuries viewed as models of excellence in western Europe because of the literature and thought which these languages expressed; and the study of modern languages is still influenced by the practices of generations of classical linguistic scholars. But all languages have a literature, even those which have never been written down. And oral performances encountered in some of these languages, once transcribed, stand proudly alongside the classics of established literate societies.

The idea that one's own language is superior to others is widespread, but the reasons given for the superiority vary greatly. A language might be viewed as the oldest, or the most logical, or the language of gods, or simply the easiest to pronounce or the best for singing. Such beliefs have no basis in linguistic fact. Some languages are of course more useful or prestigious than others, at a given period of history, but this is due to the pre-eminence of the speakers at that time, and not to any inherent linguistic characteristics. The view of modern linguistics is that a language should not be valued on the basis of the political, economic, religious, or other influence of its speakers. If it were otherwise, we would have to rate the Spanish and Portuguese spoken in the 16th century as somehow 'better' than they are today, and modern American English would be 'better' than British English. When we make such comparisons, we find only a small range of linguistic differences, and nothing to warrant such sweeping conclusions.

At present, it is not possible to rate the excellence of languages in linguistic terms; and it is no less difficult to arrive at an evaluation in aesthetic, philosophical, literary, religious, or cultural terms. How, ultimately, could we compare the merits of Latin and Greek with the proverbial wisdom of Chinese, the extensive oral literature of the Polynesian islands, or the depth of scientific knowledge which has been expressed in English? Rather, we need to develop a mindset which recognizes languages as immensely flexible systems, capable of responding to the needs of a people and reflecting their interests and preoccupations in historically unique visions. That is why it is so important to preserve language diversity. There are only 6,000 or so visions left (p. 336).

71
How to look
after languages:
recognizing functions

The same arguments that require us to respect language diversity apply within a language. Here the focus is on the different functions that language performs in society, and on the regional dialects, social and occupational varieties, and individual styles that make up its expressive range (§§45–50). The identification of language functions is a result of asking the question 'Why do we use language?'

The question is so basic that it seems hardly to require an answer. But, as is often the way with linguistic questions, our everyday familiarity with speech and writing can make it difficult to appreciate the complexity of the skills we have learned. Language has a wide range of functions, each of which manifests itself in an individual set of principles and norms of practice, and demands the application of individual standards of judgement.

Dictionaries would give the impression that the 'why' question has only a single answer: there is one function of language, the definitions of language suggest, and that is to communicate our ideas, to transmit information from one person to another. Certainly, this is the most widely recognized linguistic function. Whenever we tell people about ourselves or our circumstances, or ask for information about other selves and circumstances, we are using language in order to exchange facts and opinions. This function is often referred to as *referential*, *propositional*, or *ideational*. It generates the kind of language which will be found through-

How Language Works

out this book, or in any spoken or written interaction where people wish to learn from each other. But it would be wrong to think of this as the only way in which we use language. There are several other functions where the communication of ideas is a marginal or irrelevant consideration.

Expressing emotion

When someone walks into a door and curses the door, the language used can hardly be classed as the 'communication of ideas', for the door is in no position to understand and respond. The example illustrates one of the commonest uses of language – a means of getting rid of our nervous energy when we are under stress. It is the clearest case of what is often called an *emotive* or *expressive* function of language. Emotive language can be used whether or not we are alone. Swear words and obscenities are probably the commonest signals to be used in this way, especially when we are in an angry or frustrated state. But there are also many emotive utterances of a positive kind, such as our involuntary verbal reactions to beautiful art or scenery, our expression of fear and affection, and the emotional outpourings of certain kinds of poetry.

Expressing rapport

When someone says *Bless you!* after hearing a sneeze, this hardly seems to be a case of language being used to communicate ideas, but rather to maintain a comfortable interpersonal relationship. Its sole function is to provide a means of avoiding a situation which both parties might otherwise find embarrassing. No factual content is involved. Similarly, the use of such phrases as *Good morning* or *Pleased to meet you*, and ritual exchanges about health or the weather, do not 'communicate ideas' in the usual sense. Sentences of this kind are usually automatically produced, and stereotyped in structure. They require a special kind of explanation, and this is found in the idea that language is here being used for the purpose of maintaining rapport. The anthropologist Bronislaw Malinowski (1884–1942) coined the phrase *phatic communion* to refer to this social function of language, which arises out of the basic human need to signal friendship – or, at least, lack of enmity. For someone to withhold these sentences when they are expected, by staying silent, is a sure sign of distance, alienation, even danger.

Expressing sound

There are many situations where the only apparent reason for a use of language is the effect the sounds have on the users or listeners. We can group together here such different cases as the rhythmical litanies of religious groups, the persuasive cadences of political speechmaking, the dialogue chants used by prisoners or slaves as they work, and the voices of individuals singing in the kitchen or the bath. Perhaps the clearest cases are the lyrics of popular songs and the range of phonetic effects which can be encountered in poetry. Unintelligible names, words, and phrases are commonplace in the oral poetry of many languages, and can be explained only by a universal desire to exploit the *sonic* potential of language.

Playing

When people tell each other jokes, make puns, recite limericks, or put on silly voices, they are doing far more than communicating ideas. They are enjoying the way in which the rules of language can be manipulated for humour or entertainment. And when people do a crossword puzzle, play Scrabble, or work out how many words can be found in *delicious*, they are enjoying a challenge which has the same point as any other competitive exercise, where winning is all. These are just some of the hundreds of everyday *ludic* uses of language, where the aim is not primarily to communicate meaning but to draw attention to the way the normal rules of language can be bent or broken to convey novel effects. A ludic function also lies behind a great deal of professional language use, notably in advertising, newspaper headline-writing, and literary expression.

Controlling reality

All forms of supernatural belief involve the use of language as a means of controlling the forces which the believers feel affect their lives. The various prayers and formulae which are directed at God, gods, devils, spirits, objects, and other physical forces are always highly distinctive forms of language. In some cases, the language might be regarded as a form of ideational communication, with a supernatural being as the recipient – but if so, it is a somewhat abnormal type of communication, for the response is usually appreciated only in the mind or behaviour of the speaker, and there may be no evident response at all. In other cases, the function of the language is to control matter, or the reality which the matter is supposed to represent. For example, the gardening ritual of the Trobriand Islanders involves a series of formulae which 'charm' the axes, making them effective tools. Several other situations, apart from the magical and the religious, illustrate this *performative* function of language (p. 277) – such as the words which name a ship at a launching ceremony.

Recording facts

When someone consults a reference book it would appear to be another ideational use of language; but the situation in which the communication takes place is actually quite different in several respects. When information is stored for future use, it is impossible to predict who is likely to use it – indeed, much of the material may never be referred to again. There is therefore no 'dialogue' element in the communication. The information has to be as self-contained as possible, for it is impossible to predict the demands which may one day be made upon it, and in most cases there is no way in which the user can respond so as to influence the writer. Accordingly, when language is used for the purposes of *recording facts*, it is very different from that used in everyday conversation – in particular, it displays a much greater degree of organization, impersonality, and explicitness. This function of language is represented by all kinds of record-keeping, such as historical records, geographical surveys, business accounts, scientific reports, parliamentary acts, and public data-banks. It is an essential domain of language use, for the availability of this material guarantees the knowledge base of subsequent generations, which is a prerequisite of social development. In this function, criteria of explicitness, clarity, and precision are paramount.

Expressing thought processes

People often feel the need to speak their thoughts aloud. If asked why they do it, they reply that it helps their concentration. Authors often make similar remarks about the need to get a first draft down on paper, in order to see whether what they have written corresponds to what they had in mind. The French thinker Joseph Joubert (1754–1824) once said: 'We only know just what we meant to say after we have said it.' Perhaps the most common use of language as an instrument of thought is found when people perform mathematical calculations 'in their head'. Very often, this supposedly *mental* act is accompanied by a verbal commentary. However, it is not essential that language used in this way should always be spoken aloud or written down. Often, people can be seen to move their lips while they are thinking, but no actual sound emerges. Language is evidently present, but in a *sub-vocal* form.

Expressing identity

Our use of language can tell our listener or reader a great deal about ourselves – in particular, about our regional origins, social background, level of education, occupation, age, sex, and personality. The way language is used to express these variables is so complex that it requires separate discussion (§48), but the general point can be made here, that a major function of language is the expression of personal *identity* – the signalling of who we are and where we 'belong'. These signals enter into the whole of our linguistic behaviour, so much so that it is often a problem distin-guishing the identifying function of language from that used for the communication of ideas. In a public meeting, for instance, Mr A may make a speech in support of Mr B, and it may be difficult to decide whether the reason for his speech is to make a fresh point, or simply to demonstrate to all concerned that A is on B's side. The arena of political debate is full of such manoeuvrings, as individuals strive to express their solidarity with (or distance from) each other. Many social situations display language which unites rather than informs, such as the chanting of a crowd at a football match, the shouting of names or slogans at public meetings, the stage-managed audience reactions to television game shows, or the shouts of affirmation at some religious meetings.

Meeting technological demands

Technology has always exercised a major influence on the development of language, as can be seen in the way the printing press, telephone, radio, television, and computer have extended our communicative opportunities. At the same time, the constraints introduced by each technology have fostered the use of conventions whose purpose is to maximize the efficiency with which the medium is used. For example, the broadcasting medium demands different norms of articulation if its output is to be universally understood; newspapers operate with different sizes of type; telephones motivate idiosyncratic forms of greeting and person identification; and the limitations on screen size force computer and mobile-phone users to devise new techniques of layout and abbreviation. In some cases, the contrast with previous norms of communication might be quite dramatic, as in the introduction of new symbols (emoticons) or the relaxation of rules of spelling, punctuation, and capitalization in some styles of e-mail, chatroom, and instant-messaging communication.

Working with functional diversity

Recognizing the diversity of language functions is not just a theoretical exercise. It has several practical consequences in the way we work with and evaluate language. The criterion of clarity, for example, is often cited as an absolute consideration in using language; but this criterion is relevant only in certain functions. It is critical in a function such as 'recording facts', but it is irrelevant in the function of 'expressing rapport'. We do not judge someone's *Bless you!* in terms of its clarity of meaning.

Similarly, we should strive to avoid ambiguity when 'communicating ideas', but the function of language to 'express emotion' often relies on multiple meanings to achieve its effect. Much of the semantic impact of a poem arises from the way in which we can explore the text to find multiple meanings. Few lines of poetry have just one meaning.

We would therefore expect to find considerable differences in the way these various functions exploit the lexical, grammatical, phonological, and graphological resources of the language. Some of these functions demand a rigid adherence to the rules of standard English: most kinds of record-keeping, for example, need to be expressed in formal grammar and conventional spelling and punctuation. On the other hand, most kinds of language play achieve their effect precisely by breaking the rules of standard English. And in the case of technologically motivated expression, we may find completely new directions being given to language (§24). Any theory of language management has to be able to cope with the expressive richness and divergent norms introduced by this array of intralinguistic diversity.

72
How to look after languages: recognizing varieties

A language management policy needs to include much more than the need to recognize the different languages and regional dialects within a country (§45). The familiar expression 'They don't seem to be talking the same language' acts as a reminder that there is a further dimension of linguistic variation, independent of regional identity, that can act as a barrier to communication. Within this dimension we encounter a wide range of occupational purposes to which language can be put, each of which has evolved a distinctive variety of expression, and these raise important questions for anyone concerned about how we 'look after' a language.

There is no theoretical limit to the number of occupational varieties in a language. As society develops new facets, so language is devised to express them. In recent times, whole new areas of expression have emerged, in relation to such domains as computing, broadcasting, commercial advertising, and popular music. Over a longer time-scale, special styles have developed associated with religion, law, politics, commerce, the press, medicine, and science. And we are at the very beginning of a new era of linguistic innovation associated with the various technologies that comprise the Internet.

This section reviews a selection of important varieties, briefly illustrating the kind of general social and educational issues which arise. In addition, concerns have emerged which cut across these occupational divisions. All of this has to be taken into account by policy-makers involved in language management.

Expressing science

The aim of science is to determine the principles governing the physical universe. Progress towards this end, however, is to a large extent dependent on the use of language. The knowledge base of a subject, upon which all scientists depend, is accessible only if previous generations have managed to express their findings in a precise and unambiguous manner. Similarly, present-day scientists, hoping to make their own contribution to this knowledge base, must satisfy the same linguistic constraints if their work is to be correctly interpreted and accepted by their peers. Research findings are of limited value, until they are written up and published.

The gap between scientific and everyday language is a large one, which it is difficult to bridge. Scientists are often unable to express themselves in terms the lay person can understand, or are too busy to bother. There is frequently a need to maintain secrecy, in such areas as national security or industrial invention. Not surprisingly, therefore, there is a widespread mistrust of scientific language, which is only partly alleviated through popular science publications and radio or television programmes. It is still the exception to find popularizations of science that maintain intelligibility while avoiding oversimplification, and that come to be acclaimed by specialist and lay person alike. But for the languages that are widely used in science – and especially for English, used in some 80% of scientific communication – such work is essential.

The language of medicine

The field of medicine, more than any other, forces a confrontation between scientific and everyday language. Outside the world of the research laboratory and clinic, there exists the daily routine of medical practice – a communication situation in which a doctor attempts to understand the problems of a patient, and the patient attempts to understand the doctor's diagnosis. Language is involved at all points in the medical consultation. The initial statement of symptoms is of critical significance, as it guides the doctor's search for the clinical signs of the condition. Similarly, the doctor's explanation of a problem, and the recommendations for treatment, need to be clear and complete if the patient is to understand and follow the correct course of action.

Studies of medical language have brought to light several types of situation in which there has been a breakdown of communication, and where the consultation has had an unsatisfactory outcome. Regional, social, and cultural differences between doctor and patient can all be sources of linguistic difficulty (especially in the case of immigrant patients). A perspective on communication is an essential part of medical training.

Language and religion

The close relationship between language and religious belief pervades cultural history. Often, a divine being is said to have invented speech, or writing, and given it as a gift to mankind. Religious associations are particularly strong in relation to written language, because writing is an effective means of guarding and transmitting sacred knowledge. At the centre of all the world's main religions lies a body of sacred writing, revered by believers. Scrupulous attention is paid to identifying or preserving the linguistic features of the original texts. Often, the texts are accompanied by a long tradition of commentary, which may itself take on special religious significance.

Not all religions favour the translation of their sacred books. Judaism, Hinduism, and Islam stress the sacredness of the language itself and resist translation, whereas Buddhism, and especially Christianity, actively promote it. But ultimately, all major religious works are translated – either from one language into another, or from an older variety of language into a modern variety. The formal process of religious translation is a long-term, painstaking and frustrating task, usually carried out by committee. Translators have to satisfy two criteria, which are always incompatible, because one looks backwards and the other forwards. First, the translation must be historically accurate, faithfully representing the meaning of the source, insofar as this can be known, and integrated within the religious tradition of which it is a part. Secondly, it must be acceptable to the intended users of the translation – which, in practice, means that it must be intelligible, aesthetically pleasing, and capable of relating to current trends in religious thought, social pressures, and language change. No translation can ever satisfy the demands of all these factors, and all translations are thus to some extent controversial.

The language of the law

'The law is a profession of words.' Whatever the legal domain – government legislation, courtroom activities, or the documentation that constrains our daily lives (contracts, conveyances, regulations, by-laws, etc.) – we are faced with this fundamental principle: the words of the law are, in fact, the law. There is no other variety where the users place such store on the nuances of meaning conveyed by language, where unstated intentions are so disregarded, and where the history of previous usage counts for so much.

The overriding concern for precise and consistent linguistic interpretation has, over the centuries, produced a highly distinctive style whose complexity is particularly apparent in the written language. This style has frequently been criticized by the lay public, on the ground that much of legal language is unnecessarily complex, and could be simplified without loss. There is a persistent call for change in legal language by eliminating archaic or Latinate expressions, simplifying grammatical structure, and adding punctuation. Those in favour of change argue that this would make legal language more intelligible to consumers, saving much time, anxiety, and money, and would also greatly simplify the job of lawyers themselves. Those who defend the complexity of legal language argue that its characteristics are the product of centuries of effort to devise an unambiguous, reliable, and authoritative means of regulating human society and resolving conflict. In their view, the need for consistency in legal interpretation, and for confidence in judgements (which, they argue, can save much time, anxiety, and money), far outweigh the gain that would come from an increase in popular understanding.

The language of advertising

The aim of advertising is to draw attention to a product or service in order to sell it. Whether we are shopping, reading the paper, travelling to work, watching television, or simply lazing around, we cannot avoid seeing advertisements. They come in an extraordinary range of forms and contexts. The largest and most noticeable group belong to commercial consumer advertising; but there are also such categories as trade advertising (from manufacturers to retailers), retail advertising (from shops to customers), prestige advertising (e.g. by government departments), classified advertising (want ads, house sales, etc.), and direct mailing. The activities involve posters, signs, notices, showcards, samples, circulars, catalogues, labels, wrapping paper, price tags, tickets, footballers' shirts, and many other devices. The ears can be assailed as well as the eyes, with slogans, jingles, street cries, loudspeaker messages, and the range of auditory effects heard in radio and television advertising.

The field of advertising is a controversial one, as people dispute the ethics and effects of 'hard' selling tactics, fraudulent claims, commercial sponsoring in sport, the intrusiveness of advertisements, and their effect on children. Its language therefore needs careful investigation and monitoring. But it is not an easy field to make generalizations about. Its boundaries blur with other forms of persuasive language, such as speeches, sermons, and public announcements. And within the genre, there is so much variation in subject matter that it is impossible to maintain a single attitude that will encompass everything. Whatever our view about advertisements for cigarettes, washing powders, or cough remedies, it is unlikely to be the same as the view we hold about advertisements dealing with the dangers of smoking, the sale of houses, or the needs of the Third World.

The language of broadcasting

Broadcasting, as a national medium, has existed only since the 1920s; but its popularity and power have been so great that it has already given language several new varieties. People now take for granted such styles as newsreading, weather reporting, programme announcing, disc-jockey patter, and sports commentary, and they can easily forget that these styles are only three generations old. The medium has also greatly increased popular awareness of linguistic diversity. An evening's listening or viewing provides an encounter with many regional accents, social dialects, and occupational uses of language. Only the seasoned traveller would have encountered such a linguistic range a century ago.

There is, accordingly, no such thing as a single homogeneous 'language' of broadcasting. In aiming to inform, educate, and entertain, the medium reflects all aspects of contemporary society and incorporates most of its language. The result is a range of linguistic variety that exceeds even the heterogeneity of the press: discussions, news reports, soap operas, situation comedies, games, popular science, cartoons, plays, children's programmes, and much more – including, of course, a considerable proportion of recent cinema output.

Because we can see speakers and context, the language used in television programmes plays a less prominent role than it does on the radio. With radio, speech is everything. Sound effects, music, and silence are of course important; but radio is par excellence the speaker's medium. Nowhere else does the human voice receive such undivided attention. And as a consequence, great care is needed both to maximize its effects (especially through a lively use of prosody, §12) and to avoid idiosyncrasies (which radio tends to exaggerate). Above all, broadcasters have to pay special attention to the problem of how much listeners can hear and take in at a time. There is no opportunity for immediate playback if something is misunderstood. As far as possible, therefore, broadcasting language has to be clearly organized, and make use of sentences that are relatively short and uncomplicated.

For the linguist, radio has uniquely interesting features. It is person-to-person communication that is mouth-to-ear, but not face-to-face, and where direct feedback is not possible. The totally auditory world of disembodied sound can involve the emotions and imagination of the listener in ways that have no parallel. Its simultaneous reception by millions promotes the language it uses as a standard (e.g. 'BBC English') and gives it an unequalled status and authority within a community (p. 428). The question of the kind of language professional broadcasters should use is therefore a controversial one, and in several countries the relative merits of standard vs. regional and formal vs. informal usage continue to be debated.

Managing professional usage

A recurrent theme of the present section has been the concern and controversy that can arise when people encounter the powerful influence of language in special settings. Between professionals, of course, there is no problem: whether the subject matter is medicine, science, or baseball, the ability to use a specialized variety of language is a necessary part of professional competence. The difficulties arise only when others come into contact with it, by accident or design, and find themselves threatened by its lack of familiarity or clarity, as happens so often in such fields as science, medicine, religion, and the law. Proposed solutions are complex, and range from large-scale recommendations for reform to proposals that accept the linguistic complexity, and introduce children to these varieties while at school.

In the case of the mass media, the issues are somewhat different. Here the chief anxiety relates to the use of language to convey the truth. Whether we are faced with a newspaper editorial, a radio news report, a film documentary, or a piece of television advertising, we are confronted with the results of language selection: someone has made a decision about what shall be communicated and what withheld. Inevitably, then, questions arise about the reasoning used, and the form of its linguistic expression. Suspicion about motives is universal: 'Don't believe everything you read/hear.'

These issues vary in seriousness, depending on the subject matter and the kind of society in which they are raised. There is an extensive everyday terminology that illustrates the many ways in which the abuse of linguistic power shows itself. At one extreme we are faced with such 'mild' notions as sales rhetoric, exaggerated claims, and sensationalism; at the other we find a wide range of strongly pejorative labels, such as bias, prejudice, propaganda, misinformation, censorship, indoctrination, brain-washing, and psychological (which usually means linguistic) warfare. These words are used in all kinds of social situations where people are in conflict – most commonly when the conflicts are 'organized', as in politics, religion, and trade union negotiations.

Popular anxiety over special uses of language is most markedly seen in the campaigns to promote *plain* speaking and writing – notably, the Plain English movements of Britain and the USA. The main aim of these campaigns is to attack the use of unnecessarily complicated language (*gobbledegook*) by governments, businesses, and other authorities whose role puts them in linguistic contact with the general public. The campaigners argue that such language, whether spoken or written, should be replaced by clearer forms of expression.

Campaigns of this kind focus especially on such everyday consumer products as forms, official letters, licences, leases, contracts, insurance policies, and guarantees. In Britain, annual publicity is given to the Plain English Awards competition, which gives trophies to organizations that have produced the clearest documents, and booby prizes (the Golden Bull Awards) to those whose materials are least intelligible. In the USA, similar interest is shown in the annual Doublespeak Awards, awarded by the National Council of Teachers of English to 'American public figures who have perpetrated language that is grossly unfactual, deceptive, evasive, euphemistic, confusing, or self-contradictory'. The investigation of such claims forms a critical part of the practice of language management.

73
Teaching people to look after languages

How do we learn about good practice in language management? Presumably in the same way that we learn about good practice in everything else: in our first years at home, in our early years in school, and in the practice of good citizenship throughout life. So how is information about language acquired, in these different domains?

An important clarification needs to be made at the outset: *learning about language* has to be distinguished from *learning language*. The latter is a familiar topic in linguistics courses, usually going under the heading of *child language acquisition* (or, more generally, to allow for ongoing language growth in later years, *developmental linguistics*). But that is not the relevant topic when we want to do something about the range of linguistic issues outlined in §§70–72. Learning about language, which also means learning a way of talking about language (a *metalanguage*), is the topic which must now come to the fore.

There are two dimensions: learning to talk about the structures of a language – the grammar, vocabulary, sound system, and (if the language has been written down) writing system – and learning to talk about the uses to which the language can be put. It is sometimes thought that this is a set of abilities which can be learned only in school. In fact, the foundation for the acquisition of linguistic metalanguage is laid down in the home. In particular, some of the factors governing our sense of *appropriateness* in language use are established at a very early age.

Learning about language at home

It is surprising just how much metalanguage is used by caretakers when they are talking to young children. Of course, this is not the kind of technical terminology we associate with language study at later ages. When children are learning their language's sound system (§§13–14), vocabulary (§31), and grammar (§40), parents do not comment on what is happening using the terms of phonology, syntax, or semantics. *That was a lovely prepositional phrase, darling! Wonderful plosive consonant! Nice lexeme!*

But some very general words for talking about language do occur in caretaker speech. A verb like *say* is often used, as are *ask* and *tell*. Words to do with naming occur, such as *name* and *called*. Many auditory words will be heard, such as *quiet*, *loud*, *shout* (plus the important negative *don't*), *listen*, *talk*, *cry*, and *voice*. Mothers use such language even to their newborns, mock-scolding them for the *noise* they are making, for example, or drawing attention to the auditory quality of burps and other vocalizations. In such circumstances, even such words as *big* (in such phrases as *big voice*) can become metalinguistic.

Some basic parameters of linguistic manners will be laid down, usually from around the age of three. In particular, there is a steady inculcation of the social factors that govern a successful conversation – such as the correct use of forms of address and markers of politeness – *please*, *thank you*, *sorry*, *pardon?* (not *what?*). Children are introduced to basic rules of behaviour, such as not to talk while food is in their mouths, not to interrupt, or not to swear (though tolerance levels vary greatly between families). They also learn to anticipate points of potential breakdown (carry out conversational *repairs*, p. 273), such as by asking for clarification (*What do you mean?*) or repeating utterances that are unclear.

If the child is given an early exposure to books, the basic terminology of reading will also be heard. There will be words identifying the entities and attributes involved in reading, such as *book*, *read*, *page*, *turn over*, *word*, *top* (of a page), and *picture*. Some parents will go into more detail at this point, using such words as *line*, *big letter*, *sentence*, and *full stop*, as well as the letters of the alphabet. Their role now overlaps with that of the teacher.

Learning about language in school

When children arrive in school, they experience a different linguistic world. They meet for the first time children from different regional, social, and ethnic backgrounds, whose linguistic norms are not the same as their own (§§45–48). They encounter a social situation in which levels of formal and informal speech are carefully distinguished, and standards of correctness emphasized (§69). The educational setting presents them with a variety of unfamiliar, subject-related styles of language. They have to learn a new range of linguistic skills – reading, writing, and spelling (§§19–21). And they find themselves increasingly having to talk about what they are doing.

Educationists now recognize the complexity of the language demands being made on the young schoolchild, and realize that progress in many areas of the curriculum is greatly dependent on a satisfactory foundation of linguistic skills. The traditional emphasis on *literacy*, the ability to read and write, has been supplemented by an emphasis on *oracy*, the ability to speak and listen. Teachers pay increasing attention to a child's pre-school linguistic experience, seeing this as a foundation on which they can build. Special efforts are made to relate different kinds of linguistic learning: the task of writing is brought closer to the child's experience of reading; reading, in turn, is brought into contact with the ability to use spoken language; and oral skills are supplemented by work on listening comprehension. Above all, teachers stress that children's linguistic ability is a major factor influencing their success in the learning of other subject areas, such as science, mathematics, and history.

In the 1970s, this central, integrating role of language work promoted a host of new language schemes, materials, and approaches, and a philosophy which is best summarized in the phrase *language across the curriculum*, which became something of an educational slogan in Britain, following the UK government's publication of the 1975 report on the teaching of English in schools, *A Language for Life* ('The Bullock Report'). Since then, other aspects of the role of language have come to be better appreciated – not least, the need for a corresponding emphasis on children's 'vertical' development, as they move between classes and schools and encounter different kinds of language experience in a variety of subject areas.

The learning of a foreign language is a major factor in all of this. Over and above the value of learning other languages as ends in themselves, there is an implication for our first language. As literary critic George Steiner once said:

> Is it not the duty of the critic to avail himself, in some imperfect measure at least, of another language – if only to experience the defining contours of his own?

He was talking about literary criticism, but his point applies to everyone.

From the children's point of view, a great deal of language work must seem fragmentary and inconsistent, if no effort is made to ensure a coherent frame of reference that will accompany them as they move through the educational system. This rather abstract statement hides a multitude of points of concrete detail, such as ensuring that the same descriptive terms are used – that the teacher at Grade 6 doesn't describe words like *this* and *that* as *demonstratives* if the teacher of the same children at Grade 7 calls them *determiners*. Because of its diverse terminology, the teaching of grammar has been particularly affected (§36). Research into the best means of achieving a coherent linguistic approach is thus a major aim of the rapidly developing field of *educational linguistics*. The whole perspective is often summarized under the heading *KAL*, or *knowledge about language*.

Since the early 1990s, in the UK, the National Curriculum in English has provided a focus for introducing children to language management. Most schools have taken the language message on board, introducing ideas about linguistic diversity, rights, and tolerance, teaching children about the fundamental principles and functions of language, and giving them training in analysing and appreciating language variety as a frame of reference for instructing them in the special properties and power of the standard language. There is widespread variation between countries, in this respect, some of which are notorious for their conservatism in linguistic practice; but the UK has taken a lead in thinking through the question of what it means to implement an educational language policy.

Learning about language as adults

Language has been an object of fascination and a subject of serious enquiry among adults for over 2,000 years. Often, the observations have been subjective and anecdotal, as people reflected on such topics as the nature of meaning, ideals of correctness, and the origins of language. But from the earliest periods, there has also been an objective approach, with scholars investigating aspects of grammar, vocabulary, and pronunciation in a detailed and organized way. At the end of the 18th century, the subject attracted an increasing number of specialists, so much so that it rapidly became possible to see the emergence of a new field of scientific research with language analysis as its focus. This approach, first known as *philology*, dealt exclusively with the historical development of language. In the 20th century, the field broadened to include the whole range of subject matter represented in this book.

The field is now known as *linguistics*, or *linguistic science*, and the short answer to the question 'how to learn about language as an adult' is simply: 'take up linguistics'. Anyone who has reached this point in the book has, of course, already begun to do so, for 'how language works' is the main question that linguistic science tries to answer.

The scientific emphasis is important. Linguistics shares with other sciences a concern to be objective, systematic, consistent, and explicit in its account of language. Like other sciences, it aims to collect data, test hypotheses, devise models, and construct theories. Its subject matter, however, is unique: at one extreme, it overlaps with such 'hard' sciences as physics and anatomy; at the other, it involves such traditional 'arts' subjects as philosophy and literary criticism. The field of linguistics includes both science and the humanities, and offers a breadth of coverage that, for many aspiring students of the subject, is the primary source of its appeal.

Only a small number of people become professional linguists, but everyone can acquire a linguistic temperament. Perhaps – especially after reading this far – you already have it. But it is possible to check, by reflecting on your mindset in relation to a set of principles which would form the foundation of any philosophy of language management. I list them here in no especial order, and stop at ten only because of illustrious precedents.

I *Are you concerned about endangered languages?* The concern can take many forms – aside from doing the actual work of linguistic documentation – such as lobbying for political support, providing help at community level, and fund-raising. All speakers, and especially those whose languages are not in any danger (at present), should be reflecting on this, and doing something about it.

II *Are you concerned about minority languages, even if they are not in any global sense endangered?* All languages express the identity of the people who speak them, but for those who find themselves to be a small part of a large community, the role of language is especially important. They want to see their language treated with respect by the dominant culture; they want opportunities (which usually means funding) to use their language in public and see it valued. It would be intellectually dishonest to take pride in the achievements of our own language while denying the same opportunity to others.

III *Are you interested in all accents and dialects within a language?* Here I am talking about a readiness to accept the variety of forms a language takes as it varies from one part of a country to another. You do not have to personally like all these forms, of course, any more than you have to like all kinds of music or literature. But linguistically aware people do not go round, as many have done, condemning some (usually urban) dialects as ugly, rough, or slovenly, or their speakers as unintelligent or criminal. *Eternal vigilance* was once the watchword of a puristic and prescriptively minded linguistic age. The watchword of the new century should be *eternal tolerance*.

IV *Are you concerned about the expressive range of language?* This means valuing all varieties and styles in a language, whether spoken or written, formal or informal, regional or social, domestic or professional. It means being concerned over standards of excellence, while recognizing that language reflects many needs and activities. One of the purposes of language is to express identity, as we have seen; another is to foster mutual intelligibility. This means that language has to be clear, care has to be taken to avoid ambiguity, and subtleties of expression have to be carefully managed. There has long been a concern in schools for children to master a standard language, in which the focus is on the sounds, grammar, and vocabulary that facilitate national (and, these days, international) intelligibility. In the past, this was all too often seen as a replacement for a local dialect. The new mindset sees the value of both.

V *Are you multilingually minded?* There are still too many cultures which are monolingual in temperament. These are the disadvantaged ones. Although culturally dominant, reflecting their colonial pasts, they are missing out intellectually by failing to make a second language a routine part of growing up. In the words of American essayist Ralph Waldo Emerson: 'As many languages as he has, as many friends, as many arts and trades, so many times is he a man.' Or woman. And the benefits, as people are beginning to learn, can be economic as well as personal.

VI *Do you accept change in language as a normal process?* This means not seeing it as decay and deterioration, and complaining about it to the press, the prime minister, or whoever will listen. There is probably more time wasted on this issue than on any other in the world of language. Language change is inevitable, continuous, universal, and multidirectional. Languages do not get better or worse, when they change. They just – change.

VII *Are you concerned about those who are having difficulties learning their mother tongue – whether for medical, psychological, or other reasons?* As many as 10% of the child population can be affected by disabilities in listening, speaking, reading, or writing. Deafness, cleft palate, dyslexia, and language delay are just some of the conditions which form the world of another cadre of language professionals, the speech and language therapists – or pathologists, as they are often called. That is a world where there is a shortage of funding too.

VIII *Are you concerned about those who have lost their ability to use a mother tongue in which they were once proficient?* This is the language pathology world also, but now I am talking about the linguistic consequences of strokes, and other forms of brain damage, among the adult population. Aphasia is one of the best-known syndromes.

IX *Do you want to foster the link between the study of language and the study of literature?* All too often, schools, universities, and language-teaching institutions introduce a sharp boundary between the two domains. 'The language' is taught in one class; 'the literature' in another. We need to allow more language awareness into the literature class, and more literary examples into the language class. Both sides, after all, have a focus on creativity. The creation of new words and sentences is how a language develops and changes; the creation of new discourses is how literature does.

X *Finally, do you appreciate, truly appreciate, the value of language in human development and society?* Languages should be thought of as national treasures, and treated accordingly. If you do, this book is just one of many you will read. If you do not, return to page 1, and try again.

Further Reading

Aitchison, Jean and Diana M. Lewis (eds.). 2003. *New Media Language*. London: Routledge.

Aronoff, Mark and Janie Rees-Miller (eds.). 2001. *The Handbook of Linguistics*. Oxford: Blackwell.

Baker, Colin and Sylvia Prys Jones. 1998. *Encyclopedia of Bilingualism and Bilingual Education*. Clevedon: Multilingual Matters.

Baron, Naomi S. 2000. *From Alphabet to Email*. London: Routledge.

Brumfit, Christopher. 1995. *Language Education in the National Curriculum*. Oxford: Blackwell.

Carter, Ronald. 2004. *Language and Creativity*. London: Routledge.

Cook, Guy. 2000. *Language Play, Language Learning*. Oxford: Oxford University Press.

Coulmas, Florian. 1989. *The Writing Systems of the World*. Oxford: Blackwell.

Crystal, David. 2004. *The Language Revolution*. Cambridge: Polity Press.

—— 2004. *The Stories of English*. London: Penguin.

—— 2004. *Making Sense of Grammar*. London: Longman.

Daniels, Peter T. and William Bright (eds.). 1996. *The World's Writing Systems*. New York: Oxford University Press.

Duranti, Alessandro. 1997. *Linguistic Anthropology*. Cambridge: Cambridge University Press.

Fletcher, Paul and Brian MacWhinney (eds.). 1995. *The Handbook of Child Language*. Oxford: Blackwell.

Frawley, William J. (ed.). 2003. *International Encyclopedia of Linguistics*, 2nd edn. Oxford: Oxford University Press.

Hughes, Geoffrey. 1988. *Words in Time*. Oxford: Blackwell.

Laver, John. 1994. *Principles of Phonetics*. Cambridge: Cambridge University Press.

Mugglestone, Lynda. 2003. *Talking Proper: the Rise of Accent as Social Symbol*, 2nd edn. Oxford: Oxford University Press.

Nettle, Daniel and Suzanne Romaine. 2000. *Vanishing Voices*. Oxford: Oxford University Press.

Price, Glanville (ed.). 1998. *Encyclopedia of the Languages of Europe*. Oxford: Blackwell.

Wardhaugh, Ronald. 1993. *Investigating Language*. Oxford: Blackwell.

Index

The alphabetical order of this index is letter-by-letter

abbreviations 117, 227
Academies 452–3
accent (in pronunciation) 290, 309–10, 326–7, 482–3
accent (in words) 75
accidence 236
accommodation 294, 325–7
acoustic cues 46–7
acoustics 32–8
acquired vs developmental disorders 143
acronyms 227
activity, communicative 322, 327–8
    types 327
acuity 45
Adam's apple 26
adjacency-pair 155, 270
adjectives 242, 245–6
adjective phrases 250
adverbs 242, 244
advertising language 473
affixes 226, 238
affricates 61
African-American English Vernacular 306–8
African languages 397–402
Afro-Asiatic family 400–402

age (of a person) 283–4
agent omission 280
agglutinating languages 238, 369
agraphia 143
air streams 20–23, 51
Albanian family 372–3
Albee, Edward 128
alexia 143
Alford, Henry 458
allographs 106
allomorphs 239
allophones 68
alphabetic writing 113–18, 357–8
Altaic family 380–82
alveolar ridge 28, 59
alveolar sounds 59
Amarasimha 213
ambiguity 468
amelioration 228
American languages 403–8
American Name Society 222
American Sign Language 160–61, 164
Amer-Ind 167
Amerindian languages 403–8
amplitude 35
analogy 363

analytic languages 369
anaphoric relations 261
Anatolian family 373
animal communication 2, 9
anthroponomastics 218
antonymy 196
aperiodicity 37
aphasia 143
apostrophes 120, 455
apotropaic names 219
appropriateness 323, 477
approximants 57
aptitude in language learning 434–5
areal linguistics 292
Aristotle 187
Armenian family 373
articulation 27–31
    disorders 94–6
    ease 362
    manner 52, 60–62
    place 52, 58–9
articulatory description 51–65
artificial languages 423–6
associations between words 195
atlases, dialect 296–9
Atlas linguistique de la France 297
attitude in language learning 435
audibility 44
audience 325
    in reading 137
    in speech 263
audio-lingual method 439
auditory perception 44, 79–80
aural-oral method 439
auricle 39
Austin, J. L. 276
Australian family 395–6
Austro-Asiatic family 387–8
Austronesian family 393–4
authorship studies 320
auxiliary languages 345, 423–6

babbling 83
babies' perception 79–80

Balto-Slavic family 374
Basic English 426–7
Basque, attitudes to 304
behaviourism 433
Bell, Alexander Graham 35
Berko, Jean 87
bilabial sounds 59
bilingualism 303–4, 337–8, 409–15
    dictionaries 213–14
    programmes 448–50
black-letter writing 101
blend 227
blogs 264
Bloomfield, Leonard 147, 184, 241
body language 4, 5–10
body posture 7
Bopp, Franz 365
borrowing 224–5
boustrophedon 98, 108
bow-wow theory 350
brackets 119
brain and language 142, 171–9
breathy voice 13–14
British Sign Language 161
broadcasting language 474–5
Broca, Paul Pierre 174
Broca's area 174–8
Brown, Roger 87
buccal voice 23
Bullock Report 480
by-name 219

calligraphy 100
calques 225
Camden, William 220
capital letters 100, 106, 117, 217–18
cardinal vowel diagram 62–3
caretaker speech 271–2
Carolingian minuscule 101
caste 310
cataphoric relations 261
Caucasian family 382–3
Cawdrey, Robert 214
Celtic family 375–6

Central American families 405
cerebrum 171–3
channel, communicative 322
characters (in writing) 111–12
Charlemagne 101
chatrooms 153–7
Chaucer, Geoffrey 358
cheremes 163
cherology 163
child language 477
    conversation 271–4
    dialect awareness 296
    grammar 254–9
    reading 133–6, 145–6
    sounds 79–96
    vocabulary 204–9
    writing 136–9
Children of a Lesser God 161
Chinese languages 331, 388–9
Chinese Sign Language 160–61
chirography 99
choice
    in pragmatics 275
    in stylistics 317
Chomsky, Noam 232–3, 253
Christian names 218
clarity 467–8
class, social 309–10, 454
clauses 251, 256
clay tokens 107
cleft palate 56
Clerc, Laurent 164
click languages 22, 292, 400
click sounds 21–2
clipping 227
coarticulation 52–3
cochlea 42
cocktail-party phenomena 45
code, communicative 322–3
code switching 414–15
codification 446
cognate languages 365
cognitive skills 135, 433–4
coherence 261

cohesion 261–2
collocations 194–5
colons 119
commas 119
commissives (speech acts) 277
common nouns 217
communication 321
    modes 3–4
communicative teaching 439–40
comparative method 357–8, 364–70
comparative philology 365
comparison 262
complementary terms 196
complex tones 37–8
compound words 226
comprehension 80, 174–5, 204
computer-assisted language learning 442
computer-mediated communication
    153–8
conjunctions 242
conjunctive relations 261
connectivity, sentence 257, 261–2
consonantal alphabets 115
consonants 56–7
    described 58–62
    learned 85–7
constatives 277
contact languages 343
contact societies 6, 370, 409–10
context 150, 322–8
contours 74
contrastive analysis 433
conventionalist view of meaning 187
convergence, speech 326
conversation 267–74
    by computer 153–4
    learning 271–4
    repairs 478
    turns 155, 265–6, 268–71, 478
    with babies 80–81
converse terms 196
conversion 227, 243
cooing 82–3
coordinate clauses 251, 256

coreference 261
Cornett, R. Orin 168
corpus 212, 214, 232
corpus planning 445
cortex 171–3
Corti, Alfonso 42
creaky voice 14
creativity 484
creole languages 345–9
cries, baby 82
Cro-Magnon 353–5
cued speech 168
cultural assimilation 337–8
cultural change 361
cultural studies 441–2
cuneiform 111
cursive writing 100
cycles 34
cyclical relationships 197

dactylology 167–9
Dahl, Roald 205
Dalgarno, George 168
dashes 119
deafness 159–70
decibels 35
declarations (as speech acts) 278
decreolization 346
deep dysgraphia 145
deep dyslexia 144
definitions 189, 199–203, 207–9
Defoe, Daniel 452
deixis 150
dental sounds 59
derivational morphology 237
descriptive grammar 231–2
descriptive linguistics 454
developmental disorders 143
developmental linguistics 477
diacritical marks 65
dialect 289–301, 306–15, 482–3
    accent vs 290
    atlases 296–9
    awareness 296

chain 291
continuum 165, 291
family 338
geography 295
in sign language 164–5
in spelling 116
language vs 291–2, 329–35
mixture 293
dialectology 295–301
    social 299–301
    urban 300
dialogues 262–6
Diamond Sutra, The 103
diaphragm 20
dichotic listening 43
dictionary 190–91, 199, 210–16
    coverage vs treatment 211
    evaluation 211–13
    history 213–16
diglossia 312–13
ding-dong theory 351
diphthongs 64
diplomatics 99
directives (as speech acts) 277
direct method 438
discourse 183, 260–66
    prosody 77
discrimination, auditory 44–5, 80
displacement 10
distance zones 6
distinctive features 69, 106
divergence, speech 326
diversity, linguistic 338, 449, 459, 467–8,
    474, 482–3
documentation of languages 338–9
Donald Duck 23
double articulation 9
Doublespeak Awards 476
Dravidian family 383–4
Dryden, John 452
dual alphabet 100–101
duality of structure 9
dysgraphia 140, 143
    types 145

dyslexia 140–46
  types 143–4
dysphasia 143
dysphonia 91–2

ear 39–43
  inner 42
  middle 40–41
  outer 39–40
eardrum 39–41
ears, two 43
Eats, Shoots and Leaves 452
Edmont, Edmond 296–7
education 296, 307–8, 479–81
  policy 446–50, 459
educational linguistics 480
egressive airflow 20–21
ejectives 22–3
electronic medium 153–8
elliptical sentences 250, 261
elocution 321
e-mail 153–4, 156–7
Emerson, Ralph Waldo 483
emoticons 156, 467
emotional expression 76, 463
emphasis 88
endangered languages 336–42, 482
endolymph 42
English
  family of languages 333, 428
  global 225, 427–8
English Place-Name Society 222
Enkvist, Nils-Erik 262
epiglottis 25
epigraphy 99
error analysis 433–4
esophageal speech 92
Esperanto 424–5
ethnicity 302–8
etymological fallacy 229
etymology 213, 220–23, 228–9
  folk 229
EURALEX 214
European Union 305

translation issues 420–21
Eustachian tube 41
Eustachio, Bartolommeo 41
exchanges, conversational 269–71
exclamation marks 120
Exner, Sigmund 175
Exner's centre 175
exposure in language learning 435
expressive range 483
expressives (as speech acts) 278
extension, semantic 227
external auditory canal 39–40
eye 121–3
  contact 6, 269
  dominance 142
  movements 121–2
eyebrow flash 7

facial expressions 6–7
false friends 160
family names 218
family tree 366–8
feature detectors 80
feedback 6, 93–4, 150, 153–4, 177, 270, 475
felicity conditions 278
female/male speech 271, 285, 362
Fielding, Henry 243
figurative language 208, 321, 325
finger-spelling 167–9
first-language 431
first names 220–21
Firth, J. R. 194
fis phenomenon 87
fixations (in reading) 121–3
flaps 62
fluency
  disorders 92–4
  in languages 412–13
  in reading 136
focal areas 299
folk etymology 229
football results intonation 88–9
foreign language learning 430–36, 480
foreign language teaching 437–43

forensic linguistics 293, 320
formants 37–8
forms and meanings 182, 187
fovea 122
Fowler, Henry Watson 231
framing 157
Francis, Philip 320
Franco, General 304
free variation 300
frequency
    of sounds 34
    of words 124
Freud, Sigmund 229
fricatives 61
frictionless continuants 57
full stops 119
functional shift 227
functions of language 462–8
fusional languages 369

Gallaudet, Thomas 164
Galsworthy, John 309
Gastarbeiter 304
g dropping 309–10
gender 313–15
generalization, semantic 227
genetic classification 368–70
genres 327
geographical distance 361
Germanic family 376
gestures 2, 7, 9, 163, 355
Gilliéron, Jules 296
given name 218
global languages 427–9
glossogenetics 353
glottalic sounds 22
glottal sounds 60
glottal stops 27, 60
gobbledegook 476
Golden Bull Awards 476
Gorman, Pierre 166
Gothic script 101
gradience 245
grammar 182–3, 230–59, 280

and intonation 76
approaches 230–35, 480
descriptive vs prescriptive 231–2
divisions 182–3
learning 254–9
types 231–3
grammar translation method 438
graphemes 105–6
    related to phonemes 114, 143–4
graphetics 97–100, 105
graphic contrast 120
graphic expression 97–100
graphic substance 149
graphology (in handwriting) 102
graphology (in linguistics) 98, 105
graphs (in writing) 106
Greek family 376–7
Greenberg, Joseph 397
Grimm, Jakob 365
Gutenberg, Johannes 103
gyri 171–3

hair cells 42
half-uncial writing 100
handedness 173–4
handwriting 97
    analysis 101–2
hard palate 28
harmonics 34–5
harmony in sounds 86
Hart, John 131, 358
head (of a phrase) 250
headwords 211
hearing 39–45
hemispheres, brain 171
hemispheric dominance 142, 173–4
Herodotus 352
Hertz, Heinrich Rudolf 34
Heschl, R. L. 175
Heschl's gyri 175
hierarchy in syntax 250–53
hieroglyphic writing 109–10, 402
Higgins, Henry 293
holophrases 255

Homer 213
homo loquens 355
Honest to God 325
Hsu Shen 213
humanistic approaches 440–41
hypercreolization 346
hypernyms 196
hypertext links 157
hyphenation 119, 240
hyponymy 196

iconic signs 159–60
ideational language 462
identity 466–7
    ethnic 302–8
    individual 317–19
    national 330–32, 425
    physical 282–8
    prosodic 78
    regional 289–94, 425
    social 309–15, 425
ideographic writing 110–11
ideology (of signs) 424
idiolect 290, 316
idioms 193
illocutionary acts 277–8
imitation in language learning 433
immediate constituents 251–3
immersion, language 449–50
implementation (of a language) 446
implosives 22
incompatibility 197
incorporating languages 369
indexical features 78
indirect speech acts 279
Indo-European family 364–7, 371–9
Indo-Iranian family 377–8
Indo-Pacific family 394–5
infixes 238
inflecting languages 369
inflections 236–41
information structure 77
ingressive airflow 21
initialisms 227

instant messaging 153, 155, 157
intelligence and language 287
intelligibility 291, 329–32
intensifiers 285
intensity of sounds 35–6
interchanges 269–71
interjections 242, 246, 351
interlanguage 433–4
internal reconstruction 365
International Phonetic Alphabet 53–6
Internet 153–8, 223, 469
interpreting 417, 419–20
interruptions 268–9
intonation 74, 84
    learning 88–9
inverted commas 119
irregular words 239
isoglosses 297–9
isolates 387, 407–8
isolating languages 240, 369
Italic family 378

Japanese family 392
jaw 29
Jespersen, Otto 350–51
Johnson, Samuel 214, 453–5
Jones, Daniel 62
Jones, William 364

kanji 111–12, 392
Khoisan family 400
kinship terms 188–9
knowledge about language 480
Korean family 391–2
Kurgans 371

labio-dental sounds 59
Labov, William 359, 362
la-la theory 351
language 1–4
    auxiliary 345
    awareness 436, 480, 484
    birth 343–9
    classification 368–70

language – *cont.*
  counting 332–3
  death 336–42
  delay 95–6
  edges 11–17
  equality 460–61
  first vs second 431
  functions 462–8
  immersion 449–50
  loyalty 449
  maintenance 410, 448
  management 451–84
  minority 336–42, 447–9
  mixing 414–15
  names 333–4
  nests 340
  origins 350–56
  primitive 289–90, 460
  principles 457–61
  properties 8–10
  shift 410
  simplified 426–7
  structure 9, 180–85
  vs communication 3–4
  vs dialect 291–2, 329–35
language across the curriculum 479–80
language change 346, 357–63, 458–60,
    483
  causes 360–63
  linguistic factors 362–3
  social factors 361–2
language families 364–408
language laboratories 442–3
language learning 430–36, 480
  difficulties 483–4
  reasons 431–3
  timing 436
language planning 444–50, 480–81
language teaching 202, 231, 437–43
  materials 441–2
  methods 438–40
laryngectomy 92
larynx 18, 25–7, 283
  artificial 92

lateralization 173
laterals 6
learning 77, 79–96, 128–9, 133–46,
    204–9, 254–9, 271–4, 361
  conversation 271–4
  grammar 254–9
  languages 430–36, 477
  sounds 79–96
  reading and writing 133–46
  vocabulary 198–209
learning about language 477–84
  as adults 481–4
  at home 478–9
  in school 479–81
learning disability 140
least articulatory effort 362
legal language 472–3
l'Epée, Charles Michel de 164
levels of language 181–5, 276
lexemes 193
lexical diffusion 359
lexical gaps 202
lexical items 193, 262
lexicography 210–16
lexicology 191
lexicon 183
lexicopedia 217
lingua francas 394, 397, 423–9, 445
linguistic atlases 296–9
linguistic engineering 444–50
linguistic geography 295
linguistics 3, 481
  descriptive 454
  developmental 477
  educational 480
  historical 365–70
linguistic variables 300–301
lips 29, 52
  rounding 14, 52, 62
listening 45
literacy 133, 339, 479
literary style 319, 484
loan translation 225
loan words 224–5

lobes, brain 172–3
localization 174–6
locutionary act s 277
logographic writing 106, 111–12
look-and-say 134
loudness 35–6, 73
   as prosodic feature 74–5
lower case letters 106
Lowth, Bishop 453–4
ludic language 464
lungs (in speech)
   not used 21–3
   used 20–21

machine-aided translation 422
machine translation 421–2
macro-phylum 368
majuscule 100
Makeba, Miriam 22
Malayo-Polynesian family 393–4
male/female speech 271, 285, 362
Malinowski, Bronislaw 463–4
Malouf, David 342
manual signals 15–16
mass media 475–6
meaning 3, 186–91
   analysis 192–7
   change 227–9
   meanings of 186–7
   natural vs conventional 187
   vs form 182, 187
medical language 470–71
mediums of communication 183
   electronic 153–8
   speech and writing 147–52
Medoff, Mark 161
Meso-American families 405
message form 323
metalanguage 135, 477–8
Mezzofanti, Giuseppe 416
Miao-Yao family 391
minimal free forms 241
minimal pairs 67
minority languages 336–42, 447–9, 482

minuscule 100
modernization (in language planning) 446
monogenesis 347
monolingualism 409–10
monologues 262–4
monophthongs 64
monosemic words 191
morphemes 237–9, 250–51
   free vs bound 238
morphology 182, 236–41
   inflectional vs derivational 236–7
mother tongue 431
motivation in language learning 435
motor skills
   in speech 49, 175, 177
   in writing 136–7, 175
multilingualism 409–15, 483
Murray, James 215
Murray, Lindley 453–4

names 217–23
   first 220–21
   language 333–4
   personal 218–20
   place 221–3
narrowing, semantic 228
nasality 14, 28–9, 52, 91
nasal sounds 29, 60
nationalism 303
naturalist view of meaning 187
Neanderthals 353–5
negation development 258–9
Netspeak 158
neurolinguistics 176–8
Niccoli, Niccolò 101
Niger-Congo family 398–9
Nilo-Saharan 399–400
nodes 91
nonfluency, normal 93, 256
nonphonological writing systems 108–12
nonsegmental features 73, 183
nonverbal communication 2, 4, 9
norms 445

North American families 403–5
notional syllabus 439–40
noun phrases 250
nouns 242, 244–5

obsolescence 227
occupational varieties 469–76
oesophageal voice 23
Ogden, Charles Kay 426
one-word sentences 255
onomastics 218
onomatopoeia 187, 350
opposites 195–6
oracy 479
organ of Corti 42
origins of language 350–56
orthoepists 358
oscillation 33
ossicles 41
overextension 206
Oxford English Dictionary 215, 228

Paget, Grace 166
Paget, Richard 166
Paget–Gorman Sign System 166
palaeography 99
Palaeosiberian 386
palatal sounds 59
palate 28–9
palato-alveolar sounds 59
Papuan family 394–5
parafoveal area 122
paralanguage 13–15, 74
parentheses 119
parsing 230, 233–4
participants 322, 324–5
parts of speech 242–6
part/whole relationships 197
passive constructions 280–81
patronymics 218–19
pauses 74
    between words 240
pedagogical grammar 230
pejoration 228

performatives 277, 465
perilymph 42
periods (in punctuation) 119
periphery (of eye) 122
perlocutionary effect 277
personality and language 287
personal names 218–20
pharyngeal sounds 60
pharynx 18–19, 28
phatic function 152, 464
philology 481
phonation 26
    disorders 91
phonemes 68
phonetics 51, 182
phonic mediation 123
phonics 134
phonic substance 149
phonological dysgraphia 145
phonological dyslexia 143–4
phonological rules 69–70
phonological writing systems 108,
    113–20
phonology 66–72, 182
    divisions 183
phrases 250
phylums 368
physical identity 282–8
pictographic writing 108–10
pidgin languages 343–9
    expanded 345
pinna 39
pitch 26–7, 34, 73, 283
place names 221–3
plain English 476
Plato 187
playing with language 464
plosives 60
poetry 319
Poggio 101
politeness 273, 275–6, 478
polygenesis 347
polysemic words 191
polysynthetic languages 240, 369

pooh-pooh theory 351
popular etymology 229
post-creole continuum 346
potato's 455
pragmatics 275–81
predicates 247
prefixes 226, 238
preparatory conditions (in speech acts) 278
prepositions 242
pre-reading 135
prescriptivism 147, 230–31, 452–8
prestige 361–2
Price, Vincent 14
Priestley, Joseph 454
primates 18–19, 354–6
productivity 8–9
professional usage 475–6
proficiency, language 411–12
pronouns 242, 275, 314
    sex-neutral 314
proper nouns 217
propositional language 462
prosodic features 74
Proto-Indo-European 364–7, 371–9
proto-words 84
Psamtik I 352
pseudo-dialogues 263–4, 271
psychotherapy 320
pulmonic air 20–21, 51
punctuation 106, 118–20, 248
pure tones 33
pure vowels 64

Queen's English, The 458
question development 257–8
question marks 120
Quirk, Randolph 232
quotation marks 119

racial anatomies 286
randomness in language change 363
rapport, expression of 463–4
reading 121–6, 132–9, 178

active approach 135–6
    by ear 124–5
    by eye 125–6
    disorders 140–46
    terminology 478–9
rebus 109
Received Pronunciation 64, 327
receivers, message 324–5
recognition, auditory 44
recording facts 465–6
reduplication (in sign) 162
reduplication (in speech) 87–8
reduplication (in words) 227
reference grammars 232
reference vs sense 188–9
referential language 462
reflexive noises 82
registers 327
regular vs irregular 239, 244–6, 363
relexification 348
relic areas 299
religious language 471–2
repetition 262
representatives (as speech acts) 277
resonance 27–8
    disorders 91
respiratory cycle 21
retroflex sounds 59, 292
revitalization 338–42
rewriting 127
rhetoric 321
rhythm 73, 75
Robinson, John 325
Roget, Peter Mark 194
rolls 61
root, word 238
root languages 369
rules
    breaking 464, 468
    prescriptive 453
    syntactic 249–50

saccades 121–3
Scandinavian languages 330, 376

scanning 136
Schleicher, August 365
scientific approach to language 481–2
scientific language 470
second language 431
semantic change 227–9
semantic features 201
semantic fields 193–4, 198–9
semantics 182, 186–91, 276, 280
    popular meanings 186
semantic shift 228
semi-circular canals 42
semi-colons 119
semilingualism 338
semiotics 3
semi-vowels 57
senders, message 324–5
sense 190
    associations 195
    relations 195–6, 262
    vs reference 188–9
sentences 232, 247–8
    connection 257
    identification 248
    learning 254–9
    meanings 207–8
    purpose 190
    structure 247–53
Serbo-Croatian issues 331
settings 322–4
sex (of a person) 284–5
sexism 313–15
Shakespeare 193, 224, 243, 358
Shaw, George Bernard 293
Sholes, Christopher Latham 103–4
sign languages 15, 16, 159–70
    contrived 165
    types 165–70
sign space 162
silence 74
Silent Way, The 440–41
simplified languages 426–7
Simplified Spelling Society 132
Simpson, Homer 153

sincerity conditions 278
singing 283–4
Sino-Tibetan family 388–90
situational syllabus 439
Skelly, Madge 167
skimming 136
slips of the tongue 72, 178–9
smileys 156
social class 309–10
social roles 309–13
    of the sexes 285
social status 310–11
sociolinguistics 276, 294, 299–301, 361–2
soft palate 28–9, 52, 62
sonic potential of language 464
sound pressure level 35
sound spectrum 37–8
sound symbolism 351
sound systems 66–72
South American families 405–7
spacing 118–19
spatial organization 120
specialization, semantic 228
speech 18–96
    continuity 47–8
    disability 90–96
    primacy 3–4, 16–17
    production 18–31, 82–4, 176–7, 204
    reception 39–43, 79–81, 178
    surrogates 13
    synthesis 46–7
    therapy 94–5, 321, 484
    vs electronic communication 153–6
    vs writing 147–52, 248
speech acts 276–9
    indirect 279
speech perception 44–50
    active vs passive 48–50
speech sounds 18–31
    description 51–72
    learning 79–96
speed
    in interpreting 420
    of reading 124–5

of signing 160, 167
of speech 21, 46, 73, 75
spelling 116, 127–32, 453
   disorders 145
   irregular 130–31
   reform 131–2
   variation 116
Spelling Reform Association 131
Sprachatlas des Deutschen Reichs 296
stammering 93–4
standard dialects 290, 346, 455–6
standard English 290, 428, 455, 468
status planning 445
Steiner, George 480
stems, word 238
stereotyping 287–8, 314, 344
stops 60
strategies in language learning 435
stress (in words) 75–6
stress-timed rhythm 75
stuttering 93–4
style 316–21
   dictionary labels 212
   literary 319
   senses 316–17
   variation 116, 316–21
stylistics 276, 317
stylostatistics 318, 320
subject matter 323
subject/predicate 247, 253
subordinate clauses 256
substitution (in texts) 261
substratum 361
subvocal language 124, 466
suffixes 226, 238
Suggestopedia 440
sulci 171–3
Summer Institute of Linguistics 336
suprasegmental features 73
surface dysgraphia 145
surface dyslexia 144
surnames 218
Swift, Jonathan 316
syllabic writing systems 113

syllables 70–72
syllable-timed rhythm 75
symbols 118
synonymy 195–6
syntax 182, 247–53
synthetic languages 369

tactile communication 4, 5–6, 9
Tai family 390–91
technological influences on language 467
teknonymy 219
telegraphic speech 256
tempo 75
Tennyson 243
text 260–66
   structure 261–2
text linguistics 260
theography 325
theological language 319, 325
theophoric names 219
theoretical grammar 232
thesaurus 194
thinking, expressed by language 466
thumbs-up sign 7–8
timbre 35, 74, 283
time in sign language 162
Tocharian family 378–9
tolerance 483
tone languages 76–7
tonemes 77
tone of voice 13–15, 73–8, 80, 155–6
tones 74, 77
tongue 29–31, 62
toponomastics 218
toponymy 218
traditional grammar 230, 233–5
transitional bilingualism 448–9
transition areas 299
translation 416–22, 472
   machine 421–2
   machine-aided 422
tree diagram 252–3
trills 61
triphthongs 64

Truss, Lynne 455
tunes 74
turn-taking 155, 265
typesetting 103
typography 103
typological classification 368–70

uncial writing 100
underextensions 206
unison speech 324
universal languages 423–4
upper case letters 106
Uralic family 384–5
urban dialectology 300
usage manuals 451–2
uvular sounds 60

van Buren, Paul 319
variables, linguistic 300–301, 359
varieties 312–13, 327–8, 469–76
vegetative noises 82
velar sounds 59
velum 28
verbs 242, 244
verb phrases 250
visual communication 4, 6–9
vocabulary 183, 190
    growth 205, 224–9
    learning 198–209
vocal abuse 92
vocal folds 18, 25–7, 51, 283
vocal fry 14
vocal noises 11–13
vocal organs 18–31, 286, 355
vocal play 83
vocal tract 18, 27
voice (in speech) 26
    disorders 91–2
    mutation 283
voice (in writing) 139
Voices 296
voicing 26, 51, 91
von Schlegel, August 369
vowel glides 64

vowels 56–7
    described 62–5
    learned 85–7

Walker, John 453–4
Wallis, John 358
waveforms 33
Webster, Noah 215
Wenker, George 296
Wernicke, Carl 174
Wernicke's area 174–8
Wesley, Samuel 316
whispering 13, 91
whistle languages 12–13
whistling 12
whole-word approach 134
Wilkins, John 358
Williams, Kenneth 14
word
    associations 195
    creation 224–9
    identification 240–41
    meanings 192–3
    structure 236–41
    types 240
word classes 242–6, 254
word superiority effect 125
world languages 427–9
World Wide Web 153, 156
writing (as ability) 127–32, 136–9
    disorders 140, 145
    functions 137–8
    posture 136
writing (as medium) 16, 97–158
    history 107–8
    systems 105–20
    vs electronic communication 156–8
    vs speech 147–52, 248

Yeats, W. B. 316
yo-he-ho theory 351

Zamenhof, Ludwig Lazarus 424–5
zero tolerance 452, 456